The Archaeolog

The Archaeology of Environmental Change

Socionatural Legacies of Degradation and Resilience

Edited by
Christopher T. Fisher, J. Brett Hill, and
Gary M. Feinman

THE UNIVERSITY OF ARIZONA PRESS TUCSON

First issued as a paperback edition 2011

www.uapress.arizona.edu

Library of Congress Cataloging-in-Publication Data
The archaeology of environmental change : socionatural legacies of degradation / edited by Christopher T. Fisher, J. Brett Hill, and Gary M. Feinman.
p. cm.
Includes bibliographical references and index.
ISBN 978-0-8165-2676-5 (hardcover : alk. paper)
ISBN 978-0-8165-1484-7 (paperback : alk. paper)
1. Environmental archaeology. 2. Social archaeology. 3. Environmental degradation—History. 4. Human ecology—History. I. Fisher, Christopher T. II. Hill, J. Brett (James Brett), 1960– III. Feinman, Gary M.
CC81.A69 2009
930.1—dc22 2009016346

Manufactured in the United States of America on acid-free, archival-quality paper, and processed chlorine free.

16 15 14 13 12 11 6 5 4 3 2

Contents

The Archaeology of Environmental Change

Introduction

ENVIRONMENTAL STUDIES FOR TWENTY-FIRST-CENTURY CONSERVATION

Christopher T. Fisher, J. Brett Hill, and Gary M. Feinman

WE PREPARE THE INTRODUCTION to this book in the midst of figurative and literal storms that are changing the landscapes of both our planet and the discourses that we are having about it on a daily basis. The popular media is dominated by stories of environmental crisis, as well as by stories of the villains and heroes who battle for our collective fate. The story of the day in the United States—and we could have chosen many—remains the hurricanes that battered the U.S. Gulf Coast in 2005 and their many social dimensions. The societal dimensions of this tragic tale retain their currency, underscoring the inability of decision makers to fully grasp and resolve phenomena related to coupled human and natural systems (Liu et al. 2007).

The very presence of rapidly growing numbers of people, in particular the poor, in coastal areas increases exposure to this destruction (see Haag 2007). Protective barrier islands and wetlands have been diminished and weakened by increased human settlement and industry, with predictable consequences. Even the effects of human-induced climatic changes on hurricane frequency, while still a matter of some debate, have potentially dramatic implications (see Emanuel 2005a, 2005b; Landsea 2005; Pielke 2005; Pielke et al. 2005).

Striking, then, are numerous references among the media and politicians to these events as "natural" or even "unstoppable" disasters, underscoring the widespread belief that they are outside the control of humans (Kennedy 2006). Far from an esoteric debate, this has a very real influence on the direction of public policy, the manner of Gulf Coast reconstruction, and the direction of relief and other funding. Moreover, it has had a distinct influence on the distribution of blame for the disaster, which has been predominantly focused on the competence of those who failed to respond adequately, rather than on a long trajectory of growing poverty, environmental mismanagement, and pollution (see International Federation of Red Cross and Red Crescent Societies 2001; Sarewitz and Pielke 2005).

Stories of environmental disaster and culpability are easily contrasted with stories of struggle and success. Twice in three years, the Norwegian Nobel Institute has awarded its annual Peace Prize to an environmentalist, first in 2004 to Wangari Maathai of Kenya, and again in 2007 to Al Gore and the United Nations' Intergovernmental Panel on Climate Change (IPCC). By awarding the Nobel Peace Prize to environmentalists, the Nobel Committee has both underscored the threat that global change represents and unambiguously linked social and economic development to sustainable socioenvironmental relations. Indeed, *Time* magazine likens the Gore/IPCC award to a critical mass toward broad public recognition of the threat and importance of human-caused global change, calling the Gore/IPCC Nobel "A Green Tipping Point" (Walsh 2007).

It has long been recognized that there is a fundamental connection between societal and environmental health. For example, since 1968 the Union of Concerned Scientists has published repeated calls for action against the socially and economically motivated abuse of technology and its environmental consequences. In the nineteenth century, influential scientists such as George Perkins Marsh argued that humans threatened to undermine their own well-being through exploitative attitudes that could lead to environmental degradation (Redman 1999:25–34). And even in Classical Antiquity, scholars recognized the need to balance environmental conservation with social and economic needs.

Yet today the enormity of any single environmental story, whether of disaster or accomplishment, is being overwhelmed by the sheer number and pace of new narratives. Noteworthy is the fact that we can open any major newspaper and discover accounts of compelling environmental concern to humanity. On the whole there seems to be more bad news than good, perhaps in part because the many things humans do every day that work out well are not deemed newsworthy. Problematic is the fact that the root causes underlying environmental problems, often involving a long-term and complex interplay of human institutions and ecological processes, are absent from popular discussion (Fisher and Feinman 2005).

We believe that any valid environmental explanation must take into account interactions between human decisions, environmental change, and unintended consequences at multiple timescales. From a diachronic perspective, the recent hurricane devastation bears striking similarities to past environmental crises. Most commonly, human societies failed to meet the inherent challenges associated with closely interconnected human/environment systems. The results were disasters in human terms far worse than the initial damage or threat caused by nature. Unarguably, the scope, severity, and broad reach of the Gulf Coast hurricanes make them one of the worst natural calamities in U.S. history. But in the history of our human species, such catastrophic episodes are de rigueur. All societies collapse—sometimes slowly, sometimes quickly—and poor environmental management often plays a critical role (Diamond 2005; Tainter 1990; H. Weiss and Bradley 2001; Yoffee and Cowgill 1988).

Maathai's success in encouraging poor women to plant thirty million trees in East Africa also focuses attention on our ability to improve degraded conditions and to think diachronically about human actions and environmental conditions. Land degradation, which by definition must be human generated (D. Johnson and Lewis 1995), is seldom an irreversible process, lending hope and support to modern conservation efforts. As with Maathai's initiative, peoples in the past have at times promoted programs of landscape repair and rejuvenation that can help guide and inform modern conservation efforts.

But the broader recognition that humans can fundamentally impact their physical surrounds so that even climate (once commonly thought to be outside the reach of human control) and other aspects of the environment may be significantly altered is a recent phenomenon, galvanizing scientific and public opinion and, in the process, becoming a powerful political reality (e.g., Haag 2007; Macilwain 2004). The fact that essential aspects of modern environmental problems have obvious parallels to those faced by our counterparts in the past has begun to enter the realm of "popular culture" (e.g., Diamond 2005; Mann 2002a, 2005; Montgomery 2007). And it is becoming increasingly clear to many in the scientific community that to understand the environmental present and to manage-model our biota for the future, we must consider contemporary human activities, as well as the historic sweep of past environmental change (Briggs et al. 2006; Dunning et al. 2002; D. Foster et al.

2003; D. R. Foster 2000; Gillson 2005; Lentz 2000; Liu et al. 2007; Motzkin et al. 1999; Redman 1999, 2000; B.L.M. Turner 1993; B.L.M. Turner et al. 2003).

From the millennial perspective of archaeology, episodes of collapse-settlement abandonment, dramatic regional shifts in power and population, and even cataclysmic events—are a regular feature of humankind's global history (Tainter 1990; H. Weiss and Bradley 2001; Yoffee and Cowgill 1988). In his recent book, *Collapse*, author Jared Diamond (2003, 2005) catalogs cases of what he terms "ecocide." These are unintentional episodes of ecological catastrophe through which past societies have degraded their environment, thereby precipitating social disintegration and demographic decline.

While Diamond has been criticized for his over-reliance on environmental hazards and factors in his case studies (Demoncal and Cook 2005), we do agree with the major thesis that many past episodes of societal decline were caused by a complex interplay of natural perturbations and anthropogenic or human factors that played off each other for decades, if not much longer. Encoded in past land-use history are prior solutions to (and outcomes of) environmental challenges that are similar to their modern counterparts. For millennia humans have coped with the same kinds of environmental threats as Wangari Maathi's, Al Gore's, and the IPCC's efforts are energized to ameliorate today. Familiar modern concerns of deforestation, soil erosion, desertification, loss of biodiversity, and climate change plagued our ancestors as well (R. M. Adams 1978; Denevan 1992; Krech 1999; Redman 1999). These same factors are often invoked as causal triggers responsible for the formation and decline of archaic societies around the globe (e.g., Diamond 2003, 2005; Gill 1995; see also Redman 1999).

The consequences of these processes are variable and do not always result in cultural decline. Analysis of this variability using long-term records yields insights into the outcomes of contemporary processes, often challenging long-held assumptions concerning human/environment interaction. Contemporary concerns and conservation goals do not exist in a vacuum, but instead are part of long-term trajectories that can only be understood diachronically.

The present volume of contributions from scholars active in many parts of the world is intended to provide a survey of some insights gained through socionatural archaeology. Some explore complex processes in an attempt to highlight key factors affecting change, while others provide seemingly counterintuitive interpretations that challenge prevailing wisdom. Although varied in terms of geographic location, scope, and time period, the chapters in this volume comprise three critical themes: the multi-dimensionality of explanations; new theoretical frameworks; and new answers to old questions, discussed in turn in the sections below.

Multi-dimensional Explanations

One strong sentiment that emerges from this collection is that when social and environmental aspects of societies are examined together it becomes clear that questions concerning past socionatural phenomena do not have simple answers. The new complexity is in strong contrast to past land-use histories that are often portrayed in fatalistic terms, with societies seen as making short-term decisions leading to environmental failures precipitated by some mechanism outside of human control (e.g., Diamond 2003, 2005). This new view takes advantage of our increasing ability to analyze and interpret complex datasets, inspiring some to call social science the science of the twenty-first century (Watts 2007). In the history of human-environment relations, both successes and failures are driven by phenomena more complex than just population shifts, climate changes, or other universal drivers. In reality, it is never just an environmental story, but rather a complex mosaic of human action, unintended consequence, and natural change, although some socionatural systems may be more susceptible to collapse than others (Janssen et al. 2003; Liu et al. 2007; Redman et al., this vol.; Reynolds et al. 2007).

For example, in the present volume, Simmons (chapter 8) notes the failure of simple population models to account for variability in the effects of early colonizers on the island of Cyprus, arguing instead that other factors such as land-use strategies may be more important than sheer numbers of people. Likewise, Fisher (chap. 10) re-examines the popular land degradation/population connection with new evidence from west-central Mexico, concluding that organization rather than population is the root cause behind modern degradation in the region. Dunning et al. (chap. 4) illustrate the close co-evolution of land-tenure traditions and conservation ethics with Mayan agriculture in historical and contemporary circumstances. Kusimba (chap. 6) goes a step further with evidence of historical ivory hunting in Africa to argue that humans are, in fact, an essential element in an environment that has evolved in their presence, and that their continued presence is crucial to conservation goals. Finally, Ravesloot et al. (chap. 11) argue that archaeological notions of social collapse are misguided in the context of the Hohokam and that modern Pima-Maricopa represent a successful adaptation to the environmental challenges of drought and erosion in the past.

This complexity translates to landscapes as well, and many of the contributors to this volume model past environments as highly dynamic and historically contingent. This makes modern environments palimpsests in the sense that current human-environment choices are always conditioned by previous landscape decisions in a non-linear fashion. Landscape change is immutable, altering parameters governing stability, productivity, and potential (Blaikie and Brookfield 1987:10–13). A landscape may return to a similar condition over a given period of time, but will never again contain exactly the same suite of plants, animals, and general environmental conditions (e.g., Denevan 1992; Fall et al. 1996, 2004).

Because these relationships are complex, tying outcomes to human decisions is a difficult task, and the unintended consequences of both human action and inaction serve as tipping points for many of the case studies presented here. Results that are outside the knowledge base of a given society are hard to predict, with the unintended consequences of socionatural interactions a major driver of past (and present) change (Cronon 1983, 1996; van der Leeuw et al. 1998, 2000). In addition, legacies of past land-cover change are often associated with time lags between human decisions and their consequences (Liu et al. 2007). This notion of "changing stable relationships between human groups and their environments" (Redman 2005), coupled with the unintended consequences of intentional human action, is a strong theme that runs through all of the contributions in this volume.

New Theoretical Frameworks

Given the increased media, scientific, and public attention paid to global warming and recent environmental disasters, the visibility of environmentalism has dramatically increased. Nevertheless, research on long-term human effects on the environment still falls below the radar of the general public, those who engage policy, scholars in related disciplines, and even many anthropologists. Why is this so? A major stumbling block seems to be the lack of a unified body of concepts, theories, and hypotheses from which we can construct meaningful narratives for disciplinary and public consumption. Research on human-environment relations in the past is fragmented by subject matter (especially contemporary versus historical approaches), discipline, and outlook. What is needed is a common language (*metalanguage*; see van der Leeuw and Redman 2002) that can act as a bridge between various groups pursuing these kinds of research agendas.

At present, the issue is not the lack of a paradigm, but instead the fact that we have too many competing options. It is easy to get lost among the variants of ecology (historical ecology, agroecology, political ecology) and other related approaches (eco-dynamics, resilience theory, complexity theory, coupled human/natural systems, etc.). Multiple contributors to this volume provide complementary approaches that begin to tackle this problem. Redman et al. (chap. 1) and van der Leeuw (chap. 2) illustrate the use of panarchy and resilience theory as a useful structure for integrating different disciplines with overlapping environmental research goals. Hill (chap. 7) uses evidence of hinge-points in the history of Levantine socionatural relations to find common ground between resilience theory and traditional anthropological concepts of practice theory as they relate to the significance of change. Scarborough (chap. 3) juxtaposes two different models of economic development to illustrate how broadening our views to include less Eurocentric alternatives such as labortasking provides insights into archaeological problems as well as questions of sustainability in modern contexts. Bar-Yosef (chap. 9) offers a valuable challenge to archaeologists who are reluctant to acknowledge the importance of the environment in determining human outcomes and brings our attention back to the crucial matter of large-scale climate change and its role in human evolution.

In addition, all of the contributions draw from two relatively recent changes in the way the human-environment connection is perceived that we believe could be the core of a new approach: 1) A recursive human-environment connection, and 2) non-equilibrium dynamics. For the former, over the last decade or so, there has been a fundamental shift in the way that the society-nature connection is perceived toward a non-linear recursive connection (Blaikie and Brookfield 1987; Cronon 1983, 1996; Descola and Pálsson 1996; Scoones 1999; Zimmerer 1994; Zimmerer and Young 1998). Recently, van der Leeuw and Redman (2002) traced a shift from a reactive to a proactive and then an interactive conception of socionatural connections (see also Blaikie and Brookfield 1987; Fisher 2000; Scarborough 2003a; Zimmerer 1994), replacing the traditional nature-culture dichotomy common in Western thought (see Bryant 1992; Cronon 1996; Descola and Pálsson 1996; Escobar 1999; Giddens 1984) with a recursive view of human-environment interaction.

Additionally, contributors follow a long-term shift in ecological thinking (see Botkin 1990; Perry 2002; B. L. Turner 1993; Vayda and McCay 1975; Wu and Loucks 1995; Zimmerer 1994; Zimmerer and Young 1998), rejecting notions of ecosystems in balance in favor of flux, nonequilibrium dynamics, and long-term change. This sea change emphasizes ecosystem dynamism with cyclical changes at many temporal and geographical scales (Botkin 1990; Zimmerer 1994). The result is a landscape that is viewed as a heterogeneous mosaic of patches undergoing distinct successional regimes (Perry 2002:341). Shifting cultivation is just one example of an intentional human strategy to increase environmental heterogeneity (Padoch et al. 1998). For landscapes, the seemingly contradictive normative notion of "disequilibria" means that humans constantly coped with flux while engineering more intensive production regimes on those landscapes.

Determining cause-and-effect relationships in socionatural systems depends on the units of analysis and their associated scales in time and space (K. W. Butzer 1996; Hill 2004; van der Leeuw et al. 2000:363). Consideration of shorter temporal and spatial scales masks long-term trends, but allows human action and environmental consequence to be elucidated. Larger scales allow broad patterns to be discerned, but at some loss of precision to causal discrimination. Multi-scaler, inclusive records identifying short-term events and broad-scale trends are needed for complete considerations.

For example, what appears catastrophic at an archaeological timescale may be barely perceptible at the scale of a human generation (Hill 2004: chap. 6), and a crisis at the scale of an individual actor may seem like sustainable land management when viewed from a millennial lens (van der Leeuw et al. 1998, 2000, this vol.). Likewise, Redman et al. (chap. 1) argue that it is "only with a long-term perspective that we can identify which of the seemingly beneficial near-term actions truly contribute to long-term resilience and identify the ways in which some outwardly rational choices lead, in the end, to undesirable outcomes." Ravesloot et al. (chap. 11) contribute yet another view on temporal matters, noting the varying perspectives held by contemporary groups with a different sense of connection to the past and the success of their ancestors.

All the chapters in this volume demonstrate that it is only through the *longue durée* that we can identify successful and detrimental socio-landscape strategies.

New Answers to Old Questions

When frameworks are applied that integrate humans, environments, and natural processes at many scales, counterintuitive results can often emerge. Many of the case studies in this volume challenge the seemingly straightforward connections that are frequently applied to human/environment questions. For example, following a Malthusian tradition and basic principles common to population ecology (e.g., Ives 1998), Diamond (2003) has stressed the supposed connection between population pressure and environmental degradation. Although demography is certainly important for understanding human-environment relations, it is far from a simple cause-and-effect chain. Environmental damage may result either as a product of high population densities and intensive systems of land use or during demographic nadirs when highly maintained landscapes are left unattended. Empirically, there is no universal causal link between population growth and land degradation (Fisher et al. 2003; T. J. Whitmore et al. 1990). In fact, many contributors to this volume offer evidence that human numbers are a poor predictor of degradation or its significance with regard to ecological or cultural sustainability. Highly variable demographic scenarios have played out under different circumstances, and it remains incumbent upon us to understand why.

Human culture mediates connections between driving forces and variable environmental outcomes. Critical concepts affecting this variability include "landesque capital" (Blaikie and Brookfield 1987:9; Brookfield 1984:36, 2001:55; Kirch 1994:19), strategies and beliefs affecting the relative values and productivity of humans, land, and resources (Blaikie and Brookfield 1987; Kusimba, this vol.; T. H. McGovern 1994; Scarborough, this vol.; van der Leeuw, this vol.), and conservation ethics affecting which sacrifices are made in cases of competing interest for limited resources (K. W. Butzer 1996; Dunning et al., this vol.; Hüttermann 1999; Kusimba, this vol.; Redman 1999). Each of these enables or constrains the uses of land and its consequent effects in ways independent of reductionist prime-movers.

The concept of landesque capital is used to identify landscape manipulation designed for long-term gains in productivity. Landesque capital allows labor to be environmentally banked through stone walls, terraces, drainage and irrigation systems, raised fields, or other landscape infrastructure. Such "built" capital can increase productivity for generations if it is maintained. The landesque-capital landscape is a common form of anthropogenic environment that occurs across the globe. Furthermore, factors affecting the value of land and its productivity are culturally mediated and highly variable through time and location. Thus, both actual and perceived degradation are structured by the uses land is put to, whether agricultural or pastoral, industrial or recreational. Likewise, the techniques and strategies of development are culturally variable, resulting in different means and outcomes to common goals such as increased production. Finally, ethical factors affecting perceived rights and responsibilities to land resources are variable, with consequently divergent outcomes depending on the perceived relationship of humans to nature. Many instances of land-use rationale deviating from the goals of immediate or strictly economic maximization underscore the non-linear connections between humans and environmental degradation.

A fundamental property of all of these cultural mediating factors concerns what happens to them following demographic, social, or technological change. Landesque capital depends on regular allocations of labor to ensure stability. Degradation often results from a failure to repair and maintain agricultural infrastructure. Likewise, landscapes develop over time under specific notions of use value, and degradation often results from changes in the value and intended uses of land incompatible with former ideas. Land-use ethics similarly develop over time in specific socionatural settings with resulting stabilization of human-nature relations. Subsequent disruption of such practices, often through political upheaval or conquest, often results in degradation.

A common pattern associated with built landscapes and culturally structured socionatural relations is long periods of relative stability and productivity, made possible by consistent maintenance, followed by shorter episodes of land degradation caused by disruption of traditional practices. Colonialism (which includes the introduction of new technologies and species), changes in land tenure, the collapse of long-term systems of stratification and work, and epidemics (fomenting marked demographic declines)—all have been implicated as a trigger for this sort of land degradation (Blaikie and Brookfield 1987; K. W. Butzer 1996; Denevan 2000; Dunning et al. 2002; Fisher et al. 2003; T. H. McGovern 1994; Runnels 2000; Spores 1969; van Andel et al. 1990; van der Leeuw et al. 1998; T. M. Whitmore and Turner 2002; Zimmerer 1991, 1993).

The Resilience of Built Capital

One historical lesson centers on the resilience of anthropogenic landscapes and the legacy of human capital. The built environment has proved to be a powerful resource for past human societies; to understand modern landscapes, we need to understand the cultural repertoire that people bring to the present. Landscapes are additive amalgams that represent the sum total of natural and human (both intended and accidental) modification over millennial scales (Erickson 2000a, 2000b; Fisher and Thurston 1999; Hill 2004). In this sense, every aspect of the environment is a unique entity that cannot be understood apart from its historical trajectory. Nonetheless, there are commonalities in the solutions that humans have created to solve many complex problems, including technology and socioeconomic organization (see Scarborough 2003a).

The built environment has created long-lasting legacies of socio-landscape relationships that have remained stable for long time periods but are often susceptible to unforeseen crises. At century or millennial timescales, such anthropogenic environments seem sustainable—and, indeed, by modern definitions of the term were successful—but such settings often were exposed to eventual catastrophe. Redman et al. (this vol.) suggest that this is a key reason why the concept of "sustainability" is inherently flawed, arguing instead for framing the issue in terms of more "resilient systems" with the capacity to react to unforeseen and unintended consequences in a rapid fashion.

Conclusion

There is widespread recognition that human society has created an environmental crisis through anthropogenic processes such as global warming (Gelbspan 1998, 2004), but the avenue toward resolution is far from certain. In an influential white paper, Shellenberger and Nordhaus have argued that environmentalism (or the environmental movement) in its current incarnation is dead (Shellenberger and Nordhaus 2005). They call for the creation of a "third wave" of environmentalism framed around investment rather than conservation or regulation. Shellenberger and Norhaus point to the narrow definition of environment and what is environmental and note that both are defined as categories "separate from and superior to the 'natural world.'" Policy solutions will come in the form of holistic endeavors that will move beyond narrowly defined environmental parameters. Absent from this discussion is the inclusion of past successes and failures in human-environment relationships and the holistic manner in which human-environment relations have now been modeled in the social sciences. As the chapters in this volume conclusively illustrate, socionatural relations in the long view not only can make a substantial contribution to the "new environmentalism" but also ought to be a significant component of this emerging approach.

Part I

New Frameworks for Interpretation

1

The Resilience of Socioecological Landscapes

LESSONS FROM THE HOHOKAM

Charles L. Redman, Margaret C. Nelson, and Ann P. Kinzig

THE JUNCTION BETWEEN present and future societies lies in the global common, the shared physical, biological, and intellectual resources of the planet—the environment. There is no greater challenge than to seek a better understanding of the operation of our environment and to use that knowledge to preserve, nurture, and perhaps even to improve upon this gift. Society maintains academic research and rewards university departments for a variety of reasons (see van der Leeuw and Redman 2002 for a fuller discussion). At the top of the list is that research may help solve present-day problems such as the above or enhance our standards of living. Also important is that research may enrich our lives through a deeper appreciation of fundamental issues. Although it could be argued that archaeology contributes in various ways to the second of these objectives, we are almost never asked to contribute our knowledge and perspective to the solution of present-day problems, including those related to the environment, even though we consider that one of our specialties.

Relevance, Interdisciplinarity, and Reality

The challenge, therefore, is to identify specific issues of widely recognized importance that archaeology can contribute to in a meaningful manner and then to pursue those issues with energy and creativity. We cannot expect decision makers outside our discipline, who are already involved in the intriguing issues of our day, to identify our contribution for us—that is up to us. The penalty for not doing so is the marginalization of our discipline. Few among us do not already recognize that our academic departments are losing their relative prominence within the university structure and that government funding for archaeological research has not kept pace with the money available for disciplines deemed more relevant. If we continue on our current trajectory, it is inevitable that the decline of our relative position will continue. A second, more ominous threat is that archaeology will attract a decreasing proportion of the most creative students, as they feel the need to be engaged in solving the crushing problems facing society today. Ultimately, the stagnation of archaeology as an intellectually active discipline would be disappointing to us as practitioners, but more importantly, it would lead to the erosion of one of the tenuous links our modern societies have established with the past (van der Leeuw and Redman 2002).

We should tackle present-day issues, such as reversing the collision course society seems to be moving along with the environment. Although this issue has attracted wide public attention only in recent decades, the underlying, worldwide trends are millennia old and derive in part from the legacies of past choices and actions. These trends can best be understood from a perspective that takes those long-term dynamics into account and that addresses questions from an integrated, often interdisciplinary perspective on human societies and biophysical environments (McIntosh et al. 2000; Redman 1999). In theory, archaeology is ideally suited to make an invaluable contribution in this area. In practice, however, few synergies have materialized. There is a rich intellectual history of archaeologists interested in human-environment relations. Among them are the cultural ecologists who contributed a series of important studies (K. W. Butzer 1982; Crumley 1994; Moran 1990; J. Steward 1955; Vayda 1969; Watson and Watson 1969). Despite this active intellectual tradition within archaeology and anthropology, few funding agencies or colleagues in the life or earth sciences think of archaeologists as essential collaborators when designing large-scale environmental research programs (see Barker 1995; Lipe and Redman 1996; Sisk and Noon 1995 for similar calls to action).

Contributions of Archaeology: Getting Beyond "Listen to Me!"

Before we as archaeologists rush onto the scene proclaiming our importance, it is essential to think through what we have to offer that is not already provided by other scientists. We suggest below domains where our contributions are important, and sometimes unique.

First, contemporary studies usually have to content themselves with investigating an historical cycle that is truncated—that is, not having completed a cycle—while archaeological case studies can provide not only completed cycles but also multiple completed cycles. This allows greater understanding into the dynamics of linked cycles and permits more in-depth monitoring of the slow-process, low-frequency events that appear to be the keys to ultimate system resilience (S. Carpenter et al. 1999; Scheffer et al. 2001). Although ecologists know that ecosystem structure and function may take decades or centuries to fully respond to disturbance, ecological studies almost exclusively examine ecosystem dynamics over intervals of a few days to a few years. Rare centennial-scale studies suggest that some human impacts are enduring, yet few integrative ecological studies of human land use cover timescales longer than two hundred years (D. Foster et al. 2003; Heckenberger et al. 2003; Mann 2002b; Roberts 1998).

Second, the "deep time" perspective allows us to understand the ultimate, rather than the proximate, causes of the collapse of social and ecological systems. Biologists have historically viewed land use as a human impact, without addressing the social dynamics that lead humans to alter the landscape in diverse ways. Collaborations with social scientists who seek to address these dynamics will allow ecologists to understand the ultimate rather than the proximate drivers of human-environment interactions (Collins et al. 2000; McGlade 1999). In particular, the long-term history of human-environment interactions contained in the archaeological record reveals that many human responses and strategies, while apparently beneficial in increasing resilience in the short term (even over a few generations), nonetheless led to a serious erosion of resilience in the long term, resulting in the collapse of both environmental and social systems (Kirch et al. 1992; T. Kohler 1992a; T. H. McGovern et al. 1988; Redman 1999; Rollefson and Köhler-Rollefson 1992; van Andel et al. 1990). It is only with the long-term perspective that we can identify which of many seemingly beneficial near-term actions truly contribute to long-term resilience, and identify the ways in which some outwardly rational choices lead, in the end, to undesirable outcomes. The converse of this is that some social adaptations or cultural traditions may appear inefficient or "illogical" when viewed in the short term, but reduce risk and increase resilience in the long term (K. W. Butzer 1996).

Third, an examination of human-environment interactions over sufficiently long timescales allows one to examine "true transformations" or truly novel situations (Brand 1999). These can be globally novel situations—such as the first-time emergences of agriculture, urban living, or industrial societies. Or they may be locally novel—not entirely new, but new to the people of a certain place and time. It remains to be seen whether today's "Information Age" will represent a fourth revolution for modern humans (the first three being agriculture, urban living, and industrialization), resulting in fundamental transformations in the organization of human society and human-environment interactions, but if it does, our understanding of the dynamics of past transformations, and the implications for resilience, may prove crucial in navigating the coming changes.

Fourth, the field of archaeology, when supplemented with the anthropological perspective, allows a rich understanding of the linked dynamics of social and ecological systems across a range of organizational scales—from individual households to hamlets, villages, cities, and civilizations. Few other social sciences encompass such a broad spectrum, preferring instead to concentrate more narrowly on "bottom-up" (e.g., household, village) or "top-down" (e.g., nation, state) levels of organization. If the dynamics of a system are predicated on the links between scales—particularly the interaction of "fast" and "slow" variables—then examination of these linkages from both social and ecological perspectives will be crucial. Archaeological perspectives can provide critical bridges to fill some of the gaps left by present-day or near-historic studies focused on a narrower spectrum of human organizational scales.

Finally, the archaeological record allows us to identify those emergent features that appear to be inevitable—or at least highly probable—in societies increasing in complexity, including social stratification, compartmentalization of information, and, at certain scales, ecological simplification. The challenge before us will be to distinguish those features of social systems, and human interactions with the environment, that can be altered to achieve more desirable social and ecological outcomes and those that are so much a product of history, human development, and biological, social, and cultural evolution that we must accept their constraints in fashioning our visions of the future. An archaeological perspective can contribute to meeting this challenge.

To accept the relevance of episodes from the past for dealing with problems of the present and future, two additional points must be made. First, for at least the last twenty to forty thousand years, people have been biologically and mentally indistinguishable from those of us alive today; and second, people in the past faced real environmental crises. There is little question that during the past ten thousand years we have modified, with increasing speed, our cultural trappings and social organizations, creating in the ensuing years environmental problems of increasing severity that are more global now than they were in the past. We must not, however, underestimate the impact environmental crises had on people in antiquity (K. W. Butzer 1982; Crumley 1994; Redman 1999). Having environmental degradation force the abandonment of a homeland in which several generations of one's ancestors lived and died is a disaster that few of us face today. In terms of human decision making and the operation of socionatural ecosystems, the past has a great deal to tell us about how people confront threats to sustainability of relationships between social systems and environmental systems.

Partnerships and New Perspectives

We have argued that archaeologists should be ready to collaborate and that we have important perspectives to bring to interdisciplinary and multidisciplinary teams. We also believe that many environmental scientists, ecologists in particular, are ready today, more than ever before, to welcome our participation. Over the last five decades, ecologists, archaeologists, and other scientists have dismantled two longstanding theoretical constructs. Ecologists have rejected the "balance of nature" concept in favor of a view that ecosystem stability and change result from interactions between persistent ecological processes and contingent historical events (including human action) (Scheffer et al. 2001). In this new view, the human components are dynamic and the relationships to environmental components are recursive. Similarly, archaeologists have dispelled the myth that indigenous people were in "harmony with nature," using evidence that for millennia humans substantially altered and often degraded their environments (Bottema et al. 1990; K. W. Butzer 1996; Kirch et al. 1992; Leveau et al. 1999; McIntosh et al. 2000; Redman 1999). Recent research is suggesting that human modification may stabilize ecosystem functions, but with drastic consequences for human and ecosystems when the social structures that support these practices collapse (Fisher et al. 2003).

The ever-increasing influence of human activity on biophysical processes demands that human society be able to assess and cope with rapidly accelerating anthropogenic environmental change. This task is difficult because environmental changes and their repercussions may play out over long time spans and across multiple spatial scales. Two current projects at Arizona State University (ASU) involve collaborations between ecologists and archaeologists. The first, "Legacies on the Landscape," is focused on the environmental consequences of two episodes of human population expansion in a relatively small segment of land, the Agua Fria National Monument in central Arizona (Briggs et al. 2006). The second, "Long-Term Coupled Socioecological Change," is broader in time and space, examining the relationship between vulnerability and transformation across a span of one thousand years in the American Southwest and northern Mexico (Hegmon et al. 2007). Both projects engage multidisciplinary teams in addressing problems that practitioners from any one discipline could not address alone.

"Legacies on the Landscape" is focused upon understanding the long-term legacy of prehistoric and modern human land use on the ecology of desert grasslands in the southwestern United States (Briggs et al. 2006). The case study is situated on the Agua Fria National Monument, just north of the Phoenix Basin, a location adjacent to the heartland of Hohokam society that we will be discussing later in this chapter. The project addresses an essential question concerning the ecological implications of human action: What are the ecological and social conditions under which human land use results in long-lasting transformations of ecosystem structure and function? Answering this question is fundamental for an understanding of the current condition of the world and for any attempts at managing it for sustainability. At a more general level, the combination of a long timescale and a sophisticated understanding of the economic, social, and political drivers of land-use change will gain ecologists an unprecedented ability to model human-environment interactions as a complex dynamical system.

The project proposed by Spielmann and her colleagues, "Alliance and Landscape: Perry Mesa, Arizona in the Fourteenth Century," is designed to overcome the long history of examining landscapes from dichotomous, natural- and social-science perspectives (Fairhead and Leach 1996; Head 2000) by focusing on the recursive relationship between human action and ecosystem-scale change and by considering the long-term ecological impacts of less intensive prehistoric human action. We know from ethnography (Bar-Yosef and Khazanov 1992; Fowler 2000) that even highly mobile hunter-gatherers managed plants and animals on their landscapes. What we do not know is the degree to which the accumulated actions of relatively low-density populations resulted in permanent transformations in ecosystem structure and function, and how these changes then condition current choices. This kind of long-term analysis of coupled socioecological change may demonstrate that many apparently "pristine" environments were in part structured by past anthropogenic alteration. We inherit many conditions that constrain our present-day alternatives and the impacts that contemporary choices will have on future landscapes. Thus, the ecosystems in which the majority of contemporary ecological field research is being carried out are, in fact, the products of both human and natural processes.

The second ASU collaboration, "Long-Term Coupled Socioecological Change," recognizes that there is a degree of irreducible uncertainty about how the dynamics of coupled social and ecological processes unfold and a legacy of intertwined socionatural processes of differing duration, intensity, and geographic scope. These intertwined processes give rise to complex dynamics on multiple temporal and spatial scales—change followed by relative stasis, followed by change. There are both understandable patterns and irreducible uncertainties in this cycle; neither stability nor transformation can be taken as the norm, and extant conditions must be seen as the product of long-term processes. For scientists, this means that theories of stability or vulnerability and transformation need to be unified to describe different aspects of a single, legacy-laden dynamic, rather than divided and treated as descriptors of separable phenomena. For society, this means coming to terms with the legacies of the past and being aware of those we will leave for the future. And for both scientists and society at large, it means recognizing the inevitability of uncertain changes and the need to develop strategies for coping with change rather than attempting to maintain rigid control (Hegmon et al. 2007).

Examining long-term human-environment interactions in several archaeologically documented case studies in the American Southwest and northern Mexico, the interdisciplinary project seeks to answer the question: What key social and ecological variables and interconnections foster stability or promote transformation in coupled socioecological systems? For each case, the recursive relationship between cultural practices and the structure of the local environment is examined, addressing specifically the role of diversity and complexity in promoting transformation. Moving to a regional spatial scale, the interconnections among local trajectories and processes are systematically investigated with attention to how we can understand the temporal coincidence of dramatic cultural transformations in different locales. Stepping back and comparing the local trajectories, the group seeks a generalized understanding of the environmental and social conditions that tend to foster stability or contribute to transformation. Finally, these deep-time case studies are compared to similar studies of resilience in present-day and near-historic case studies.

Resilience Theory and Archaeology

We believe that to work most effectively within an interdisciplinary framework and to have results that can be incorporated into important debates about social future, archaeology should examine the utility of perspectives derived from resilience theory, as we have in the "Long-Term Coupled Socioecological Change" project. Resilience theory seeks to understand the source and role of change—particularly the kinds of change that are transforming—in systems that are adaptive (Holling et al. 2002:5; Levin 1999). It is a theory of linked dynamic cycles across spatial and temporal scales. At the core of resilience theory is the adaptive cycle, which is represented by a "figure eight" as shown in fig. 1.1 (Holling 2001:394–395). Individual adaptive cycles are nested in a hierarchy across time and space (fig. 1.2). These nested hierarchies may have a stabilizing effect due to the fact that they provide the memory of the past and of the distant to allow recovery after change occurs. They may also have a destabilizing effect when dynamics across scales become "over connected" or "brittle," allowing small-scale transformations to "revolt" and explode into larger-scale crises. Taken together, this theoretical framework is called panarchy (Gunderson and Holling 2002).

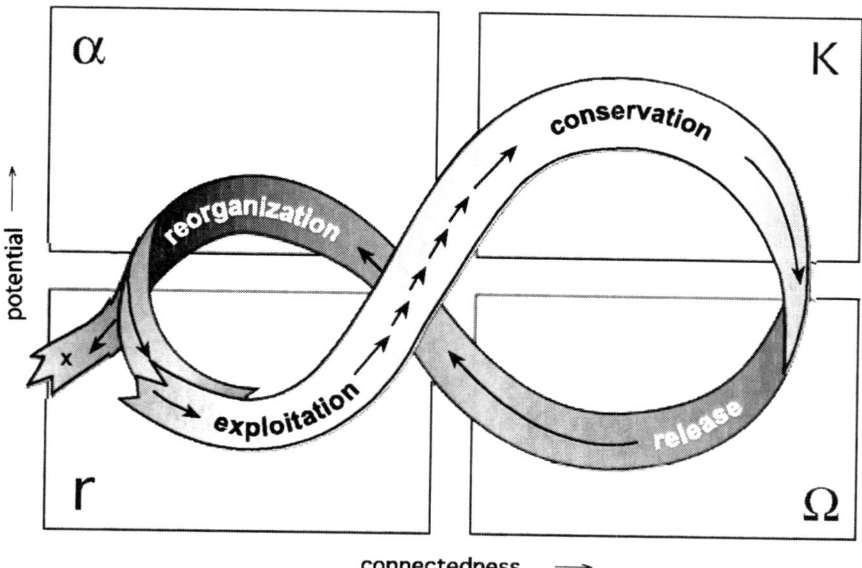

FIGURE 1.1. A stylized representation of the four phases of an adaptive cycle as discussed by resilience theorists (adapted from Holling and Gunderson 2002).

Four key features of ecosystems provide the underlying assumptions of resilience theory (Holling and Gunderson 2002:25–27; Redman and Kinzig 2003), and we believe these features and assumptions are worthy of evaluating for coupled socioecological systems. First, change is neither continuous and gradual nor consistently chaotic. Rather, it is episodic, with periods of slow accumulation of "natural capital," punctuated by sudden releases and reorganizations of those legacies. Episodic behavior is caused by interactions between fast and slow variables. Second, spatial and temporal attributes are neither uniform nor scale invariant; rather, patterns and processes are patchy and discontinuous at all scales. Therefore, scaling up from small to large cannot be a process of simple aggregation. Third, ecosystems do not have a single equilibrium with homeostatic controls; rather, multiple equilibria commonly define functionally different states. Destabilizing forces are important in maintaining diversity, flexibility, and opportunity, while stabilizing forces are important in maintaining productivity, fixed capital, and social memory. Fourth, and finally, policies and management that apply fixed rules for achieving constant

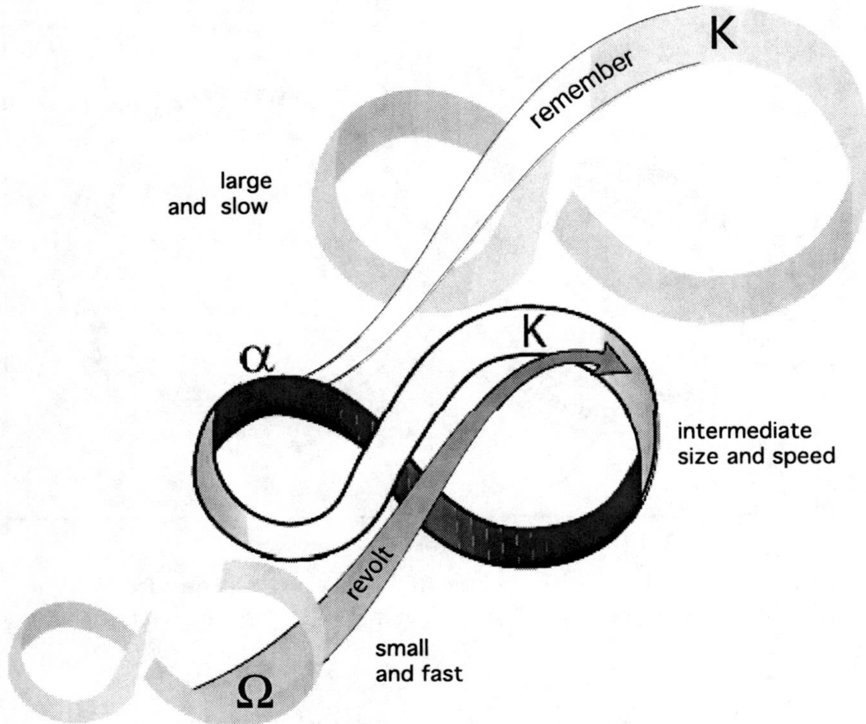

FIGURE I.2. "Remember" and "revolt" cycles across levels of the panarchy. Resilience theory emphasizes a synchronic interpretation of interactions in which small-and-fast, intermediate, and large-and-slow cycles are simultaneously operating.

yields, independent of scale and changing context, lead to systems that increasingly lose resilience—i.e., to systems that suddenly break down in the face of disturbances that previously could be absorbed. Ecosystems are moving targets, and therefore management has to be flexible, working at scales that are compatible with the scales of critical ecosystem and social functions. These critical scales may themselves change over time. The key for enhancing system resilience is for individuals, their institutions, and the society at large to develop ways to learn from past experiences, and to accept that some uncertainties must inevitably be faced.

In contrast to 1970s-style systems theory (Flannery 1968), resilience theory emphasizes the inevitability of both stability and transformation.

Neither stability nor transformation is assumed to be the norm; rather, systems are seen as moving between the two in what has been termed an adaptive cycle (Holling 1973; Holling and Gunderson 2002). Subsequent iterations of the cycle can repeat previous patterns, or transformation can be revolutionary, leading to fundamentally new configurations, possibilities, and dynamics (S. R. Carpenter and Gunderson 2001; Westley et al. 2002). Thus, we concentrate both on those configurations and linkages that promote stability and on those that engender transformation. Resilience theory also offers a framework for understanding that transformations—even the most socially and environmentally dislocating changes—are not chaotic and idiosyncratic, but rather are governed by particular dynamics, conditions, and opportunities (Folke et al. 2002).

In more traditional views, ecosystem succession is seen as being controlled by three functions: release (omega phase in fig. 1.1), in which the tightly bound accumulation of biomass becomes increasingly fragile until suddenly released by external agents; exploitation (r phase in fig. 1.1), in which rapid colonization of recently disturbed areas is emphasized; and conservation (K phase in fig. 1.1), in which slow accumulation and storage of energy and material are emphasized (Holling and Gunderson 2002:33–35). Resilience theorists add a key fourth function: reorganization (alpha phase), in which resources are reorganized into a new system to take advantage of opportunities. The innovation here is that this "new" system may resemble its predecessor, or have fundamentally new functional characteristics (see M. Nelson et al. 2006 for an archaeological treatment of this aspect of the resilience perspective). These four phases have been organized into an "adaptive cycle" metaphor that allows one to analyze specific ecosystem trajectories against this theory.

Resilience theory has added two additional features to our understanding of succession in particular, and system dynamics more generally. The first is that change is ultimately inevitable and repeated, although repeated cycles may not follow the same pathway or result in analogous systems. The triggering event of release can occur as the result of an internal change in the system, and the K phase is no longer viewed as a stable phase interrupted only by external perturbations. The second feature is one already mentioned—that these adaptive cycles appear to occur across scales, but not continuously. Instead, it is assumed that there are only a handful of spatio-temporal scales—ranging from small-and-fast to large-and-slow—that exhibit strong signatures in the system, and it is the interaction among adaptive cycles at these different characteristic scales that determine resilience dynamics.

As shown in fig. 1.2, small-and-fast adaptive circles may go through frequent periods of creative destruction; in many cases, the "memory" imposed by large-and-slow adaptive cycles would mean the small-and-fast levels would re-enter the same or similar adaptive cycles ("remember" arrow). (For example, families may disintegrate due to divorce, but reconstituted families follow the designs deemed "acceptable" by cultural or religious institutions, including, most prominently, parent-child nuclear families.) In some cases, however, tight connections among small-and-fast cycles, or between small-and-fast and intermediate cycles, might mean that creative destruction at the smallest levels precipitates concurrent destruction, and potential flips into fundamentally new adaptive cycles, at larger levels (the "revolt" arrow). This might occur, for instance, if enough families adopted fundamentally new household arrangements to force changes in higher levels of social arrangements.

Long-Term Transformation in the Hohokam Socioecological System

One of the cases explored by ASU interdisciplinary groups is the prehistoric, farming occupation of the Sonoran Desert of central and southern Arizona, referred to as "Hohokam." Our work focuses on the Phoenix Basin. Beginning by at least AD 700, human populations gradually modified their terrestrial and fluvial landscapes through a diverse array of agricultural and water-management strategies (Howard and Huckleberry 1991). Hohokam settlements eventually spanned a territory exceeding 100,000 km^2 (Doyel et al. 2000; fig. 1.3), when the Phoenix Basin contained the largest canal irrigation network north of Peru (Doolittle 2000). This period of gradual growth and relative stability ended in the twelfth century (the Preclassic to Classic transformation) when some villages were depopulated, new styles of monuments with restricted access were constructed, and populations were increasingly concentrated along perennial water sources, abandoning many interior desert areas (Bayman 2001; S. Dean 1994). This reorganization is associated with regional climatic events and possibly with changes in river-channel morphology

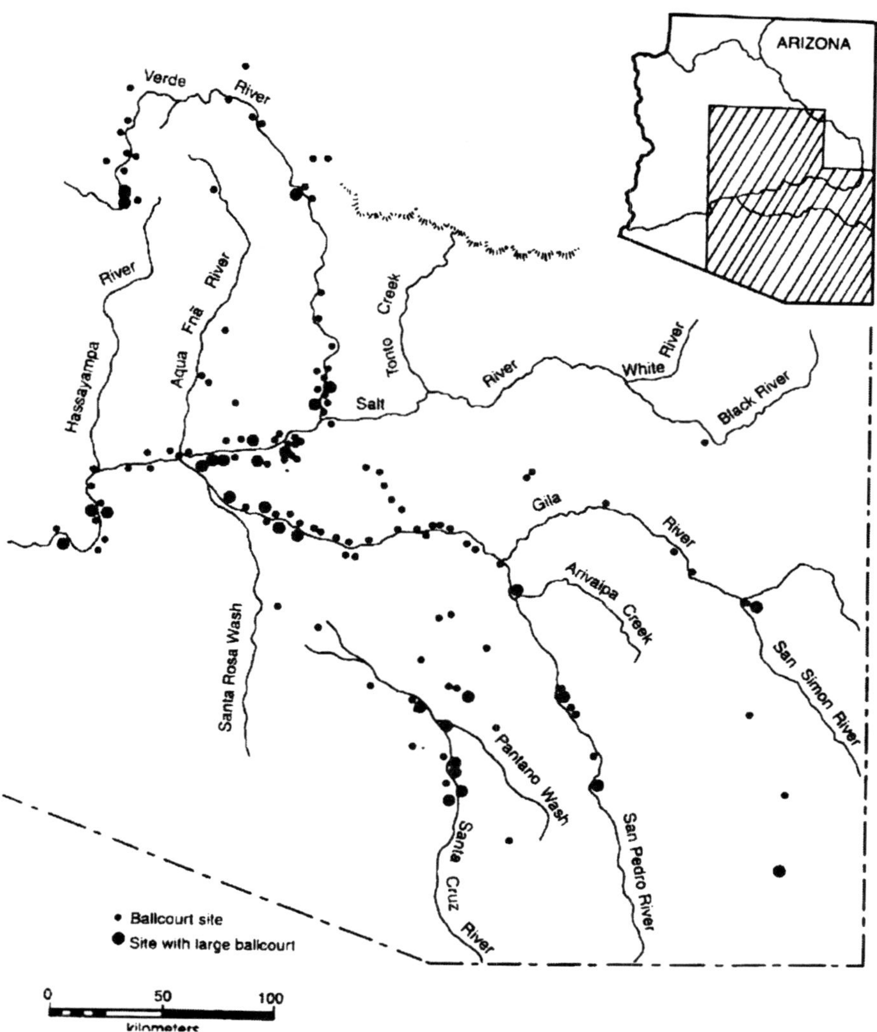

FIGURE 1.3. Location of sites with ballcourts as an indication of the geographic range of Hohokam-influenced settlements during the late Preclassic period.

(Howard and Huckleberry 1991; Waters and Ravesloot 2001). Irrigation agriculture, a key point of articulation between social and environmental processes, provides a window through which to examine the rapid transformation (e.g., Nials et al. 1989). Also, the mid-twelfth-century transformation involved change in the social order, including development of a more hierarchical structure and a decrease in access to ritual/public spaces (Abbott 2000; Bayman 2002; Bayman and Shackley 1999; S. Fish and Fish 2000; G. Rice 1998). Thus, the transformation provides a context in which we can investigate issues of social organization and resource management, including the development of models relating the scale and structure of decision making and responses to environmental perturbations.

An enormous amount of archaeological research has been conducted in the Hohokam region during the past twenty years, and this is supplemented by excellent paleoclimatic records derived from several sources. The initial impression derived from the record is that short-term political stability and economic maximization were achieved only by weakening the capacity of the productive system to react to internal and external challenges and, hence, undermined long-term survival of Hohokam irrigation farming and social constructions (Redman 1992, 1999). It is informative to look at each domain of evidence we have on the Hohokam, how it changed or did not change across this time period, and the implications for the socioecological system. Whether this is a sharp transition that took place very quickly or is a slower evolution that took one or more human generations is yet to be determined, and this may vary according to domain of evidence and processes involved. For the sake of this chapter, we will treat this transition as sharp, contrasting the two periods when there are differences and not emphasizing continuity. Another approach might emphasize the continuities that were evident in the reorganization.

The regional distribution of population is one pattern that has been often reported on and prompts us to think of this transformation as a fundamental reorganization of the society. Preclassic Hohokam settlements and constellations of Hohokam attributes are found at sites from Flagstaff (150 km north of Phoenix) to the U.S.–Mexico border (200 km south of Phoenix). Some would argue that the evidence found in these far-flung settlements did not necessarily indicate that biologically identified "Hohokam" were living there, but often the assemblage of architecture, artifacts, and burial customs does suggest that the population would have socially identified themselves as what we refer to as the Hohokam. Over the intervening years, this broad geographic spread contracted, with settlements in distant locations (such as Flagstaff or Payson) no longer exhibiting Hohokam traits and, within the geographic core, a gradual abandonment of agriculturally less-desirable areas in favor of those that could be irrigated and intensified. Hence, during the Classic period, the population concentrated in the Phoenix Basin and a few scattered, large settlements in the south and west.

Some Hohokam settlements were occupied for only a few generations, but in selected locations, such as the basin occupied by the modern city of Phoenix, Hohokam communities existed for a millennium, up until at least AD 1450. Although the population density of the Phoenix Basin ebbed and flowed, the persistence of these desert dwellers is truly impressive. The centerpiece of their success was their irrigation system, which was built around the two rivers—the Salt and the Gila—that traversed the broad Phoenix lowland basin. These rivers ran year-round, but their volume varied dramatically in response to runoff from rainfall and snowmelt in the upland catchments. The Hohokam took advantage of this resource by building hundreds of kilometers of canals, some as long as 30 km, to bring water and sediments to increasingly distant fields (Abbott 2000; Bayman 2001; Crown and Judge 1991; Doyel et al. 2000; Howard and Huckleberry 1991). Interestingly, archaeologists believe that the Phoenix Basin's enormous irrigation system had already attained nearly its maximum extent early in Preclassic times. Hence, these major irrigation systems were in operation in both periods. Over the course of the Preclassic to Classic transition there is a filling-in of the existing canal works with smaller distribution canals, thereby bringing water to new fields. Interlinking canals may have been built later, allowing for the shift of water from one system to another that would be important if the head gates of one system did not function effectively. The Hohokam developed ballcourts and, later, platform mounds at local centers that focused community ceremonial and civic activities. Community organization provided the framework for allocating water from canals and mobilizing labor for constructing and maintaining the canal system.

The actual spatial layout of settlements and form of residential architecture between these two phases changed substantially. In the Preclassic, villages had large amounts of open space and were comprised of pit houses arranged in small groups around open space referred to as a courtyard. Each courtyard cluster was separated from adjoining ones by substantial open space. During the Classic period, settlements characterized by rectilinear, multi-room surface architecture were built, and the villages became more densely arranged. The population per village was not only nucleating but also, in many cases, overall village population grew. In addition, many villages and parts of larger settlements were situated within enclosure walls.

A shift in public architecture has been one of the key attributes associated with the change between these two periods. In the earlier phase, the existence of large and small features identified as ballcourts has come to be the hallmark of whether a settlement should be considered "Hohokam." With the passage of time, ballcourts continued but decreased in frequency, and a new construction—the platform mound—became the most recognizable public architecture in Classic period sites. These mounds started small, but by the fourteenth century, they dominated the settlements, with ritual activities and elite residences on top. Some of the largest Classic settlements had multiple platform mounds and, at a few, multistory Great Houses. Platform mounds were almost always set within walled compounds, enabling the restrictive performance of ceremonial activity.

A few changes in artifact style and burial treatment are worth noting. Ceramics are always a favorite way of differentiating between temporal periods, and this is true for Hohokam prehistory as well. Whereas red-on-buff pottery, produced primarily along the Gila River, dominated the decorated assemblage throughout the Preclassic, the onset of the Classic is identified by its replacement with Salado polychromes, much of it made in areas to the east of the Phoenix Basin. Burials and ritual items also changed, with some forms more restricted. The Preclassic is characterized by cremation burials and ritual items—such as censers, palettes, shells, and fired-clay figurines—associated with what are interpreted as cremations of high-status individuals. With the beginning of the Classic period, inhumation became increasingly popular. The ritual inventory remained similar, with the addition of ritually important items such as conch-shell trumpets and stone batons. The distribution of these items changed substantially: cremations have few ritual items, while some allegedly high-status inhumations have ritual items. Additional ritual materials are found on or associated with the platform mounds.

Although we believe that climate remained relatively stable throughout the Hohokam sequence and up to the present, some changes in patterns may have had significant impacts on irrigation agriculture. Because local precipitation in the Phoenix Basin averages about seven inches a year, far less than is needed for maize agriculture, we have focused on the volume of stream flow in the Salt and Gila Rivers that would have been available for diversion into irrigation canals as they passed through the settled areas. One important difference between the two rivers is that although they both were fed by catchments that received bi-annual precipitation (summer and winter), the winter signal was much more intense in the Salt catchment than in the Gila, thereby providing several times the volume of runoff. The second pattern is one that appears to have changed during the course of the Preclassic to Classic transition (Nials et al. 1989). In simplest terms, the pattern seems to have been for more consistent levels of stream flow punctuated by infrequent flood and drought during the Preclassic, with a change in the Classic to significantly more variable stream flow levels and more frequent flood and drought years (fig. 1.4).

Evidence concerning native plants used and animals eaten enables some insights into the changing nature of the local and regional environment and the resources available to the Hohokam. Desert species supplemented the corn, beans, and squash that were transplanted from Mexico. Local varieties of beans were grown, agave was harvested for food and fiber, and other crops like cotton and little barley also contributed (P. Fish and Fish 1992). Animals hunted were usually small, such as rabbits, and could be found in the vicinity of settlements. Trapping them may have been a regular part of the daily farming regime. Over time, there was a shift in the type of rabbits eaten—from cottontail to jackrabbit—reflecting an environmental change to increasingly open habitats (James 2003). Larger artiodactyls, like antelope and deer, were also hunted when available, but over time it appears that long-distance hunting parties were needed to bring back these animals, implying that they were no longer available locally. The overall picture one can reconstruct from this indirect evidence is that during the Preclassic the landscape may have been a mosaic of irrigated fields and areas that retained their Sonoran Desert vegetation. Along the river there probably was dense riparian vegetation, and perhaps it extended along some of the canals as well. However, after centuries of occupation of the area with shifting farm fields and continual exploitation of resources, the habitat

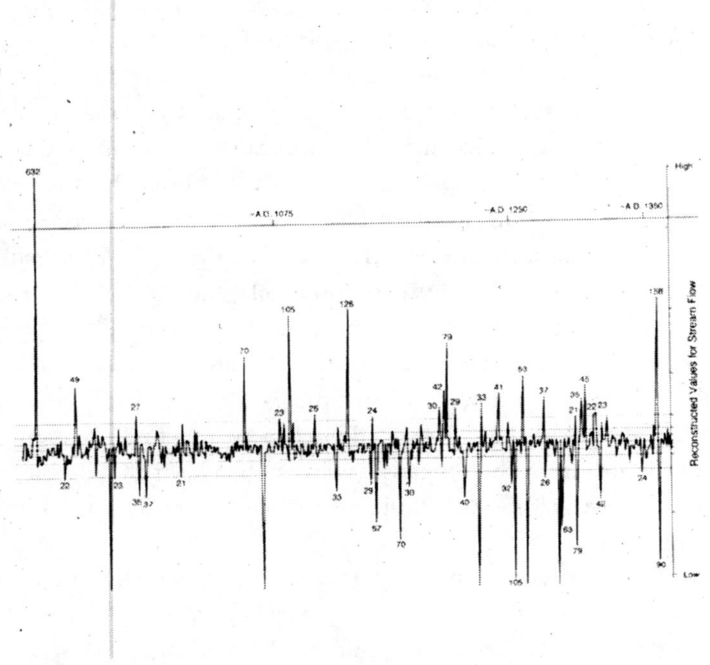

FIGURE 1.4. Reconstruction of stream flow of Salt River during Hohokam occupation (adapted from Nials et. al. 1989).

must have lost much of its native vegetation and become more continuously open and homogeneous.

Archaeological evidence does reveal that there was a dramatic increase in riparian species consumed by the Hohokam during the Classic period, perhaps because of the pressure on the other terrestrial fauna in the vicinity of settlement (Kwiatkowski 2003). We expect that the Salt River would have had some water year-round and that it would have flowed actively for substantial periods of time. Lakes and swamps may have persisted along the river courses, and the riparian areas may have been lush and large when water was abundant. Nevertheless, the use of muskrat, beaver, aquatic birds, and fish implies a food crisis for the Hohokam, or at least an intensification of their procurement strategies that left no potential resource unutilized. Fish ranked behind rabbits as a source of animal protein for the Classic period Hohokam (James 1994). In measuring the size of the fish taken during Classic Hohokam times, James found that they were smaller than the modern examples, suggesting that already these fish were under pressure and that the larger ones had been systematically fished out.

We believe that the major forces driving Hohokam society through the adaptive cycle and offering stability to many residents up until AD 1450 or so derived from the interaction of environmental factors and human strategies: climate variability, floodplain dynamics, irrigation strategies, and social integration and differentiation. An essential aspect for understanding these dynamics is attention to the varying spatial and temporal scales at which they occurred. In particular, a long period of relatively stable annual stream-flow volumes allowed for the construction and subsequent expansion of irrigation systems on the Salt and Gila Rivers that were essential to the growth in population and social complexity that characterized the Preclassic period Hohokam adaptive cycle (ca. AD 700–1150; fig. 1.5 map). Although settlement densities were highest near perennial streams, the Hohokam also used a diverse suite of agricultural and gathering strategies in areas without perennial streams. A long period of increasing variability of water flows and possible down cutting of the riverbed stressed the irrigation system and possibly the hinterland; at this time, Hohokam society experienced a serious transformation toward more social differentiation and hierarchy, resulting in what archaeologists characterize as the Classic period (ca. AD 1150–1450; Nials et al. 1989; G. Rice 1998). We hypothesize that this represents a release and revolt reorganization in the system, projecting it through a new adaptive cycle (fig. 1.6), one that Abbott (2003) suggests led to decline. The geographic extent of the region contracted from north and south, even though population may have continued to grow (Ingram 2008); community-level social organization fragmented, yet the sociopolitical leadership became more institutionalized and hierarchical, as demonstrated by the construction of platform mounds and "great" houses associated with compounds in which only a few resided. At the household level, people probably had less autonomy, with their activity spaces becoming more structured and concentrated. Overall, we believe that flexibility at the household level had diminished, while community organization had become tighter and operated at larger social and landscape scales.

Populations increasingly concentrated along perennial water sources, and with some exceptions, the non-riverine deserts were substantially

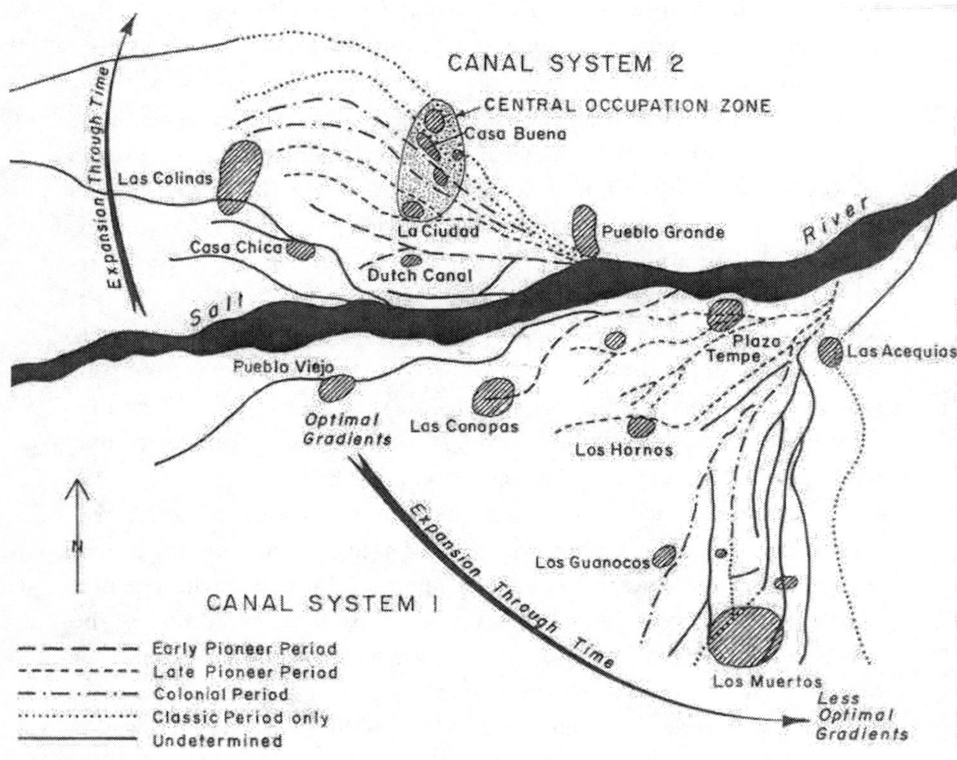

FIGURE 1.5. Outline of some of the major canals and Hohokam settlements in the Phoenix region (adapted from G. Rice 1998).

depopulated. Although this reorganization stabilized social relations and allowed continuation of irrigation farming, it was not sufficiently resilient to maintain the Classic period institutions and settlements beyond AD 1450. When the Spanish arrived after AD 1540, many areas in the major river valleys were no longer occupied, and populations had greatly waned since Classic period highs.

Throughout the sequence of stability-transformation-stability in social relations, farming strategies inhibited radical changes in field and settlement location. Irrigated fields, when purposely watered or accidentally flooded, received a load of nutrients and new silt that served to regenerate the soil fertility. This is extremely important in the Southwest where soil development is slow and soils remain shallow. Large settlements

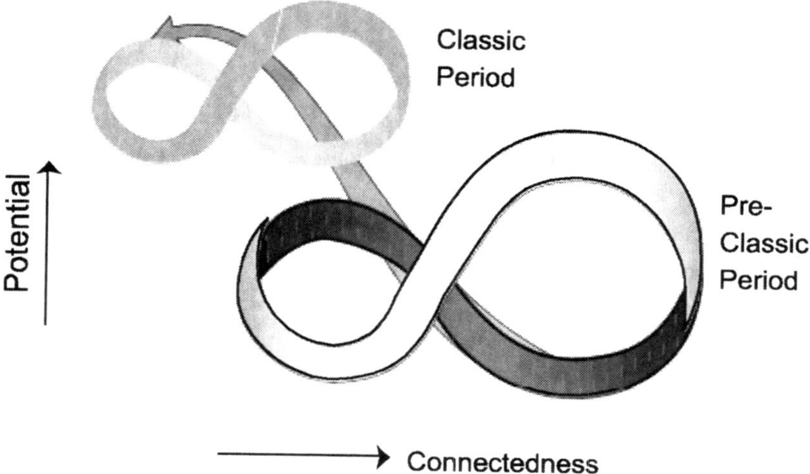

FIGURE 1.6. Proposed adaptive cycles related to a state flip in Hohokam society occurring during the Preclassic to Classic period transition (adapted from Redman and Kinzig 2003).

focused in the wide valley bottoms, while smaller settlements were located to take advantage of the sloping uplands, the bases of alluvial fans, and the arroyo bottoms where storm runoff could be channeled, bringing substantial organic and sediment additions to the desert soils (P. Fish and Fish 1992). Wide flat valley bottoms with available surface water were extremely localized, and farming locations with suitable water diversion potential in association with arable flatlands were even more restricted. Investments in modifying field locations and the limited distribution of essential features for farming made frequent resettlement disadvantageous. This focused residential stability created increased need for Hohokam settlers to conserve the long-term productive potential of the surroundings and to develop diverse and efficient strategies for provisioning the growing population. The fact that intensive agriculture results in reduced mobility for human groups is key to understanding the Hohokam and the human-environment interactions of many other groups around the world.

The growth of irrigation canals during the Preclassic and the shift in regional population during the Classic period influenced the ability of farmers to diversify. The expanding irrigation system brought water to areas away from the floodplain of major rivers, increasing productivity. However, the construction of canals and cultivation of domesticated plants altered the landscape in ways that may have decreased ecological diversity and modified ecosystem function and structure. When the canals were carrying adequate water, productivity was high, but in times of drought or when floods damaged canals, an ever-broader swath of the landscape would have been relatively barren. During the Preclassic, Hohokam farmers extended far north to the Mogollon Rim, but by the Classic period, the Hohokam region had contracted toward the Phoenix Basin and was much less topographically diverse, which had implications for the diversity of plant and animal resources available to Classic period farmers (James 2003; Kwiatkowski 2003).

Explanatory Priorities: Separating Cause from Effect

In considering the classes of transformations of socioecological systems that are fundamental to the condition and sustainability of the world, two in particular come to mind. The first are those of the r through K phases of the adaptive cycle that represent periods of growth and maintenance of complex systems, often with the accumulation of both capital and vulnerabilities. Second are those of the omega phase of the adaptive cycles that involves episodes of degradation of landscape and sometimes the collapse of the social system. In the literature concerning these two fundamental transformations, we find substantial uncertainty as to the priority of cause and effect. A closer look at these ambiguities may lead researchers to consider the relationship of social and ecological factors in more sophisticated ways.

Archaeology provides many examples of each of these transformations, and archaeologists have repeatedly suggested particular explanations for these socioecological changes. What is most interesting to us is that specific historical situations have been explained by archaeologists in fundamentally contradictory ways. Looking back at the Hohokam case, we have found two very different explanations offered in the literature for the sequence of growth in Preclassic and Classic periods. The explanation we put forward ourselves is built upon the earlier work of Nials et al. (1989) and others (Bayman 2001; Redman 1992; G. Rice 1998) who suggest that growth in population and social complexity characterized the Preclassic period and that it was made possible by a long period of relatively stable annual stream-flow volumes in the rivers that fed their canal system. The following long period of increasing variability of water flows was key in encouraging the reorganization of the Preclassic socio-ecological system through what may have been an omega and alpha phase into the Classic period system where the geographic extent and the population contracted. With some variations, this explanation is repeated by several scholars and has attained a reasonable level of acceptance.

However, Ingram has recently presented a set of analyses that lead to a different explanation of the same historic episode (2008). By compiling a phase-by-phase inventory of excavated residences in settlements along one of the largest of the Salt River irrigation systems, he calculated population trends that contrast with previously accepted reconstructions. His conclusion is that the population in the Classic was higher than that of the Late Preclassic. In addition, he looked at stream flow using more detailed parameters than had been used previously and confirmed low variability in the Preclassic and high variability and more frequent serious floods and droughts during the Classic. Hence, the correlations he proposed link the period of high variability with increasing population, and the more stable period of stream flow with lower population. This exciting contrary proposition forces one to consider what could have driven this counterintuitive correlation. Ingram suggested it might be that serious floods in fact have positive ecological impacts by restoring soil nutrients and reducing the threat of salinization that outweigh the traditionally cited negative impacts. Other explanations might rest at a larger geographic scale where the same climatic pattern that led to variable stream flow in the valley may have caused even less desirable conditions in the uplands, leading people to migrate into the valley. This perspective is consistent with other studies suggesting that efforts at risk minimization lead to new organizational structures operating at scales not previously incorporated into the system (Sanders and Price 1968). Whatever the causes and whether or not these patterns hold up to future examination, this trial formulation is exciting because it challenges the accepted logic and forces us to look beyond intuitively obvious relations to more complex couplings that might be operating at different scales and prompting changes in the social ecological landscape.

The second class of transformations that archaeologists often attempt to explain is episodes of environmental degradation and their relationship to social collapse. As the literature on human impacts on ancient environments has grown, an explanatory pattern has emerged Redman 1999): increasing population numbers, increasing aggregation, and increasingly hierarchical sociopolitical organizations over time create excessive pressure on surrounding landscapes, eventually leading to cycles of degradation and loss of productive potential. This then results in an inability to provide the surplus production to support the hierarchical political structure, and the society is seen to collapse, or at least the central authority is truncated and some of the cities are depopulated. Hence, when describing the collapse of the Ur III Dynasty in early Mesopotamia, the demands put on the productive landscape by the central authority are argued to have led to an over-exploitation of the land and destructive salinization of fields that ultimately led to the sociopolitical breakdown of the centralized authority (R. M. Adams 1978; Redman 1992). Similarly, many have drawn the inference from the study by O'Hara et al. (1993) of late prehistoric sediments in the Lake Pátzcuaro Basin of west-central Mexico that the rise of the Tarascan state, with its high population density and hierarchical political organization, led to episodes of serious soil erosion and loss of agricultural potential, undermining the society (K. W. Butzer 1993; Redman 1999). This pattern of excessive use by high populations, especially those in a hierarchically organized society where consumption patterns are intensified by the existence of elite groups, is one that makes intuitive sense, especially in the context of contemporary environmental discourse that suggests modern exploitation patterns may also lead to socioecological collapse. Implicit in some of the suggestions for the eventual abandonment of the Phoenix area by the Hohokam in the fifteenth century is that the extended period of high population density in the region undermined the productivity of the landscape so that people could not effectively respond to crises like a large flood or serious drought and were forced to leave the area.

However, other researchers are suggesting a contrary pattern where dense population and complex social and political organization facilitated the investment of labor and capital in maintaining sophisticated agrarian systems, such as terracing, raised fields, or large-scale irrigation works. These systems enhanced productivity by directing water and organic deposits to new areas. When the central authority failed, for social or political reasons, the ability to keep the sophisticated agrarian system intact was lost and production took a nosedive. Eventually, the deterioration of these capital improvements may also have meant a degradation of the landscape through soil erosion, salinization, or some other peril that the high level of labor input had held in bay. Fisher (Fisher et al. 2003, this vol.) provides new evidence on the Lake Pátzcuaro Basin, suggesting that the episodes of high soil erosion in fact followed the downfall of the Tarascan state rather than caused it. Similarly, Fall et al. (2004) suggest that the periods of highest productivity in the Levant were during episodes of strong central authority and that the fall of hierarchical government often led to a deterioration of the agricultural infrastructure and a drop in productivity (see van Andel et al. 1990 for a similar discussion of early Greek landscapes). Determining the correct historic pattern of environmental degradation—whether the fall of high civilizations was caused by environmental degradation or the fall of those civilizations subsequently caused environmental degradation—may be a case-by-case situation and demands careful chronological and landscape reconstructions. We are not trying to settle that argument here, but rather point to the complex and recursive relationships that existed within the social and ecological system. Not only are both important in their own right but also one cannot be understood without understanding the reflexive relationship it has with the other.

Acknowledgements

This chapter has benefited from several National Science Foundation research projects.

Abbott, D. and K. Spielmann (co-PIs). "Alliance and Landscape: Perry Mesa, Arizona in the Fourteenth Century." National Science Foundation, BTS-0613201.

Hall, S. and J. Briggs. "Legacies on the Landscape: Prehistoric Human Land Use and Long-Term Ecological Change," NSF DEB-0614349.

The project "Long-Term Coupled Socioecological Change in the American Southwest and Northern Mexico" is supported by National Science Foundation "Biocomplexity in the Environment (BE): Integrated Research and Education in Environmental Systems," BCS-0508001.

Redman, C. and A. Kinzig (co-PIs). "Agrarian Landscapes in Transition: A Cross-Scale Approach." National Science Foundation, BCS-BE-216560.

Ann Kinzig was partially supported by a grant from the James S. McDonnell Foundation.

2

What Is an "Environmental Crisis" to an Archaeologist?

Sander E. van der Leeuw

The contribution of anthropology and archaeology to the problems of our own society is very limited unless we can learn from studying different instances of social processes in the past and in distant places. Such learning depends in turn on our capacity to formulate what happens elsewhere in terms of concepts, models, and theories that also help us understand the processes and problems we ourselves are involved in.

One such set of processes and problems that has recently emerged is "the crisis of the environment." The Rio de Janeiro Conference on the Environment in 1992 placed environmental concerns very high on the agenda of governments, companies, and societies in various parts of the world. As a result, the 1990s and early 2000s saw several international treaties, the creation of ministries of the environment in many countries, and recently the inclusion of the precautionary principle in the constitution of the French Republic.

But it seems that we have not yet really come any further in defining this so-called "environmental crisis." Why? There are many possible answers. Some of the more superficial concern the role of the media, politics and politicians, and societal dynamics. But the nature of the term "crisis" itself has made it difficult to advance our understanding, as it refers to a feeling, a perception, rather than to specific events or processes. The term may also have dramatized the situation to such a point that our attention strayed from the topic because it seemed unsolvable. And finally, the term "environmental crisis" inherently escapes definition because of its intrinsic ambiguity.

The questions that pose themselves at a more fundamental level are no easier to answer. What is a crisis? Do we have a purely environmental crisis on our hands, or should we rather be speaking of a socioenvironmental crisis concerning the interaction between society and its natural environment? If that is the case, do we know other examples of such crises? Can we distinguish their causes? Are they environmental, societal, or mixed?

Altogether, there are many questions, and few answers. In the disciplines I am familiar with—such as ecology, history, anthropology, and archaeology—the notion of crisis is in effect rarely studied, poorly defined, and poorly understood. I would therefore like to contribute some ideas derived from fifteen years of multidisciplinary research on instances of environmental crises as coordinator of a research program (ARCHAEOMEDES) on "Understanding the natural and anthropogenic causes of desertification and land degradation in the Mediterranean Basin."

Comparing Two Examples

To begin, I will argue that "environmental crises" are in effect crises in the relationship between a society and its environment. To that effect, I will briefly present, and compare, two case studies of environmental problems. Whereas the first is experienced as an environmental crisis, the second is an instance of the successful avoidance of such a crisis.

The Argolid is situated in the southeastern Peloponnese. This small catchment basin was up to the 1940s one of Greece's richest areas and is now considered to be the locus of a major environmental disaster. The events leading to that disaster began in the 1950s, when fear of rural abandonment led the government to grant subsidies to keep young farmers on the land. But instead of young potential farmers (for whom they were meant, but who never heard about them), landed urbanites (bankers, notaries, dentists, etc.) claimed the subsidies, asserting they were farmers. Because they could not spend much time farming, they chose to plant an "easy" crop, requiring little labor or supervision: citrus. Their fruit sold well throughout Europe, and they became rich. That tempted many of the farmers in the region to plant citrus also.

Forty years later, this dynamic has resulted in major problems because citrus requires huge amounts of water. By 1990, groundwater levels became so low—400 m in some places—that water and soils have become salinized, the microclimate has been altered, crop and plant diversity has been severely reduced, and recurrent crop pests are increasing. All these "environmental" problems have led to the introduction of technological "solutions": pumps, air-mixers, etc.

Moreover, the changes have created a regional dependency on distant markets and have led to social upheavals and to increasing subsidies for political reasons. In the early 1990s, the European Union's political will to give such subsidies declined, and as a result, the area is a social disaster in the making. Yet, this totally unsustainable socioenvironmental system is not due to any one of these single factors, but rather to the interaction of natural and social dynamics, which created a series of positive feedback loops leading to non-linear dynamics.

The Baixo Mondego encompasses the middle and lower catchment of the Mondego River, between Coimbra and Figueira da Foz in central Portugal, and has plenty of rain. Until the 1960s, holdings were infinitely small and dispersed over the valley and the surrounding foothills. Most farms exploited two ecosystems. The main crops were corn, rice, and horticultural crops, as well as some eucalyptus forest (if one can call that a crop).

Political intervention also has dominated the scene here since the 1960s. The government first built a hydroelectric dam to protect the floodplain from flooding, as well as new road and irrigation systems. In the 1980s, it began to re-allocate land; at present, this is partially completed. Together, these initiatives changed the socioenvironmental system profoundly. They focused agriculture in the valley and led to the concentration of land in the hands of a few people. Large parts of the uplands were given over to the exploitation of eucalyptus, which heavily degrades the soil.

As small-scale agriculture became less profitable, most families found a solution by taking on a job in one of the towns, or living off a pension. But that would not have happened but for four particular circumstances. The first is the proximity of the two urban economic centers that provided jobs for the rural population (Coimbra and Figueira). Secondly, the valley had a very good (rail and road) transportation system to facilitate daily commuting from rural homes to the urban workplace. Third, the existence in the valley of two urban economic centers provided a large number of jobs for the rural population. Finally, the transition occurred while Portugal was still relatively isolated from the rest of the European Union. Hence, neither emigration nor tax-free exports nor subsidies were available to mitigate the problems. This enhanced the resilience of the local system, which now flourishes.

Are these "crisis" problems truly environmental? In the Argolid, subsidies linked an independent agricultural system into a wider political, social, and economic system. They initiated choices that were not environmentally sustainable, and eventually transformed the economic and social dynamic compromising its resilience. In the Baixo Mondego, the system seems to owe its resilience to its relative isolation. The socioeconomic structure had the opportunity to initiate a shift to pluri-activity thanks to good transportation and small distances. Problems began to occur as the new hydro-system neared completion, when the government wanted farmers to change from rice cultivation to herding. That never worked, because the transition was not well organized . . . and went against a long-standing tradition.

In these (and many) other cases, the problems seem to lie in the interaction between society and the environment. Most environmental phenomena are not "simply" "events that occur in our environment." They are part of a co-evolution between people and their environment that links, in many insufficiently understood ways, social dynamics to the natural (i.e. "non-social") dynamics occurring in the environment.

For millennia, the human race managed to survive a permanently changing environment. During that period, wherever we have solid evidence, it can be argued convincingly that the societal dynamics caused problems through a prolonged sequence of "unintended consequences" of human impact on the environment.

Indeed, one is tempted to generalize that after a long period of interaction between a society and its natural environment, the former has selectively transformed the latter according to its worldview, using the resources the society has identified and ignoring all others. In the process, the two spheres have become so intertwined that the society can no longer find a way out of the problems its appropriation with its environment has brought about.

What Do We Mean by "A Crisis"?

In an initial approximation, one could define an environmental crisis as an instance of extreme degradation of the relation between a society and its natural environment, a time when that relationship functions very poorly, or not at all. Either the society or its environment changes at such a quick pace that the society can no longer maintain the kind of adequate relationship with its environment that enables its continued existence.

Why is the burden of maintaining that relationship entirely on the society? Luhmann (1992) reminds us that people do not communicate with their natural environment, but communicate among themselves about that environment. The society defines its environment, its environmental problems, how it addresses them, and whether the result is an improvement or not. The problems are thus inherent in the relationship between the society and its environment, rather than in the natural dynamics of the environment. They are due to the inevitably incomplete and thus inadequate perception and handling of the environmental dynamics and the cognitive and information-processing capacity of the society. If the society was always able to perceive emergent environmental problems in time to solve them, there would never be any environmental crisis. Hence, one could also define an environmental crisis as a temporary inadequacy of the information-processing capacity of the society that deals with transformations in the relationship between itself and its environment. At such a time, the society can no longer maintain a profitable relationship with its environment.

What Brings Environmental Crises About?

One could argue that environmental crises are triggered by an unusually important deceleration or acceleration of one or more of the processes constituting the dynamics of the socionatural system. That process or processes must be important enough to entail changes in a sufficiently large number of enough other processes to cause the system to lose its coherence.

From that perspective, the investigation of the trajectories that may lead up to such sudden changes are important. Those trajectories are not linear, and are the result of the complex dynamics by which societies deal with many, partially contradictory, phenomena. Only an important number of case studies may be able to shed light on the "topology of the possible" (Fontana 2002) that governs such trajectories. Such a study cannot succeed without answering three groups of general questions, as well as a wealth of many more detailed ones concerning the individual trajectories.

1. What drives any socioenvironmental system periodically towards a crisis? Can we distinguish typical "pre-crisis" and "post-crisis" system states? If so, what characterizes them?
2. Under which conditions do such crises occur? We need to identify the necessary as well as the sufficient conditions. Are there generic indicators that could warn us of impending crises?
3. How do crises manifest themselves? Is there a finite set of trajectories linking each "pre-crisis" state to a "post-crisis" state? If so, how could these be described?

There is of course no guarantee that the approach that underlies these questions—viewing crises as inherent in the relations between a society and its environment—is a good one. But our characterization of such crises as caused by the environment alone has prompted more questions than it has answered. We have never tried to test the hypothesis, for example, that there are stages in (or states of) socioenvironmental dynamics that are more vulnerable to environmental crises than others. But, in view of the current state of our knowledge, we have in my opinion little to lose, and much to gain, by considering these questions.

What Drives Socioenvironmental Systems Regularly towards a Crisis?

It is of course impossible to answer this question without an important number of case studies of crises, and that is where, in my opinion, the difficulties begin. There are indeed many of them, but virtually all are formulated descriptively, rather than in terms of a general theory of socioenvironmental crises. We are therefore unable to identify similarities and differences between the instances observed or to distinguish, in each case, the fundamental processes from incidental ones. We urgently need a general theory to describe the individual occurrences of socioenvironmental crises in general terms.

At least four research domains converge on the construction of such a theory of the dynamics of socioenvironmental systems. The natural sciences have contributed to the ideas that are sometimes called "the science of complex systems" (e.g., Bak 1996; Kauffman 1993; Levin 1999; Prigogine 1980). Social anthropology has contributed "cultural theory" (M. Thompson et al. 1990), and the sciences of organization and information have contributed an understanding of the dynamics of social structures (e.g., Huberman et al. 1988; Pattee 1973; H. Simon 1981; H. White 2001). Some of their ideas have been adapted by ecologists (e.g., Allen and Hoekstra 1992; Allen and Starr 1982; O'Neill et al. 1986). Finally, the first attempt at a synthesis of these different ideas comes from collaboration between ecologists and social scientists (Gunderson and Holling 2002; Holling 2001).

In their "Resilience Theory," Gunderson and Holling (2002) conceive of socionatural systems as self-organized systems consisting of a relatively small set of essential processes that create and maintain such organizations. Many other processes can be superimposed on these, few, essential ones, but they depend on the latter for their survival. According to Holling (2001), the trajectories of such complex systems consist of an endless reiteration, at all hierarchical levels, of a cycle that moves through four states: "exploitation or growth," "conservation or accumulation," "creative destruction or re-structuration," and "reorganization or renovation." The levels at which they these cycles occur not only range from individual cells to the biosphere but also from the local to the global in space, and from the momentary to the millennial (or more) in time. At any time, and whatever the state of the individual levels, there are interactions between all levels. But the nature of these interactions varies with the state of the system at each interacting level.

This approach thus combines the idea of spatio-temporal hierarchies of processes with that of adaptive cycles. H. Simon (1981), Allen and Starr (1982), and Allen and Hoekstra (1992) propose that complex systems consist of hierarchies of semi-autonomous levels of processes that can be distinguished according to the spatio-temporal scales that constitute them. Each level exchanges energy, matter, and information with the levels above and below it. Together, these levels constitute an edifice of levels at which the dynamics can vary within certain limits, maintaining an overall coherence that is flexible due to the exchange between levels. Simon's idea is that in such an edifice each level serves two functions. A level stabilizes the lower levels, while innovating at its own.

Three characteristics determine the state of the cycle and its future.

1. The *potential* of the system that is available to be transformed. It determines the range of options open to the system as it moves forward through time. One might call it the system's "richness."
2. The *connectivity* between the levels and, consequently, between the internal control variables and the processes that operate in the system. It determines the control that the system has over itself, and the degree of flexibility (or rigidity) available to the system's dynamics.
3. The *adaptive capacity* of the system, that is to say its resilience. The resilience of a system is also a measure of its vulnerability to unexpected perturbations.

Together, these three characteristics of self-organizing systems constrain the range of responses available to socioenvironmental systems, institutions, and individuals: their connectivity limits the extent of the system's self-control, its "richness" constrains the range of its future states, and its resilience determines its vulnerability to sudden perturbations.

During the part of the trajectory that includes the phases of "exploitation" and "conservation," the connectivity and the stability of the socioenvironmental system augment. The system also accumulates (ecological, economic, cultural, and social) capital at this time, such as nutrients, biomass, physical structure, know-how, customs, trust, and all other elements that allow it to grow and flourish. Simultaneously, it accumulates a number of mutations and innovations that await the (partial) dissolution of the structure that constrains them. But that dissolution is delayed by the increasing connectivity between the different elements of the dominant regime, which allows it to harness increasing quantities of resources, and thus to reinforce its robustness. In this the process phase, the system becomes less flexible. In Holling's words (2001:403): "It becomes an accident waiting to happen."

The (sudden) release of these innovative forces is usually triggered by an (internal or external) perturbation that is sufficiently profound to break the dominant regime's hold over its resources. These then become available to the forces of change. Innovation and experimentation increase and spread throughout the system. The ensuing battle between endogenous and exogenous perturbations will ultimately decide the fate of the system.

The part of the trajectory that begins with "creative destruction" and ends with "reorganization" first sees a loss of connectivity between different levels that is inherent in the re-structuration. Hence, the costs of experimentation are relatively lowered, and the system becomes more resilient (that is, it accepts with ease any necessary adaptations relatively easily). But as these different innovations take hold, and they mobilize resources that are therefore no longer available to other such innovations, the system re-stabilizes in another state.

"It is," says Holling, "as if two different objectives dominate one after the other. The first is the production and accumulation of capital, and the second is innovation and re-structuration. These two objectives cannot be attained at the same time. And the system's success in achieving the first objective determines the success it will have in attaining the second" (Holling 2001:403).

I must end this paragraph with a warning. Holling, Gunderson, and others have thus presented us with a set of descriptors that enable us to understand better and to envision the dynamics of socioenvironmental systems and the incidence of crises. But their work is not yet sufficiently advanced to be able to provide us with a classification of types of "creative destruction" that might apply to environmental crises.

Under Which Conditions Do Socioenvironmental Crises Occur?

I have argued that, in general terms, one could say that adequacy between societal dynamics and environmental dynamics ensures stability in socio-environmental systems. But the level of adequacy varies with the evolution of both domains, because of time lags and interference between the natural and the societal dynamics that are together jointly responsible for adaptation to new circumstances.

To keep things simple, I will here distinguish three states of the relationship between the societal and the natural components: robustness, resilience, and vulnerability. Robustness refers to the state of the system in which its structural and circumstantial characteristics enable it to resist all perturbations, both endogenous and exogenous. Elsewhere in the literature this state is called "resistant" (S. F. Carpenter et al. 2001). Following Holling (1973, 1986), I think that the capacity to adapt itself to changing circumstances by making changes without interrupting the continuity of the system's trajectory is one of the fundamental characteristics of living systems. Holling (1986) calls this capacity the resilience of the system. But the dynamics of socioenvironmental systems may also be vulnerable to destruction at particular times. "Windows of vulnerability" are phases in which neither the robust nor the resilient characteristics of a system permit it to survive without structural transformations; either the system changes fundamentally, or it loses its coherence.

The dynamics of socioenvironmental systems thus oscillate between necessity and chance. At certain times, they are impervious or indifferent to perturbations because their internal dynamics are sufficiently coherent and robust to be able to ignore that state. At other times, such socioenvironmental systems are so vulnerable that any perturbation, large or small, could cause an irreparable loss of coherence. In that state, the system will only survive if, by chance, there are no perturbations. But in the intermediate state, in which systems survive by adapting themselves, the occurrence of socioenvironmental crises not only depends on the nature of the perturbations but also on the resilience of the system.

Much depends upon the strength of the perturbations relative to the resilience of the system concerned. Firstly, a system's resilience varies with the degree of connectivity between the different dynamics of the system. In the Valdaine (southern France), Berger et al. (2003) were able to monitor socioenvironmental dynamics in great detail for the whole of the Holocene. This study led him to conclude with clarity that at the beginning of the Holocene the connection between the societal and the environmental dynamics was so weak that environmental crises did leave few traces in the landscape. Such traces are only first observed from the sixth millennium BC onwards, when the cumulative effects of anthropogenic deforestation, agriculture, and herding brought climate oscillations into focus. But from then on, the progressive appropriation of nature by society gradually increased the connectedness between the societal and the environmental components of the regional system to the extent that in the last few centuries, the slightest climatic or anthropogenic perturbation triggers environmental consequences of important proportions.

Another factor that determines the resilience of a socioenvironmental system to a considerable degree is the speed with which its different component processes can adapt to one another. That in turn depends first upon the speed with which the temporalities and the character of the natural dynamics are capable of change. As this speed is mainly dependent upon the constraints inherent in the local and regional conditions of the environmental component of the combined system, one can evidently not generalize about it. But the resilience of the system also depends on the speed with which the society can identify and analyze changing circumstances, and deal with them. If we may, for the sake of argument, consider the biological information-processing speed of human beings as being more or less constant through time, the effective speed of information processing depends among other things on

1. The form in which the information is transmitted and processed. This involves variables such as the level of education in the society, the semantic structure of the language concerned, the level of abstraction of the concepts available, etc.;
2. The length and the configuration of the trajectories followed by the messages, and thus the structure and configuration of the communication networks in a society;
3. The coherence of the society from a political, economic, social, and cultural point of view, on the assumption that a coherent society will need less time to agree on the new measures to take than a fragmented or divided society.

Finally, the history of the system is important. As it evolves between its past and its future, it always includes structural elements inherited from its past. These may be material, such as a road network, an irrigation system, or an urban system; but they may also be institutional, such as its administrative and political structure; or sociocultural, as in the case of its values or worldview. Often, many such elements are closely integrated, particularly in a society's technological means of responding to crisis. They thus determine a system's resilience to an important extent. The material legacies among them are often easier to change than the social or cultural ones, as the former are more tangible and less embedded in the core of the culture.

However important the capacity to change might be, one should also consider that a system that innovates too rapidly might endanger its future, as such a system may be overwhelmed by the unintended consequences of these innovations. That will destroy just as certainly the adequacy between the societal and the environmental dynamics as undue conservatism will.

How Do Socioenvironmental Crises Manifest Themselves?

In the last part of this chapter, I will try to show how one might generalize from a description of events to a systemic interpretation of the dynamics leading up to a socioenvironmental crisis. I will present first the recent history of a third of the other regions we studied as part of the ARCHAEOMEDES project: Epirus in Greece. I will then describe that history in terms drawn from the perspective I have just outlined. Space constraints force me to present this case study in the form of a heavily simplified historical account that enables me to add important elements to the explanations presented so far, as well as sketch its impact on the population.

The Epirus Crisis[1]

Until World War II, the inhabitants of any Epirote village formed a small, isolated, and closed group in a very isolated rural area where people lived off the land and the herds it sustained. The technical, social, and economic differences among the inhabitants were relatively small, and the information pool was very homogeneous (everyone knew everything about everyone else); most decisions were made on a consensus basis. Their socioenvironmental system had been functioning for a long time, so that the people knew the area intimately, and their ways of dealing with the environment were closely matched with local circumstance. In effect, over the centuries, a long-term sustainable strategy had evolved.

After World War II, the area was the focus of a civil war that in many ways was more destructive of society than the world war itself, and it triggered widespread emigration among a population that had always been very mobile, often spending many years away from home only to come back to retire among relatives and friends. At about the same time, the division of Epirus between Greece and Albania led to the construction of paved roads in the area. These two processes triggered a cascade of complex transformations in the society, its relationship to the landscape, the spatial structuring of the latter, and the means of existence of the population.

The paving of the roads triggered increasing contact between many of the isolated villages. As people started moving along the roads, information from the outside began to influence village life: stories and observations on how things could *also* be done. Because not everyone shared the urge to visit, the information pool began to differentiate. At the same time, the roads brought increased contact between the countryside and the provincial capital, Ioannina. That linked the villages to a whole range of different administrative hierarchies and facilitated the meddling of regional and supra-regional institutions into village affairs. The appointment of village headmen, for example, gave the authorities in Ioannina some influence over village activities and simultaneously gave the headman a status of his own and a communication channel to the outside. Ultimately, the spatial macro-structure was transformed from one based on tribal territories into one based on the roads, and nodes linked to the urban system were "seeded" farther and farther into the countryside.

It was a long-standing tradition in the area, dating back to the Turkish occupation, that many men would for long periods earn money elsewhere in Greece, in the Ottoman Empire, or abroad, but come back regularly to their ancestral village. The civil war increased such emigration, and thus contributed to 1) the reduction and aging of the rural population, and 2) fundamental changes in lifestyle and in perspective on society and its future. Notably, it accelerated the social and economic differentiation of the population, so that not everybody knew everything any longer about everybody else, leading to occasional conflicts of interest between people and/or groups within villages.

Changes in perspective on the landscape also occurred. Seasonally trans-humanent people who used to consider their hilltop village as their "real" home, and the valley as a temporary (winter) abode, now generally considered themselves as living in the valley and their hilltop houses as temporary (summer) places of residence. As a result, residence in the valley became longer, and hilltop grazing less intense and less localized. A newly imposed existing interdiction to burn the hillsides regularly to provide grass for the animals would in itself not have had any particular spatial effects if the herds would have continued to graze the same grounds every year, as they would have kept all non-grass vegetation short or out. But under the changed perceptual circumstances, thorny bushes in the uplands immediately saw their chance, and an important part of the uplands became inaccessible almost overnight, even to goats. This forced the herdsmen to bring the animals ever closer together in other upland areas, which were thus overgrazed. That in turn led to erosion on the very vulnerable (tectonically highly active) slopes. In effect, outside authority and local changes in perception colluded to allow "garrigue" growth and increased gulley erosion (because brushwood barriers were no longer maintained). Ultimately, the abandoned uplands were colonized by various species of trees, reducing the amount of water in the karstic aquifers and causing a shortage of drinking water.

The increased dependency of the population on valley cultivation triggered changes in the economy. Cash became more important, as "urban" ways, norms, and ideals penetrated the countryside and stimulated people to acquire other material goods, transforming the herding economy of the hills and mountains into a (sedentary) economy based on fodder production cultivation and consumption in the valleys. This increased the dependency on the commercial aspects of the national and supranational economic system, and the vulnerability that such dependency entails. Young people deserted the rural lifestyle, and the increasing dependency of the region on the outside world multiplied. It became easier to protect oneself against natural calamities, but more difficult to escape the distorting consequences of imported economic crises or of the European Union's agricultural subsidies.

The emigration had important consequences for the local economy and lifestyle, as the lack of competent laborers led the Epirotes to reduce their dependence on goats and sheep and to increase the number of pigs, which require less supervision. To increase their income, certain villages tried to promote tourism by building the necessary infrastructure with European money. With or without European subsidies, the region pursued the development it was now locked into. A tertiary sector developed itself in Ioannina, and along the paved roads, the region became increasingly dependent on money coming from the outside, notably the contributions of the émigrés who amassed a degree of wealth elsewhere. And that, in turn, changed the equilibrium between the different powers in the villages, and in the region as a whole.

Generalizing the Description in Terms of Resilience Theory

In the case of Epirus, our post-war observations begin at the end of an "accumulation" phase that lasted several centuries. A local agro-pastoral economy developed, centered on the individual villages and, at a higher level, on the tribes that occupied the territory. That economy had two connections to other regions: long-distance trans-humanence and temporary emigration of the male population. Both originated during the Ottoman occupation. As a result, the socioenvironmental system of the Epirotes had exchanged much of its initial resilience for a high level of interconnectedness among all aspects of daily life. It had become thus more efficient and profitable, but it had lost much of its diversity and flexibility. In one word, it had become "hyper-coherent," an example of "an accident waiting to happen," and had survived by virtue of the absence of major perturbations.

The double shock of World War II and the Greek Civil War (1943–1949), affected the dynamic structure of the socioenvironmental region at all levels simultaneously, interrupting so many processes at the same time that the upper levels of the system, with their slow dynamic, were no longer able to play a role and stabilize the lower levels. In other words, the perturbation was so great, and the society not resilient enough, that the society could not absorb it and keep its fundamental, historical structure intact. It was not resilient enough to absorb a perturbation of this size. The societal dynamics were no longer able to adequately respond to the environmental ones, and the socioenvironmental system thus found itself in a "window of vulnerability" in which the societal dynamics were no longer able to adequately respond to the environmental ones.

Despite the ravages of the world war, emigration at the end of the civil war temporarily increased the total quantity of resources (the "capital") at the disposal of the Epirotes, while also reducing the traditional control of the traditional structure over these resources (that had been damaged by the two wars). These two tendencies have, together, forced the society toward innovation, while at the same time reducing the social and economic cost of such innovations. The ensuing reconstruction occurred under the external pressure of the very rapid urbanization of the last fifty years; it was facilitated by the creation of the new transport infrastructure that broke the tribal geography of the region. By introducing new communication networks, the road network changed the traditional flows of information that had maintained the coherence and the connectivity of Epirote society. We observe this, for example, in the information-exchange patterns in each and every one of the villages. Traditionally, the villagers had not given much credibility to news brought to them by strangers, believing only what they heard from the inhabitants of their own village. But from the 1960s, and beginning in the villages closest to Ioannina or along the roads, the rural Epirotes forged privileged links with certain "townsfolk." They learned to believe what such contacts told them and, relatively quickly, preferred such information over the "gossip" they were told by their fellow villagers.

As a result, new social and information networks became the foundation on which the society reconstructed itself. But these new networks were not woven sufficiently quickly to avoid the fact that during a whole generation, the Epirotes experienced this transformation as a "crisis." The demographic downturn may in part explain this, because it reduced the potential connectivity in the region. But the feeling of "crisis" experienced by the population was also due to the need to negotiate new connections around new concepts and new ways of life, even a radically different worldview. This phase of "creative destruction" lasted around forty years. In that period, many different solutions were pursued in order to try to end the crisis. In those years, the natural environment was profoundly transformed, calling into question the perspective of the villagers on their own place in the landscape and in society. The herdsmen of the heights transformed themselves into farmers in the valleys. Their means of subsistence, as well as the nature of their crops and their herds, changed; garrigue and forest replaced the deserted meadows, leading to shortages of drinking water for some villages.

But new connections developed everywhere, albeit initially very slowly, and in the end the socioenvironmental system reconstructed itself on a different basis, consisting of subsidies, ecotourism, the export of milk products and craft objects, and a certain degree of industrialization (mainly in Ioannina). In the 1980s and 1990s, the socioenvironmental system thus entered into a phase of "reorganization."

The Contribution of Cultural Theory

The anthropologist and historian Thompson and his colleagues (M. Thompson et al. 1990) attempt to set another step in the same direction by emphasizing the fact that the societal dynamics, as conceived by Holling in 1986, also have a cognitive component. The arguments underlying this convergence of the two theories is as simple as it is convincing: any society that finds itself in a certain state will develop a perspective on the world that is adapted to that state, and will transform its environment accordingly.

According to them, one may distinguish four fundamentally different kinds of worldview among a large sample of societies and cultures. These differ with respect to the extent to which the individuals who express them are integrated into a larger group of people with whom they share their values and their beliefs, and according to the degree to which their roles are weighed down by the society's institutions. On this basis, Thompson distinguishes four perspectives.

In a period in which an exploitative dynamic prevails, an "individualist" perspective has the opportunity to develop itself in a stable world with ample resources. The identity and the social position of the individual are determined by his (her) own effort, know-how, and courage. This worldview is formulated in terms of opportunities and potential advantages; problems are viewed as challenges, fear is not admitted because it paralyses, and human beings are deemed to be very adaptable.

In phases of consolidation or accumulation, a "hierarchist" perspective often develops. It considers the world less stable and takes into account that resources are not limitless. Social norms are often transgressed at the cost of overexploiting the resources. It is therefore necessary to put mechanisms in place to inform, to regulate, and to control. Hence, the predominant perspective imposes its norms, as well as the administration apparatus and the procedures, to ensure that they are respected. Society accepts the need for such an authority with power that reinforces the rules adopted in order to ensure the correct functioning of the socioenvironmental system.

A "fatalist" perspective develops in situations of social isolation in which one people loses all hope that the observed dynamic is manageable, in that blackest of times when change is around the corner. These are the times that Holling et al. (2002) call "creative destruction." The world is experienced as incomprehensible and out of control, and life as a game of chance. Individuals are deemed impotent when faced with such a situation, and their actions as having no effect whatsoever. Both the material and the social costs of innovation, are reduced to a minimum, and many new approaches can be tried and initiated.

An "egalitarian" perspective develops in the unstable circumstances that characterize phases of reorganization, among people whose existence is still very precarious. Each change can bring about inevitable catastrophes. In this perspective, the fragility of nature is accentuated, and the probability that natural or social disasters will occur preoccupies everyone. The feeling dominates that all individuals are equal in the face of the sheer size of the events and that solidarity is the best way to mitigate the impact of events.

Each of these worldviews carries the seeds of its own destruction. An excess of hierarchism leads to a legalistic attitude. That in turn becomes less and less profitable and leads to the decline of the state-controlled socioenvironmental system. Similarly, a resulting excess of individualism leads inevitably to a situation of frequent conflict that, in turn, triggers a return to a more stable and just society. In this sense, the evolution of a society does not fundamentally differ from the evolution of the socionatural system of which it is a part.

Of course, none of these perspectives is ever the only one to occur in a society, or even to dominate unchallenged. The continuity of the existence of any society is ensured by the fact that there are many different ways to react to any events that occur. The exact mix varies according to the recent history of the society concerned. That variation impacts on the dynamics of the socioenvironmental system at the same time as it undergoes its consequences. But as the dynamics in question are complex, and occur at different time frames, there will always be delays, time lags, oscillations, and even moments of extreme volatility. Complete adequacy between the mixture of perspectives and the systemic dynamics of the moment is never more than momentarily achievable. Moreover, the necessary adjustments inevitably incur social costs (negotiation, innovation, restructuration), as we have amply seen in the case of Epirus. Those costs are not always easy to identify, and even less easy to compensate, and that can in turn prolong the delays.

Indeed, in order for the society to survive common perturbations, it is essential that it must be heterogeneous, not only from the perspective of its resources but also from that of its social and cognitive diversity. There are two important reasons for that. Firstly, each oscillation, whether due to endogenous or exogenous perturbations, appeals to a range of reactions that try to correct the observed disequilibrium. These reactions have very different effects, according to their nature, their strength, and their temporal span. Those that occur most quickly mobilize the least effort. If they manage to correct the imbalance, the affair is closed. But if they are insufficient, more costly stabilizing mechanisms take over and so forth until a new dynamic equilibrium is reached. Hence, the vulnerability of the system is inversely proportional to the diversity of the solutions that can be mobilized at all concerned levels.

The other important characteristic of a resilient system is that it "makes errors"; that is, it does not always find the best response to the circumstances of the moment. This quality is necessary to ensure that it maintains the requisite diversity in the face of the emergence of new challenges. A system that would respond perfectly to the conditions at time t_1 could not also respond perfectly to the conditions at time t_2. In other words, the system must at any time simultaneously explore new solutions and exploit others that it already knows. The required multiplicity of responses to perturbations is guaranteed by the fact that different perspectives co-exist in any socioenvironmental system.

Conclusion

This chapter is explicitly programmatic. I have tried to outline my answer to the question, "What is the nature of environmental crises?" and to summarize the reasons why I adhere to an approach based on the concept of "socioenvironmental system." Similar approaches are currently under development by researchers in different countries, not only around such journals as *Nature, Sciences et Sociétés* in France, and *Ecology and Society* and *Ecosystems* in the United States but also in the long-term environmental research movement worldwide and at a limited number of universities and research organizations elsewhere. In my own case, I have chosen to base my current work on that of the Resilience Alliance.

We are at present very far from a robust conceptual model that is directly applicable to the analysis of socioenvironmental interactions. The skeptics will say that, for the moment, all this is no more than a metaphor. What encourages me to persevere with this approach is the fact that I currently observe in the environmental sciences a phase of "creative destruction." Awareness is spreading of the fact that our current research will not provide us with the solutions to the socioenvironmental problems that we so urgently need. A trans-disciplinary community is shaping up that includes physicists and mathematicians, biologists and agronomists, economists, anthropologists, historians, and archaeologists, to name but a few of the research domains involved. That community has begun to negotiate the questions it wishes to ask from a trans-disciplinary perspective and to open the doors to their "disciplinary kitchens," which they have kept for so long hermetically closed.

To conclude, I will summarize some aspects of this approach to the question of "environmental crises" that seem particularly interesting to me. To begin with, we need to transform our anthropocentric perspective—which views socionatural relations either as people's *adaptation to* the environment, or as their *spoliation of* the environment—into a more balanced one, in which humans are nothing but "another unique species." As a consequence, we will have to abolish the distinction between "society" and "environment." Both then will be viewed as intimately related as the two faces of Janus.

As a result, the research then becomes focused on *interactions between* different kinds of dynamics, at different scales. The perception of the environment by individuals and groups, the relation between environmental perception and human action, and the consequences of the dynamics of human intervention in the environment will thus become important objects of study. Understanding them will involve the cognitive sciences and the sciences of communication, as well as the study of techniques as the interface between perception and action.

Interestingly, the responses of human beings to changes in the environment, for example, will turn out to be shaped in two steps. First, the observed patterns are simplified into abstract conceptions, theories, or models. Because these are derived from close observations during a period of a certain length, they present the best summary of the risks to the system at all spatio-temporal levels observed. But they are, nevertheless, much simpler than the observed reality. In the second step, people's intervention into the ongoing dynamics introduces new interactions in the latter, and renders the processes concerned ever more complex. The net effect of each of these two steps is that it further reduces our understanding of what is actually going on.

It is therefore not surprising that our interventions in the environment always have unexpected and unintended consequences. Their unpredictability is further aggravated by the fact that we know those phenomena best that occur most frequently, but are the least disturbing. As we do something about these risks, we shift the temporal spectrum of risks from frequent to less frequent, from better known to less well known. The cumulative effect of that over longer periods is the following: as many unknown, infrequent risks are created, eventually the probability that these will link up (or collide in time) and cause a cascade of changes (a crisis) is very high indeed! Environmentalists have called this effect that of "time bombs"; I would prefer to speak of "risk barriers," borrowing the image of what happens when sound waves cumulate into a "sound barrier."

In that light, we must not only ask, "What kind of an environment do we want for ourselves in the future?" (Lévèque and van der Leeuw 2003) but also, "What is an environmental risk?" and, more importantly, "What is an acceptable environmental risk over such and such a period?" And there we come up against a very major challenge indeed, which involves archaeologists and anthropologists, ecologists, and all others who deal with the issue of sustainability: how to translate our lessons from the past into lessons for the future. We observe the past as "closed," formulated in terms of certainties, cause and effect, defined concepts and categories, etc. But we view our future in terms of uncertainties, chance, opportunities, open-ended concepts and categories, and we have a very underdeveloped set of tools to transform one perspective into the other. Statistics is only a very partial help, limited to very closely defined cases. Developing such tools seems to me one of our most urgent priorities.

But it is only a beginning. We will need to develop a truly transdisciplinary field of "sustainability studies" that builds the theoretical foundations to integrate the study of social and environmental dynamics from one and the same perspective. This undoubtedly will transform profoundly parts of the social sciences into a more quantitative, computational, model-based field that, among other things, truly studies the foundations of societal dynamics from an information-transmission and -processing perspective, probably in terms of multi-net dynamics (e.g., D. White forthcoming).

Archaeology will play an important part in that development, as it is the only discipline that provides us with detailed enough knowledge about the very-long-term socioenvironmental dynamics.

Note

1. For a more encompassing description of these events, see van der Leeuw 1998 and van der Leeuw et al. 2003. This part of the present chapter presents a general perspective that is complementary to the one offered in van der Leeuw (2000). The latter paper describes the Epirus events in terms of self-organizing information flows.

3

Beyond Sustainability

MANAGED WETLANDS AND WATER HARVESTING IN ANCIENT MESOAMERICA

Vernon L. Scarborough

ONE OF ANTHROPOLOGICAL archaeology's persistent strengths is its fundamental interest in environmental reconstruction and the role that ancient society has played in transforming it (Denevan 1992; Scarborough 2003a). Drawing on that lasting contribution, this chapter examines the interface between socioeconomic and sociopolitical change and the engineered landscapes from ancient Mesoamerica. A little touted, but pivotal, Mesoamerican legacy was the management of wetlands and the harvesting of unpredictable water sources (Scarborough 2003b, 2006a, 2007; T. M. Whitmore and Turner 2002:chapter 7; cf. Pandey et al. 2003). Through this context and case study, variable environments are shown to affect variable economic logics—or how groups make a living and the social organizational strategies they employ. The two different economic orientations, or pathways, discussed here open new ways for assessing aspects of social evolution and perhaps useful ways of evaluating social structures as well as truly sustainable and productive alternative resource-use strategies.

Ecosystems, Social Systems, and the Economy

An overwhelming interest in human ecology by archaeology and its emphasis on technologies to exploit the environment have resulted in the kinds of temporal, spatial, and interpretative typologies we have all grown to accept in the discipline—ceramic and lithic types illustrative of temporal divisions have the oldest pedigree, but the "social life of things" includes insights into "econiche" specializations as well as ethnic and gender production and consumption differences. Studies based on

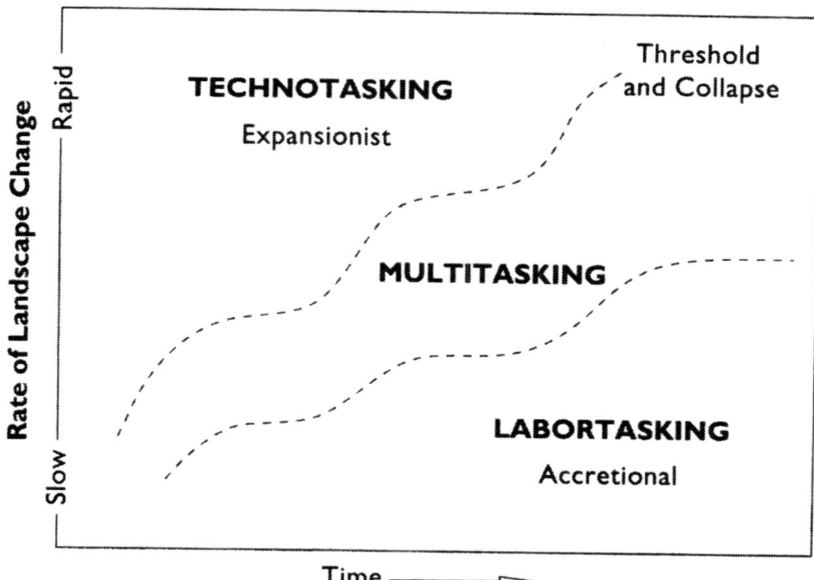

FIGURE 3.1. Rate and process of landscape change. Technotasking and labortasking are discussed in the text. Multitasking is a third landscape modification process or economic logic employed by subordinate rural population and is difficult to identify in the archaeological record. It is not further discussed in this presentation. (From Scarborough 2003a: fig. 2.1).

the preserved technologies of society generally provide accurate interpretations of the past, but they are frequently couched in an overarching model of technological change and advancement. Elsewhere, I have referred to aspects of this cultural process and rate of change as *technotasking* (Scarborough 2003b; fig. 3.1). Nevertheless, other economic orientations exist and provide archaeology with other ways of assessing past economic behaviors.

Technological Intensification, Rate of Change, and Biophysical Exploitation

Generally speaking, archaeology implicitly conflates human ecology and human economy and assumes that only one principal definition of economy exists (cf. Halperin 1994; Scarborough 2003b). As discussed elsewhere (Scarborough 2003b, 2005a), technotasking explains human behavior by emphasizing the exploitation of the biophysical environment via complex technological manipulation and acceptance. Economic success is measured by the predictability and abundance of the yield, or resource concentrations, an approach frequently challenging the natural laws of diversity and succession by employing technology to homogenize aspects of the biophysical environs (Scott 1998).

Although technological intensification is a subset of technotasking, the latter emphasizes rapid rates of environmental and social change couched in a context of exploitative resource extraction and consumption (fig. 3.1). The rapidity of this change prefigures some of the earliest experiments in socioeconomic and sociopolitical complexity and the initiation of the archaic state. The earliest states emerged from the semiarid biophysical environs of the Old World, near the banks of several of the planet's most productive river systems. The initial abundance of arable land made possible from these canalized sources permitted the landscape transformations by sedentists of otherwise economically wasted desertscapes. Although many vectors converged on a landscape in allowing the development of the first states and their accompanying cities, the technological mastery of early hydraulic practices was foundational. The impact of urbanism and the centralizing of natural resources in refined concentrations were stimulated by a rapidly acquired and widely accepted set of technological innovations including the wheel, the sail, and expanded use of beasts of burden as well as land-use intensification emphasizing canalization. Nevertheless, with accelerated social and environmental change, the drive to control and expand into the semiarid environments of the earliest states was frequently interrupted because of environmental overreach by their growing populations. Southern Mesopotamia, for example, has a very broken trajectory of precipitous state rise followed by as precipitous a collapse (R. M. Adams 1981; Postgate 1992). In part, this is a direct result of resource abundance followed by resource depletion based on a technotasking economic logic that promoted rapid, sometimes radical growth and landscape expansion implicitly anticipatory of new or better modified technologies used to acquire and develop arid lands. Salinization coupled with significant sedimentation problems was not well understood or solvable and exemplifies technological overreach in spite of the advances in other technological spheres (M. Gibson 1974;

Jacobsen and Adams 1958; Powell 1985). Over the short term, however, newly colonized lands were increasingly settled using an enhanced corpus of hydrological knowledge and the sizable tracts of land that became productive with hydraulic innovation (cf. R. M. Adams 2006). Today, technotasking is the principal economic logic on earth suggesting the innovations or breakthroughs that have carried and sustained it—it is now tightly intertwined with a Western worldview of the biophysical environment and the acquisition of huge concentrations of refined resources.

The drive to employ technology as a means of reducing the drudgery of work is the essence of Brookfield's classic essay (1972) distinguishing innovation stimulated by abundant surplus as opposed to intensification excited by population growth and shortened fallow cycles. Such nuanced trajectories may well drive many early complex societies and their underlying economic logic (Kirch 1994; Nichols 1987; Nichols et al. 2006; cf. Doolittle 1990). But what if we reassess our notions of economy and not assume that it is always organized around the quest for technological superiority?

Labor Intensification, Rate of Change, and Biophysical Harvesting

The economic logic that emphasizes strong attachments to reduced parcels of land coupled with sizable population aggregates and slow rates of societal change is *labortasking* (Scarborough 2003b, 2005a). Today, aspects of this economic orientation are widespread throughout Southeast Asia, associated with rice paddies and intensive labor investments frequently organized around the extended family and immediate community. Bray (1986; cf. Scarborough 2003b) refers to these systems as "skill-oriented economies" because they focus on highly specialized agricultural skills dependent, in part, on age and gender differences. These skills are labor intensive and learned generationally, permitting highly stable yet resilient food production and harvests. A key to this economic logic is a set of highly interdependent social relations that make many technological breakthroughs less necessary and less acceptable. Large concentrations of biophysical resources are less apparent when compared to technotasking adaptations. Nevertheless, deployments of large numbers of laborers over small plots with limited productivity frequently result in a careful monitoring and an adequate harvesting of resources. Productivity is measured by not only by yield but also by the ability to reinvent the landscape (soils and microclimate) and stay within its constricting natural parameters—though the slowly altered, regional built environment is often changed dramatically and productively from its initially colonized appearance. Such systems permit us to examine early states in another light and assist in reassessing economic and political evolutionary trajectories.

Labortasking encompasses the notion of labor intensification, but it also emphasizes the slow and constrained rate at which an environment and the society within it are altered through time (fig. 3.1). It frequently develops within less-resource-abundant, human-altered environments than associated with societies practicing more technologically oriented economic adaptations. Although difficult to retrieve from the ancient material record, some findings suggest that the earliest states in semitropical settings were preadapted to the slowly evolving and imposed stability of resource harvesting from within a fragile biophysical system (Scarborough 2000, 2005a). Labor-oriented economic strategies tend to develop less-centralized institutions for organizing the economy than do technologically oriented economic logics.

As I have previously argued (Scarborough 1998, 2000, 2003a, 2005b) for semitropical settings, species diversity abundance is counterpoised by a reduced abundance of any one species at any specific locality, resulting in difficulties for human exploitation and our need to concentrate biophysical resources. When coupled with thin (though frequently productive) soils, seasonal drought, and, in Upper Central America, the disturbing absence of permanent and accessible water sources, semitropical environs might be construed as an unlikely setting for early civilization and social complexity. Given high humidity and temperatures, organic storage and associated resource concentrations are difficult to maintain. Nevertheless, several archaic states arose from these ecological circumstances; in the case of the ancient Maya, a labortasking economic orientation developed (Scarborough 2003b).

Although labor intensification associated with incremental landscape change leading to long-term scalar modifications and a stable built environment evolves under several sets of social and environmental parameters, it is generally associated with relatively high population densities in the rural hinterlands complemented by only slightly larger population nodes identified at the region's towns and "cities." Our recent ethnoarchaeological investigations in Bali (Scarborough et al. 1999), for example, indicate that colonizing attempts by eleventh-century elites to centralize sociopolitical control as well as to concentrate primary resources in this otherwise resource-dispersed, semitropical setting failed. Sizable populations of hinterland rice farmers, however, organized to accretionally alter the fragile island's soils and watercourses over several centuries in producing the dizzying, contour-meandering, stair-step rice-paddy system of today. This regionally populous settlement and land-use adaptation reflects a predictable trajectory associated with the natural distribution of biophysical resources in some semitropical environments.

Humans, like the entire biological community, are initially organized by dispersing themselves to best harvest from the many different semitropical microenvironments. Here, centralized and concentrated resource accumulations are less emphasized or developed than apparent in a technotasking pathway. Under these conditions, dispersed labor-oriented economic adaptations develop to alter a selection of the microenvironments and enhance their resource productivity for humans. With modest population growth, plant associations are modified to produce more and better varieties of food and fiber. Continued community growth and associated needs result in a progressively engineered landscape and the advent of sizable towns for coordinating growth and societal change, as well as hinterland environmental alterations designed to enhance agricultural productivity. Because of the diversity of microenvironments and the indigenous adaptations to these settings, careful attention to the process of production is emphasized in addition to the immediate abundance of the resource. The fragility of the setting demands frequent environmental assessments and compatible resource substitutions to prevent rapid and catastrophic degradation. Productivity is contextualized in a set of interdependent conditions that require year-round monitoring through social coordination and environmental review.

Mesoamerica

The case study I employ to elucidate the economic dichotomy introduced is Mesoamerica (fig. 3.2). It is selected for three reasons: 1) my familiarity

FIGURE 3.2. Map of Mesoamerica. (From Scarborough 2003a: fig. 4.24).

with the culture area as much of my fieldwork experience draws from the region, 2) it captures extreme environmental variability within a relatively limited area when compared to other settings globally, and 3) it identifies the kinds of economic logics discussed. Nevertheless, Mesoamerica, indeed the New World, was primarily identifiable by a Stone

Age technology—and without the wheel or sizable tractable animals (camelids were the exception in Peru)—a condition that seemingly narrows the dichotomy between technotasking and labortasking. However, the dichotomy I have drawn does grade between the two extremes with a continuum of characteristics weighing a culture into one economic logic over the other. Mesoamerica shows how different environments were used to cultivated different economic logics without complex implements. The separation between technotasking and labortasking in Mesoamerica focuses on the rapidity and control with which resources were exploited or harvested respectively, as revealed by the kinds of settlement identified and the land- and water-use techniques employed.

Wetlands and Water Harvesting

The modification and use of swamp-like settings is one of ancient Mesoamerica's significant legacies. Biological abundance in wetland settings is immense, and when modified to emphasize the production of those resources most important to humans, wetlands represent perhaps the richest reservoir of food and fiber known. The most celebrated intensive use of the wetlands comes from highland Mexico during the Aztec period (AD 1350–1519). The chinampas of the lakeshore settings within the Basin of Mexico indicate the tremendous productivity of these artificial island planting surfaces, or elaborate raised fields. Nevertheless, the ancestry of ditched and raised plots—if not their precise form—is identifiable 2,500 years earlier in present-day Belize (Pohl et al. 1996).

Maya Lowlands

The Maya Lowlands encompass about 250,000 sq. km, of which 30 percent is seasonal wetlands. Given the population density throughout the region during the Classic period (AD 300–900) and the proximity of the largest cities and towns to these swamps, the ancient Maya clearly incorporated wetland environs into their economic organization. Although recent compelling arguments exist for increasing the cultivation period of upland slash-and-burn plots and thus permitting greater cropping yields through time, especially during the late Classic period (AD 550–900) (K. Johnson 2003), problems persist with the swidden hypothesis

(T. M. Whitmore and Turner 2002). Both in conjecturing the amount of pest damage associated with lengthened periods of annual cultivation and the likelihood that several kinds of cropping methods were used to accommodate the specific attributes of the diverse set of semitropical microenvironments, dependency on swidden agriculture alone falters. Furthermore, significant effort was invested in markedly altering the agricultural landscape, suggesting that creative mulching and manual grass-weed removal were insufficient in promoting adequate food production for the many growing communities, though such techniques were surely used when appropriate.

Our recent investigations within the Three Rivers region of the east-central Yucatán Peninsula reveal the range of engineering modifications that allowed the intensification of the agricultural base (Scarborough et al. 2003a). Low-lying berms of cobble and earth functioned as diversionary features in directing seasonal runoff (Hageman and Lohse 2003; Kunen and Hughbanks 2003), several varieties of terrace construction captured and reclaimed eroding sediments as well as retained moisture for extended periods (Dunning et al. 2003; Hageman and Lohse 2003; Kunen and Hughbanks 2003), and drained field platforms designed to use swamp-like margins are identifiable throughout portions of Belize and adjacent Quintana Roo best documented within riverine floodplain margins (Dunning et al. 2003; Guderjan et al. 2003; Harrison 1993; Harrison and Turner 1983; Pohl et al. 1996). These intensifying techniques reveal the variety of forms employed by the ancient Maya in modifying the immediate microenvironments in which a group lived. Within the sizable centers, additional landscape engineering occurred by way of great labor investments in creating lasting water- and land-use systems for sustaining larger populations in proximity to the main plazas (King and Shaw 2003; Scarborough 1993; Scarborough and Valdez 2003; Scarborough et al. 1994, 1995). The flexibility in employing a precise selection of land-use techniques to best harvest a resource promoted the resource-specialized community in portions of the Maya Lowlands.

Many of the agricultural features identified in the Maya Lowlands date to the Classic period. However, we now have good evidence that at least some of the seasonal swamps of the region were formerly permanent shallow-water wetlands during the Late Preclassic period (400 BC–AD 200) with their margins put to agricultural ends (Dunning

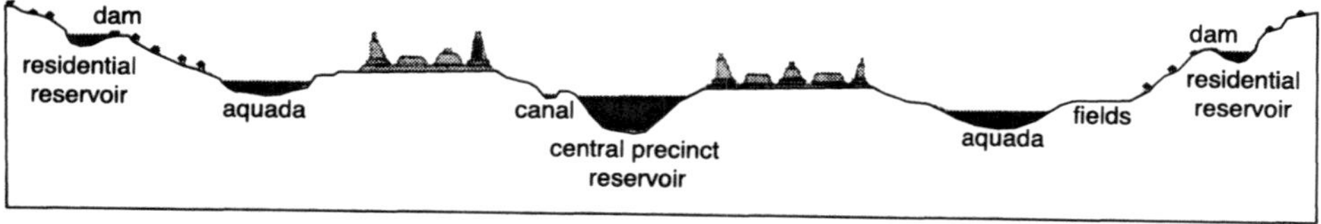

Concave Microwatershed

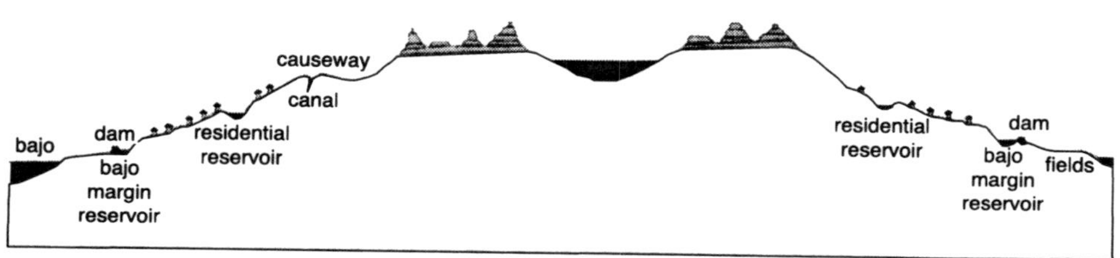

Convex Microwatershed

FIGURE 3.3. Microwatersheds in the Maya Lowlands. (From Scarborough 2003a: fig. 7.1).

et al. 2002; Dunning et al. 2003; Hansen et al. 2002). Our investigations indicate that several Petén plateau *bajos* (sizable, internally draining depressions) of northern Guatemala and adjacent portions of Belize and Mexico above 100 m asl were natural bodies of water with rich semitropical biota. Populations were drawn to these settings because of the seasonality of the rainfall and the lack of surface water elsewhere (Puleston and Puleston 1971; Scarborough 1994). Dubbed *concave microwatersheds*, these settings were expanded, exploited, and altered to retain as much water as possible during the dry season (Scarborough 1993, 1994, 1998; fig. 3.3). As Late Preclassic populations rapidly adjusted to the naturally abundant, though formally variable, catchment shapes and sizes, degradation of the surrounding forests and soils increased. Descendant populations attempted to control the erosive effects of agricultural overuse by employing the kinds of swidden intensification suggested above for the Late Classic period. The slope margins of the perennial wet bajos were terraced to contain degrading sediments, and rectilinear berms were constructed to channel runoff to adjacent fields and to further curb erosion (Scarborough et al. 2003b). Temporally, these widely incorporated features appear by the Early Classic period (AD 300–550) and continue throughout the subsequent Late Classic period (AD 550–900), a time of significant settlement change.

By the Early Classic period, we see marked changes in the environments of the bajos. The former perennial wetlands are now buried by tons of degraded sediment and a displaced hydraulic budget (Dunning et al. 2002, 2003; Scarborough 1993), the latter partially induced by a climatic drying trend (Gill 2000; Gunn et al. 1995; Hodell et al. 1995). These stressful circumstances resulted in an innovative adaptation in which the Classic period Maya relocate the cores of their settlements to hillocks and ridges frequently in proximity to and above the same bajo locations that their Late Preclassic ancestors had colonized. Although the abundance of the perennial wetlands was markedly diminished, flood recessional techniques, coupled with the slope-management methods of terrace and berm construction provided renewed productivity. At the core of these slope-management systems was a reinvented water-distribution system based on rainwater catchments and diversion into huge elevated storage tanks (Scarborough and Gallopin 1991; figs. 3.3, 3.4).

The Classic period introduces a new settlement organization at many communities in the lowlands. A *convex microwatershed* developed with the displacement of Late Preclassic *concave microwatersheds* (fig. 3.4). Large communities like Tikal, Kinal, and La Milpa organized around excavated reservoirs quarried from the relatively soft limestone, the latter used to erect the towering pyramids and rectilinear administrative structures (Scarborough 1993, 1994). The seasonal rainfall regime permitted the newly constructed and elevated tank system to fill with runoff during the heavy rains of September through December and then provide a gravity-flow release of the potable supply during much of the remainder of the year. Several central precincts of the largest centers were carefully planned to direct rainy season runoff onto canted plaster surfaces, moving water into the adjacent tanks or the former quarry scars. Large plazas as well as steep-sided pyramids shed massive volumes of water, much of it contained by the reservoir system (cf. Scarborough and Gallopin 1991; fig. 3.4). During the dry season, water was released by sluice gates frequently built into sizable dams—also functioning as causeways through the site area—allowing groups and subgroups below the summit administrative center to access

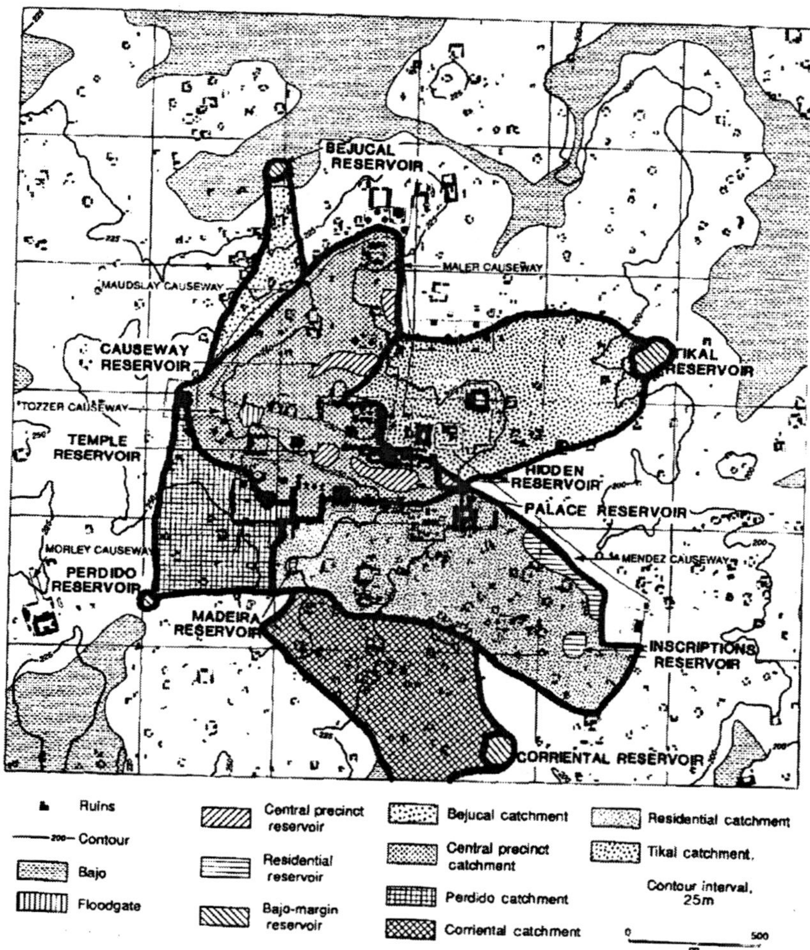

FIGURE 3.4. Convex microwatershed at Tikal with main rainfall catchment areas.

running water. Because most of the urban Classic period population was positioned near the sloping margins of the transformed hillocks or ridge system occupied by the sizable centers, water access was predictable and controlled. Gray water was likely reused near the foot of the site core and along the former margins of the wetland bajos that sustained continued agricultural productivity (fig. 3.4). The recycled wastewater was collected in large low-lying tanks, providing a small but significant third crop from the sediment-infilled Preclassic wetland margins (Scarborough 1993, 1994, 1998).

During the Classic period, we (Scarborough and Valdez 2003) argue that resource-specialized communities pervaded the settlement system in portions of the Maya Lowlands. This highly interconnected information and goods-transfer system complemented the changing landscape adaptations based on a labor-oriented economic strategy. As a partial consequence of the semitropical backdrop, the sizable, sometimes huge, architectural centers of the Classic period were not occupied by the extremely dense population aggregates associated with some other early experiments in archaic statecraft. Classic period centers operated as much to coordinate and redistribute information and goods as to centralize and control resources and labor. The role and influence of the self-organized and heterarchical communities in the Maya hinterlands permitted the frequent monitoring and long-term sustainability of the entire lowland setting. A myriad of micro-landscape adjustments used to harness the diverse biophysical setting required direct and relatively open linkages between the sizable centers and the rural communities, an adaptation less emphasized by non-tropical early states.

The environmental realignment made by Early Classic populations from an earlier Late Preclassic adaptation is accompanied by several seemingly unrelated changes in the material culture. Carved stela erection, polychrome ceramics, elaborate masonry palace construction, and formalized writing indicate a new/renewed emphasis on kingship introduced during this temporal and environmental juncture. Given that the newly engineered environs were precipitated by the overexploitation of a growing Late Preclassic population and the necessity for an alternative built landscape, the causal arrow suggests that the new material trappings resulted from a new cultural adaptation induced in part by the forced relocations and subsequent alterations of the engineered landscape (Scarborough 2003a).

The long-term changes to the landscape during the Classic period in the Maya Lowlands indicate a relatively slow, highly adaptive alteration of a semitropical environment that was overexploited by an earlier set of Preclassic occupations. The initial attraction to the perennial wetlands of the Late Preclassic period triggered a relatively brief phase of rapid exploitation of the biophysical semitropical resources that was unsustainable.

However, subsequent economic developments emphasized a classic labor-tasking adaptation that drew on the lessons learned from the failed technotasking economic logic associated with the overuse of the Late Preclassic wetland setting.

Highland Mexico

The environmentally rich and resource-abundant Basin of Mexico is another celebrated region in which the archaic state evolved. Unlike the lowland Maya, however, portions of highland Mexico developed highly centralized and lasting societies, which rapidly exploited the highly resilient and abundant natural setting. The circumstances for development were initially moored on a similar Late Preclassic (Late Formative) perennial wetland adaptation. Although semiarid, a sizable though shallow lake basin surrounded by a number of springs provided the natural resources for a long trajectory of settlement near the lake margins (Niederberger 1979). By the Late Formative, at least two sizable centers developed within the basin: 1) Cuicuilco in immediate proximity to the southwestern lakeshore, and 2) Teotihuacan located a bit farther from the lakeshore to the northeast, but positioned on a large concentration of springs (Sanders et al. 1979). Monumental architecture as well as a nucleated settlement pattern identified both early cities. Because of the volcanic activity of a nearby volcano, Cuicuilco was destroyed by the end of the Late Formative, with a portion of the surviving population likely relocating to the rapidly ascending primate center of Teotihuacan (Sanders et al. 1979). Conventional wisdom suggests that Teotihuacan was supported by classic irrigation schemes based on the 80–100 springheads irrupting at or in immediate proximity to the center (Sanders et al. 1979). A review of the literature, however, suggests that drained or raised fields were constructed at the springheads, a resource adaptation that likely influenced the extremely high concentration of population identified at Teotihuacan (Millon 1973; cf. Scarborough 2003b). Evidence supports the use of raised agricultural beds along the southern lakeshore margins of the basin by Late Formative times and perhaps at other lakeshore localities (Armillas 1971; Coe 1964; Palerm 1955:35).

By way of example, the Aztec period (AD 1350–1519) island capital of Tenochtitlan was the densest concentration of humanity in Mesoamerica, together with the nearby southern lake margins of Lake Xochimilco and Lake Chalco (Sanders et al. 1979). Tenochtitlan was highly ordered by a gridded street and canal pattern, not unlike the more controlled street layout at ancestral Teotihuacan. When chinampas were concentrated as a consequence of limited water-source access (Teotihuacan) or limited amounts of arable land (the island of Tenochtitlan [and adjacent lake margins]), strict urban planning was the result. When coupled with the overall resource abundance of highland Mexico, a rapidly expanding and exploitative economic and political organization evolved.

Although a Stone Age technology, Teotihuacan was organized as a technotasking economic logic based on the rapid processing, distribution, and consumption of resources. Because of the incredible abundance and fertility of the basin, unlike the fragility of large portions of the Yucatán Peninsula for resource use and concentration, the basin's occupants were less capable of overexploiting their environment given the limitation of their Stone Age tools.

Lowland Maya and Highland Mexico Compared

The precipitous rise of state-like complexity in Mesoamerica is frequently associated with the Late Preclassic period. Two of the principal nuclear areas developing statecraft were ecologically grounded on perennial wetlands. Although central and southern Mesoamerica are both viewed here as legacies of wetland management, the trajectories of the two regions were significantly different. The Maya Lowlands were a vast wetlands and seasonal swamp setting that was colonized by sedentists who likely positioned themselves near perennial bodies of water to best allow for concentrated agricultural activity and population growth (Puleston and Puleston 1971; Scarborough 1994). Some researchers have suggested that many of the earliest Late Preclassic villages and towns were highly compacted settlements (centralized) when in proximity to productive wetland settings (Cliff 1982, 1986; Wilk and Wilhite 1982), with settlement only subsequently dispersing during the highly active landscape transformations associated with the Classic period. The reconstructions of the huge Late Preclassic Maya center of El Mirador indicate a city of rectilinear layout occupied by a highly compacted support community

(Hansen, personal communication 2001; Matheny 1987). Given the volume of monumental architecture from pyramids to palaces, a construction mass for the city is estimated to be of the same order of magnitude as Teotihuacan. In fact, El Mirador may be a sister city at the other end of the subcontinent organized on very similar principles to those of Teotihuacan (cf. H. Wright 2005). We do not know the precise constitution of the settlement in the Mirador Basin, though significant wetland management is demonstrable. In many ways these two cities appear to arise from similar environmental backdrops, based on the proximity of wetlands and altered low-lying depressions (cf. Hansen et al. 2002). Nevertheless, El Mirador as well as several other Late Preclassic cities and towns were abandoned by the Early Classic period.

A portion of the vast natural wetland terrain in the Maya Lowlands changed to a less productive set of seasonally inundated bajo sediments when the Early Classic occupants attempted to harvest the environs. The tremendously altered landscape eventually based on elevated civic reservoirs and grand displays of public architecture further excited erosion, leading to plant and soil degradation. In turn, the wetlands were infilled with sediment and allowed to desiccate. Even though a third of the Maya Lowlands is seasonal swamp today, suggesting that seasonal wetland management was a principal environmental resource for the ancient Maya, current research does not reveal a strong argument in favor of major labor deployment and its landscape signatures deep within these depressions during the Classic period. Bajo settings were clearly used for flood recessional agriculture as well as natural harvests of animals, plant fibers, and chert nodules, but significant alterations to potential lake levels or chinampa-like fields are not well supported. Accretional landscape modification associated with sizable but dispersed human populations during the Classic period emphasized a labortasking economic organization.

Although the evidence for intensive agriculture in highland Mexico is frequently reduced to the Postclassic lakeshores of Xochimilco and Chalco—the seat for Aztec-period chinampa fields—wetland management was much more widespread through time and space (cf. T. M. Whitmore and Turner 2002). The early appearance of wetlands in proximity to Teotihuacan, more than 60 km from the shores of Xochimilco, suggests extensive raised fields that influenced colonization and settlement density at this inland location. Ironically, it is at precisely this site area (the

Basin of Mexico)—argued as being supported by conventional canalization efforts—that our best case for perennial wetland control flourishes for at least 1,500 years. The Maya Lowlands, however, emphasize wetland management even earlier. Because of the fragility of their environs, the ancient Maya eventually developed a highly variable range of agricultural methods and practices less dependent on raised fields, though continuing to harvest the wetlands and their margins (cf. Berry and McAnany 2007).

The Maya developed the huge urban center of El Mirador in complement to Teotihuacan, only to have the former site collapse during the Early Classic period within its uncertain bajo surroundings. The initial dispersed abundance of the semitropical, lowland Maya wetlands promoted an apparent rapid and exploitative economic logic that attracted Late Preclassic colonists to the perennial wetlands. In the case of El Mirador, a technotasking-like adaptation was not sustainable in the jungle ecology and abandonment followed. This was subsequently followed by a slower Classic period accretional harvesting of the diverse yet fragile resource base. The Maya example emphasizes both the fragility and flexibility embedded in a tropical ecosystem and the continuum of cultural actions demonstrable in any economic logic. During the Classic period, the trajectories of the Mexican Highlands and Maya Lowlands went their divergent ways, the former only enhancing the wetland legacy through exploitative resource extraction in the context of extreme resource abundance, the latter incrementally altering the fragile semitropical environs to harvest the diversity of wide-ranging resources (Scarborough 2000, 2003b).

Conclusions

The issue of resource sustainability not only highlights one of the most significant concerns of our time and place but also forces a reasoned assessment of what we mean by economy. Under technotasking logic, societies will organize to generate more and greater tool-making inventories, an adaptation affecting decisions as fundamental as the rate and process of landscape alteration. A Western model that now pervades all of the developed and much of the less-developed world champions the rapid exploitation of resources based on the precipitous growth of complex technologies. Following from this is the view that sustainability attempts to maintain the same crop yield on a landscape unless a more effective technology—an outside vector like pesticide, fertilizer, or genetic alteration—is introduced to allow increased abundance. Given that technology frequently inserts itself in fits and starts, a general adaptation to increased production demand is the rapid clearing of both old and new agricultural lands to make way for technological enhancements—even when the anticipated technology is not immediately available. In any event, sustainability of yields within technotasking logic is not immediately or inextricably connected to the condition of the landscape; yield is always the independent variable.

A labortasking logic suggests a different way of processing the greater landscape—not just the yield. For several reasons noted, societies incrementally alter their landscapes to produce a built environment better than the year before. Sustainability develops at several levels—including the harvest—but also in association with the conditioned and reconditioned appearance of the landscape itself. The environment becomes better adapted to the needs of humans from the moment of colonization until the massive modification, for example, of terraced rice paddies (Scarborough et al. 1999). The hills and dales, soils and redeposited sediments, are transformed over generations into highly productive and increasingly sustainable settings (Scarborough 2003b, 2005b).

I have presented ancient Mesoamerica as a case study of how varied environments—even those in intra-continental proximity—were transformed differently. Although heuristically presented as polar extremes, the two environments shared wetland adaptations and, in the case of the ancient Maya, switched economic logics as a consequence of less predictable cultural and environmental decision making (Scarborough 2003b). Nevertheless, the Maya Lowlands and their wet-dry rainforests evolved land- and water-use strategies that reflect the variability encompassed by a labortasking economic orientation, while the Mexican Highlands revealed a focused exploitation of resources reflective of technotasking logic. These different resource-use strategies provide at least two separate economic logics and indicate another way to assess social evolution.

From my vantage, the technotasking logic has pervaded archaeology and human ecology circles for two generations and prevented an anthropology of social evolutionary principles from discarding the simplicity of bands, tribes, chiefdoms, and states and the technological and material indicators that archaeologists use to type cultures.[1] Most of us realize the futility of the sequence when working with real data and problems, but no clear alternative view presents itself (Scarborough 2005b). Nevertheless, if we recast economy as the way humans make a living and not immediately assume that technology and specific kinds of ecology are required subsets of economy, another way of interpreting the past arises. Some groups did not embrace technology in the manner that we do today, and they evolved in ecosystems much different than our own or those environs in which few of us search for the origins and maintenance of statecraft. It may well be that the received wisdom which argues that some combination of band-to-state development did occur in several semiarid and temperate environs and was associated with strong hierarchical—perhaps hegemonic—political and economic systems. These were the successful technotasking societies from Teotihuacan to Uruk, Iraq (Scarborough 2000). However, another economic pathway emphasized labortasking and the highly structured community organization associated with the ancient Maya. Here, an early experiment in technotasking may have occurred at a city as impressive as El Mirador, but by the subsequent Early Classic period, communities in the Maya Lowlands could not uniformly harvest/exploit water and land in that earlier manner. A heterarchical adaptation arose that permitted dispersed populations to alter their ecological settings at the level of the microenvironment. Resource-specialized communities evolved, and a self-organizational schema developed (Scarborough and Valdez 2003). Labortasking emphasized community coordination and perhaps the parsimonious acceptance of tools through time. The ancient Maya preoccupation with time may well be a consequence of this focus on community coordination and its scheduling practices (cf. Freidel et al. 1993; Leon-Portilla 1988). Regardless, such an evolutionary trajectory does not fit well with the band, tribe, chiefdom, and state sequence. In fact, it is the frequent and implicit incorporation of labor and its organization into more conventionally described technological change in societies that compromises the classic sequence of social development nearly everywhere.

To best understand the past and perhaps affect the present, archaeologists and anthropologists must broaden their view of what technology is. It is NOT an independent variable, and it is not necessary for all societies to incorporate more sophisticated versions of it. All of us enmeshed with technology know its potential for human improvement as well as disaster. We are less aware that it is not and was not an inevitable result of cultural development. This simple assumption has limited our abilities to think imaginatively about what may have been and what may yet come. True sustainability entails many complex economic aspects beyond technology; how the community is organized and responds to its diverse needs frequently can rest with the structured coordination of labor through time.

The wetland legacy of ancient Mesoamerica reveals several lessons in sustainability. In the case of the lowland Maya, sustainability was a labortasking product of a fragile environmental setting. When the Maya asserted rapid and exploitative methods for changing their environment, collapse was imminent. When they followed the slow and incremental harvesting pathway, sustained growth in the context of a "domesticated" environment resulted. The ancient Mexican Highlands demonstrate a kind of technotasking "sustainable" by virtue of a naturally abundant ecological setting. When and where technotasking succeeds, a rich environment must be assumed or artificially created. In the case of Lower Mesopotamia and the earliest city-states, the fortuitous insertion of canalization over the desert-scape allowed the latter; in the case of highland Mexico, the extremely rich volcanic soils and lakeshore setting accommodated a seemingly endless replenishment of resources and permitted the former. Rapid and unrelenting exploitation of biophysical resources, however, does have limits, and in both cases of technotasking presented here, collapse eventually occurred.

In today's world, the nation-state is able to exploit resources from several quarters of the globe to maintain the necessary biophysical resource concentrations to sustain a technotasking pathway.[2] Obvious technological breakthroughs have allowed the rapid extraction and distribution of these resources to highly centralized and concentrated places. But how long can this definition of sustainability last? Because a labortasking pathway is a different approach to economy and sustainability with demonstrable long-term success under changing environmental circumstances, perhaps aspects of it can be emulated or grafted onto our most present worldview. Can a technotasking pathway and the decision-making apparatus it implies sustain us as we enter the planet's uncertain future? There are other ways to think about sustainability and longevity modeled from a lost socioeconomic/sociopolitical pathway.

Notes

1. One of the difficulties with evolutionary anthropological archaeology is our explicit denial of the sequence band, tribe, chiefdom, and state, while continuing to couch our arguments with little useful alternative method or theory. We frequently move the sequent categories around and add or drop subdivisions of these categories (cf. T. K. Earle and Haas 1991; A. Johnson and Earle 1987; Sanders and Webster 1978), and all the time object to the old, tired types that Service (1962, 1971) gathered and identified for us nearly two generations ago. These categories may well prove effective in some cases, but in such situations, we are examining a society wedded to technotasking—as the categories are rooted in J. Steward's (1955) early notion of cultural cores with technology the underlying identifier. Nevertheless, we can still follow a grounded evolutionary approach and broaden our view of economy by presenting another economic logic less attracted to technological innovation with or without surplus stimulation.

2. The Great Collapse of the southern Maya Lowlands continues to receive tremendous attention, fueled by recent climatological data. Nevertheless, the demise of such a long-lived civilization was precipitated by several factors, both external forcings as well as internal social dynamics. Elsewhere, I (Scarborough 2003c, 2006b) indicate that a Mexican Highland version of technotasking was emulated by the last Late Classic period Maya rulers that interrupted the fundamental heterarchical linkages between centers and peripheries and corrupted the ecological success of the longstanding labortasking pathway.

Part II

Multi-dimensional Explanations

4

Creating a Stable Landscape

SOIL CONSERVATION AND ADAPTATION AMONG THE ANCIENT MAYA

Nicholas Dunning, Timothy Beach, Sheryl Luzzadder-Beach, and John G. Jones

SCHOLARS HAVE PRAISED the ancient Maya for creating and sustaining an elaborate civilization in a tropical rainforest environment (e.g., Drew 1999) and also have criticized them for devastating that same environment (e.g., Abrams and Rue 1988; D. Rice 1993). Similarly, views about the environment of the Maya Lowlands have ranged from fragile and with very limited agricultural potential (e.g., Meggers 1954; Morley 1946) to diverse and replete with niches well suited to all manner of agricultural intensification (e.g., Harrison 1990; B. L. Turner 1978a). Such contrasting views also reflected very different beliefs and different knowledge regarding the size and density of ancient populations, environmental carrying capacity, and the impacts that these populations had on the lowland environment (Dunning and Beach 2004). While we are far from a consensus on these fundamental aspects of ancient Maya civilization, a number of critical variables are coming into clearer focus. It is clear that the Maya Lowlands environment is indeed quite varied, with a mosaic of regional and microenvironments presenting challenges and opportunities for human adaptation (Dunning, Beach et al. 1998; fig. 4.1).

It is also clear that the environment was far from static during the course of Maya civilization, with both natural and anthropogenic changes making adaptation an ongoing and recursive process. As part of this process, the relationship between population size, density, and environmental disturbance was not always simple and direct, a finding that is becoming increasingly evident in other parts of the world as well (e.g., Fisher, this vol.; Simmons, this vol.). In this chapter, we review data bearing on the relationship between population and environmental change in the

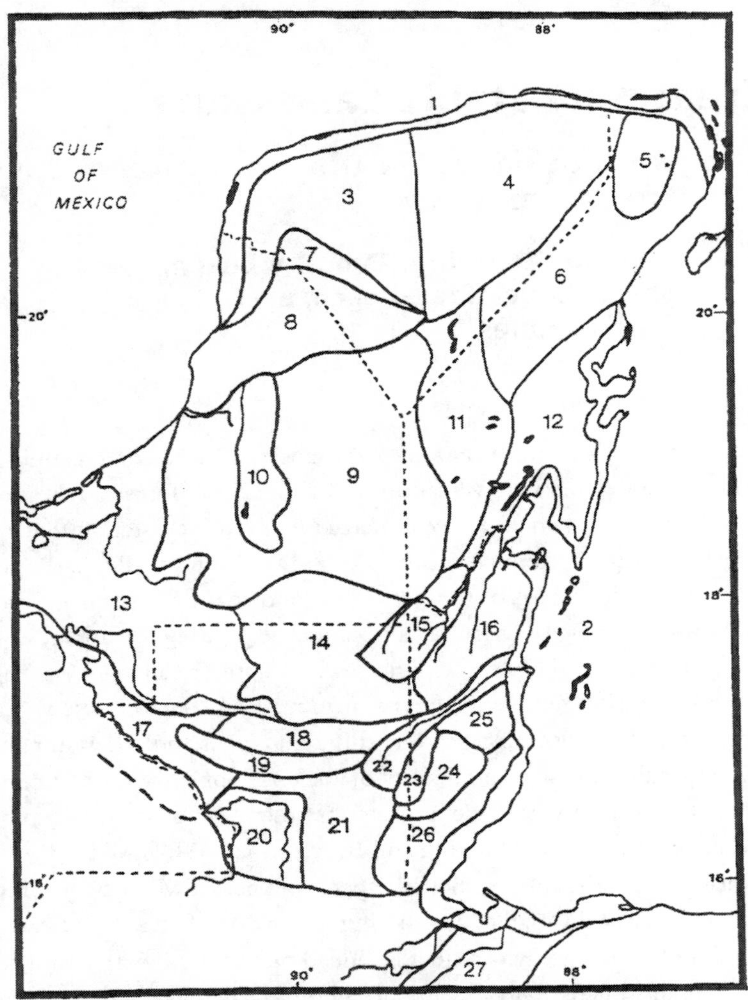

FIGURE 4.1. Environmental and adaptive regions of the Maya Lowlands. 1) North Coast, 2) Caribbean Reef & Eastern Coastal Margin, 3) Northwest Karst Plain, 4) Northeast Karst Plain, 5) Yalahau, 6) Coba-Okop, 7) Puuc-Santa Elena, 8) Puuc-Bolonchen Hills, 9) Central Hills, 10) Edzna-Silvituk Trough, 11) Quintana Roo Depression, 12) Uaymil, 13) Río Candelaria–Río San Pedro, 14) Petén Karst Plateau, 15) Three Rivers, 16) Rio Hondo, 17) Lacandon Fold, 18) Petén Itza Fracture, 19) Libertad Anticline, 20) Río de la Pasión, 21) Dolores, 22) Belize River Valley, 23) Vaca Plateau, 24) Maya Mountains, 25) Hummingbird Karst, 26) Karstic Piedmont, 27) Motagua and Copan Valleys (after Dunning, Beach et al. 1998:fig. 1).

Maya Lowlands. We give greatest attention to the Three Rivers region of the east-central Yucatán Peninsula, but also consider comparative information from other parts of the lowlands. While in some instances there does indeed seem to be a direct relationship between rising populations and rising impact, in others relatively small populations generated considerable local environmental destruction, whereas population increases often spurred conservation efforts (Beach, Dunning et al. 2006). Judging from any history of conservation, the extent and success of conservation was apparently as much the result of variation in social factors as in environmental differences, relationships that are also apparent in contemporary agricultural colonization (e.g., Beach, Luzzadder-Beach et al. 2006). Our review here focuses in particular on episodic periods of soil loss and conservation and variation in levels of land stewardship. However, before presenting our analysis, we briefly consider the changing views in scholarly theory on human-environment relationships in ancient Maya Lowlands that should be considered.

Changing Views on the Ancient Maya and the Maya Lowlands Environment

Scholarly views on the Maya Lowlands environment and ancient Maya society and agriculture have changed greatly over the past fifty years (B. L. Turner 1993). A paradigm persisted until the mid to late 1960s that saw ancient Maya civilization as an apparent anomaly in world history: namely, a complex civilization supported by rotating, long-fallow (swidden) agriculture in a relatively homogeneous, environmentally limiting tropical-forest setting (e.g., Morley 1946; J. H. Steward et al. 1955; J. Thompson 1954). After all, the Yucatán is generally flat and geologically uniform and was blanketed by a poorly understood tropical forest. This model also saw ancient Maya population levels as necessarily low and dispersed, and Maya "cities" as mostly vacant ceremonial centers. This view was a product of the site-center-focused nature of Maya archaeology before the 1960s and a very limited view of the lowlands environment (N. Hammond 1978; B. L. Turner 1978b), as well as the overarching influence of two scholars, Sylvanus Morley and Eric Thompson, who championed strongly utopian views of Maya society, perhaps as an intellectual retreat from the horrors of the mid-twentieth-century world (Schele and Miller 1986:18–25). It is also now clear that early scientific thinking about the pre-Hispanic Maya was strongly influenced by the effects of centuries of colonial and post-colonial changes to the Maya world that normalized long-fallow swidden agriculture and discounted indigenous land rights.

Over the last three decades, archaeological investigations began to look more widely, including at areas beyond site centers, at the same time that modern forest clearance was exposing large areas of terrain and aerial imagery was becoming increasingly available. Modern investigations were also aided by a growing array of scientific techniques from environmental sciences and geosciences that became increasingly integrated into archaeological investigations. These combined sources produced evidence for much more densely settled rural and urban populations, and for intensive agriculture as manifest in field walls, terraces, and visible wetland fields across many parts of the Maya Lowlands. In this way, a new view emerged that emphasized environmental heterogeneity and diverse agricultural systems, replacing the old, deterministic orthodoxy (Harrison 1990).

However, B. L. Turner (1993) challenged the "new orthodoxy," largely because it assigns too great a role to human agency and ingenuity and excessively minimizes the limitations posed by both perennial (e.g., groundwater hydrology) and variable (e.g., climate change) components of the natural environment. In response, contemporary archaeological investigations often address human-environment relationships as a core question and employ a battery of archaeological, geoarchaeological, and paleoecological methods. Out of these investigations, and spurred by the intellectual debate between more envirocentric and anthrocentric perspectives, a new paradigm has emerged in environmental studies that recognizes the inherent instability of the biophysical environment and the dynamic flux that characterizes human-environment interactions (Dunning and Beach 2004). This model sees human-environment interactions as between states of relative stability and instability with changes brought about by adjustments in both human and biophysical factors. Hence, cultural adaptation must be constant and continually successful, but even continual adaptation may be met with acute or chronic decline, sometimes becoming catastrophically maladaptive. Similarly, because of the different trajectories of Maya Lowlands history, we should understand Maya adaptive systems to have varied tremendously across space and time (Beach et al. 2002; Beach, Luzzadder-Beach et al. 2006; Dunning, Beach et al. 1998).

The Maya Lowlands Environment

The cultural region of the Maya Lowlands includes the karstic Yucatán Peninsula, contiguous low-lying river valleys of Central America, and a small area of higher elevation and crystalline geology of the Maya Mountains of Belize. The chief environmental factors that create a mosaic of habitats across this region include variation in rainfall, ecological succession and disturbance, water table depth, water quality, soil and geomorphic processes, and the slope gradients and drainage caused by structural geology (Dunning, Beach et al. 1998; Luzzadder-Beach and Beach 2009). Humans are imbedded in all factors, of course, especially in this region of four millennia of profound human modifications.

Annual rainfall totals generally grade from a low of about 500 mm on the northwest coast of Yucatán to a high near 2,500 mm in the southern extremes of the lowlands, but with a few noticeable anomalies generated by convergent wind systems, orographic precipitation, and rainshadow effects. High rainfall averages do not preclude the region from significant drought hazard, because annual and seasonal variation is quite high. Annual rainfall is also highly uneven, with a pronounced and variable winter dry season generally from December through April.

Most of the Maya Lowlands has carbonate (chiefly limestone) bedrock, a simple fact that profoundly affects human settlement because of its influence on the movement of water and the development and fertility of soil. These parent material and climatic factors largely explain the pan-regional distribution of soils across the lowlands. Soils in the north tend to be shallow, well-drained, clayey, and calcareous, whereas soils in the south tend to be deeper, more poorly drained, clayey, and calcareous, but also more leached. However, this trend is not gradual, with many sharp contrasts in soil cover at both regional and local scales. Within the various subregions of the lowlands, geologic structure and time of pedogenesis (soil age) are also important factors creating variation in the spatial distribution of soils. Faulting, erosion, and dissolution have created a landscape with enough drainage variation to have produced a range of land surfaces varying from well-drained uplands with generally shallow but fertile Rendoll soils, to older, well-drained uplands with deep red Alifisols (or Terra Rosa), to areas of seasonal inundation with deeper Vertisols and some perennially flooded wetlands with water-logged, organic Histosols. Over time, humans have also played an enormous role in regional soilscape formation, inducing erosion, aggradation, and changes in soils chemistry and morphology (Beach 1998a, 1998b; Beach et al. 2003, 2006).

Geologic structure also largely governs the regional availability of surface and subsurface water, creating both severe limitations and excesses. Surface and spring-fed rivers drain the margins of the wetter southern half of the peninsula, but perennial surface water is virtually absent, and groundwater is accessible only with great effort throughout much of the hilly central portions of the peninsula and northern karst plains. Nonetheless, along many coastal margins and even in the interior, cenotes, springs, perched water tables, and caves make water more accessible and indeed locally plentiful.

Natural vegetation across the Maya Lowlands generally follows patterns of rainfall, though edaphic factors, like soil drainage and chemistry, and lithologic factors are also influential (Flores and Espejel Carvajal 1994; Gomez-Pompa et al. 2003; Greller 2000; Hartshorn 1988). Beginning on the northwest coast of the peninsula, beach ridges merge into a 10–20 km swath of swampy estuarine wetlands, then give way to a thorn woodland-savanna that in turn grades into a tropical, deciduous seasonal forest. Moving southward on the peninsula, the deciduous forest then grades into a band of semi-evergreen forest and an evergreen seasonal rainforest (also called tropical very dry forest) that stretches from central Yucatán to the northern Petén. This dry forest in turn breaks up into a savanna zone around La Libertad in the north-central Petén, which grades southward into the species-rich tropical moist forest of the southern half of the Petén. These forests are not actually tropical rainforests, but they have diverse species assemblages that tend to increase southward with available water supply (Gomez-Pompa et al. 2003; Greller 2000; Hartshorn 1988).

Recent geochemical coring studies of the Caribbean's Cariaco Basin indicate dramatic swings in climate during the Archaic and Preclassic periods from about 4,000 to 2,000 years ago (Haug et al. 2001), and we do not yet know how this affected the Maya Lowlands. Several studies that have analyzed the geochemistry and oxygen isotopes of sediment cores taken from a variety of lakes within the Maya Lowlands showed a long period of regional aridity developing, beginning around 3,000 years ago and intensifying most notably during the time of the Classic collapse between AD 800 and AD 1000 (Brenner et al. 2002). Also, embedded within this drying trend there appears to have been a 208-year-long cycle of drier periods (Hodell et al. 2001). These data are clearest from two lakes (Chichancanab and Punta Laguna) in the northeastern part of the peninsula, where ancient settlement was comparatively light. In areas of heavy settlement, such as the central Petén, lakes' human-disturbance signals simply overwhelm any evidence for natural oscillations, which tend to be more subtle (Brenner et al. 2002). At this point there is insufficient paleoenvironmental evidence to make statements such as "The drought of AD 910 was most severe in regions A, B, and C of the Maya Lowlands, and less severe in regions X, Y, and Z" with a great degree of certainty. While there may indeed have been significant spatial variability in drought severity across the Maya Lowlands, it has not yet been well mapped. Similarly, our understanding of the cultural factors that may have contributed to drought vulnerability in some areas more than others remains nascent. Furthermore, the many transformations that occurred within Maya civilization during the protracted demise of the Classic period are far too complex to be generalized as simply drought-caused depopulation and collapse (Demarest et al. 2004; Webster 2002).

Population and Environmental Change in the Maya Lowlands

Mid-twentieth-century views of the ancient Maya estimated overall population densities in the Petén "heartland" of the lowlands to have been on the order of 40–80 persons/sq. km, a level consistent with food production derived from long-fallow swidden agriculture (Cowgill 1961; Morley 1946). By the late twentieth century, many scholars had come to favor much higher estimates of population densities (Culbert and Rice 1990). Within the central Petén, peak overall Late Classic population densities have been variably estimated at 121/sq. km (B. L. Turner 1990), 196/sq. km (Culbert and Rice 1990), and 221/sq. km (specifically for the Petén lakes area; D. Rice and Rice 1990). Somewhat higher densities have been proposed for the Río Bec (282/sq. km; B. L. Turner 1990) and Puuc (290/sq. km; Dunning 1992b) regions. The highest regional population estimates come from the Petexbatún (486/sq. km; O'Mansky and Dunning 2004) and Copan Valley (640–880/sq. km; Webster and Freter 1990), although we think densities were higher in these areas because of political conflict and environmental circumscription. A recent, much higher estimate of population at the central 10 sq. km of urban Chunchucmil of at least 2,650/sq. km is interesting, for this is the most unlikely of Maya Lowlands environments to sustain a high population (Dahlin et al. 2005). This Classic period site lies on the northwest coast of Yucatán, where soils and rainfall are the least, but groundwater is close to the surface (Beach 1998a; Dahlin et al. 2005; Luzzadder-Beach 2000). This estimate seems out of line, but Dahlin et al. (2005) made their conservative estimate considering three central critiques that Maya population estimates might be too high: 1) artificially high person/structure numbers (Becquelin and Michelet 1994), 2) no consideration of the seasonality of some populations (Dunning 2004), or 3) failure to adequately account for the mobility of population within archaeologically discernable time periods (Inomata 2004). Nevertheless, such high populations at Chunchucmil could have been sustained through a combination of multiple-resource-zone exploitation, market-center trade, or development of alternative food sources and systems. Regardless of the actual populations that ranged across the Maya Lowlands in pre-Hispanic times, it is clear that meeting subsistence needs was often a challenge that had considerable environmental impacts and that generated numerous attempts to increase sustainability.

A general model showing a direct correlation between the growth of population and increasing levels of environmental degradation has been outlined for the central Petén lakes region during the course of Preclassic through Classic Maya civilization (ca. 500 BC–AD 900) (M. Binford et al. 1987; Deevey et al. 1979; D. Rice 1996; fig. 4.2). Although cautioning that research strategy and data analysis homogenize inter-lake basin variations and that the data may have been to a degree forced to fit a relatively small number of reliable radiocarbon dates, D. Rice (1996) stands by the general pattern described in the model of escalating environmental disturbance up until the collapse of population around the lakes in the ninth

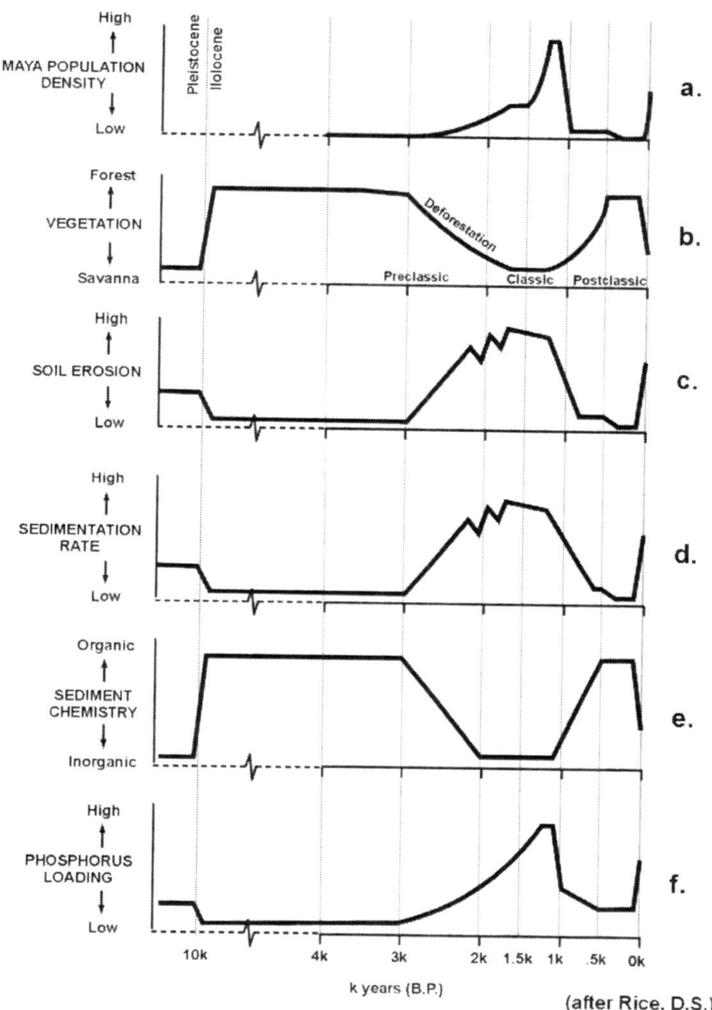

FIGURE 4.2. Summary of the long-term impacts of Maya settlement on the terrestrial and lacustrine environments of the central Petén lakes (modified from D. Rice 1996 and M. Binford et al. 1987).

century AD. By this time, the central Petén landscape was essentially deforested, with most available land given over to agriculture, though lake cores can be biased to more intensive land uses surrounding lake watersheds. In addition to the need for agricultural land, regional forests were undoubtedly depleted by a growing demand for construction materials and firewood and possibly abetted further by climatic drying (Brenner et al. 2002). In denuded areas with appreciable slopes, soil erosion was increasingly stripping sloping land surfaces to bedrock. Unfortunately, despite considerable research, we still know comparatively little about the precise nature of Classic Maya agriculture around the central Petén lakes because very few vestiges of field walls, terraces, or wetland fields have yet to be identified there. In fact, the apparent lack of such relicts may in part account for the severity of erosion experienced in these lacustrine watersheds during the course of their ancient occupation. Nevertheless, the tropical forest surrounding the lakes recovered substantially during the Postclassic (AD 900–1500), despite continued occupation of the watersheds by a sizeable, albeit reduced, population (D. Rice 1996; P. Rice and Rice 2004).

The general trajectory of cultural and environmental history outlined above for the Petén lakes region does appear to apply loosely to some other areas, but it would indeed be reckless to use it as a general model for the entirety of the Maya Lowlands. For example, some parts of the lowlands experienced population crashes and abandonments near the end of the Preclassic (ca. AD 100).

Many of the urban centers (such as Nakbe and El Mirador) of Mirador Basin within the Petén Karst Plateau were largely abandoned at this time, possibly because of earlier severe environmental degradation (Hansen et al. 2002; Jacob 1995) or climatic instability. Meanwhile, in northern Belize, rising water table levels may have influenced cycles of abandonment and adaptation of wetland field systems and related settlements through the Preclassic and Classic (Luzzadder-Beach and Beach 2009; Pohl et al. 1996; Rejmankova et al. 1995). Ironically, sea level rise and attendant water table rise may have ended wetland agriculture in the far northern Belize coastal plain in the Preclassic, but made it possible in the Classic period farther to the south at Blue Creek (Luzzadder-Beach and Beach 2009). Water table changes may have similarly adversely affected the Yalahau region of northern Quintana Roo at end of the Early Classic (ca. AD 500), triggering another regional abandonment (Fedick et al. 2000). Nevertheless, in many parts of the Maya Lowlands, populations continued to rise through the Late Classic period (AD 550–800), and in some areas growing population appears to have indeed triggered environmental problems. For example, in the Copan Valley, expanding Late Classic populations began deforesting surrounding hillsides, generating severe soil erosion (Abrams and Rue 1988; Wingard 1996), although the degree to which the valley subsequently experienced rapid or gradual depopulation is debated (Fash et al. 2004; Webster et al. 2004). Yet in many areas like the Petexbatún and Caracol, rising populations seem to have triggered significant soil conservation as part of agricultural-intensification efforts. As noted elsewhere in this volume by Fisher for the Lake Pátzcuaro Basin in Mexico and by Simmons for early Cyprus, the sheer numbers of people on the land may well be much less significant than how they are organized and what land-use strategies they employ. In order to shed better light on the nuances of environmental change, population trends, and cultural adaptations, we will examine one subregion of the Maya Lowlands in greater detail below.

The Three Rivers Region and La Milpa

The Three Rivers region comprises the eastern margins of the large Petén Karst Plateau, a hydrologically elevated limestone area characterized by rugged, free-draining uplands and seasonally inundated, clay-filled depressions (*bajos*), but also includes the upper margins of the coastal plains and the low-lying valleys of the Río Bravo and Booth's River, areas of low, limestone ridges and large, perennial wetlands (Dunning et al. 2003; Luzzadder-Beach and Beach 2009). The moderately large urban center of La Milpa is situated atop a topographically prominent ridge on the upland plateau far from any perennial water courses, but in close proximity to bajos of various sizes (fig. 4.3). Soils on the limestone uplands are fertile but shallow Rendolls, vulnerable to erosion where significantly sloping. Bajo soils vary from deeper, cumulic Mollisols to deep, clay Vertisols and organic mucks (Histosols). Regional native vegetation ranges from perennial herbaceous swamps (chiefly in riparian areas), to seasonal swamp forest (in most bajos), to tropical wet/dry deciduous forest across the uplands (Brokaw and Mallory 1993). The latter reflects the powerful influence of seasonal wet-dry regional climate. The severity of the dry season poses a significant obstacle to human occupation of the karstic uplands, where perennial water sources are few and far between.

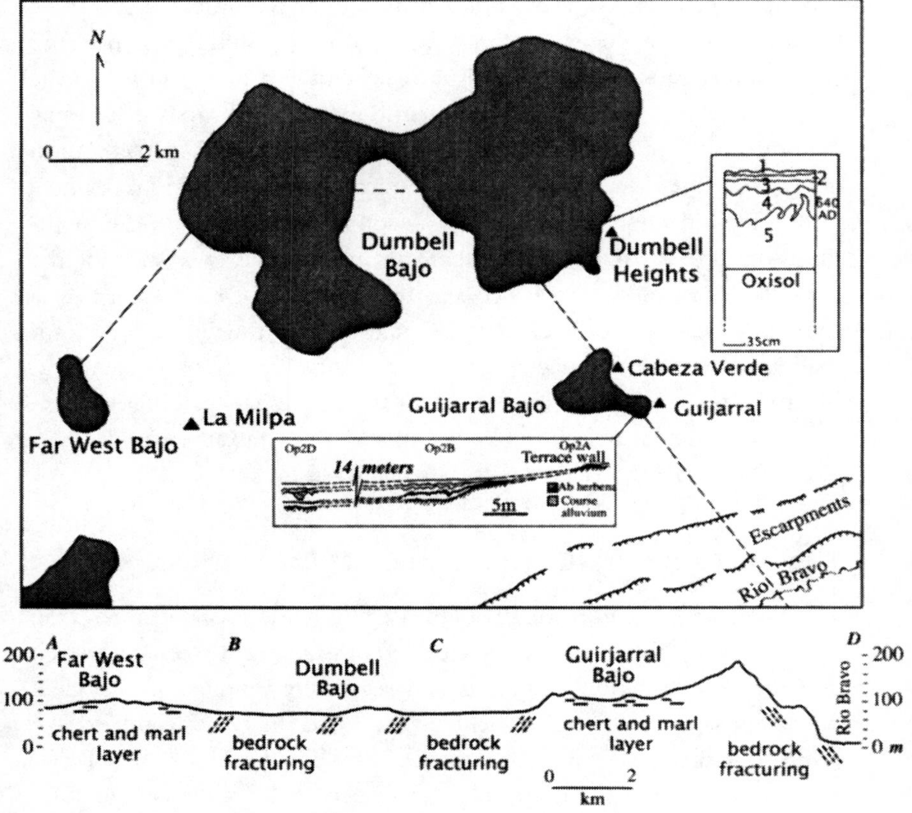

FIGURE 4.3. Map and cross section of elevated interior *bajos* near La Milpa in northwestern Belize, and excavation details from the Guijarral and Dumbbell Bajos.

In 1995, we began a program of geo-environmental archaeological investigations in the bajos of the region, with a particular focus on the relatively small Far West Bajo on the northwestern margin of the La Milpa urban area. Our investigations clearly revealed that this bajo contained a perennial wetland and shallow lake until around AD 100 (Dunning et al. 2002, 2003), a habitat similar to those known to have been highly attractive to early Maya settlers (Pohl et al. 1996). Over the course of several centuries, erosion on surrounding uplands choked the bajo with huge quantities of clayey sediment, burying the Preclassic soil surface and hydrologically transforming it into a seasonal swamp, a process that may have been helped by general regional climatic drying trends. We subsequently recovered complementary data from additional bajos in northwestern Belize and the eastern Petén, leading us to posit a general model of anthropogenic environmental change within many bajos towards the end of the Preclassic (Beach et al. 2002; Dunning et al. 2002). Fieldwork undertaken in 2003 has caused us to modify our views somewhat. Further excavations in the Guijarral Bajo northeast of La Milpa produced data similar to those of the Far West Bajo. However, in the large Dumbell Bajo north of La Milpa, we found no evidence to suggest that this depression ever held a lake or substantial perennial wetland (although we did uncover a buried late Pleistocene savanna surface; Dunning et al. 2006). We attribute this variation to the hit-and-miss nature of erosion and sedimentation and a probable difference in the subsurface hydrology of the region's bajos, variability that is not surprising in a karst region (fig. 4.3). Environmental variability between and within bajos undoubtedly played a significant role in their relative attractiveness as settlement loci both at the onset of Preclassic agricultural colonization (Dunning et al. 2006) as well as later, in their altered states, during the Classic (Kunen et al. 2000). It is also clear that, as noted by Kusimba (this vol.) for East Africa, human activities are an essential element of these wetland environments, having evolved in part as the product of human involvement. A similar sequence of events occurred in the perennial, coastal-plain wetlands around Blue Creek (Luzzadder-Beach and Beach 2009). Here ca. 6 sq. km of rectilinear field and canal patterns date to the Classic period and hold evidence for several important food and other economic taxa. But like the bajos, these wetlands hold a more complicated chronology. Numerous excavations through them show this landscape's intensive agricultural surface was 1–2 m lower, with an equally lower water table, in the first half of the Preclassic. But in the later Preclassic, the water table rose through flooding (human or climate-driven) and sea level rise, and erosion, sedimentation, and gypsum precipitation from saturated water aggraded the landscape by 1–2 m by the Classic period. These processes created a perennial wetland, which Maya farmers adapted to by building ditches and managing fields (Luzzadder-Beach and Beach 2009).

While the environmental degradation of nearby bajos may have contributed to the demise of the large Preclassic urban centers of Nakbe and El Mirador (Hansen et al. 2002; Jacob 1995), at La Milpa and many other southern lowlands centers, the Maya successfully adapted to their changing environment. Ironically, while rapid sedimentation severely degraded many bajos as water sources, in many locations it also created significant areas of prime farmland (Dunning et al. 2002; Gunn et al. 2002). We have found that the margins of many bajos contain large areas of deep, colluvial soils resulting from erosion upslope during the Preclassic. These colluvial aprons became a primary focus of intensive agriculture in the Classic, as evident in numerous field walls and terraces that helped build up soils (Beach et al. 2002; Dunning et al. 2002).

The site of Guijarral is best described as a relatively dispersed agricultural village spread along one flank of a bajo of the same name (Hughbanks 1998; Kunen and Hughbanks 2003). Although there is archaeological evidence for occupation at the site extending back into the Late Preclassic, much of the residential (as well as modest monumental) construction at Guijarral dates to the Late Classic when numerous field walls and terraces were also built. Geoarchaeological investigations extending into the Guijarral Bajo indicate that this depression contained a perennial wetland when the area was first settled in the Preclassic (Dunning et al. 2006). Although Preclassic population was sparse, it appears to have cleared significant areas of forest, exposing slopes to erosion and resulting in the rapid aggradation of the bajo with clayey sediment (fig. 4.3), a finding consistent with data from the Far West Bajo and other investigated bajos (Dunning et al. 2002). In at least some parts of the Guijarral Bajo, channel incision (probably during the Early Classic) indicates that the bajo had begun to flush out some accumulated sediment. However, aggradation of these channels in the seventh century AD suggests the renewal of soil erosion during the Late Classic, followed by the construction of terraces to help stem the downslope movement of soil. Closer to La Milpa, our investigations also suggest a period of soil recovery during the Early Classic when population growth was very low and a resumption of erosion in the Late Classic (despite terracing and other conservation measures) when population grew rapidly (Beach et al. 2002; Dunning and Beach 2000).

Another adaptation made by the Maya to the sedimentation and drying of bajos was the construction of urban reservoirs at many sites, beginning towards the end of the Preclassic (Scarborough et al. 1995). This development probably contributed to growing social and economic inequalities in Maya society by vesting symbolic and, to a limited degree, actual control over a vital resource (water) as well as by increasingly skewing land values in favor of the site center and elite landholders (Dunning

1995, 2003). Nevertheless, smaller-scale water-management features and more soil- and water-conservative forms of agriculture came to characterize the cultivated areas of the La Milpa urban area as well as rural farmsteads throughout the region (Beach et al. 2002; N. Hammond et al. 1998; Hughbanks 1998; Lohse and Findlay 2000; Weiss-Krejci and Sabbas 2002), particularly as population growth accelerated in the Late Classic. Other than the few modest urban reservoirs, there is little evidence at La Milpa or elsewhere in the region for centralized control of water or soil resources. Rather, these resources appear to have been largely managed at the household or local group level (Dunning 2004; Hageman and Lohse 2003; Tourtellot et al. 2003; Weiss-Krejci and Sabbas 2002), though wetland field ditching near Blue Creek shows clear evidence of north-south linear ditches of ca. 600 m with many crossing ditches that cover large areas (Luzzadder-Beach and Beach 2009). Notably, many of the areas of highest rural population concentration in the Three Rivers region were along ecotonal boundaries such as escarpment edges and bajo margins, which offered good possibilities for diversified as well as intensified agriculture and subsequent risk reduction (Dunning et al. 2003).

Recent pollen analysis of a short sediment core recovered from an *aguada* (Lagunita Elusiva) located near the eastern margin of the La Milpa settlement zone offers a glimpse of changing vegetative cover in the area beginning (at the base of the organic portion of the core) in the fourth century AD (fig. 4.4). Not surprisingly, pollen evidence indicates considerable deforestation and cultivation (with a great abundance of maize) for the Late and Terminal Classic periods, followed by gradual reforestation after regional depopulation around AD 830 (J. Jones and Dunning n.d.). The intensity of cultivation in this area is also indicated by a network of field walls adjacent to the aguada.

At La Milpa, population growth was very rapid, particularly in the second half of the Late Classic after AD 700, leading to speculation that the region may have experienced an influx of migrant peoples, perhaps from the Petén, who may have initially been a boon for the city, but who may have eventually overwhelmed local resources (N. Hammond et al. 1998; N. Hammond and Tourtellot 2004). However, researchers now see the city thriving up until its demise: a demise that was quite sudden as evident in several abandoned, incomplete construction projects in the site center (N. Hammond and Tourtellot 2004). Urban population at

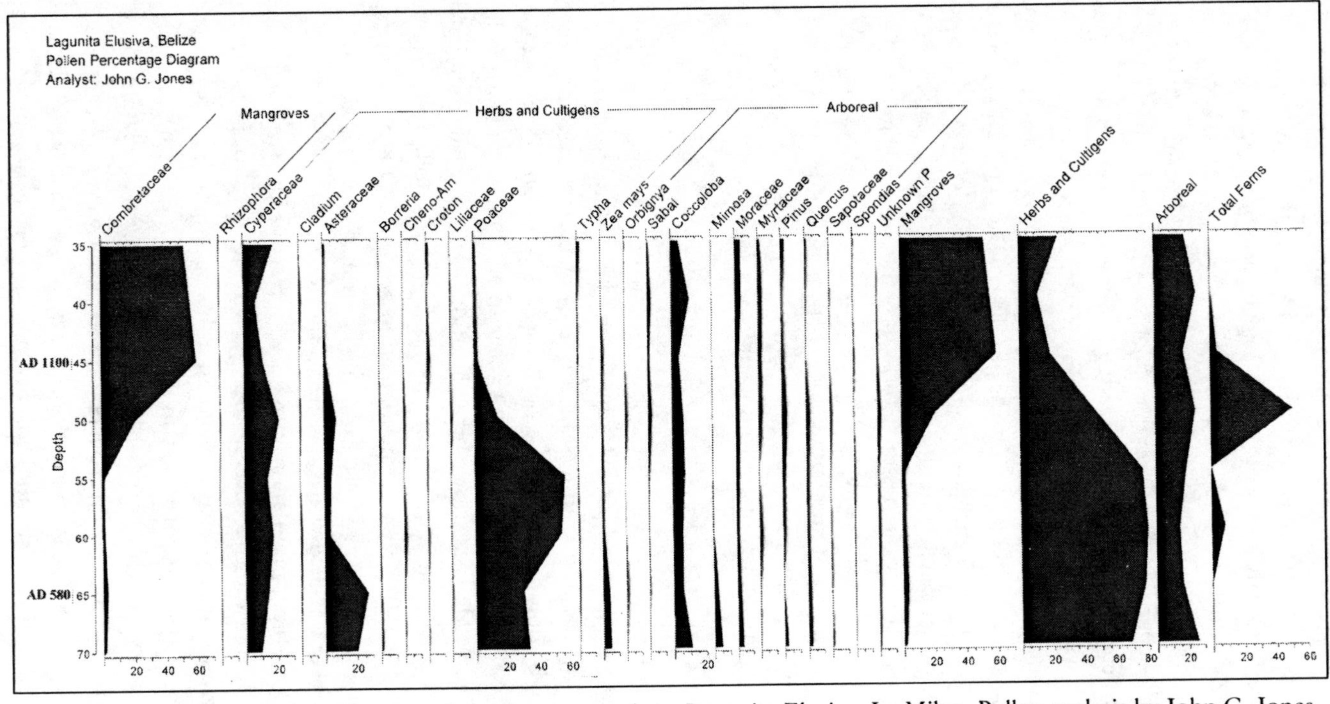

FIGURE 4.4. Pollen frequency diagram of a sediment core from Lagunita Elusiva, La Milpa. Pollen analysis by John G. Jones.

La Milpa may have reached 46,000 by the early ninth century AD, but crashed rapidly around AD 830 for reasons that remain unclear. If this part of the lowlands was indeed beset by severe drought, the rapid abandonment of the water-poor karst uplands is not surprising while some centers situated on perennial coastal rivers to the east (e.g., Lamanai) continued to be occupied.

Discussion

Certain of our findings have parallels in other parts of the Maya Lowlands. Two general conclusions about the Maya Lowlands are that populations were extremely high in the Classic, especially the Late Classic, and also that environmental impacts started early, before the highest populations of the Classic period. We see strong evidence for Preclassic erosion and aggradation in many Petén and Belize sites, but we also see in some sites like Cancuén in the far southern Petén, environmental impacts only in the Late Classic (Beach, Dunning et al. 2006). Elements of these findings support both Malthusian and Boserupian models for population and environment, but an alternative model applies better, one of pioneer degradation followed by adaptation of conservation or by decline. Around El Mirador and Nakbe, the changed bajo environments of the Early Classic correlated with decline (whether or not related), whereas the altered bajos of the Three Rivers region became new environments for manipulation in the Classic. But almost all the sites met with decline by the tenth century.

The Petexbatún (part of the Río de la Pasión region; fig. 4.1) offers an interesting comparison to what we have found in the Three Rivers region. In the Petexbatún, we found clear evidence of significant Preclassic deforestation and severe soil loss in two watersheds of differing size: the small Aguada Catolina and the much larger Laguna Tamarindito (Beach and Dunning 1995; Dunning and Beach 1994, forthcoming; Dunning, Rue et al. 1998). Similar findings of Preclassic soil erosion are reported from Laguna Las Posas farther to the south and Petén Itzá farther to the north from the Río de la Pasión region (Anselmetti et al. 2007; Johnston et al. 2001). Preclassic populations appear to have been quite small in the Petexbatún and reliant largely on swidden agriculture. Although there is palynological evidence from Laguna Tamarindito that fallow periods progressively decreased over several centuries during the Preclassic, we have found no indications of significant soil conservation attempts. As with the Three Rivers region, there is substantial evidence that the Maya of the Classic period inherited a landscape severely altered by their ancestors (Dunning and Beach 2000). In cores taken from Laguna Tamarindito, we also found evidence of some forest recovery when regional populations either declined or became more spatially concentrated during the Early Classic (Dunning and Beach forthcoming; Dunning, Rue et al. 1998).

The Petexbatún is justifiably famous for the intensity of warfare that racked the region between AD 632 and AD 810 and is documented by the Maya in numerous inscriptions and militaristic monuments (Demarest 2004; Houston 1993). During the Late Classic, elevated land around and between the major centers of the Petexbatún (Dos Pilas, Tamarindito, and Aguateca) was partially divided by a field wall system. Some of these agricultural areas were naturally defensible and others had defensive systems nearby, testifying to intensive competition for arable and defensible territory and leading to tremendous population concentration and agricultural intensification (Dunning et al. 1997; O'Mansky and Dunning 2004). On the other hand, adjacent low-lying areas (both well drained and poorly drained) were less densely populated and were not divided by walls, nor were they easily defended. Late Classic agriculture in the Petexbatún was, thus, concentrated by social forces onto limited land that was intensively cultivated, including significant terracing efforts. The paleoecological record from Laguna Tamarindito indicates lower soil erosion rates substantially in the Preclassic despite larger, more densely settled populations and the survival of appreciable areas of forest (Dunning, Rue et al. 1998; Emery et al. 2000).

Archaeological evidence from Tamarindito indicates that agricultural terracing may have begun at that urban center as it grew from a small village into an important town during the Early Classic (Dunning et al. 1997; Valdés 1997). This situation parallels a more general trend in the southern Maya Lowlands during the Early Classic that saw increasing levels of urbanization, reservoir construction, and agricultural intensification—especially terracing (Dunning 1995). Probably the most dramatic example of agricultural terracing in the Maya Lowlands was developed at the city of Caracol on the Vaca Plateau of the Maya Mountains in Belize. This urban agricultural system of terraces sprawls over tens of square kilometers and shows some of the best evidence for centralized direction of agriculture in the region (Chase and Chase 1998).

In contrast, the region within the Maya Lowlands exhibiting the most widespread use of agricultural terracing is the Río Bec area of the Central Hills district (fig. 4.1), an area that displays such little evidence of centralized control and so few urban areas that it gave rise to a model of Classic Maya sociopolitical organization patterned on feudal Europe, including a ubiquity of small towns and manor houses (R. E. Adams and Smith 1981). Nevertheless, this decidedly rural landscape was thoroughly partitioned by field wall systems, and almost all hilly terrain was terraced (B. L. Turner 1983). Similar to the Three Rivers region, agricultural terracing appears to have been managed at the household or small corporate-group level and did not result from central planning.

If there is a common factor involved in the conditions giving rise to soil conservation among the Classic period Maya, it would seem to be the stability of land holding (Dunning 2004). At Caracol, stability came in the form of centralized organization. In the Río Bec area, the security of an established rural land-holding system offered comparable stability. In the Three Rivers region, both urbanization and concomitant intensification of land use as well as the development of a stable rural land-holding system are discernable (Beach et al. 2002; Hageman and Lohse 2003; Lohse 2004; Scarborough 1993). On the other hand, in the politically fractious Petexbatún region, competition and warfare may have forced the development of a conservation ethic to intensify defensible small holdings. In all cases, however, there was a clear investment on the part of those who controlled land to create a sustainable system of cultivation.

Looking across the Maya Lowlands, a tremendous variety of adaptive responses to a varied and changing soilscape indicate that the ancient Maya developed a considerable indigenous pedological knowledge (Dunning, Beach et al. 1998; Dunning and Beach 2004). Some of this knowledge has persisted even into modern times as manifest in such forms as folk soil classifications and cultivation techniques; however, a tremendous amount of adaptive knowledge has been lost due to depopulation and regional abandonments associated with both the Classic collapse and Spanish Conquest, and with the disenfranchisement of many Maya groups from their lands in post-Conquest times. Maya groups who have managed to remain in the same areas for centuries clearly have an adaptive advantage in the form of useful environmental knowledge to those now colonizing largely vacant land (Beach and Dunning 1995; Dunning 1992a). Such indigenous, generational knowledge has, indeed, been the key to resilience of Maya populations in the *longue durée*. While investments in "landesque capital" surely aided in the creation of a more sustainable agricultural base during periods of Maya history, in the longer term, it has been indigenous environmental knowledge that has given greater resilience to Maya agricultural adaptations (cf. Redman et al. and van der Leeuw, this vol.).

In contrast, many agricultural colonists also face an equally daunting barrier to developing a stable landscape: lack of clear or irrevocable land title. Our work in the Petexbatún region has allowed us to observe a number of significant soil-conservation problems associated with a lack of land stewardship. Since many of the colonists moving into this area hold rather insecure title to their land and are surviving largely on a harvest-to-harvest basis, their commitment to conservation is typically minimal (Secaira 1992). We have seen horrendous examples of modern soil loss, with whole hillsides being denuded of their soil cover within a few years (Beach 1998a; Beach and Dunning 1995; Beach et al. 2006; Dunning and Beach 1994, forthcoming). There is considerable and unfortunate irony in the fact that as forests are cut down across the region, hundreds of relict agricultural terrace systems have been revealed—terraces that could be usefully resurrected under more favorable political and economic circumstances. At the same time, in Belize, European settlers have equally devastated landscapes, burning and bulldozing uplands and lowlands directly across any cultural feature in their paths. Ancient wetland field patterns, conservation features, and houses have been leveled, and some steep slopes have eroded to below bedrock in a few years. They have recently, as has been done earlier in so many other places around the world, veneered the Maya Lowlands with the pastures and livestock of European rural landscape. As with the Preclassic Maya pioneers, the instability of this recent European soil erosion will in time decline with new landscape stability and with the reduction of the source of erosion, upland soils (Beach, Dunning et al. 2006).

Many centuries ago, relatively small numbers of Preclassic Maya agricultural colonists cleared forest and destabilized many regional soilscapes. Over the centuries, and as populations grew in the Classic period, the Maya in many areas developed conservation practices that helped to stabilize many regional landscapes. In some areas of the Maya World, enough cultural continuity remains for us to glimpse some of the beliefs that underlie Maya land ethics. For example, for many traditional Yucatec Maya farmers, the earth, or *luum*, is believed to impart *itz*, "sap" or "the holy substance of life," to growing plants and other things (Dunning 2003). This is part of a cyclical system in which *yiitz ka'an*, "the holy substance of the sky," is believed to bring fertility to the earth in the form of rainfall. These beliefs, deep-rooted in pre-Hispanic Maya culture, appear to have evolved hand in hand with Maya agriculture, adapting to and reflecting changes in the environment and society and persisting in contemporary Maya farming communities in areas where historical circumstances have allowed for the retention of traditional practices and beliefs. These beliefs and practices include a well-developed conservation ethic rooted in abiding ancestral ties to the land. For the traditional Maya, it is in the cultivation of this ancient ethic through the solidification of land rights that the future of soil conservation in the Maya Lowlands lies, for only those people who can see their futures in the local soilscape will invest in its stewardship.

This synthesis also provides evidence that geoarchaeology holds an important group of techniques to extend our paltry records of environmental change and to plan better for a larger range of future events. Moreover, unlike most techniques, it also provides evidence of human response and adaptation. We have presented evidence for climate change, sea level rise, erosion and aggradation, groundwater and water quality changes, as well as evidence for successful and unsuccessful human response over five thousand years of Maya Lowlands history. What this record shows in some cases are large-magnitude events that had regionally destructive impacts in the Preclassic, end of the Preclassic, and the Terminal Classic periods. The Maya as a people persisted through adaptation and migration, though with very high costs. This is far from a rosy picture, given these high costs of population declines and cultural losses. But it does show that even in what was once thought a fragile environment or a "Green Hell," the Maya adapted to soil loss, water deficiency, rising water tables, climate change, and other forces of nature. These lines of evidence thus underscore the important role of geoarchaeology in sustainable development, restoration ecology, understanding recurrence intervals of large events, and understanding the deep roots of cultural patrimony.

5

Farming the Margins

ON THE SOCIAL CAUSES AND CONSEQUENCES OF SOIL-MANAGEMENT STRATEGIES

Tina L. Thurston

Contemporary Problems and Insights from the Past

Considering the profound impact humans can have on soils, it is remarkable that until recently humanly altered soils have no standardized characterization within classification systems used by modern soil scientists. Recently, Dudal et al. (2002) proposed the term *anthropogenic soils* to describe soils radically transformed from their natural state—both enriched and depleted by human activity (Dudal 2002:1). The 10*th* edition of the USDA Keys to Soil Taxonomy finally addressed this issue (Soil Survey Staff 2006). This is a timely effort, as soil poverty remains high on the list of problems with the world's food supply today.

In the following discussion, I consider enrichment and depletion, examining the modern history of the movement first toward artificial, then toward "organic," soil augmentation worldwide. Guided by the belief that the laboratory of the past contains important insights for the present, I examine the origins and long-term use of such methods by exploring the role of anthropogenic soils in pre- and proto-historic sequences in the marginal farming environments of the North Atlantic. I offer evidence from both "homeland" regions—Norway, Sweden, and Denmark—and the islands of the Norse diaspora. Across these islands, between AD 700 and AD 1100, a colonization era or *landnam* (land-claiming) targeted some extraordinarily soil-poor and marginal lands.

A great deal has now been written characterizing the soils used or created by the farmers of the North Atlantic. Far less has been written contextualizing their agricultural economy within the social and political conditions of their times: the *anthro* in *anthropogenic* has been seen primarily in technological and ecological terms. After examining extant paleoecological research, I offer contextualization via two avenues: first, through analogy between soil-related successes and problems of recent farmers in marginal regions; and second, through my own case study in which anthropogenic-soil creation and use is embedded within a thorough examination of the political, social, and economic issues confronting farmers in the North Atlantic state of Denmark. Through this combination, I offer new avenues toward understanding agro-pastoral variation in one region, while also addressing the broader socionatural issue of soil management.

The Past-Present Interface

Until about thirty years ago, most archaeologists believed that hunger, due to poor natural conditions or lack of technology, was behind the initial turn to agriculture and later farming intensification (Childe 1928; Cohen 1977). This was based on then-current notions that modern people starve due to similar food-production shortages, a key part of mid-century thought on world hunger. Improved technology was largely seen as the answer. To address this dilemma in our own times (the embarrassment of a rich global dinner table with too few seats), the so-called "Green Revolution" of the 1960s and 1970s was inaugurated—a scheme in which Western, mechanized, chemical-based farming was introduced to "underdeveloped" societies worldwide in hopes of feeding the undernourished and, after creating dependence on Western methods and products, making money off third-world farmers and their governments.

By the late 1970s, this revolution was both a success and a failure: In Asia, it produced "miracles" in food production; in Africa, it had almost totally collapsed. Yet even where the Green Revolution was successful, biodiversity narrowed, and small family farms and the indigenous knowledge they preserved were overwhelmed by agribusiness conglomerates, while fertilizers, pesticides, and high-tech irrigation systems were both beggaring ordinary farmers and poisoning the land. Most disheartening was that even as production rose, more people starved, even when food supplies in their own nations were at overflow levels (Altieri and Rosset 1999), not because food was scarce, but because of resource inequality.

New and advanced technologies, hybrid crops, and Western systems of agricultural organization could do nothing to alter extant systems of unequal economic, political, and social power, especially the purchasing power, for land and food of the poor or marginalized. Around the same time that agroecology proponents began to recognize this, the "social hypothesis" on the origins and expansion of agriculture was first proposed (i.e., Bender 1978), an idea that considered the past in light of observation rather than intuition: early agriculturalists also suffered resource inequality, even among the earliest farming people. A dialectic between past and present was opened, and appreciation of past complexity increased dramatically. Today, archaeological thought on this subject has developed enough to offer insights for contemporary planning and development.

Failure in the Developing World

The Green Revolution's failure lay in unequal relations in regions where it produced increased yields, and in areas where it failed to do so, especially in Africa, unforeseen cultural and natural conditions were to blame. Much of Africa has largely infertile soils (Asiema 1994), poor in nitrogen and phosphorus, exacerbated by drought. Chemical fertilizers and high-tech irrigation alone do not correct this (Lal 1987) since they are costlier then the crop they produce. Additionally, Western manufacturers ignored popular Africans cultigens—yam, cassava, millet, and sorghum—despite low interest in wheat, the focus of Western research (Thomson 2001).

Perhaps most significantly, in the mid-twentieth century, Western companies and aid programs operated in cultural vacuums, introducing new methods via male household heads, who agreed to recruit "non-working" women and children into new agricultural schemes without thought of who would do their traditional jobs (FAO 1997, 1998). Elsewhere, food supply was disrupted when companies introduced new crops onto previously infertile land through men, who were incorrectly assumed to control production, when women, who held rights to land and traditional crops, were in fact the primary farmers (FAO 1998; Jiggins 1986a, 1986b; Lipton and Longhurst 1989). In other cases, redirection from subsistence to cash crops fouled up farmers' responsibilities for providing food when crops or market conditions failed (FAO 1998). Finally, corrupt or ineffective governments, as well as war in many regions, created impossible conditions (J. Stone 1998).

Failure in the West

While a stable food supply in the so-called developing world is important, there is also a rising recognition of similar problems for the developed world:

> When tractors entered the agricultural scene in the early part of the twentieth century, fields got larger, and fewer farms kept animals and spread manure on fields. The Dust Bowl was the most dramatic result of this mechanization, and brought renewed interest in managing the tilth and organic matter of soil. After World War II, the use of pesticides and "artificial manure" exploded, and the living characteristic of soil was again neglected. In the 80s, the cost of chemical inputs began rising significantly. Interest in better management . . . and the potential of soil-specific farming technology increased. (Lewandowski et al. 1999:11)

The Second Revolution

Green Revolution failures in multiple worldwide contexts spawned many organizations through which indigenous knowledge and low-tech methods were promoted. Development NGOs (Non-governmental organizations), such as the International Development Research Centre (IDRC) and the International Food Policy Research Institute (IFPRI), research and implement sustainable/resilient farming in Africa, Latin America, and Southeast Asia.

The United States Department of Agriculture, Canadian Ministry of Agriculture and Agri-Food, and many local agencies now recommend a return to sustainable agriculture for first-world, mechanized farmers, citing a need for integrating chemical, biological, and cultural methods as opposed to "chemical alone."

Testing the Second Revolution

Today, the terms development, sustainability, and resilience are associated with the recognition that the need for improved agriculture, combined with lack of funding for hi-tech agro-technologies, requires innovative solutions that focus on people's needs rather than on finding markets for expensive or artificial products. Technologically improved, organically amended soil quality, anti-erosion methods, and water management are the most important issues (Lal 1987).

Now that several decades have passed, development authorities believe they are well informed about the success or failure of these sustainable alternatives in contrast to Green Revolution ideas. Confidence is rampant in the technology and its implementation, as well as in social policies in tune with the environmental, economic, and sociopolitical conditions (Asiema 1994; Lal 1987). Yet, in reality, while new programs are touted as great successes, they may in the long term resemble the Green Revolution—initially promising, eventually failing. Typical "long-term" plans for development are five or ten years, while true sustainability and resilience operate on scales of decades, centuries, or longer.

Archaeological Insights

In addressing the utility and use-life of amended soils for modern farmers, archaeology has great predictive power. Current "innovations" include methods that can be traced back for millennia and are the subject of numerous archaeological studies. One natural experiment that can test the success of low-tech soil management, in addition to addressing social issues surrounding it, lies in the so-called *plaggen* soils found across northwest Europe (i.e., England, Scotland, Scandinavia, the Atlantic Islands, Germany, Belgium, the Netherlands), where poor soils were augmented to increase soil fertility, or good soils were improved to prolong sedentary farming.

Manure, household waste, and composted animal stall bedding were spread onto marginal lands, over time creating thick, almost completely humanly made soils (I. Simpson, Dockrill et al. 1998:744). The vast majority were formed between AD 700 and AD 1200, with a few rare examples dated as early as 600 BC (Pape 1970).

Archaeologists can determine the impact of soil-related strategies—not for ten or twenty years, but for centuries—and how much they "cost" versus how they improved (or failed to improve) agriculture. The outcomes—continued settlement with farming, continued settlement with "replacement" subsistence strategies, or complete abandonment of the marginal landscape—should be of interest to those promoting modern use of similar techniques in marginal regions.

Constituents of Soil-Management Traditions

There are several ways to assess the presence of fertilizing practices and their intensity. One is visual and manual inspection of soils for relatively darker color, greasy texture, and inclusions of cultural material from household refuse. Another is through soil phosphate, which becomes highly elevated when animal bones and animal or human manure are plowed into soil over long periods. Green manure—non- or under-composted plants (other than remnant crops) purposely planted in place or brought from elsewhere—has been used since at least the fifth century BC (McGuire 2003:6) and is detected through phytoliths, pollen, macrofloral remains, and the preserved "outlines" of turf bricks. Kelp, common in the Atlantic region, deposits tiny seashells that adhere to seaweed.

Based on older methods, Carter and Davidson (1998) were pessimistic about soil micromorphology's ability to identify ancient cultivation practices, stating that berms, canals, and stone walls are the most secure indicators of past farming practices. In the last decade, new methodologies make these concerns obsolete.

Some new techniques involve study of manure lipids retained in soils over long periods. Lipid extracts, like phosphates, additionally reflect differences in the use of space through manuring intensity—high around farmsteads and declining with distance (Bull et al. 1999; I. Simpson et al. 1999).

Specific manures are identified through bile acids: campesterol, sitosterol, and 5 beta-stigmastanol implicate ruminant animal manures (Bull et al. 1999), while coprostanol reflects omnivorous animals. Pig manure contains hyodeoxycholic acid (Bull et al. 1999), while dog droppings, lacking the microorganisms required to create them, do not contain 5[Beta]-stanol biomarkers. Human feces contain 3[alpha]-hydroxy-5[Beta]-cholanoic acid (lithocholic acid) and are dominated by deoxycholic acid (Bull et al. 1999).

Historical Contexts of Soil Augmentation

Soil augmentation has a circuitous history, only tangentially related to its ultimate use, undoubtedly impacting its long-term use by current farmers, since farming is as much a value-driven occupation as other trades. If archaeological case studies are to be of any use to modern problems, the social settings of past and present people must be more than superficially understood. In Nordic cultures, agricultural practice was strongly shaped first by kinship and gender relations, and later by politics and patronage. These have parallels in similarly transforming relationships in recent times. It is typically imagined that Africans in marginal regions have always gone hungry. Few outside the specialist community understand that indigenous farmers produced adequate food from arid and soil-poor contexts for millennia, until colonialism destroyed or disrupted indigenous farming.

Causes of success or failure with soil augmentation in the present (Chianu and Tsujii 2004) are almost identical to what archaeologists have determined for the past: methods introduced from outside, or learned in one context and applied in another, are often subject to collapse, through farmer unfamiliarity and different, often inappropriate, combinations of necessary materials. Environments differing from regions where methods originate may provide too few manure sources or suitable green substitutes. The physical transplantation of farmers from areas where such methods are not used into new areas where they are required also presents problems. The origins of manuring in North Atlantic Europe are thus an important preface to later discussion.

The Complex (Pre)History of Farming the Margins

Manuring within North Atlantic communities was actually an unintended byproduct of purely social processes, rooted not in Iron Age or medieval agriculture, but in earlier sociopolitical conditions among people who were primarily pastoralists. Anthropogenic soils were a part of a sequence where human impacts altered nature, creating anthropogenic landscapes that in turn recursively impacted people, who once again created new conditions and adjusted to the fruits of their own actions. In this volume, Hill, Fisher, and Feinman characterize this ongoing dialectic as the "socionatural connection"—which may further be understood as part of the structuration process (Giddens 1984, 1993) through which one can link soil, augmented with garbage, to intensification, migration, social structure and social change, taxation, and back to soil again in a cycle linking the local, regional, and global, and the material and ideational across time and space (Bourdieu 1977, 1990; Ortner 1984, 1989; Pred 1984, 1986; S. Turner 1994).

Society and Agroeconomic Practice in the Early North Atlantic

Across Europe, complex cultures flourished during the Bronze Age, in Scandinavia from ca. 1700 to 500 BC. Monumental grave mounds of the Nordic Early Bronze Age (ca. 1700 BC) contain richly furnished men and women; later "princely" burials (1100–500 BC) were more extravagant. Petroglyphs and figurines indicate musical instruments, and wheeled cult objects were used in elite ceremonies (Coles 2003). They also show oxen harnessed to plows or chariots, or in herd-like groups.

Average and monumental longhouses echo class differences. Late Bronze Age houses of up to 50 m were divided into byre and living areas, while houses up to 100 m long could have three sections, with a central byre for twelve to sixteen animals (Bech and Mikkelsen 1999:74–75). Some probable chieftains' farms feature separate cattle-houses and animal pens. Evidence points to chiefly labor mobilization (T. Earle 2002, 2004) for a number of industries including hide-working (Bech and Mikkelsen 1999). Cattle may have been slaughtered before winter, when hides were worked for use as currency in the active pan-European trade.

Paleoecology reveals that pasturage and fodder were the focus of management (Callmer 1991:339). Pollen diagrams indicate increasing clearance, predominantly supporting grazing, indicating a steady rise in cattle populations over time, but only a small amount of field farming in areas of just 300 to 1000 sq. m around farmsteads (Andersen 1992).

Many archaeologists and agricultural historians wrongly connect initial Bronze Age use of byres with the desire to collect manure. Until the Bronze Age ended, despite undoubted abundance of manure, little or no manuring was practiced. Instead, swidden cycles of two to five years for fields and thirty to fifty years for cropping areas were used (Callmer 1991:339).

Why, then, were cattle given "houses" in the Bronze Age? Oft-cited intuitive explanations include the erroneous ideas, recently debunked by Zimmerman (1999), that cattle should be warm and dry for optimum milk production (Charles 1994:5), when this actually suffers in warm conditions; that cows provided warmth for humans, which experimental work has disproved; or that byring saved labor, when it necessitated extremely labor-intensive foddering practices (Zimmermann 1999:307).

Theoretical Ideas on the Origins of Byring

Traditional models are environmental, linked to a colder and wetter climatic minimum around 500 BC, roughly corresponding to the Bronze Age–Early Iron Age transition. The conclusion: climate change encouraged byring (Olausson 1999). Kristiansen (1988) hypothesizes that climate change and land degradation from grazing, combined with population growth, compelled intensification, leading to the realization that manure improved soils.

Myrdahl (1984, 1988), also in a Boserupian vein, further links technological changes to demographic-driven intensification. He suggests that manure, more easily collected from byres, necessitated hay-meadows for fodder, which leads to increased use of iron for scythes, rakes, and other tools.

Yet byring began early in the warmer Bronze Age, and manure was not used to augment soil until a millennium later. No "population pressure" is indicated by the Bronze Age's sparse and low-density settlement, and in the Early Iron Age, it became more ephemeral—500 BC to AD 1 is sometimes called "the period of no finds."

Byre, Manure, and Plaggen Soils

Recently, social theories link byring not to environment- or population-driven intensification, or even to agriculture at all, but instead to sociopolitical changes during the Bronze Age, when status and prestige were in large part manifest through cattle wealth and feasting (Fokkens 1997), hinging on ever-larger herds (Olsson 1991). Zimmerman (1999) proposes that byring has roots chiefly in competition and the increasing ideological value of cattle, depicted in petroglyphs in the same contexts as warships, armed or mounted warriors, and mythological scenes.

As cows were recast into precious status markers (Zimmerman 1999), warlords may have engaged in competitive cattle raiding. Recent cattle-focused ethnic and national rivalries continue to initiate feuds and massacres (Dawes 1999; Ross 2003), while traditional intergroup status-related raids continue (Evans-Pritchard 1940; R. C. Kelly 1985; Moore and Puritt 1977; Spencer 1973)—some violently transformed by modern armaments and new political motives (Fleisher 1998; Gray et al. 2003).

Raiding may have instigated construction of secure animal housing, similar to the East African *kraal*, as protection from both predators and rival groups (Tarayia 2004). Common peoples' cattle also require housing, as they could have been targeted as symbols of local elites' power to protect their constituents. Similar arrangements between commoner cattle-herders and local paramount and sub-chiefs are seen in Africa (Moritz et al. 2002:137). Elite sequestration of animals may have made the housing of cattle socially attractive, imitated by non-elites with (or with pretensions to) higher social standing than their neighbors (Olausson 1999).

In byres, manure began to literally pile up; at the very end of the period, it was finally used for intentional fertilizing (Zimmerman 1999). Increased Bronze Age feasting, trading, and support of a semi-permanent warrior class may relate to intensified production for both food and alcohol, found in many elite graves.

Byring is thus linked not to non-environmental factors, but rather to a value system in which prestige and social mobility were derived primarily from keeping cattle *at any cost*. If cattle were kept not institutionally as status items, but rather pragmatically for meat and dairy, the byre, manure, and all subsequent uses may well have been deemed too labor intensive for early farmers to even consider, as field-farming was a minimal occupation. Even if soil improvement is demonstrated, if the methods are outside a system of labor and values, long-term sustainability is uncertain, as seen episodically throughout the Green Revolution.

From Manuring to Plaggen Soils

In the Terminal Bronze Age and Early Iron Age (ca. 600–500 BC), manuring finally appears in the archaeological record as an increase in nitrogenic weed seeds, increased soil phosphate levels, and manure residues (Bull et al. 1999). During the Iron Age, as permanent settlements increased and swiddening was abandoned, field-system soils were profoundly transformed.

Before AD 700, enrichment was focused on good soils. Although soil augmentation was clearly not "invented" in order to colonize deficient sub-Arctic soils, between AD 700 and 1200 manuring would become important in the spread of Vikings and later Norse into the marginal North Atlantic. Simultaneously, internal colonization occurred in the homelands, either onto good, uninhabited lands or nearby marginal areas. It is easy, but overly simplistic, to imagine that diasporic North Atlantic farmers set out to "grab" impoverished land due to homeland overpopulation combined with the advent of the Medieval Climatic Optimum (AD 700–1100), as is commonly argued (B. Berglund et al. 1991:436; G. Jones 1987:272). While the so-called "Medieval Warm Period" had above-average temperatures more hospitable for farming, the North Atlantic was still cold for agriculture, and had little tree cover and limited farming soils. Most specialists agree that complex political clashes at home, as Nordic states emerged from chiefly societies, combined with traditions of exile and exploration, lie at its root.

Migratory populations practiced the North Atlantic mixed-farming economy, combining cereal cultivation and pastoralism with marine and other wild resources, enabling farming in such unthinkable places as the Shetland Islands, the Faroe Islands, Iceland, and even Greenland. As Adderley and Simpson (2005) have noted, "Effective management of the land area surrounding the domestic settlement, the home-field, was essential to sustain settlements" in the North Atlantic, precisely because of the poor soils. This even allowed some colonies to survive, in a diminished or retrenched mode, into the Little Ice Age, while some were unable to overcome truly severe environmental changes.

While scanty ethnohistoric and historical data exist, most knowledge about this unlikely expansion comes from archaeology and its associated sciences. Using such data, I now explore the cultural and ecological causes and consequences of the North Atlantic sequence.

The North Atlantic Region

The North Atlantic (fig. 5.1) is comprised of Arctic and sub-Arctic areas above the 50th parallel bordering the Atlantic Ocean; its adjunct seas,

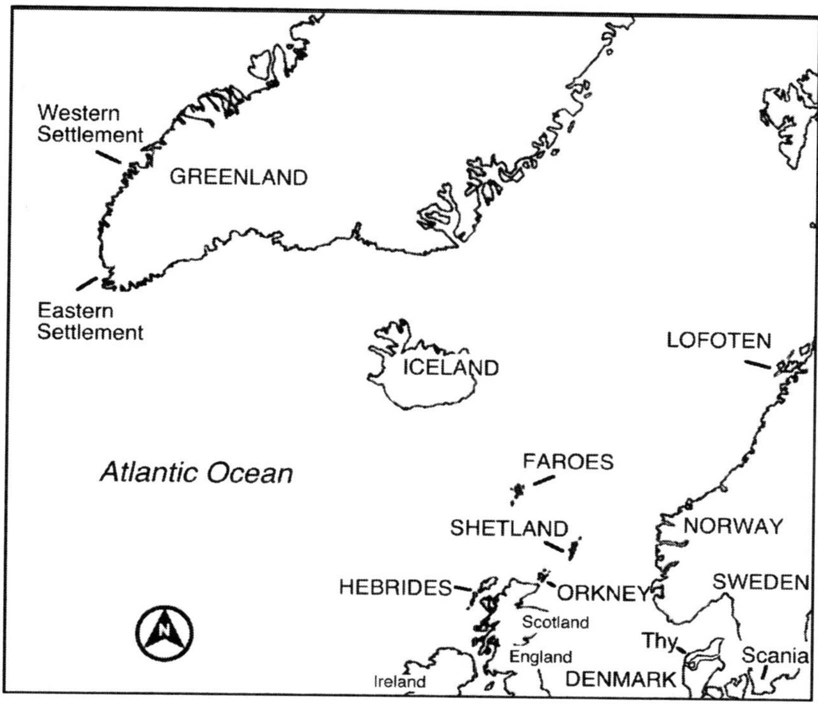

FIGURE 5.1. The North Atlantic region and Norse settlement.

the North, Arctic, Norwegian, and Baltic Seas; and Hudson Bay. The region's past cultures represent groups of all types: hunter-fishers, agro-pastoral "tribes" and "chiefdoms," and state-level societies.

One similarity experienced by all who farm here is the rarity of large expanses of suitable agricultural soils. This results in two strategies: 1) make intensive use of good soil where it is found, and 2) enrich poor soils when possible. One of most interesting revelations of this comparative study is that attempts at anthropogenic-soil creation across the early North Atlantic were not automatic or without implementation problems, even within what many would assume was an "ethnically homogeneous" population who broadly shared their indigenous farming knowledge.

Norway

In Norway, homeland of many migrants, enrichment was a common strategy beginning in the Iron Age, even above the Arctic Circle in the

Lofoten Islands, which are barely viable for farming. The Gulf Stream plays a part in warming the North Atlantic climate more than the latitude suggests, with Lofoten at its outer range. Steeply sloping terrain permits only small fields on sandy, eroding terraces, which have been studied at two Iron Age farming locales, Orsnes and Hov, typifying locally available soils (I. Simpson, Bryant et al. 1998:1188).

Micromorphology reveals that above virgin peaty/sandy topsoils lie disturbed and well-mixed loamy sand topsoils, 30–50 cm thick, resulting from human manipulation. Portions of turf-built retaining walls lie at their downslope boundaries in "a deliberate attempt to trap eroding soils to create a soil for cultivation" (I. Simpson, Bryant et al. 1998:1189). Thin sections reveal excremental pedofeatures, or manuring, plus scattered midden material: ceramic fragments, charcoal, fish and animal bone, and dark, thick-cut turf bricks brought from elsewhere to thicken the soil (I. Simpson, Bryant et al. 1998:1188).

These relict soils date to around AD 700, but ethnographic accounts indicate similar practices prevailed until one hundred years ago (I. Simpson, Bryant et al. 1998:1192). Sharp spades were used to mix peat topsoil with sand across many small fields, cumulatively providing a substantial farming area, rotated in a two-year fallow system (I. Simpson, Bryant et al. 1998:1192). These were amended with mineral fertilizers, in contrast to prehistoric manures.

The Faroe Islands

Several projects examine soil improvement in the marginal Faroe Islands (Adderly and Simpson 2005; Hannon et al. 2001). Here, pre-Norse settlement, around AD 700, involved heavy sheep grazing, causing rapid and widespread vegetation shifts, the loss of sparse but important tree cover, and degradation of land into peat heathlands. The Norse, arriving at around AD 870, established infields or home-fields surrounding individual farms, vital for growing fodder and cereal, but were limited by prior degradation and the rugged geographic setting. Adderley and Simpson (2005) discovered intensive Faroese Norse soil augmentation, optimizing the limited and impoverished land, in turn permitting long-term sustainability around three settlements studied on the islands of Suđeroy, Sandoy, and Eysteroy. A low-yield baseline is seen in the era of original Norse settlement, but with management, yield improved steadily through the twelfth century (Adderly and Simpson 2005). Soil management eventually acted as a buffer against climatic downturns in terms of cereal and hay yields.

Orkney

On the Tofts Ness peninsula of Sanday, Orkney, radiocarbon dating and stratigraphic relationships indicate anthropogenic soils with greatly enhanced phosphate levels originating in the Bronze Age, with continuous formation into the Iron Age (I. Simpson, Dockrill et al. 1998:734, 739). Further analysis comprised thin section micromorphology, stable carbon isotope analysis, and analysis of free soil lipids (I. Simpson, Dockrill et al. 1998:729).

The soil was formed through application of green manure—grassy turf material (I. Simpson, Dockrill et al. 1998:743)—combined with ash, domestic waste, and manure derived from a ***human*** source (I. Simpson, Dockrill et al. 1998:744). Faunal material consisted of cattle and sheep, and as such manure was not applied directly to fields, it may have provided fuel, emphasizing a marginality necessitating "the utilization of all available resources to enable continuity of settlement" (I. Simpson, Dockrill et al. 1998:744). On Westray, Orkney, Norse fields were manured and fishing was also intensified, perhaps to supplement flagging terrestrial production (I. Simpson et al. 2005).

At Marwick, additions of manure, grassy turf, and seaweed are evident, beginning between AD 1200 and 1300 and continuing until the early twentieth century (I. Simpson 1997:365–380). Yet this site tells a very different and potentially significant story in terms of modern implementations. Marwick's grassy turf material was stripped exclusively from adjacent hill land used for pasturage, employed as animal bedding, and then composted. Soils near early farms have total phosphate values between two and three times background levels (I. Simpson 1997:365–380). Marwick's farmers were, in fact, too successful—the land was improved beyond what was necessary for the highest possible crop yields. And, as turf was stripped from hill land, summer pastures were significantly damaged, without any real payoff. This is an example of poor overall land management, despite the creation of a successful anthropogenic soil.

Shetland

In Shetland, over-enthusiastic soil enrichment created comparable problems. On Papa Stour Island, soils were manured at levels exceeding requirements for increasing and maintaining high yields, also at the expense of surrounding pasture highlands, again with no real gain. This strongly and negatively impacted available biomass for summer grazing (Adderley et al. 2000:429). One explanation is that as manuring produced higher yields, Papa Stour became an exporter of grain to other parts of Shetland (Adderley et al. 2000:429), creating a cycle based on *hoped-for* yields that were even higher. The authors note that a "lack of long-term cultural knowledge on how much organic carbon application was required to maintain arable systems" is apparent (Adderley et al. 2000:429). Soil should have been enhanced during the first 150 years, after which the frequency and intensity of augmentation could have been lowered.

Iceland

Another, different, cultural problem can be observed in Iceland, colonized largely by Norwegian farmers in the late ninth century AD. This farming is usually conceptualized by archaeologists and historians as marginal and at subsistence levels (I. Simpson et al. 2002:424). Treeless today, recent research indicates Iceland had a fair but fragile tree cover at settlement, denuded by early pioneers, leading to land degradation and erosion (Dugmore et al. 2005; I. Simpson et al. 2001).

The eventual failure of field farming on Iceland, which occurred by the 1500s, is frequently characterized as a result of climatic deterioration. This long-held idea recently has been challenged through soil thin section micromorphology and soil phosphate studies. At sites where agricultural activity is known to have occurred, manuring was low or non-existent, and grain yields were, in fact, at subsistence levels. Attempts at using seaweed as green manure could not adequately enrich soils (I. Simpson et al. 2002:434). Phosphorus levels between 180 and 309 parts per million (ppm) compare poorly with Faroese soils, where farmers created levels of 700–1,700 ppm. Computer modeling indicates short-term climate fluctuations reflecting slight observed variations in past crop yields, but no indication that the climatic deteriorations of the late AD 1200s or 1400s led to the low yields (I. Simpson et al. 2002:434). Total lack of soil management rather than climate was the primary limiting factor for cereal crop production (I. Simpson et al. 2002:435).

Why did the Icelanders fail, while those in Faroe Islands, Shetland, Orkney, and Arctic Norway succeeded? The eradication of tree cover and grazing of sheep on fragile grasses led to erosion and soil degradation, making it impossible to keep enough manure-producing livestock to augment the soil. Extant animals were pastured in the mountains in summer, where their manure could not be used for enriching lowland fields (I. Simpson et al. 2002:440).

The Icelanders *did* have other options—human manure, terrestrial and marine animal bones, and ash—but did not use them. Here, a shortage of labor might be indicated, or simply a lack of tradition-based indigenous knowledge from the founders, who largely were comprised of upper-class migrants propelled by civil unrest, whose land, left behind, had been of good quality.

Greenland

A familiar yet oft-debated chapter in the Norse expansion involves the Viking discovery of Greenland in AD 982 by Erik the Red, who brought several hundred colonists from Iceland. As many as 3,000–4,500 people may have occupied the Eastern Settlement until the 1400s. The Western Settlement, farther north along the Davis Strait, probably was home to 1,000–1,500 people and was occupied until about 1350. The earlier-settled Eastern Settlement had favorable livestock conditions during the Medieval Climatic Optimum, which ameliorated Greenland's climate even farther north than Norse areas by around AD 1020 (Kuijpers et al. 2001).

There is no doubt that the Little Ice Age (AD 1350–1850) ultimately caused the colony's final abandonment, but many other issues contributed to its failure. It was long believed that no agriculture was attempted in either region and that pastoralism and hunting, augmented by trade, comprised the entire economy, but new evidence points to hay farming and possibly some grain farming.

In 1990, the Farm under the Sand site (Gården under Sandet or GUS) was discovered in permafrost under aeolian sand in the western region, preserving organic material of all types (J. Berglund 1998:8). A large complex of buildings from the eleventh to the fourteenth century was explored, spanning the entire settlement period (J. Berglund 1998:9). Due to erosional threats, the site became the focus of a multidisciplinary, multinational, multiyear research program.

Geoarchaeological work included extensive soil analysis (Cameron 2004; Schweger 1998). Unlike the Eastern Settlement, where no augmentation has yet been demonstrated, at GUS a thick cultural layer is found not only near structures but also in infields where crops would have been grown—cereal processing is evident through grinding stones from the early period (J. Berglund 1998:10). Substantially increased soil phosphates, from manure application, raised fertility enough to support continuous cultivation (Cameron 2004:108); stable isotope analysis excludes seaweed as an input (Cameron 2004:107).

Soils and farming in the Eastern Settlement, where more work has been done, are topics of debate. While dung was used to fertilize infields at GUS, little or no evidence yet indicates the use of manure in the Eastern Settlement where many cattle were producing dung, though it is possible that extreme dryness may have led to irrigation attempts (I. Simpson, personal communication 2004).

Past research suggested that windblown sand horizons resulted from erosion linked to Norse farming activities (Fredskild 1978; Jakobsen 1991; Sandgren and Fredskild 1991), producing assertions that the Norse were "bad farmers" in marginal regions, but recent marine coring indicates aeolian layers resulted from increased storm activity beginning around AD 1300 (Lassen et al. 2000). Mikkelsen et al. (2001) studied such interstratified soil and sand near Norse farms in Søndre Igaliku, Eastern Settlement, and found that as at GUS storm-related windblown sand degraded farming activity long before the Little Ice Age became problematic.

Recent studies using shallow seismic survey and deep-tow side-scan sonar (Kuijpers et al. 1999) reveal that during five centuries of Norse occupation large stretches of fertile lowland bordering fjords became submerged, as postglacial isostatic rebound was followed by subsidence. Near the Viking settlement of Brattahlid, a 100 m band of coastline disappeared during the last millennium. At the Norse Episcopal residence of Gardar, "a gradual loss of useful land areas due to the relatively fast sea-level rise must have had a destructive effect on the farming and (grass) cultivation potential of the successive Norse generations in the area" (Kuijpers et al. 1999:64). Some inland Inuit settlements, as well as the Norse Herjolfsnes graveyard (Nørlund 1924), are now partially inundated (Rasch and Fog Jensen 1997). The bay at Søndre Igaliku today is inundated during high tides by 1–2.5 m, while largely dry at low tide. Mikkelsen et al. (2001) note that this "vast area" of once-fertile lowland was used for Norse production of winter hay for cattle (Mikkelsen et al. 2001:67).

Some research examines whether Norse inability to adapt to worsening climate worked against them. As time went on, Norse Greenlandic diet, originally terrestrial, included more marine resources (Lynnerup and Nørby 2004). Others suggest that in the end they were too attached to the European "farming" lifestyle to essentially become hunter-gatherers like the local Inuit, and thus survive eventual severe climate downturns (T. McGovern 1990, 1992).

During five hundred years of settlement, highly valued cattle became difficult to feed; why then was there no use of manure, bone, or seaweed to improve farming in the Eastern Settlement? Manuring evidence may lie underwater, but alternately, since many Greenland settlers came from Iceland, we may look to Iceland's problematic lack of manuring as a model. Perhaps east and west Greenlanders had different origins, strategies, and levels of knowledge about intensification.

Denmark

Archaeologists with corresponding specialties routinely link broken pots, stones, bones, and other daily detritus with the larger processes of economics, politics, and religious beliefs. Environmental archaeologists, however, often describe the impact of grazing, manuring, and plowing on sensitive landscapes, but rarely link social, economic, and political conditions with observable data on farming and intensification strategies "in a historic context to explain the basis of human activity" (I. Simpson et al. 2001:175). In the remainder of this chapter, I link soils and fertilizers, as a class of archaeological materials, to these larger structures and processes. In the Danish example, differing natural conditions, agricultural strategies, and local and state political and economic interests together clarify differential use of soil augmentation.

Between 1992 and 2006, my fieldwork lay within Viking Age and medieval Denmark: modern Denmark, northern Germany, and Scania, now southern Sweden. The Danes, who colonized England and Normandy, had the largest expanses of good farming soils in all the homelands. Within Denmark, however, there is tremendous variation in soil quality.

Scanian fieldwork between 1988 and 1994 included extensive soil chemical survey between 1992 and 1994. The area, historically and currently, remains "a rich agricultural region with level and even clay fields of a pronounced 'plains' character" (Ekström 1950:57).

Between 1997 and 2006, my work lay in northwestern Jutland's Thy region (pronounced "tew"), where highly drained, low-nutrient soils formed in the glacial outwash sands (Sømme 1968:103, 116). In the Iron Age and Middle Ages, windblown sand sometimes covered entire settlements and their field systems (Marseen 1959:66). Such conditions encourage formation of Podzols (spodosols)—sandy, nutrient-leached soils, and Histosols with 75 percent or more organic matter, mainly peat (FAO 1978:24). In Thy and across western Jutland, sandy heathland flourished until nineteenth-century modifications rendered it into croplands. Western Jutland's large expanses of Atlantic coastal fluvisols, recently drained and reclaimed for farming (FAO 1981:67), previously were marshy hay meadows suitable for grazing or fodder cutting.

In earlier times, only Thy's eastern bayside shore offered good farmland, formed in an old moraine. This sharp divide, leaving two-thirds in heath and about one-third in richer soils, is seen throughout Jutland, making Thy a microcosm of the peninsula. This stark landscape boundary in turn affected land use (fig. 5.2).

Thus, soil quality is a primary basis for subsistence and settlement choices. Larger-scale swiddening in the early Iron Age later gave way to small manured infields for subsistence grain production, primarily of barley, rye, and oats. Jutland settlements moved short distances every 175–250 years, although soil fertility is not hypothesized as a cause. Since farmers were manuring, they were maintaining nutrient levels, and since the village often only moved a couple of hundred meters, the same field systems were in use. Unknown beliefs about village founders, use-life, or other factors may be indicated.

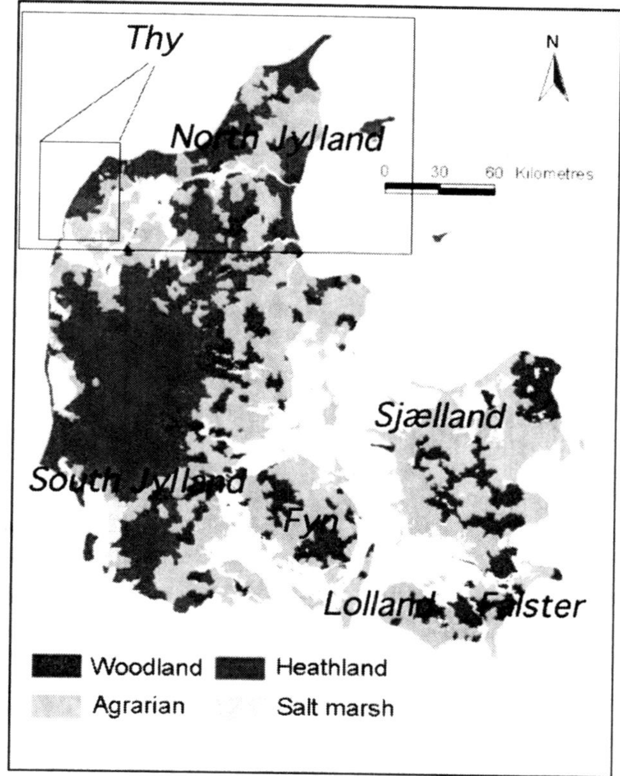

FIGURE 5.2. Denmark's core and outlying provinces.

The Historic Context of Danish Farming Strategies

Augmented soils in Scania and North Jutland were largely formed and used during a sequence of state development in Denmark. Ethnohistoric records indicate that active dissent characterized this period, as uncooperative, hostile peer polities were unified into a state controlled by a "core" area. By the Late Viking Age—early medieval transition, there were two dissenting outliers remaining: Scania and North Jutland. Their stark ecological contrasts, but shared political situations, within the unification trajectory were the basis of study.

How did central state pressure to unify and contribute taxes, labor, and tribute impact these differently oriented regions? To study dissent,

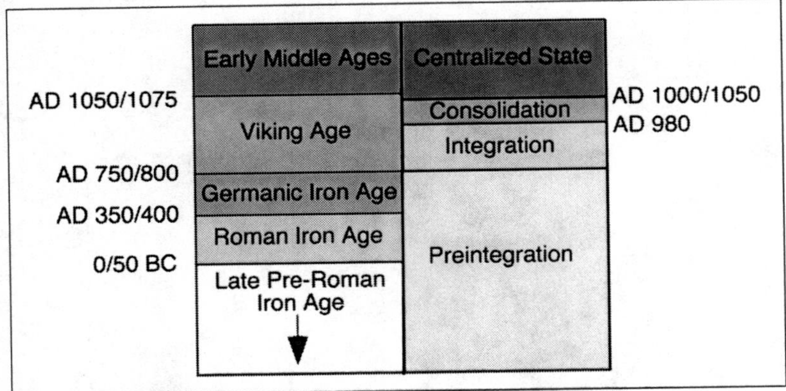

FIGURE 5.3. Chronology/phases for Danish state development.

carefully interpreted ethnohistories are helpful, as are archaeological indicators of the state's various strategies of cooperation, cooption, or coercion. Please note the traditional culture-historic chronology in contrast to the project's entirely different parallel chronology, based on political changes and corresponding socioeconomic shifts. Thus, I refer to the Preintegration phase, the Integration phase, and the Consolidation phase, followed by a more centralized medieval state (fig. 5.3).

Scania. Around AD 1000, during the Consolidation phase, archaeological evidence for statebuilding in Scania includes construction of central-state fortified administrative locales and urban centers in the previously non-urban region, and the disappearance of local chiefly compounds that had earlier controlled it (fig. 5.4). Rural change is also evident. In Scania, older villages, unchanged since foundation, were reorganized, contracting up to 60 percent to conform to a new linear "street" plan, probably connected to new forms of record-keeping for taxation and military obligation (Riddersporre 1988; Thurston 2001). Simultaneously, from AD 1000 to 1100, across Denmark, but with especial density in Scania, thousands of *torps* were founded: tiny, dispersed agricultural settlements, many with preplanned linear street layouts, substantially increasing arable land and yields.

Ethnohistoric documents record Scanian complaints to the king over new taxes and military obligations, silenced when some dissenters

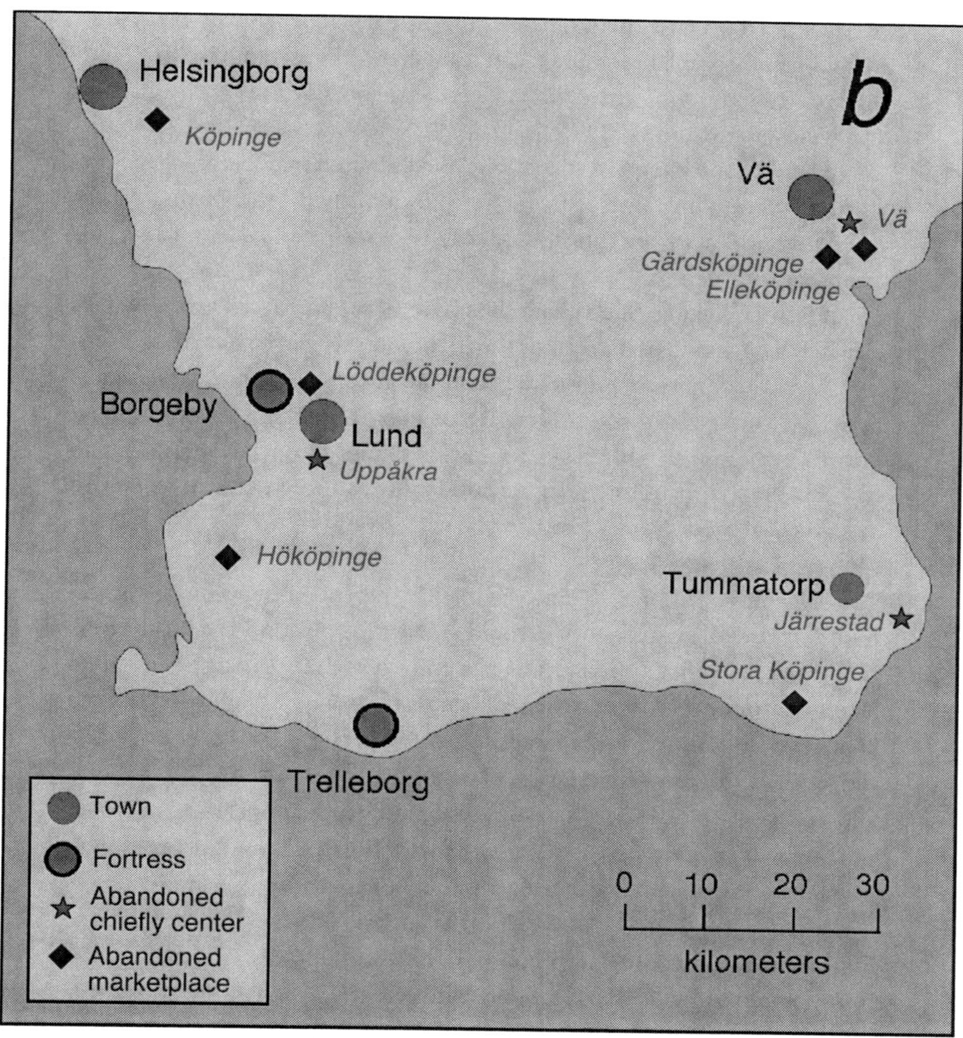

FIGURE 5.4. Scanian towns and fortresses, ca. AD 1000.

were executed; these texts describe acrimony on the part of farmers and brutality from the state. Landscape changes seem to reflect this, as they display the most extreme version of the "power of place": razing of chiefly centers, destruction and transplantation of older villages, a wave of pioneering agricultural hamlets, and the creation of new urban central places at state-determined locales. In Scania, angry confrontations between farmers and the king occurred in the 1080s, and by 1180, after many formal complaints, they elected their own king and rebelled, leading to a bloody two-year conflict. The Scanians lost this confrontation and were assimilated.

In Scania, soil chemical surveys were conducted over eight village territories surrounding one of the state-founded towns, integrating earlier archaeological work and phosphate data to examine an additional six, for a total of fourteen.

In Scania, Viking Age village sites have between 10 and 30 ha of soils elevated well above background, the highest levels within 250 m of dwellings. In Scania, natural phosphate levels lie at 50 to 150 ppm, while semi-managed outfields (through grazing of manure-making cattle) contain 400 to 900 ppm or more. Systematically manured outfields yield 1,000 to 1,500 ppm. Infield manuring created truly artificial plaggen soils with 2,000 to 6,000 or more ppm.

Thy, Northern Jutland. Unlike Scania, where no indigenous or state-founded towns existed until around AD 1000, prior to the Consolidation phase, Northern Jutland was not entirely rural. Although remaining largely autonomous, it experienced state-sponsored urban inroads from an early date. Centers and markets emerged in the eighth century, while the tenth century saw foundation of major urban locales at Århus, Viborg, and Aalborg. In Scania, when intrusive state-towns appeared, fortresses of similar type were constructed in North Jutland simultaneously with Scania, also around AD 1000 during the Consolidation phase.

While agriculturally poor, North Jutland had essential strategic importance, controlling the economically and militarily vital fishing and transport conduit of the Limfjord. Aalborg town, the Aggersborg fortress, large marketplaces like Sebbersund, the Skaggerak canal (enabling naval movements), and at least one major *ledung*, or military levying-place for wartime fleets, indicate North Jutland was the focus of elite political, rather than subsistence, intensification during state-building (fig. 5.5).

A decade of archaeological work in Thy sought understanding of how, when, and how far the central state penetrated this region, revealing that, unlike in Scania, local people maintained control of important naval levy-places, and "old" centers were reused, rather than being razed

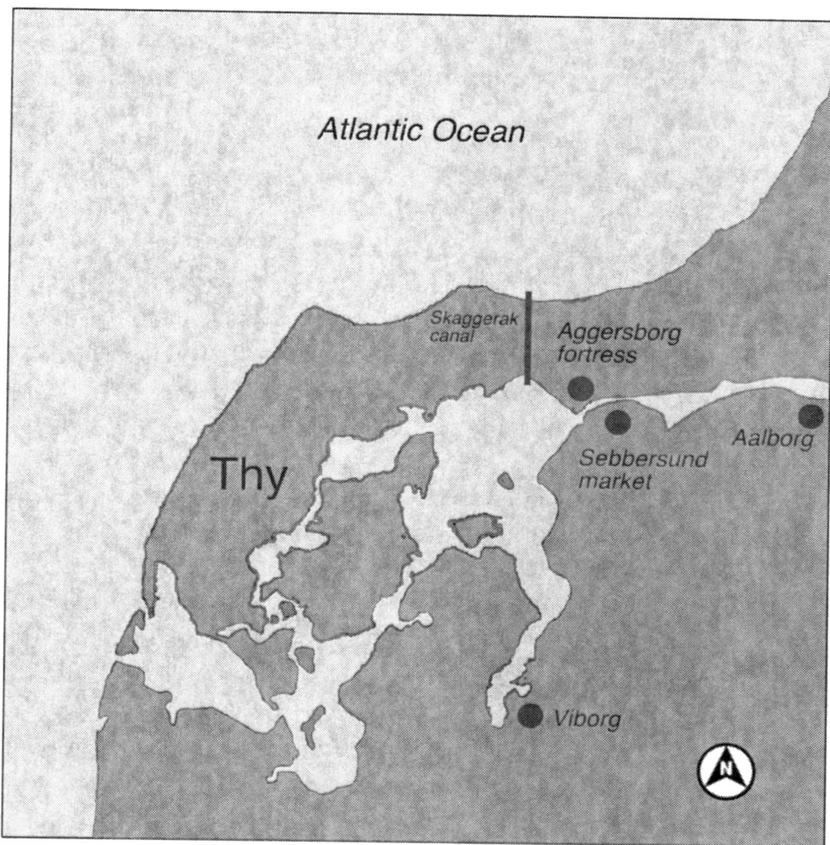

FIGURE 5.5. West Danish towns.

and replaced by central foundations (Thurston 2006, 2007): reuse rather than destruction suggests a different political climate.

Another question addressed whether forced abandonment or continued use was seen in rural contexts. In Scania, older villages underwent massive internal reorganization around AD 1000, and hundreds of torps simultaneously appeared. Neither phenomenon occurred in Thy. In the twenty-three rural village territories tested and at several major excavations, farming villages of the eighth to eleventh centuries were directly overlain by early medieval phases of the same villages, none apparently regulated or planned. This contrasts with Scania, but also differs from south-central Jutland and the rest of the core area, where they invariably moved as far as one kilometer to an entirely different location at this time. Thy's villages probably shifted to current locations in the later Middle Ages.

Additionally, torps were founded in Thy, but much later: no material earlier than the twelfth–fourteenth century characterizes them, unlike Scania, where material from around AD 1000 is typical. As the state consolidated power across Denmark, opening new arable land was clearly less important or less achievable in Thy than in Scania. Less interference and regulation may indicate less taxation during state building.

North Jutland's livestock orientation may explain why the later wave of torp intensification sites was smaller as well. Herders typically increase production through short-term strategies such as pasturing more animals on the same amount of land, necessitating fewer changes in settlement. Modern pastoralists commonly do this to pay taxes or raise cash. This is far less disruptive than what must occur among cereal-crop farmers to raise yields.

In terms of soil augmentation in Thy, the picture is also different than in Scania. The same patterns are evident, with higher amounts of anthropogenic additions closer to the dwelling areas, indicating infields, outfields, and undeveloped village lands, but Thy's levels are distinctly lower. The highest infield levels reach 1,800 to 2,000 ppm, but most lie between 800 and 1,500, while outfields average between 400 and 700. Offsite readings lie between 10 and 150 ppm. Thus, natural phosphate levels in "good" soils are similar between regions, while poor soils were augmented to a good, but not excessive level. While most Jutland villages shifted location a short distance every 175–250 years, lower phosphate levels are not explained only by dislocation: field territories did not really shift, and augmentation could have produced much higher levels.

The ethnohistoric evidence for North Jutland also tells a story different than Scania's. In the 1080s, the North Jutlanders rejected the Danish king—the same time that the Scanians first came into conflict with the crown. Contemporary chroniclers note similar reasons—rising taxes and labor demands—remarking upon North Jutland's relative poverty (Pålsson and Edwards 1986). Here, the North Jutlanders departed in strategy from the Scanians. Instead of quieting after state threats, North Jutlanders invaded the core area with an army, killing both the king and his entourage of advisors and warriors.

Discussion

Uprisings in both Scania and North Jutland were led by local elites with farmer followers. Historical and archaeological evidence indicates that wealthy Scanian farmers did not immediately rebel during initial hardships in the 1080s. The aftermath of Scanian uprising one hundred years later was immediate, brutal retaliation.

Relative poverty may have created intolerable conditions for the Jutlanders, forcing more immediate armed confrontation to dethrone a perceived tyrant; their pastoral organization, perhaps more segmentary, may have aided their ability to organize. No retaliation for the rebellion is recorded, perhaps for fear of further regicides by the still-forming state. Unification, perhaps on the Jutlander's terms, soon followed.

The state did not interfere materially with Jutland's local organization, and long-time cooperation is apparent in the cumulative foundations of state towns and military installations. Ultimate resolution and acceptance of state authority may also relate to poverty: state markets, centers, and fortresses made good economic partners for less-wealthy regions.

There are also marked differences in soil management between the two regions, with much higher levels of augmentation in Scania despite already good conditions for farming. These differences can be explained in three ways. First, the Scanian soils already had higher nutrient levels than much of Jutland's soil, although limited areas were comparable. Second, Scanian villages, once established, never or rarely moved. Swiddening ceased around AD 500. Thus, constant additions continued to raise soil phosphate levels to outstanding heights. Yet in Jutland, even with village dislocation, maximal augmentation could have produced higher levels of soil phosphate.

Third, and perhaps most importantly, grain-crop production was of utmost importance in Scania, especially with the advent of state taxation and church tithing in close succession (Thurston 2001). Thus, a farmer's perceptions of where assets should be applied would have been centered around improving crop production. In Thy and much of Jutland, since animal production was most important, manuring would have been aimed at satisfaction rather than maximization—or *perceived* maximization; since Scanian farmers, like those in Shetland, clearly were over-manuring, creating soils ten to twenty times higher than necessary to efficiently raise yields. As in Shetland, indigenous knowledge that manuring raised yields may have been combined with a false expectation that even more manuring would create even higher yields, perhaps desperately hoped for under such severe pressure to pay taxes. Although many torps were founded in Scania, opening even more fields would have been a better strategy than over-manuring extant ones.

While Thy had lower-quality soils to begin with, their augmentation reflects a better overall land-management strategy, as the levels attained easily maintained and improved crop production. They avoided immediate taxation burdens through rebellion, and later probably paid their tribute through more easily intensified animal resources, reflected in the high number of animal prefixes in the names of Jutland's torps and known droving roads and cattle markets on the peninsula (Thurston 2006).

Conclusions

As argued elsewhere (Thurston 1999), linking ordinary, even lowly, materials and practices to the larger conditions of the state is implemented best through local and regional research, combined with theories normally outside of environmental archaeology: practice and structuration theory (i.e., Bourdieu 1977; Giddens 1984, 1993; Ortner 1984, 1989; Pred 1984, 1986). Social life lies neither in individual micro-activity nor only in events at the macro-level (Giddens 1984). The micro- and macro-scales—human agency and social structure—must be studied as a dialectic relationship (Gauntlett 2002). Interpersonal interactions, artifacts of daily life, and familiar geographic locales structure people's worlds, as they travel through life on a course of ordinary, continuous praxis that fuels social reproduction. Giddens imagined social structure created from ingrained institutions, legal and moral codes, traditions, and "ways of doing things," yet such practices can also be ignored, replaced, or reproduced differently, through choice, neglect, or dislocations like migrations, thus changing their social milieu (Gauntlett 2002). The state can also step in to change both practices and structures, often in more visible, disruptive, and unwanted ways. In the tension between ordinary people and the state lie explanations for soil chemical data and the farming strategies that created them.

Today, similar struggles between ordinary people and their states are still being played out as people rise to demands for taxes and commodities for the local and world marketplace, except today's mantra includes not only chemicals but also genetically engineered plants and animals:

> Faced with an estimated 786 million hungry people in the world, cheerleaders for our social order have an easy solution: we will grow more food through the magic of chemicals and genetic engineering. For those who remember the original "Green Revolution" promise to end hunger through miracle seeds, this call for "Green Revolution II" should ring hollow. Yet Monsanto, Novartis, AgrEvo, DuPont, and other chemical companies who are reinventing themselves as biotechnology companies, together with the World Bank and other international agencies . . . will save the world from hunger and starvation if we just allow these various companies, spurred by the free market, to do their magic. (Rosset et al. 2000)

Despite recognizing these drawbacks, farmers in the developing world must produce for themselves and the marketplace. How they do so largely rests in the social context of their economic choices. Development NGOs engage in research and implementation of sustainable and resilient farming in Africa, Latin America, and Southeast Asia. Their work indicates that, as in the past, agricultural innovation must be driven by the needs of farmers, both real and perceived, not the mere availability of technology. They cite adoption of sustainable methods as ways to lower monetary and labor costs, and improve weed and pest situations (Buckles, Triomphe et al. 1998). Farmers, they state, especially in West Africa (Bationo 2004; Buckles, Etèka et al. 1998), but also in Latin America (Buckles, Triomphe et al. 1998; Bunch 2002) and Southeast Asia (Oyen 1995), are innovators, willing participants in field trials, resulting in what the IDRC says are easy-to-adopt, resilient technologies.

This is encouraging in the short term, but as demonstrated, even in presumably culturally homogenous zones such as the North Atlantic, farmers do not always adopt even useful technologies when they are not part of long-term, locally developed cultural repertoires, a fact exacerbated by migration from home regions. The differences between the Eastern and Western Settlements of Greenland may highlight this. Farmers may overuse or underuse technologies, either through wrongly perceived benefits, as in Shetland, Orkney, and Scania, or because locally they lack some necessary resources, as in Iceland. Why alternative resources go unused in cases like Iceland and Greenland's Eastern Settlement is unknown, possibly linked to an inability to imagine other solutions, more probably to extremely short-term perspectives: getting through the next season with enough to eat. Studies with more contextual, culturally embedded views of observed technological changes are needed in the North Atlantic.

Today, as in earlier times, the lowly dungheap is, in chainlike fashion, actively connected to state policies and institutions. No simple models can characterize why some farmers easily incorporate new practices and others do not, and outcomes are linked as much to historic traditions as to promised or expected improvements. Development must consider long-term trajectories, cultural differences, and different historic traditions, even within culturally similar regions. Lessons from the past on the successful creation and use of anthropogenic soils can shed light on their likely success today.

6

The Human–Wildlife Conundrum

A VIEW FROM EAST AFRICA

Chapurukha M. Kusimba

AFRICAN WILDLIFE CONSERVATION managers are mired in a vicious conflict between people and wildlife. National parks and game reserves are among the leading foreign-exchange earners in Kenya and Tanzania, where the economic value of preserves and parks is inspiring attempts at eco- and archaeotourism (Musiba and Mabulla 2003). Some scholars and local people, however, have been critical of tourism-inspired development initiatives because they fail to benefit the local communities that are neighbors of tourist-designated areas. Moreover, the critics argue that wildlife conservation policies generally ignore local communities (D. Anderson and Grove 1987; Eriksen et al. 1996; Hitchcock 1994, 1995). This chapter will examine the long-term history of human ecological impacts in the arid lowland grasslands and bush in and around Tsavo National Park in southeastern Kenya, with special attention to iron-smelting and elephant-hunting impacts on the environment. By considering the varied history of human action in this ecosystem, we will debate the actions of indigenous peoples of Tsavo as "natural conservationists" (E. Smith and Wishnie 2000).

It is now evident that modern cultural and natural landscapes have evolved as a consequence of human interaction with animal and plant life. As such, conservation programs that promote dialogue and show a keen understanding of, and sensitivity to, the cultural values, mores, and conservation practices of indigenous people are more likely to succeed (Musonda 1989).

This chapter draws upon examples from archaeology and ethnohistory to evaluate the impact of technology and culture on the environment. Archaeology coupled with ethnohistorical and archival evidence suggests that post-sixteenth-century Tsavo was characterized by periodic droughts, which were accompanied by famine, disease, and warfare (Kusimba 2004; Kusimba et al. 2005; Merritt 1975). What role did people play in shaping the East African ecological and cultural landscapes? To what extent were ecological and social crises in part caused by unsustainable exploitation of the region's resources? I use data drawn from iron working, the ivory trade and its impact on elephants, and subsistence in Tsavo in the last three hundred to four hundred years to show the complex relationships between technology, economy, and the environment. Although a strong case has been made concerning the role of preindustrial iron production in shaping the African environments, my reevaluation of archaeological evidence seems to suggest that East African environments are likely to have been shaped by the use rather than the production of iron. Technological advances and economic growth in Eurasia increased elite demand for luxury items including African ivory, gold, and enslaved labor (Kusimba 2004). Thus, I argue in this chapter that technological, economic, social, and political transformations in Eurasia beginning from the sixteenth century more likely played a far greater role in the shaping of East African ecosystems than traditional land-use and resource-exploitation strategies.

The Role of Iron Production and Use in Shaping the East African Environments

Preindustrial iron production in Africa was a complex technology carried out in many communities by guilds of highly specialized workers across the continent (e.g., P. Schmidt 1978, 1997). Iron bloom and its finished products, including hoes, axes, machetes, daggers, swords, spears, arrows, and knives, were traded far and wide (Kusimba 1993; Kusimba and Killick 2003; P. Schmidt 1997; P. R. Schmidt and Mapunda 1997). As one of the principal wealth-creating technologies, ironworking and its components were a much-sought-after sphere of knowledge, and the few who controlled access to this technology prospered (De Maret 1985). Local elites invested in the craft and supported royal guilds, which made prestige as well as ritual and utilitarian objects (De Maret 1985).

The recovery of high-quality bloomery and crucible steel at a number of coastal sites suggests that East Africa served as an important center for iron production during the Late Iron Age (ca. AD 500–1500) (Kusimba

1993; Kusimba et al. 1994; Kusimba and Killick 2003). The political economy at this time emphasized the utilization of locally available resources, with some participation in a wide range of exchange networks. Interaction between coastal and foreign societies is indicated by a greater variety of imported pottery when southwestern and southern Asian artifacts become more common (Abungu 1990; Chami 1994, 1998, 2002; Chittick 1974, 1984; Horton 1996; Kusimba 1997a, 1997b, 1999a; Middleton and Horton 2000). Wealth accumulated from regional trade provided local entrepreneurs the means for elevating social status. Economic and political elites in early East African cities like Malindi, Kilwa, and Sofala likely financed large-scale iron-smelting and -forging industries, which supplied most of the iron needs of urban residents and hinterland communities (Kusimba 1999a, 1999b). Abundant evidence for iron production and use at virtually all excavated sites on the coast supports this perspective (Abungu 1990; Chami 1988, 1994; Horton 1996; Kusimba 1993; Kusimba et al. 1994; P. Schmidt 1995). Due to its high quality, East Africa iron became a much-sought-after commodity that was exported to places as distant as southern and western Asia (Freeman-Grenville 1962; Kusimba 1993) and was critical in the evolution of village-level societies into city-states and urban centers (Chami 1988, 1994; Kusimba 1999b; P. Schmidt 1995). I illustrate this section with an archaeological and ethnographic example.

Ironworking at Mount Kasigau and Environs

Mount Kasigau, hereafter Kasigau, forms one of four prominent hills in the Tsavo ecosystem, commonly referred to as the Taita Hills (fig. 6.1). Historically inhabited by the Taita people who call themselves Wakasigau, the area has a fragmented ecosystem of native and non-native vegetation and areas of primary and secondary forest. Old and long-abandoned mango, tamarind, coconut, citrus groves, and terraced fields in the hills, and baobab, *Adansonia* sp., in the plains tell tales of a once-dynamic domestic landscape in various stages of returning to the wild.

For 1,500 years, Kasigau was the first major stopover inland, being about three days' journey from coastal villages and towns. For those headed into the interior, Kasigau was a stop for replenishing provisions before setting off into the far interior towards Taveta, Chagga, Pare,

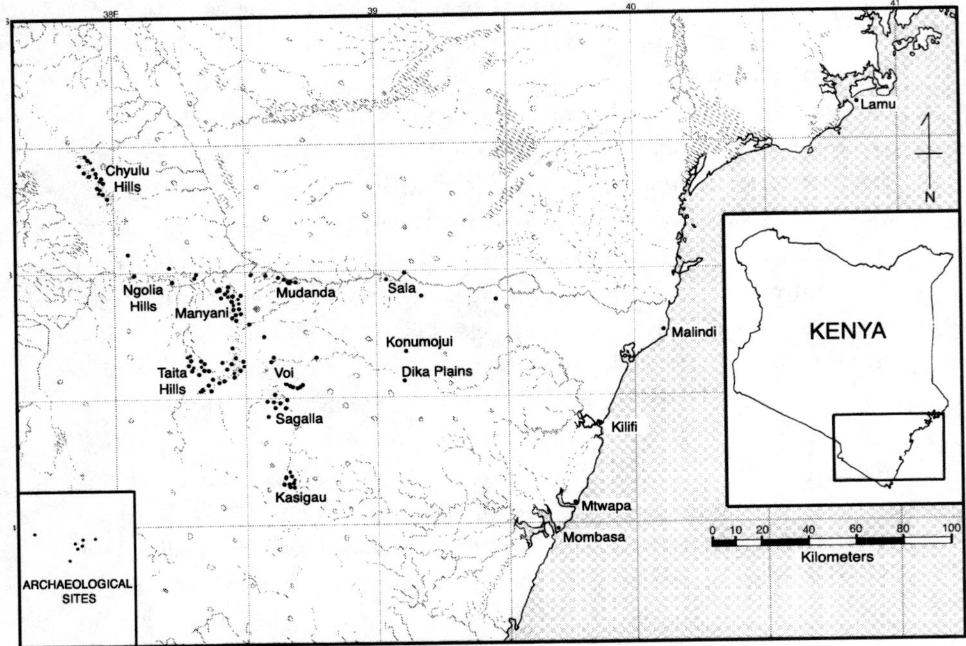

FIGURE 6.1. The Tsavo Region, showing known archaeological sites.

Ukambani, and beyond (Wakefield 1870). Among the items traded in Kasigau were ivory (raw and cut), iron bloom, rhinoceros horn, rock crystals, poison, bows and arrows, hides and skins, honey and beeswax, milk, butter, buttermilk, and other animal products. The trade items desired by the peoples in Kasigau were beaded products, cloth (both South Asian textiles and Swahili), marine shells, ostrich eggshell, and marine and glass beads (Kusimba 2004; Kusimba et al. 2005; Kusimba and Kusimba 2001; table 6.1).

Archaeological surveys located more than forty sites, mapped and extensively excavated at eight rockshelters, a terrace, and an iron-smelting site. Magnetite ore outcrops abound in Kasigau. Here, we recovered two large iron-working sites, one at Rukanga and the other at Kirongwe. The sites cover large areas of more than two acres. Our research concentrated on the Kirongwe site where we mapped one locality, K7, and excavated a rockshelter, K1, which turned up evidence for intensive iron

TABLE 6.1. Coast–Interior Trade

To Coast	From Coast
Ivory and rhinoceros horn	Cloth and textiles
Rock crystal, tsavorite, and tanzanite	Beads–marine and glass
Enslaved persons	Marine shells
Iron and bloom	Dry fish
Skins and hides	Trade ceramics
Dry meat and buttermilk	Coconut oils
Honey and beeswax	Copper, brass, silver and gold artifacts
Animal skins	

TABLE 6.2. The Chronological Sequence of Kirongwe 1

Site	Cal. Ages (2 Sigma)	Uncal. Ages Years BP	(Lab No.)
Kirongwe 1	1501–1955 AD	260 ± 70	ISGS-5227
Kirongwe 1	1444–1797 AD	360 ± 70	ISGS-5222
Kirongwe 1	1047–1382 AD	840 ± 70	ISGS-5228
Kirongwe 1	1033–1273 AD	910 ± 70	ISGS-5212
Kirongwe 1	904–1257 AD	990 ± 70	ISGS-5203
Kirongwe 1	902–1223 AD	1000 ± 70	ISGS-5210
Kirongwe 1	733–1138 AD	1140 ± 70	ISGS-5205
Kirongwe 1	722–1130 AD	1150 ± 70	ISGS-5208

production spanning eight hundred years. The chronological sequence based on nine radiocarbon determinations places K1 from the present back to 1150 ± 70 BP (table 6.2).

Furnace technology was primarily of bowl furnaces. Excavated artifacts at rockshelter K1, including a stone anvil, a large volume of tuyere fragments, slag, and both finished and unfinished tools, attest to the complexity of iron production in Tsavo. Table 6.3 illustrates the total volume of finds and their stratigraphic distribution.

The significant volumes of slag and slag-wetted tuyeres found in levels 7 through 11 correspond to 840 ± 70 to 1150 ± 70 years BP, or the eighth to twelfth centuries AD. Archaeological evidence from coastal

TABLE 6.3. Volume of Finds at Kirongwe 1, Kasigau

Level	1	2	3	4	5	6	7	8	9	10	11	12
Slag (g)			25	200	175	686	3030	4222	6255	7400	4900	650
Iron					2		1	8	4	1	111	0
Tuyeres					7	14	44	42	27	10		17
Ceramics	1	5	6	10	26	35	84	160	290	105	101	200
Beads	3	13	13	7	18	9	1	4	1			0
Bone	29	62	113	97	151	130	107	45	20	45	47	
Stone tools	4	29	1	52	27	99	69	14	11			

urban settlements provides incontrovertible evidence that rapid urban growth occurred in the region during this period as well (Abungu 1990; Chittick 1974; Horton 1996; Kusimba 1993).

Obviously, iron was an important craft and exchange item. Tsavo's iron was likely used in the manufacture of household and farm ware as well as weapons used primarily for hunting and in provisioning the demand for hinterland items by the coast. Iron accelerated intensification in terrace farming and livestock husbandry in Tsavo (Kusimba and Kusimba 2001). Iron enabled people to kill elephants, whose ivory was in high demand in Eurasia (Pearson 1998). The technical quality of iron made in Tsavo was impressive. The few arrowheads and spear blades recovered have excellent cutting and penetrating qualities and were created primarily for hunting rather than offensive and defensive weapons. Thus, besides farmers and herders, the other most significant clientele of Kasigau ironworkers were, without doubt, the professional hunters who provisioned ivory to coastal merchants, as well as to local farmers.

Iron Production and Environmental Degradation

The fuel needs of pyrotechnological industries are assumed to have been the primary cause of preindustrial deforestation (Braudel 1967; DeBarros 1988). Some scholars maintain that the forests of Europe and of several parts of Asia were formerly denuded by their iron industries, thus setting the stage for acute industrial and domestic fuel shortages. For Europe as a whole, the traditional picture of worsening fuel crises during the sixteenth through eighteenth centuries is summarized by Braudel (1967:269–271). For Britain, the case for an absolute shortage was formulated by Ashton (1924), Nef (1932), and Schubert (1957). Similar pictures of metallurgy-induced forest destruction are painted by Hartwell (1963:95) for northern China, by Horne (1982) for northeastern Iran, by DeBarros (1986, 1988) for West Africa, by P. Schmidt (1978) for the Great Lakes region of East Africa, and by K. Butzer (1981) indirectly for the fall of the Ethiopian state of Aksum.

Ethnographic observations among modern African ironworkers support the position that ironworking causes deforestation. In 1989, I carried out ethnographic research among modern ironworkers on the

TABLE 6.4. Types of Trees Used as Biofuel by Coastal Ironworkers

Trees Exploited	Blacksmiths (out of 18)	Percentage
Mgogo	2	11
Mkoma	15	83
Mkwanju	14	78
Mkanda	5	28
Mchuubi	5	28
Mkondee	7	39
Muembe	10	56

Kenya coast (Kusimba 1993, 1996). My primary goal was to elucidate the context of iron and its relationships to the development of long-distance exchange and the development of urbanism in the region. My secondary goal was to test the notion that traditional ironmaking techniques are harmful to Africa's ecosystem because strategies for harvesting of forests for biofuel are unregulated.

I interviewed eighteen modern blacksmiths on the Kenyan coast in 1989. Coastal smiths use charcoal from several species of trees as the only source of fuel. The amount of charcoal used by each smith depended on the scale of production, demand, time of year, and the type of trees from which the charcoal was prepared. Table 6.4 shows the smiths' responses on the type of trees they exploited for charcoal.

Coastal blacksmiths preferred charcoal that burned slowly, generated much heat, and yielded little ash. They claimed that ash insulates heat, resulting in fuel wastage. Most smiths use charcoal from the *mkoma*, *mkwanju*, and *muembe* trees. *Mchuubi*, *mkanda*, and *mkondee* trees are less often exploited. Only two blacksmiths exploited the *mgogo* tree, which the respondents said was scarce. Mkwanju is easy to fell, cheap to buy, fast growing, and fuel efficient because it burns slowly when exposed to the bellow blast. The mkoma yields more heat than the mkwanju, but it burns fast and was considered less favorable in comparison to mkwanju. A 35 kg bag of mkwanju charcoal lasts three to four days and makes a total of sixteen hoes, while a similar amount of mkoma charcoal lasts less than two days and makes only six hoes. Some smiths compared charcoal from mkwanju and mkoma trees to diesel and petrol gas, respectively.

Mchuubi, mkanda, and mkondee were exploited by smiths only on the northern Swahili coast, partly due to overharvesting and governmental regulation on the southern coast. Mgogo is available only in the nearby Arabuko Sokoke Forest, one of the last indigenous forests on the Swahili coast. Consequently, blacksmiths have turned to previously underexploited trees for charcoal, especially the mkwanju and muembe. During Karisa Masha's (1920–1990) boyhood, trees like the mkondee, mchubi, and mkanda, now restricted to the Lamu archipelago and Bajuni Islands, were abundant, but they are depleted now in the Kilifi, Mombasa, and Kwale districts. Not surprisingly, a report by the World Resources Institute states that in the 1980s Kenya lost 71 percent of its total forest, including 70 percent of the mangrove forests.

Charcoal Making and Deforestation

Determining the impact of traditional forest-harvesting strategies on the ecosystem can be difficult. Fortunately, while undertaking archaeological excavations at an ironworking site of Galu (Kusimba 1993; Kusimba and Killick 2003; Kusimba et al. 1994), I collected data on the ratio of trees and charcoal from a local charcoal maker. The informant had made and supplied charcoal to nearby tourist hotels for twelve years. Based on his account, two large trees of approximately fifty years old took seven days or one week to burn and yielded ten bags of about 40 kg each.

Assuming that the charcoal maker worked continuously, he would cut down 2 trees every week. In one year, he would cut down 104 mature trees, which would yield 520 bags or 20,800 kg of charcoal. Since the informant had been making charcoal in the area for twelve years, he may have cut 1,248 mature trees, which yielded a total of 6,240 bags or 249,600 kg of charcoal. Traditional charcoal making for iron production selectively harvested specific trees. By contrast, modern charcoal-burning practices indiscriminately harvest all mature trees (see also van der Merwe 1980:488). If, as one blacksmith suggested, 1 bag forges only 16 hoes, then 10 bags of mkondee charcoal would forge about 160 hoes. It takes the smith 40 days to use 10 sacks of charcoal if he makes 4 hoes per day. In one year, the smith is capable of making 1,460 hoes, taking 92 sacks of charcoal or 19 mkondee trees. Table 6.5 estimates the exploitation of trees

TABLE 6.5. Postulated Number of Trees Exploited for Hoes over Two Millennia

Days	Years	Charcoal Bags	Trees	Hoes Produced
10		2.5	0.5	40
40		10	2	140
80		20	4	320
365	1	91.25	18.25	1,460
36,500	100	9,125	1,825	146,000
182,500	500	45,625	9,125	730,000
547,500	1,500	136,875	27,375	2,190,000
730,000	2,000	182,500	36,500	2,920,000

for two millennia years by one smith family, assuming no interruption in production.

My postulation assumes a constant pace of forest exploitation and no intervening factors and bears some obvious errors. First, let it be known that my estimates are low because I do not take into consideration other uses of forests, including boat making, firewood, and house construction (see also van der Merwe and Avery [1988:250]).

In what ways does this ethnographic example apply to preindustrial contexts in East Africa? The overexploitation of forests on the coast is a by-product of increased demand and unregulated harvesting of forests, much of which occurred only in the past three hundred to four hundred years.

The Elephant in Tsavo

The intensification of iron production beginning from the eighth century affected the East African environment less directly, through its effect on the number and distribution of elephants. The elephant has an important presence in African culture as image and material, and it is often represented in folklore and art. Its most important effect on humans, however, lies in the fact that it has shaped much of the natural African landscape, rendering it more fit for habitation by human beings. Klein (1983) speculated that the first significant interaction of elephant and human lineages may have been during the Pliocene, when loxodonts and other proboscideans created the first woodland environment where australopithecines evolved. Since then, elephants have played a pivotal role in human affairs and an important role in shaping the ecosystem of African and Asian environments.

As they forage, elephants create and maintain broad paths through impenetrable bamboo and elephant grass belts, and in forested areas, they keep extensive glades in permanent state of "early success" (Wilkie 1989), not only breaking down trees but also tearing up acres of saplings for their roots. They excavate and weed out water holes and "garden" interconnected glades and clearings into tangled vegetation. Thus, elephants open up habitats for ground-dwelling mammals. Such habitats are more productive, by reason of access to both sun and water, and more ecologically diverse than either deep forest or open grasslands. A major advantage of elephant-maintained environments from a human standpoint is that they are not hospitable to the tsetse fly, the vector of trypanosomiasis, which requires deep shade for survival. Elephants have opened up much of tropical Africa, particularly lowland areas, for pastoralists and agro-pastoralists. The Tsavo ecosystem, like many East African grasslands, has changed over time as a result of human activity. Pastoralism, agricultural practices, and hunting and gathering all impact the environment. A long history of archaeology shows that we can no longer see the relationship between humans and grasslands as antagonistic.

Lamprey and Waller (1990) showed how pastoralist burning kept bushlands to a minimum, allowing higher-quality grasses to grow and creating opportunities for wild and domestic ungulates. Tsetse is reduced by burning as well, obviously rejuvenating areas for pastoralist use. The population diversity of ungulates is also improved by pastoralists' extensive strategies of grazing and burning, which open up areas to a variety of wild grasses (Little 1996).

Precolonial Africans used a variety of techniques to hunt and kill elephants. Trapping through use of pits and snares, seemingly the safest technique, was limited in application, because of the intelligence of the prey. Hence, traditional elephant hunters often had to rely on attacks on animals that were more or less freely moving and able to defend themselves, although perhaps partially immobilized by vegetation, terrain, or fire-ringing. Such attacks were dangerous and required long periods of training. They also required weapons with excellent cutting and penetrating qualities.

The introduction of high-quality iron and steel made possible the creation of effective elephant-killing weapons. A heavy iron spear or an arrow with an iron point slowed or incapacitated the elephant, and this was what first made the routine hunting of elephants possible.

Hunting peoples of southeastern Kenya of many ethnic backgrounds attribute their hunting skills to methods developed by Waata hunters of Tsavo, who developed long bows, their trademark, and an *Acocanthera*-based poison that was eventually adopted by the Wakamba and others (Parker and Amin 1983; Steinhart 2000). Among the Wakamba, specialized hunting parties sought the elephant on the Yatta Plateau and along the Galana River. With the growth of ivory trade in the eighteenth and nineteenth centuries, specialized ivory hunting developed and was socially organized around leaders of both hunting expeditions and trading organizations called *kuthuua*, who not only led hunting expeditions but also supplied coast-bound caravans with the ivory. These hunter/trader Big Men also developed relationships with Waata. Trade activity increased social stratification and created prestige positions like the trader/hunter Big Man.

The rise of the hinterland-coastal trade in ivory, both for use by local elites and for export, was a powerful motive for wealth-seeking traders. Historical sources make it clear that substantial quantities of ivory were being shipped to West Asia and the Mediterranean and probably to South Asia as well by the twelfth century (Thorbahn 1979). The trade must already have been in existence during the ninth century, when cities oriented toward overseas commerce first appeared on the East African coast (Horton 1996; Kusimba 1999a, 1999b; Middleton and Horton 2000; Pearson 1998).

This early demand for substantial quantities of ivory was the cause of an initial decline in elephant populations in the more accessible parts of the East African interior. Conducted largely by peripatetics like the modern Waata (Parker and Amin 1983:24), Kamba (Steinhart 2000), and Okiek (Merker 1910:251–252), armed with high-quality iron weapons obtained through regional trade and exchange, this early phase of the ivory trade must have caused significant rearrangements of the elephant population. It was evidently not as devastating as the nineteenth-century elephant trade, which was assisted by guns and gunpowder and managed directly by Swahili caravan drivers, who worked with Big Men directing hunting parties of one hundred persons or more driven increasingly north and west of Tsavo to game-rich areas like Baringo in search of rarer elephants—a clear indication that Tsavo's herds were decimated (Little 1996; Steinhart 2000). The first-phase hunters left a good many elephants for the second-phase hunters to kill. But any level of sustained, selective predation is enough to alter the distribution of animal populations, perhaps especially when the animals are as intelligent and as capable of intra-species communication as elephants are.

The thinning out of local elephant populations would have led to important changes in vegetation. Dense forest cover developed in areas with sufficient rainfall and along rivers, and elephant grass and thorn bush developed in drier savannas. Tsetse flies increased in numbers, and with them trypanosomiasis. This, plus the decrease in available forage, had a strongly negative effect on the survival not only of humans but also of the domestic ruminants on which the majority of recent East African societies depend. Increase in bushland would have discouraged pastoralist use of these areas; although cattle-keepers are known to use fire and grazing to maintain high-quality browse growth in many areas, they doubtless depended on similar results from elephant foraging (Lamprey and Waller 1990; Little 1996).

Iron use facilitates the cutting down of trees, but much more importantly, it allows humans to kill elephants, who are major sustainers of tsetse-free grasslands. Numerous other factors, naturally, would also enter into the schistosomiasis-human relationship: local and regional shifts in rainfall quantities and distribution; degree of non-human and human predation on other grazing animals; intensity of swidden cultivation; the deliberate burning of forest and grasslands; non-industrial uses of wood by humans; the availability of tools capable of cutting sod and tilling established grassland; the presence of other effective elephant-killing methods (for instance, through development of effective poisons); and so forth. However, where iron tools were used intensively to hunt elephants, iron may have played an important and even central role in promoting the spread of trypanosomiasis. This may have been far more important, in both environmental and human terms, than changes in plant cover caused by the search for metallurgical fuel.

Living in Tsavo during Troubled Times: The Kisio Rock Shelter Evidence

My second example comes from a small rockshelter called Kisio Rock Shelter, hereafter KRS, located in Tsavo West National Park. My excavations here in 1998 revealed that KRS was inhabited intermittently during the past one thousand years BP. The evidence for human occupation, accumulation, and modification includes the abundance of lithic material, bones, pottery, beads, and iron artifacts. There were several cup-shaped hollows at the site, indicating site use for food processing. The fauna analyzed by Briana Bopiner and the stone artifacts analyzed by David Braun showed KRS residents were hunter-gatherers who neither owned nor used domesticated animals. In this chapter, I only discuss the fauna.

From her analysis, Bopiner concluded that most of the fauna at KRS was introduced by humans. The presence of human-induced bone-surface modifications such as cut marks, percussion marks, and percussion notches, and the presence of many long-bone shaft fragments (n = 39) and the absence of complete long-bone shafts, indicated human processing for marrow extraction (e.g., Blumenschine 1995; Blumenschine and Selvaggio 1988; Marean 1991). The bones at KRS had many limb epiphyses and small, compact bones (n = 78) and exhibited no carnivore tooth marks, suggesting that people were their primary accumulators and modifiers. This contrasted with other evidence from similar rockshelters in East Africa, where carnivores such are porcupines, hyenas, and leopards are known to be the primary bone accumulators (e.g., Blumenschine 1985; Brain 1981; Cavallo and Blumenschine 1989; Hughes 1958; Maguire et al. 1980). Bone accumulators often leave archaeologically visible signatures on specific skeletal-part profiles and bone-surface modifications including a paucity of limb epiphyses and small, compact bones and the presence of tooth marks (e.g., Blumenschine 1985; Capaldo 1995; Marean 1991; Marean and Spencer 1991).

KRS residents' prey included the dik-diks, eland, kudu, impala, alcelaphine, warthog, and zebra. Most interestingly, the large mammals present in the assemblage were juveniles (see table 6.6). Birds, hyrax, terrapin, frogs, chameleons, snakes, elephant shrews, rats, and gerbils constituted a major protein source of KRS people. The cut marks and percussion

TABLE 6.6. Faunal Remains from Kisio Rock Shelter, Tsavo West National Park, Kenya

Species	Common Name	Excavation Level(s) Present
Anas hottentota	Hottentot teal	10–20
Oena capensis	Namaqua dove	0–10
Tockus erythrorhynchus	Red-billed hornbill	0–10, 10–20, 10–25, 20–30, 50–60, 60–70, 70–80
Tockus flavirostris	Yellow-billed hornbill	0–10, 10–20, 10–25, 20–30, 50–60,
Coturnix delegorguei	Harlequin quail	0–10
Aepyceros melampus	Impala	0–10, 10–20, 20–30, 50–60
Syncerus caffer	Buffalo	10–20
cf. *Cephalophus harveyi*	Harvey's red duiker	25–35, 70–80
Madoqua kirkii	Kirk's dik-dik	0–10, 10–20, 10–25, 20–30, 50–60, 60–70, 70–80
Tragelaphus imberbis	Lesser kudu	20–30
Taurotragus oryx	Eland	0–10, 10–20, 35–45
Phacochoerus africanus	Warthog	10–20, 60–70
Heterohyrax brucei	Bush/yellow spotted hyrax	0–10, 10–20, 10–25, 50–60, 60–70
Lepus capensis	Cape hare	0–10, 10–20, 20–30
Elephantulus sp. (*rufescens*?)	Elephant shrew	10–20
Equus burchelli	Burchell's zebra	35–45, 60–70
Homo sapiens	Human	0–10, 20–30, 70–90
Cricetomys gambianus	Giant rat	0–10
Tatera sp.	Naked-soled gerbil	0–10, 10–20, 20–30, 50–60, 70–90
Taterillus emini	Gerbil	0–10
Pelosios broadlyi	Fresh water terrapin	0–10
Varanus exanthematicus	Savannah monitor lizard	0–10, 10–20, 60–70
cf. *Agama agama*	Agama	0–10, 10–20
Eryx colubrinus	Sand boa	0–10, 20–30
Chamaeleo sp.	Chameleon	0–10, 20–30
Rhamphiophis oxyrhynchus	Eastern brown beaked snake	0–10, 10–20, 20–30
Psammophis sp.	Sand snake	35–45, 50–60
Bitis arientans	Puff adder	0–10, 50–60

marks on the bones show that both the meat and marrow of bovids were exploited. All of the bovid species recovered at KRS were from resident animals, indicating that KRS residents were tethered to the area or hunted these animals during specific times of the year that coincided with the birthing season. For example, buffalo and dik-dik have seasonal breeding peaks. The former give birth at the beginning of the wet season and the latter at the beginnings of the wet and dry seasons (Kingdon 1982). This could then be evidence that KRS was a seasonal habitation site, in which the inhabitants were hunting these animals towards the end of the wet season and/or especially the beginning of the dry season and found it relatively easy to attain young dik-diks. Sampson (1998, 1999) speculated from frog and tortoise remains recovered from Late Stone Age and Late Holocene rockshelters that they might have been eaten by humans. Sampson's speculations are bolstered by Mutundu's (1998) ethnohistorical and archaeological study of the Mukogodo people of north-central Kenya, for whom hyraxes were one of the main sources of dietary protein.

The KRS residents obviously relied primarily on plant resources, especially roots and fruits that abound in Tsavo. Sept (1986) found a rich variety of plant species with edible fruits along the Voi River and adjacent alluvial plains. During the long rains, abundant trees and shrubs with larger edible fruits are at relative high densities. Some plants with edible berries are also available well into the long dry season. In addition, invertebrates such as snails can be important seasonal dietary components for hunter-gatherers. Mehlman (1989) reported that copious amounts of giant land snails were harvested, cooked, and dried for consumption during the dry season at Mumba Rockshelter in Tanzania. Seventeen kilograms of land snails recovered from the excavations at KRS suggest that they were also exploited and served as an important dry-season food source.

Environmental Reconstruction

The fauna recovered from KRS provides proxy data for reconstructing the Tsavo environment. Although the fragmentary condition of the bones limits many of the identifications of the mammals only to the family level, nevertheless some patterns in the fauna were discerned. The

TABLE 6.7. Generalized Feeding Strategy and Habitat Preference of Bovids at Kisio Rock Shelter (adapted from Kindgon [1982: 21])

Species	Feeding Strategy	Preferred Habitat(s)
Aepyceros melampus	Mixed feeder	Moist to dry savannahs/ woodlands and thickets
Alcelaphini sp.	Grazer	From moist savannahs and woodlands to valley grasslands to thickets, dry savannahs/ woodlands
Cephalophus harveyi	Folivore/frugivore (browser)	Secondary growth and montane environments (wet areas)
Madoqua kirkii	Folivore/frugivore (browser)	Thickets, dry savannahs/ woodlands
Syncerus caffer	Grazer	Moist savannahs and woodlands to drier grasslands
Taurotragus oryx	Mixed feeder	Thickets, dry savannahs/ woodlands
Tragelaphus imberbis	Folivore/frugivore (browser)	Thickets, dry savannahs/ woodlands

bovid tribes consist of Bovini (*Syncerus caffer*), Tragelaphini (*Taurotragus oryx* and *Tragelaphus imberbis*), Aepycerotini (*Aepyceros melampus*), Neotragini (*Madoqua kirkii*), Alcelaphini (sp. indeterminate), and possibly Cephalophini (cf. *Cephalophus harveyi*). The former four tribes, and especially the species represented, point towards a mixed-vegetation environment with savannah, woodlands, and a significant amount of bushy cover for browsing (table 6.7). For example, the buffalo's "need for water and dense cover, as well as grass, makes them favor mosaics and savannahs with patches of thicket, reeds or forest" (Kingdon 1997:349). The impala is found in similar habitats, generally on the boundaries between grassland and denser woodland, and requires shade, cover, and moisture.

The presence of Burchell's zebra (*Equus burchelli*) also indicates that there was water nearby, since they are very dependent on water (Kingdon 1997). Tragelaphines are woodland browsers and mixed feeders, and the lesser kudu and eland are more reliant upon browsing (Alden et al.

1995; Kingdon 1997). Kirk's dik-dik lives in areas of thornbush interspersed with open glades, browsing foliage, berries, shoots, and fruit (Alden et al. 1995). Alcelaphini are usually interpreted to represent an open grassland/savannah type of environment, but if we consider the present-day fauna inhabiting the bushland of the Tsavo region, there are hartebeest (*Alcelaphus buselaphus*), topi (*Damaliscus lunatus*), and hirola (*Damaliscus hunteri*), which have recently been translocated to Tsavo National Park. These alcelaphines are not migratory animals requiring large tracts of open grassland like the wildebeest (*Connochaetes gnu*) of the Maasai Mara/Serengeti ecosystem, but instead form resident populations and often live in the boundaries between open grassy plains and woodland or scrub or floodplains in otherwise relatively dry regions (Kingdon 1997). The absence of Reduncini is strange, considering that they are usually found in well-watered areas, often along water courses (Alden et al. 1995; Kingdon 1997). The suite of bovids found, as well as warthog (*Phacochoerus africanus*), suggests that there were resident populations of bovids that are mixed feeders and prefer to live in areas of patchy, mixed vegetation with some open areas and some thicker wooded areas—like the present-day vegetation of the Tsavo region.

The bird remains are also helpful in reconstructing the environment during the time of the accumulation of the fauna at KRS. For example, at least thirteen individuals of red-billed and yellow-billed hornbills (*Tockus erythrorhynchus* and *Tockus flavirostris*) were recovered and would have been caught through trapping and hunting (Alden et al. 1995; J. Williams and Arlott 1980). The red-billed and yellow-billed hornbills are common throughout East Africa today, frequenting dry bush country and acacia woodland and foraging on open ground for insects, centipedes, scorpions, fruit, and seeds (J. Williams and Arlott 1980). The Hottentot teal (*Anas hottentota*) is a duck that is also common throughout East Africa on fresh and brackish inland waters with abundant aquatic vegetation (Alden et al. 1995; J. Williams and Arlott 1980). The Harlequin quail (*Coturnix delegorguei*) frequents open grassland and is subject to extensive migrations when it may become extremely abundant locally in grasslands. Today, in seasons of good rains, it is very common on the Athi Plains (J. Williams and Arlott 1980). The Namaqua dove (*Oena capensis*) inhabits arid and semi-arid bush country, acacia stands (especially in sandy areas), and open dry woodland; it forages on the ground for minute seeds (J. Williams and Arlott 1980). In summary, the avian fauna, as well as the large-mammal fauna, implies mixed vegetation: hornbills, Harlequin quail, and Namaqua dove indicate dry scrub or grassland, while the presence of the Hottentot teal in the assemblage indicates that there was definitely some source of water in the near vicinity.

The presence of bush hyrax (*Heterohyrax brucei*) suggests the environment around the rockshelter was wooded. However, the presence of Cape hare (*Lepus capensis*), elephant shrew (*Elephantulus* sp.) and savannah monitor lizard (*Varanus exanthematicus*) suggests that there were definitely areas of drier, open grassy plains or shrub within the vicinity of KRS (Alden et al. 1995; Kingdon 1997). The species of *Tatera* could not be identified, since there are presently three overlapping species in the Tsavo area: *Tatera valida*, *Tatera robusta*, and *Tatera nigricauda* (Mudida, personal communication with Bopiner, 2000). Although the specific habitat of the species cannot be determined, the species of the genus *Tatera* in general inhabit well-drained, sandy areas, while *Taterillus emini* inhabits savannahs and steppe environments (Kingdon 1997).

There were four different species of snake identified from the KRS fauna. The eastern brown beaked snake (*Rhamphiophis oxyrhynchus*) lives in bushveld and is not poisonous to humans. The sand boa (*Eryx colubrinus*) is found in arid areas of East Africa, and the sand snake (*Psammophis* sp.) is found from desert to scrubland, bush, and highveld savannah, to montane grassland; neither of these snakes is poisonous to humans. However, the puff adder (*Bitis arientans*) is very dangerous to humans. It lives in all kinds of habitats except desert and rainforest, so it is not very useful in habitat reconstruction. The former three species all indicate a dry, scrub environment.

There was fresh water in or around the cave during some of the time of deposition of the fauna recovered, since many of the species present are water dependent. These include frogs (which are present in every excavation level), fresh water terrapin (*Pelosios broadlyi*), and Hottentot teal (*Anas hottentota*). It is likely that this water source served as an attraction for the animals that subsequently died there.

In sum, the area around KRS during the time of deposition of the excavated fauna was a mixed habitat of open grassy areas as well as scrub or bushy areas with some type of fresh water, probably a small seasonal pond or swamp nearby, as suggested by the absence of fish, crocodile, or hippo remains.

Conservation Implications of the Kisio Rock Shelter

What are the implications of these two case studies for understanding modern conservation strategies? The most obvious is that people are a natural part of the East African ecosystem and any conservation practices implemented there must take into consideration their role as architects of the grassland, which is more inherently fluctuating than many ecosystems where "balance" can be found (Little 1996). The aim of modern-day wildlife conservation is to preserve an ecosystem with all its dynamic interactions. Unfortunately, African national park conservation is often carried out without consulting or involving local communities. Many communities that used to live in the areas that are now national parks were forced to leave these areas when the parks were established (Eriksen et al. 1996; Musiba and Mabulla 2003; Parker and Amin 1983).

Overexploitation of habitat resources often leads to system collapse. We have pointed out that increased demand for Tsavo's animal resources, especially ivory, spurred hunters to more efficient methods and technologies. The use of iron and, later, guns led to the dwindling of elephant populations that had helped to sustain healthy habitats for people and wildlife. Previously healthy habitats increasingly became less healthy for animals, plants, and people. Oral traditions of Taita describe increasing droughts, famine, disease, and warfare (Merritt 1975). Archaeological data show large-scale regionwide abandonment of settlements. Pastoralism and farming decline and almost cease in plains. Accounts of man-eating lions, cattle rustling, and slave-inspired warfare dominating the landscape abound and tell a tale of a system imbalance (Kusimba 2004; Kusimba et al. 2005).

Nevertheless, crises that now face many national parks in Africa have compelled ecologists and conservationists to begin considering aspects of traditional and contemporary African societies' practices that promote conservation for incorporation into conservation policies (Marks 1976; Ruttan and Mulder 1999). A variety of practices are known to East African pastoralists and foragers that seem conservationist, even if they are not explicitly designed to conserve (E. Smith and Wishnie 2000). Such

TABLE 6.8. Animal Totems among the Bukusu of Kenya and Uganda

Totems	Clan	Reason for Avoidance
Esunu (klipspringer)	Babaasaba	Rescued their warrior while under pursuit by enemies by staying put at a hide-out and taking off when the pursuers arrive, thereby saving their leader
Chicken[1]	Balako, Bakhoma	They were betrayed by a cock while hiding from enemies
Emande (game bird)	Baala	Caused them misfortunes
Eng'enda (meat of a tan cow with brown or dark-colored stripes)	Batecho, Baechalo	Caused them misfortunes
Tan striped cow	Bakipemuli, Babuutu, Batukwiika, Bachemwile	Caused them misfortunes
Antelope meat	Baechalo, Bakhone	Caused them misfortunes

[1] One day they were returning from battle carrying a cock and a bundle of raffia palms when the cock betrayed them. They had hidden in the thorn bushes along the bank of the river Maanafwa when they suspected that their enemies were trailing them. All of a sudden, the cock crowed, revealing their secret hideout and so the enemies fell upon them. A handful of survivors swore never to eat the flesh of the treacherous bird (conversation with Manguliechi, Bukusu Sage, 2006).

practices include hunting taboos around pregnant or nursing wildlife, organization of hunting parties around Big Men (Steinhart 2000), and clan or lineage totems and other taboos, as well as management practices like burning. Such a strategy probably prevents overexploitation, whether this effort is intended or not (see table 6.8). Musonda (1989) reported that the Ila and Tonga of southern Zambia ritually hunted the lechwe at two to three year intervals depending on their population numbers and dynamics. The Bisa of the Luangwa Valley in Zambia only kill prime male adults, a sustainable strategy that does not effect ecologically sensitive members of the population, namely females and young (Prins 1980). In western Zambia, the Lozi participated in an annual communal hunt in which antelopes trapped on islands by rising floods were culled under strict rules (Marks 1976). Hunting large forest animals such as antelopes and boars by the Mongo of the Congo Basin was strictly regulated by cultural traditions (S. Nelson 1994).

Argument surrounds whether such practices are conservationist in their intent or merely in their effects. Small-scale societies' harvesting may seem conservationist merely because of the low off-take rates or low population densities of many of these societies relative to the abundance of game; hence, these practices might more properly be termed sustainable. Nevertheless, E. Smith and Wishnie (2000) argue that conservationist practices in small-scale societies are those that prevent or slow resource depletion and that are designed, either consciously or through long-term interaction with the environment, to be conservationist. This approach wisely considers a variety of cultural practices, both economic, ritual, and so on, that have a designed effect on maintaining resources and biodiversity.

To what extent have these cultural practices been taken into consideration when conservation policies are implemented? Colonial and postcolonial conservation policies and practices prohibit people and animals from occupying the same habitats because they presume that the two cannot coexist (Sheldrick 2000). This assumption is contradicted by the KRS data, which shows that past hunter-gatherer economies ate a wide variety of species, with small mammals, birds, plants, and invertebrates as the major resource base (see fig. 6.2). The most common mammal found at KRS is the dik-dik. Dik-diks are the smallest antelopes found in the Tsavo region today, weighing an average of about 5.3 kg (Kingdon 1997). Dik-diks, along with other small fauna such as hyrax and birds, make up the majority of the biomass exploited by hunter-gatherers at KRS. With a seasonal subsistence strategy that focused on smaller fauna, the inhabitants of KRS likely minimally impacted the overall diversity of the Tsavo ecosystem.

There are various indications of a seasonal occupation for the KRS. The attritional age profile of dik-dik (*Madoqua kirkii*) with a significant percentage of juveniles indicates that KRS inhabitants were hunting small bovids during the dry season. The abundance of edible plants and the availability of fresh water, evidenced by the presence of fresh water terrapin (*Pelosios broadlyi*) and water fowl (*Anas hottentota*), would make the Tsavo region an ideal dry-season refuge for hunter-gatherers when large

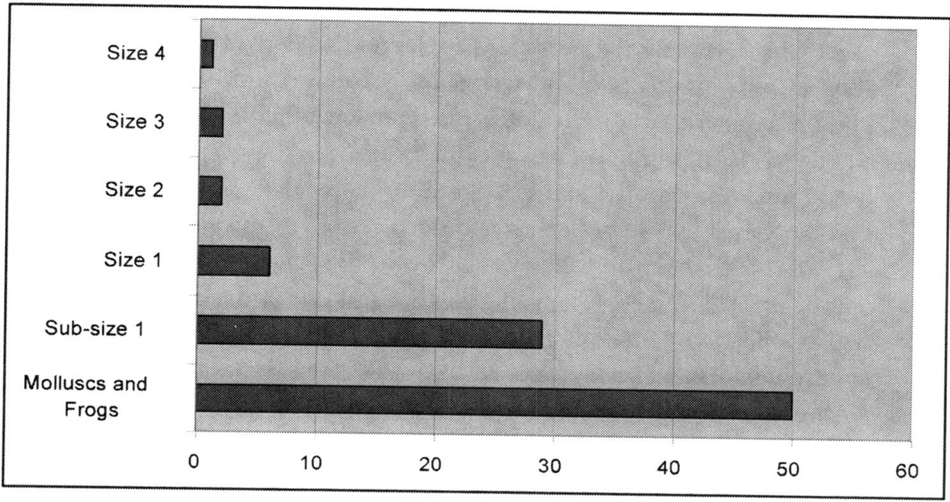

FIGURE 6.2. The Kisio Rock Shelter subsistence base: Emphasis on small fauna. Abundances in MNIs (minimum number of individuals) are shown in the horizontal bars. The MNI of frogs and mollusks are unknov n.

migratory herds disperse from the grasslands. This corresponds with a technology that conforms to previously described seasonal occupations.

This interpretation can inform modern conservation policies, which often exclude indigenous people from decisions regarding national parks under the assumption that the needs of local people are oppositional to the welfare of local wildlife populations. Similar to modern hunter-gatherers, the past inhabitants of the Tsavo area likely had developed sustainable and conservationist practices. I hope that this analysis, combined with examples of past subsistence strategies emphasizing sustainable resource utilization, may lead to a more flexible wildlife conservation policy. By incorporating indigenous knowledge into archaeological interpretations that can be applied to modern-day issues, the interactions between local people and archaeologists can be mutually beneficial.

Conclusion

My primary interest for writing this chapter was to provide a base from which a rapprochement between conservationist and indigenous peoples might begin (D. Anderson and Grove 1987). The future of conservation of African biological and cultural diversity depends on policies and strategies that incorporate the needs of peoples and wildlife (Kenya Wildlife Services 1994–1995; Lewis and Carter 1993; Western and Wright 1994). The predicament faced by wildlife management officials in East Africa highlights the most important crisis that we face in the twenty-first century: preserving cultural and biological diversity. How can people and wildlife coexist and share the same limited resources? More specifically, is it possible to maintain wildlife solely inside the park, and people solely outside parks? Can people and animals coexist if one or the other permeated boundaries? Can conservation of biodiversity occur without community support and participation?

Many studies increasingly show that conservation models developed earlier to protect wildlife from human beings have not been successful (J. Adams and McShane 1996; Akama 1996a, 1996b; D. Anderson and Grove 1987; Beard 1988). In fact, experience shows that models developed by precolonial peoples to coexist with wildlife were presumably superior in many ways to our own (Lewis and Carter 1993; Parker and Amin 1983). Indigenous knowledge fostered respect for animal abilities and led to a deliberate system of harvesting for subsistence and trade while protecting the survival of the herd. The diversity celebrated by Europeans when they first visited Africa was not a result of lack of appropriate firepower to kill wildlife. It was a deeply rooted knowledge developed over millennia of human co-evolution with wildlife. The numerous taboos that Africans have about certain animals and the many stories involving animals tell of the vast knowledge that African people had regarding wildlife. In creating wildlife sanctuaries, the colonial authorities neglected to consult their African subjects to whom they ascribed ignorance in wildlife conservation matters (cf. Sheldrick 2000). The time is ripe for us to develop a rapprochement that will incorporate both folk- and science-based ideas in developing policies that promote sustainability of biological and cultural diversity.

Acknowledgements

My research in Tsavo was supported by grants from the U.S. National Science Foundation (1996–1998, 2001–2003), the National Geographic Society (1996–1998), and the Field Museum of Natural History (1996–present). I would like to thank all the students who participated in the Tsavo research. I am especially grateful to Briana

Bopiner for the excellent analysis of Kisio Rock Shelter fauna. The hospitality of Robert Muasya, Mohamed Kheri, and colleagues at the Kenya Wildlife Services (KWS) Field Station at Manyani enabled us to undertake this research in Tsavo. Dr. David Western's mantra of "Parks beyond Parks," while he served as director of KWS, opened Tsavo National Park to archaeological research. Without the support of Isabella Ochola and John Muhanga at the KWS headquarters and Tsavo East National Park, work in Tsavo would never have taken off. They enabled us to make our first contacts with colleagues in Tsavo National Park. Finally, Joseph Kisio, Jorum Masimba, and Peter Muange took care of our team in the field.

Note

1. At the time of my research (1989–1992), several people on the coast were felling cashew trees in the area in reaction to the falling prices of cashew nuts on the world market. The farmers accused the plant's administration of mismanagement and corruption. It is probable that preference for cashew charcoal does not reflect a historical trend in its exploitation. What it does show is that smiths have shifted their attention to, and experimented with, new trees once they deplete the favored types for charcoal.

7

What Difference Does Environmental Degradation Make?

CHANGE AND ITS SIGNIFICANCE IN TRANSJORDAN

J. Brett Hill

MUCH OF THE LITERATURE on anthropogenic environmental degradation proceeds from the implicit assumption that degradation is a problem. Common usage of the term suggests a decline in utility or desirability of a landscape to living populations. Indeed, current interest in this subject among anthropologists stems in part from concerns about contemporary degradation and its causes and consequences. The concept of degradation, however, is not simple, and assumptions about its significance require closer examination. Whether it is a problem, how much of a problem it is, and to whom it is a problem are questions revealing important qualities of the socionatural connection that is the focus of this book.

What Is Degradation?

To begin, the definition of degradation must be made more explicit. To geologists, who play a critical part in many paleoenvironmental studies, a definition of degradation such as "the general lowering of the surface of the land by erosive processes, especially by removal of material through erosion and transportation by flowing water" (Bates and Jackson 1984:131), does not imply any problem at all. On the contrary, geological degradation is necessary to the development of ecologically important landforms such as floodplains that are valuable to agriculture. In some places, archaeologists have documented erosion intentionally caused for the purpose of enhancing arable lands downslope (e.g., Joyce and Mueller 1992; see also Thurston, this vol.). Such erosion clearly constitutes geological degradation and, without an understanding of its social and economic context, might be misunderstood as a problem, when in reality it had a very different meaning for those who lived with its consequences.

Similarly, the magnitude of problem posed by degradation in the past is a complex question. It is easy to imagine degradation that constituted a decline in utility or desirability of a landscape, but did not pose a very significant problem. Agriculture generally results in declining land productivity, but in many cases, this decline can be managed, for example through fallowing. The idea of degradation as a problem implies a subject who suffers detrimental consequences from it. In the absence of a subject, can degradation be considered a problem? For example, Fisher (this vol.) finds evidence that degradation in central Mexico was exacerbated after population decline and abandonment of agricultural features (see also Naveh and Dan 1973 for the Levant). Thus, it was not population pressure and intensification that led to degradation, but rather population decline and lack of terrace maintenance. This finding raises the interesting question, however: To whom was such degradation a problem? One may reasonably wonder whether native people in the post-Conquest world of population decline and land abandonment considered erosion a significant matter.

In addition to the question of who was present to suffer the consequences of degradation is the more complex question of how it was perceived. Concepts of land degradation and its consequences for human action are culturally mediated and vary in different land-management traditions. Blaikie and Brookfield (1987) discuss land degradation as a perceptual term open to multiple interpretations depending on the use of the land. They focus primarily on the land's economic uses and a combination of natural and anthropogenic processes of degradation and recovery. Emphasizing the concept of capability, their focus is on the use of the land for production and on degradation as a social matter. Van der Leeuw (1998:4–5) echoes this approach to degradation as a relative, socially determined idea and offers the example of Greek farmers who were unconcerned with large-scale erosion, but were upset by the encroachment of trees into their grazing lands. He proposes that there can be no absolute definition of degradation, but that it can be understood in specific, local circumstances. Sahlins (1981) goes further to note that the extent to which land is considered a productive resource depends on the cultural order in place, emphasizing meaning in distinctive structural categories. This focus on perception adds an element of difficulty to archaeological case studies because it is more difficult to know what people thought about their environment in the past.

From a different perspective, environmental degradation may have been problematic but difficult to identify, either by archaeologists or by those whom it affected. In the former case, archaeologists note that often it is difficult to precisely identify ecologically important processes in paleoenvironmental indices (Boardman and Bell 1992). Environmental degradation is often suspected in cases where it is difficult to identify at a scale that would cause obvious hardship. Compounding this difficulty, when processes are identified we often are unable to accurately date them at an appropriate resolution for interpretation (Bintliff 2002). In the southern Levant, disagreements about the chronology of geological deposition may result in disparities on the order of several centuries (e.g., Copeland and Vita-Finzi 1978 vs. Schuldenrein and Clark 1994; Frumkin 1997 vs. Neev and Emery 1995). Such difficulties have obvious implications for interpreting the causes and consequences of environmental change.

On the other hand, we are sometimes able to make persuasive arguments that environmental degradation was problematic in a given time and place, yet it remains unclear if anyone at the time was aware of it. For example, the Neolithic site at 'Ain Ghazal, Jordan, presents a compelling case for deforestation and erosion at a large early village (Rollefson et al. 1992). Nonetheless, the site appears to have been occupied successfully for up to two thousand years, and it is unclear whether anyone living there was aware that the landscape bore little resemblance to that of their ancestors.

How Was Environmental Degradation in the Levant Significant?

The difficulties outlined here can be categorized as 1) questions of identification, in which the timing, magnitude, or nature of degradation is unclear to archaeologists (etic), and 2) questions of perception, in which it is unclear whether any subject perceived a problem (emic). All of the issues raised above reflect on the important question of significance. In the remainder of this discussion, I explore the significance of anthropogenic environmental degradation as it applies to the area of my research on the Transjordan Plateau (see Hill 2006). This region has a long history of human-environment interaction resulting in numerous instances of degradation and modified recovery. A review of its environmental and cultural history reveals several cycles of land use and abandonment dating back to the late Pleistocene.

The title of this chapter is meant to focus attention on a fundamental aspect of the significance question. One important reason archaeologists study environmental degradation is because we think it contributed to change in some aspect of past culture. It precipitated some kind of failure, or modified behavior to compensate for declining productivity. Thus, the type and magnitude of the resulting difference bears directly on its significance and leads us to a better understanding of human-environment interaction as a process.

Differing assumptions about significance have contributed to the variety of conclusions on anthropogenic degradation in the southern Levant. One standard for identifying significant degradation is the transition from the dominance of natural causes to the dominance of human causes. For example, Goldberg and Bar-Yosef (1990) argue that significant degradation did not occur in the southern Levant until at least the Chalcolithic period. Previous degradation was deemed insignificant because it was local in scale, and because more serious environmental degradation probably resulted from climate change. Likewise, other discussions of environmental degradation in the region have focused on evidence for large-scale processes that have shaped the region's current appearance but are not easily attributed to natural causes (e.g., chapters in Bottema et al. 1990; Le Hourou 1981; Naveh and Dan 1973).

The standard of dominance is one means of assessing significance that helps with questions of identification. A common problem in environmental archaeology is discriminating among "multiple and only partially separable" causal factors (van der Leeuw and Redman 2002:600). Often, multiple environmental factors are in flux at any given time, making it difficult to ascertain the cause of degradation. Research is typically framed such that the null hypothesis is one of natural environmental change and anthropogenic causes must be demonstrated as an alternative. Rejecting this hypothesis is achieved by establishing that natural causes cannot sufficiently account for observed degradation, while identifying anthropogenic factors that could. This is a logically sound approach to the problem when considered as a binary choice in which anthropogenic degradation is uncertain but potentially important. However, in human ecology, anthropogenic degradation is neither uncertain nor in binary opposition to natural change. One might, in fact, argue that degradation is a given and that a more valid question is not of choosing between anthropogenic and natural causes but understanding how these are articulated.

For assessing the role of humans in a complex ecosystem, the status of dominance is too strict a standard for determining significance. Anthropogenic degradation might significantly alter ecosystem relations without being more important than global climate fluctuations. Simply because anthropogenic factors are not the dominant factors shaping a landscape does not mean they are insignificant. Significance is a relative term in the context of environmental change. Factors that are insignificant in shaping millennial- and regional-scale environments may be quite significant to the humans and other organisms affected by them in local, seasonal, or annual inter-relations. Furthermore, the standard of dominance tells us nothing about how degradation was perceived, or whether it resulted in any cultural change. Thus, while this standard can help identify instances of anthropogenic degradation, it can neither exclude non-dominant factors as insignificant, nor can it offer any help with questions of perception.

On the other hand, one might argue that virtually any human activity has an environmental impact that may be detrimental to some aspect of the ecosystem on some scale. Too liberal a standard of significance, including very small-scale impacts, would not be useful to researchers interested in understanding the systematics of development and change in human ecology. Given adequate data resolution, anthropogenic environmental degradation might be documented in many cases that would not help distinguish important processes of change.

One of the first conceptual issues to be clarified is the question of significance to whom. The simple answer is significance to humans, but the matter of scale remains unresolved. Do we mean individuals, social groups, or archaeological cultures? In recent decades, anthropologists have emphasized the role of individuals and human agency, and it is undoubtedly important to recognize archaeological processes as a function of individual actions. Individual actions and their effects on the environment, however, are probably too random and too difficult to discern in the archaeological record to be interpreted very meaningfully. To draw inferences about processes of cultural and environmental change, we should document change at the population level. Significant environmental degradation must affect a group of people at least at a supra-family level to be interpreted usefully in terms of human-ecological process.

A second issue relates to the type of degradation considered significant. It is easy to imagine foragers exploiting local resources to a point of diminished return, requiring movement to a new area. The depletion of local resources necessitating relocation would be important to the people who have to seek subsistence in a new territory. Yet, in most cases, such resource depletion would not interest researchers studying environmental degradation for two reasons. The cyclical nature of predator-prey relationships is considered a normal part of ecosystem dynamics. If the depleted resources recover once pressure is removed, the area would once again become a viable territory for them. Furthermore, relocation in many cases would not require a fundamentally different type of subsistence strategy. The basic properties of the population and the ecosystem could presumably remain unchanged.

G. Stone (1993) notes that cultivation almost always degrades agricultural resources and questions why this causes some groups to abandon their farms, while others intensify production to overcome the loss. Both abandonment and intensification are common strategies to deal with degradation. Given land degradation as a constant, interest is directed toward variability among cultural factors that lead to different strategies. The question of significance, however, also requires consideration of how land degradation affects culture change. The significance of anthropogenic environmental degradation is a function of its role in causing changes in the development of cultural practice. People did not always practice agriculture, agricultural intensification, or agrarian abandonment as part of their subsistence strategies. The degree to which anthropogenic degradation influenced those developments is part of the calculation of significance.

Thus, the issue of significance involves the scale of degradation and whom it impacts, as well as the type of change that results. For present purposes, I consider anthropogenic environmental degradation to be archaeologically significant if it affected supra-family social groups in a permanent way and/or resulted in a change in basic economic activity. Interestingly, such a standard potentially locates significant anthropogenic degradation earlier in time than some would have it and renders some later degradation less significant. Early degradation, such as overhunting and deforestation, appears to have resulted in profound economic changes for large numbers of people, including the rise of agriculture and nomadic pastoralism. More recent degradation, such as soil-nutrient depletion and erosion, may occur on a larger scale, but not lead to basic change in economic practice. To the degree that more recent degradation is a part of economic life in the region and is managed through established patterns of mobility and diversification, it may be considered less significant than earlier processes. K. W. Butzer (1996) proposes that the eastern Mediterranean landscape reached a new, degraded equilibrium up to four thousand years ago and that economic practice in the area today is part of a well-adapted system in that new equilibrium.

The concept of transformative change has a long history in archaeology, with contributors too numerous to mention in the space provided here. Early seeds can be seen, for example, in Thomsen's system of archaeological ages, offering support for an evolutionary view of culture change (Trigger 1989:77–79). The importance of this concept is more clearly evident in Childe's (1951) idea of "revolution," in which society is profoundly transformed by a basic change in the relationship between humans and their environment. Focus on cultural transformation is also found in archaeological discussions of systems theory (Flannery 1972) and catastrophe theory (Renfrew 1978). Of notable importance to the socionatural connection are discussions of transformation in terms of collapse and its relationship to environmental degradation (Tainter 1990:33–45; Yoffee 1991).

Related concepts are expressed in anthropological discussions of maladaptation (Rappaport 1978), resistance (Scott 1990:202–227), and practice theory (Sahlins 1981:33–66, 2000). Sahlins's discussion of culture change is particularly relevant to the present thesis, as he argues that transformation occurs when actions that are reproduced historically in one structure, or system of significant relationships, take on new meaning as their context changes in a "structure of conjuncture." Such actions constitute events, significant and distinguishable from everyday actions in that they result in a change in the existing order.

Notions of transformative change are also expressed in evolutionary biology with the theory of punctuated equilibrium (Eldredge and Gould 1972) and in ecology with the development of resilience theory (Holling 1973, 2001), the latter finding expression in recent archaeological application (e.g., Redman et al., this vol.; van der Leeuw, this vol.). In a resilience model, ecological interactions are maintained within a range of variability referred to as an adaptive cycle that has regular phases of change within a relatively fixed set of functional relationships. These cycles may be repeated in a similar manner multiple times, but periodic triggering threshold events can lead to reorganization in which these relationships are fundamentally altered.

The intersection of anthropological and ecological theory occurs in the realm of human ecology, as changes in the human relationship to the environment and economic production effect changes in the way humans are related to each other, and vice versa. In an integrated socionatural system, triggering events may come from within either subsystem or from endogenous developments in human ecological interaction. In either case, the result is systemic transformation in the quality of functional relationships. What concerns us about these transformations, as social and natural scientists, is the difference they make.

Socionatural History in Transjordan

Anthropogenic degradation predates the beginnings of agriculture in the Levant, as overhunting during the Epipaleolithic contributed to the development of broad-spectrum subsistence strategies, sedentism, population growth, and the origins of agriculture (Bar-Yosef and Belfer-Cohen 1989). These early processes establish a baseline for understanding long-term human ecology in the Levant. From the standpoint of agro-pastoralists in this region, anthropogenic environmental degradation has probably always been significant.

The depletion of local resources and the need to mitigate the effects of degradation played an important part in the early development of agriculture and pastoralism in the Neolithic, where there is evidence for overgrazing and pyrotechnology that resulted in erosion and deforestation (Rollefson et al. 1992). The abandonment of many Neolithic sites was probably due in part to drought. Yet, when precipitation returned to high levels during the Chalcolithic, sites were not typically located near previous Neolithic sites, nor were they of a similar type. A settlement pattern of relatively large Neolithic villages in valley-bottom locations was transformed to a more dispersed pattern of small, perhaps seasonally occupied farms and camps located upstream (Hill 2004). This change in settlement type is part of the transition to specialized pastoralism, which is attributed to a need to prevent herds from overgrazing agricultural lands (Levy 1983). The emergence of specialized pastoralism may have had broader environmental impacts in the southern Levant than the larger aggregated settlements of the preceding Neolithic (Fall et al. 1996).

The early Holocene environment of southern Transjordan was more humid, supporting more lush vegetation. Valley-floor morphology was less incised than at present and supported a broad and aggrading floodplain (Donahue 1985). Subsequent erosion and channel incision altered the hydrology and diminished the agricultural productivity in this region. Evidence suggests that early plant cultivation and domestic animal grazing in sensitive terrain contributed to fundamental changes, including economic diversification, the rise of specialized pastoralism, and settlement shifts to more stable areas. Changes such as these in the relationships among people and land resources were significant in that they affected large numbers of people and resulted in permanently altered economic strategies.

The end of the Chalcolithic was marked again by drought, followed by a return to relatively high precipitation during the Early Bronze Age. While climate change undoubtedly contributed to the collapse of Chalcolithic settlement, changing land use in the Bronze Age was affected by other factors as well (Hanbury-Tenison 1986). The transition between these two periods represents an important shift in material culture and settlement patterns (Braun 1989). Many Chalcolithic sites were not reoccupied in the Early Bronze Age (Gophna 1995), suggesting that such locations were unsuitable for settlement even when climatic conditions improved. In Transjordan, valley-bottom areas vulnerable to high rates of erosion were abandoned in favor of more stable upland settlement where intensive land use continues to this day (Hill 2006).

The development of Bronze Age society resulted in expansion of settlement in many areas and the rise of a distinct social and political hierarchy (Richard 1987). Through the Middle and Late Bronze Age, settlement and urbanism became focused primarily in the northern valleys and coastal regions of the Levant (Dever 1987). One important aspect of land use that changed was the role of production for external market demands. Wine and olive production, in particular, affected the Levant at this time and led to regional deforestation and a shift to economic species (Baruch 1990). The rise of urbanism and international market economies was an important change in human ecological relations that had far-reaching implications. The increasing percentage of the population not engaged in agropastoral production not only directly impacted the relationship among people and land resources but also added pressures for intensification and surplus production. Urban settlement and non-local market demand have fluctuated repeatedly over the millennia, but the changes brought about in the Bronze Age have permanently altered the economic lives of people in this region ever since.

The Iron Age saw a substantial increase in settled, aggregated life in Transjordan, as well as attention to defense. Assyrian presence in the region led to political and economic stability, and the demand for regular tribute encouraged a more settled economy to meet it (Bienkowski 1992). Technological changes also affected land use during this period. Camel pastoralism developed in the Levant during the Iron Age, subsequently changing warfare and the ability of nomadic peoples to occupy previously uninhabitable parts of the Arabian Desert (Köhler-Rollefson 1993). Concern for defense and a desire to develop pastorally productive areas away from agriculture zones led to the settlement of high, rocky terrain (Lindner and Knauf 1997).

Despite these developments, the fundamental relationships among people and their land resources do not appear very different in the Iron Age than in the Bronze Age. The greatest difference through the Iron Age and subsequent periods was the degree to which forces of political hierarchy, urbanism, and market demand established in the Bronze Age reached into peripheral areas such as Transjordan. All of these factors fluctuated repeatedly, and technological innovation repeatedly increased the effectiveness of land use. In addition, repeated cycles of political stability and security increased prosperity and population growth, leading to increased demand for agropastoral products. Large numbers of people were routinely affected by these oscillations, but their basic economic practice remained relatively constant.

The Classical Age from the Hellenistic through Byzantine periods represents a millennium of growth in population, economic production, and political complexity throughout the Levant. Following a period of rural, extensive land use and the extraction of agricultural products and raw materials in the Hellenistic period (R. Smith 1990), the Nabatean period marks the rise of the first local, unequivocally state-level polity in Transjordan. While the Nabateans distinguished themselves through their control and development of trade between the East and the Mediterranean, they also oversaw an expansion of settlement, agriculture, and hydraulic technology (P. Hammond 1973:29–30, 72–73). The development of a strong social and political hierarchy, investment in the construction of religious and royal monuments, public works, and defense placed great demands for surplus agricultural production. Settlement-pattern studies indicate avoidance of locations utilized during the Nabatean period and every subsequent period until the modern era (Hill 2004, 2006), suggesting that local environmental degradation diminished the attractiveness of previous settlement locations for reuse.

The Roman period in Transjordan remained a period of intensive settlement focused on agropastoral production, with a substantial commitment of that production to surplus. The support of a large military presence, major public works, and political elites would have continued to be an economic pressure on the land resources of the area. Historical records suggest that this pressure was increased as tax and manpower demands were increased (Graf 1997). The human population and their attitudes toward the landscape were fairly continuous from the Nabatean period, but the imposition of a large foreign power affected settlement location and type, as well as production demands.

The southern Levant in the Byzantine period experienced settlement expansion representing a peak of population and desert agriculture in the area, perhaps attributable to the spread of Christianity, public security, and prosperity (Mayerson 1994). Geomorphic evidence of erosion indicates anthropogenic factors played a substantial role in environmental degradation (Goldberg and Bar-Yosef 1990). Although the relatively large populations and intensive land use of the Classical period would have led to diminished resources, these effects appear to be of a more quantitative than qualitative nature. They undoubtedly resulted in large-scale environmental change and development of an anthropogenic landscape and would thus be considered significant from a geomorphological or biological standpoint. From an anthropological perspective, however, they do not appear to have resulted in profound changes in the relationships between people and the environment.

There was a decline in settlement activity throughout much of the Levant by the Late Byzantine period, and both population and imperial interest in the area began to decrease by this time (Kaegi 1992). During the Early Islamic period, large landowners enhanced their wealth and evaded taxes at the expense of small landowners who were forced to give up their holdings and join protest movements (Shaban 1976:90). Numerous shifts in the locus and interest of political authority throughout the Islamic periods resulted in decline and resurgence of agropastoral settlement in Transjordan (Bosworth 1967). The Mamluk and Ottoman periods were both notable for the renewed expansion of stability and prosperity in the fourteenth through sixteenth centuries, and almost all towns, villages, hamlets, and tribes of Jordan today were established by the sixteenth century AD (Adnanal-Bakhit 1982).

The early Ottoman period was a time of renewed stability and investment in Transjordan, and efforts to provide peace and better protection of peasants resulted in increases in cultivated arable land, population, and urban development (Inalcik 1997). Nomadic peoples were encouraged to settle and extend cultivation during the early Ottoman period. Much of the Ottoman period, however, was typified by a lack of effective centralized authority and domination by local tribes outside the scope of Ottoman control (McGowan 1997).

By the end of the sixteenth century, Jordan was to fall into a state of economic and demographic decline that would last for over 250 years. The causes of this decline included an imbalance between rapid population growth and limited food resources that led to land exhaustion, desertification, and epidemics (Inalcik 1997). Oppressive taxation and the threat of attack led many peasants to leave their villages. Many late-sixteenth-century settlements close to the desert fringe were given up (Hutteroth 1975). It was during the early nineteenth century that European explorers began to penetrate this region and describe it. Harlan

(1985, 1988) uses these accounts to describe a landscape largely depleted of human inhabitants, but rich in natural flora and fauna. Early European accounts typically describe the plateau as rich grassland with large numbers of wild animals and abandoned villages.

Discussion

What we see in this brief culture history is a series of hinge points when change in the basic nature of the relationship between humans and their environment follows a period of relatively fixed human ecological relations. Following a very long period of mobile hunting and gathering, populations in the Levant turned toward domestication economies and village life in the early Holocene. By the Chalcolithic, the secondary-products revolution and specialization of domestication strategies, including nomadic pastoralism, began to lead interdependent groups of people into different lifeways. In the Bronze Age, urbanism, state-level societies, and international relations began to have an effect on land use, security, and demand for agropastoral products. The Iron Age brought local political hierarchy, technological development, and large-scale, international conflict to the region. Throughout a millennium of the Classical Age, advances in technology, engineering, and science were coupled with long periods of peace and stability, leading to a high point in settlement and economic production. The Islamic Age was marked by centuries-long periods of continued advancement and prosperity punctuated by intervals of decline and abandonment as international trade and conflict oscillated throughout the region. The Late Islamic period and modern era have brought the industrial revolution and its effects on weapons, transportation, and agricultural machinery.

Major hinge points appeared with the advent of domestication and economic specialization in the Early Holocene, the rise of regional political complexity and international market economies in the Middle Holocene, and industrial technology in the Late Holocene. Millennia-long periods of relative consistency in the ecology of production have been buffeted by fluctuations in the natural and political climate, yet have remained relatively stable. Then, at a few critical junctures, the nature of human ecological relationships has been transformed in an irreversible way. In the Levant, a limited number of these triggering events, or hinge points, have led to dramatically new adaptive cycles. It has been argued that human impact on the environment has played a role in each of the four major transitions described here.

The origins of domestication are linked to population pressures on a dwindling resource base in the Late Pleistocene and Early Holocene (Bar-Yosef and Belfer-Cohen 1989). The origins of specialized pastoralism are linked to overgrazing and soil erosion near agricultural settlements, necessitating the separation of key aspects of production and new modes of mobility (Levy 1983). The rise of urbanism and political complexity are linked to anthropogenic degradation and environmental circumscription of aggregated communities (Dickson 1987). These social and economic changes have in turn led to the rise of market economies, elite non-producers, and the further separation of production from consumption (Fall et al. 1996). Finally, the industrial age has contributed to overhunting of wild animals (Jabbur 1995:357–374), deforestation (Pick 1990), and cultivation of previously non-arable lands (personal observation).

Directing our focus back to the problem of how people perceive environmental degradation, change in the functional relationships between humans and their natural environment affects both the material structures of economic production and the structures of meaning imposed by various cultural orders. Altering one aspect of these relationships brings actors into uncharacteristic conditions of conflict and contradiction with traditional structures in another aspect of their relationships, creating structures of conjunction and resulting in transformation. The result is that a cultural structure that was reproduced through time in one system of functionally significant relationships is pushed into a fundamentally new set of relationships. Thus, altering the ways in which people interact with their natural environment provides new and unanticipated meaning to common actions and familiar social frameworks. Novel opportunities are created, while established capabilities become restricted, and the expected, or "natural," order fails to reproduce itself in a predictable way. The perception may be one of either revolution or collapse, and will likely depend on one's relation to the previous order. The lesson from archaeology suggests that the production of different orders is irreversible, as each new set of relationships forever precludes a return to the former state. The significance of such change lies in the degree to which things are different and will never be the same.

Part III

New Answers to Old Questions

8

The Earliest Residents of Cyprus

ECOLOGICAL PARIAHS OR HARMONIOUS SETTLERS?

Alan H. Simmons

ISLANDS ARE OFTEN thought of as idyllic paradises, refuges for humans in search of peace and tranquility. While such stereotypes usually escape archaeological discussions of island society, islands frequently are portrayed as ideal laboratories, isolated from outside influences. This makes them exceptional locations from which to examine the effects of humans on pristine environments. Much current island research, however, is veering away from the isolationist perspective, as more and more researchers are now examining the connections between mainlands and islands as appropriate avenues of research. Nonetheless, islands continue to tell us much about how people can impact undisturbed habitats. Many of the Mediterranean islands have played a major role in scholars' interpretations of the unique relationships between humans and insular environments, and nowhere has this been more significant than in the early occupation and colonization of these places. In this contribution, I examine evidence relating to what ecological impacts the first occupants of the eastern Mediterranean island of Cyprus may have had.

The Mediterranean islands produced some of the most sophisticated ancient cultures in the world, and yet we know relatively little about their early prehistory. Explicit anthropological approaches to the processes and consequences of their colonization are relatively recent developments (Patton 1996). The traditional view is that the islands were late recipients of Neolithic colonists who imported complete Neolithic packages but left few material linkages to their homelands. As such, many researchers have considered at least implicitly that the Neolithic on the islands were isolated and quickly developed unique insular characteristics

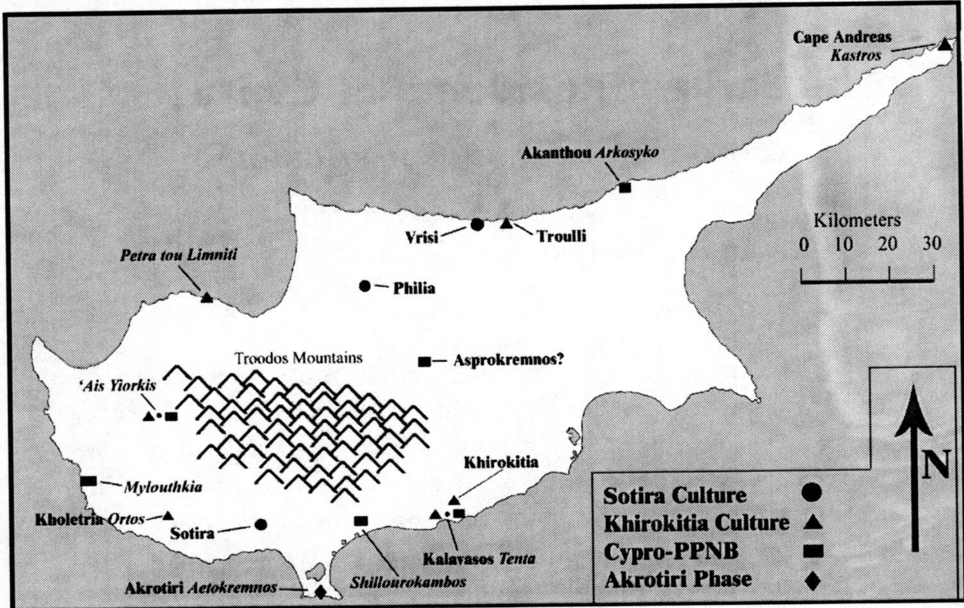

FIGURE 8.1. Cyprus, showing the location of some of the sites discussed in the text. (From Simmons 2007: fig. 9.1).

that had little to do with major developments occurring on the mainland. Recent studies, however, indicate that this was a far more complex scenario.

Exciting new research on Cyprus (fig. 8.1) is challenging traditional paradigms about when, how, and why the Neolithic spread and has brought the island to the forefront of contemporary Near Eastern research (Guilaine and LeBrun 2003; Peltenburg and Wasse 2004; Simmons 2007: 229–263, chapter 9 and Simmons 2008; Swiny 2001). Many of these new studies are still filling in crucial archaeological and chronological baseline data, and thus have not yet adequately addressed the relationship between these early people and their environments. This chapter examines suggested ecological aspects of this new research from two perspectives. First, I summarize how the initial human occupants of Cyprus had a dramatic ecological impact, in spite of only a limited occupation. Then, during the island's actual colonization during the Neolithic, and contrary to expectations, I summarize how impacts may have been relatively limited.

Akrotiri *Aetokremnos* and the Pre-Neolithic of Cyprus

The first human visitors to Cyprus, as reflected by the Akrotiri phase that is well documented thus far only at Akrotiri *Aetokremnos* (Simmons 1999), were either a late Epipaleolithic (roughly Natufian equivalent) or early Pre-Pottery Neolithic occupation. Akrotiri *Aetokremnos* assumes considerable importance because for many years claims for pre-Neolithic human occupation of many of the Mediterranean islands, including Cyprus, generally were unsubstantiated. While there are Epipaleolithic occurrences on some Aegean islands, these are relatively late. Furthermore, these islands are in proximity to the mainland (Broodbank 2000:110–117; Cherry 1990, 1992; Patton 1996:66–72; Simmons 1999:14–27). Despite the lack of evidence for true Paleolithic occupations, however, some scholars have suggested that low-visibility "para-Neolithic" or "proto-Neolithic" phases might exist, at least for Cyprus (Held 1989a:8; Watkins 1981:139), a claim that has proven prescient.

Akrotiri *Aetokremnos* challenged the traditional view, being securely dated to over 10,000 cal BC. Not only is it the oldest site on Cyprus, but more controversially, it is associated with a huge assemblage (over 500 MNI) of the endemic, and quite extinct, pygmy hippopotamus (*Phanourios minutus*), as well as smaller numbers of dwarf elephants (*Elephas cypriotes* Bate). We have argued that humans were instrumental in finalizing the extinction of these unique animals. Although the occupation of Akrotiri *Aetokremnos* apparently only lasted a few hundred years, and likely reflected only a small human population, these people had a dramatic impact by eradicating the uniquely island-adapted "mini megafauna" on the island. We have modeled that a small group of humans could have, within a relatively short period, been the trigger to extinction for remnant hippopotamus populations that may have already been suffering ecological stress due to climatic change associated with the Younger Dryas, and thus were already on the verge of extinction. Akrotiri *Aetokremnos* is a controversial site, and our interpretation, especially that of the association of cultural materials and pygmy hippopotami, is not universally embraced (e.g., Ammerman and Noller 2005; L. Binford 2000; Bunimovitz and Barkai 1996; Davis 2003:258–259). However, when all aspects of the site are examined, the most parsimonious explanation is cultural, as I have argued in detail elsewhere (Simmons 1999, 2001, 2002, 2004; Simmons and Mandel 2007).

In any event, Akrotiri *Aetokremnos* is significant for several reasons. First, it firmly establishes an eleventh millennium BC human presence in Cyprus, making it one of the earliest occupied Mediterranean islands. Even the site's critics do not question this fact. Second, it has ramifications for how islands are initially used. In this context, Cherry (1981:45–64, 1990:198–199) makes an important distinction between actual colonization of an island, resulting in permanent settlement and potential founder populations, and mere utilization of an island's resources on a temporary or seasonal basis. Third, Akrotiri *Aetokremnos* is one of the very few sites anywhere dating to the Pleistocene/Holocene boundary that shows a relationship between extinct megafauna and humans. While we know that humans have rapidly induced extinctions on islands in relatively recent times (e.g., A. Anderson 1991; Steadman 1995), Akrotiri *Aetokremnos* projects this back ten thousand years and thus causes us to revisit the controversial role of humans in Late Pleistocene extinction episodes (Martin and Klein 1984). Finally, Akrotiri *Aetokremnos* challenges research paradigms that exist on many Mediterranean islands on the nature of archaeological data. These relate to ideas that the islands were too impoverished to have supported hunter-gatherer populations and to the recognition of small nonarchitectural sites in the archaeological record (Simmons 1991, 1998a).

Within the context of this chapter, what is important is that the first human visitors to Cyprus apparently had a catastrophic impact on surviving endemic fauna. It is difficult, however, to generalize from a site as unique as Akrotiri *Aetokremnos* to a broader perspective of the ecological impacts of pre-Neolithic peoples on the limited resources available on Cyprus. Certainly, conventional wisdom is that hunter-gatherers generally have an overall low ecological impact, but where does Cyprus fit within this scenario based on present knowledge? A problem, of course, is in documenting additional pre-Neolithic sites. While there have been some claims (e.g., Ammerman et al. 2006; Ammerman and Noller 2005), these have not yet been verified with supporting data, especially relating to absolute chronology. If, however, for the moment, one accepts these

FIGURE 8.2. Overview of Akrotiri *Aetokremnos.*

as additional early sites, can they inform us on the relationship between hunter-gatherers and the Cypriot environment?

Based on the very limited published data available, the sites that Ammerman and colleagues claim are pre-Neolithic are small lithic scatters along coastal areas. These do not appear to represent substantial occupations, and even the authors refer to them as the remains of "tourists" (Ammerman and Noller 2005:541). They likely represented small groups of people making short visits to the island. Thus far, there is little if any evidence that they penetrated into the island's interior, although there is some emerging data indicating this did occur either before the Neolithic or very early into it (e.g., Pre-Pottery Neolithic A?) (McCartney 2004, 2005). Again, however, it is premature to rely too heavily on these data, although absolute dates just becoming available tend to support this placement. The point is that even if these can be confirmed as early sites, they are ephemeral, consisting primarily of chipped stone with limited amounts of fauna or features. There is little evidence suggesting a substantial built environment, and population levels likely were quite low. Thus, it seems unlikely that these early visitors to the island had much of an ecological impact.

Akrotiri *Aetokremnos*, however, is a very different type of site. It is a collapsed rockshelter overlooking the Mediterranean Sea (fig. 8.2). It also is located on the Akrotiri Peninsula, an area with limited resources. Assuming that our interpretation of the association of cultural materials and hippopotami is correct, this site represents a considerable investment in the exploitation of a species that may already have been weakened and near extinction. Akrotiri *Aetokremnos* likely was occupied over a span of a few hundred years (Wigand and Simmons 1999:209). We make no claims for sedentism of any sort, nor do we feel that this site necessarily reflects a sizeable human population. More likely, Akrotiri *Aetokremnos* was seasonally visited, with a focus on exploiting a valuable source of protein. Through this occupation, we see a stratigraphic change from an emphasis on pygmy hippopotamus (and to a lesser extent, dwarf elephant) towards avian fauna and marine shell towards the end of the occupation. We have proposed that this shift represents a demise of the terrestrial fauna, at least partially induced by overhunting. For whatever reason humans were on Cyprus during this time, they seem to have had a devastating effect on the island's remaining mammalian fauna. What happened to these people is problematic. We initially suggested that they probably left Cyrus (Simmons 1999:322), but given new developments in the early Neolithic period of the island, there is stronger evidence to argue for occupational continuity. We can now turn to some of this new evidence.

The Neolithic in Cyprus: Trouble in Paradise?

I would like to fast forward to a few thousand years past the Akrotiri phase to the Neolithic. The Near Eastern Neolithic was, of course, a tumultuous time of dramatic economic, social, and ecological change (Simmons 2007). Until recently, conventional wisdom was that the first Neolithic occupation, and the actual permanent colonization, of Cyprus, and other Mediterranean islands, was relatively late in the Pre-Pottery Neolithic sequence (ca. cal 7,000 BC), as reflected locally by the Khirokitia Culture (LeBrun et al. 1987). The Khirokitia Culture demonstrated few material links to mainland Neolithic cultures, and often was characterized as relatively nondescript, if not downright insignificant in the broader Neolithic world. In other words, it fit the typical stereotype of the Mediterranean island Neolithic. Now, however, an earlier Pre-Pottery Neolithic occupation has been documented at a handful of sites. This, the Cypro-PPNB

(Peltenburg et al. 2000, 2001), shows some material similarities to the Levantine Pre-Pottery Neolithic B (or "PPNB"), primarily in chipped-stone technology. Its earliest dates are around 8,400 cal BC, which places it relatively early in even the mainland sequence and shortens the gap between the Neolithic and the Akrotiri phase.

Even before the Cypro-PPNB was documented, we had known for quite some time that there was variation of site types during the Cypriot Aceramic Neolithic. These tended to be dichotomized into two principal types: large "core" villages, such as Khirokitia and Kalavasos *Tenta*, and smaller peripheral villages or hamlets, such as *Petra tou Liminiti* and Cape Andreas *Kastros*. The new research, however, indicates that this dichotomy is too simple, with investigations at Cypro-PPNB sites that are not typical villages, such as *Shillourokambos* (Guilaine 2003), *Mylouthkia* (Peltenburg 2003a), *Ais Yiorkis* (Simmons 1998b, 2003), and *Akantou* (Sevketoglu 2002). Both *Mylouthkia* and *Shillourokambos* contain deep wells in addition to other features (especially at the latter). In addition, Kalavasos *Tenta* (a principal Khirokitia Culture site) now also likely has a Cypro-PPNB component (Todd 2003). And, as noted earlier, a few other sites, all in the central portion of the island and as of yet unexcavated, also show chipped stone similarities to the Cypro-PPNB, or possibly earlier phases (McCartney 2004, 2005). It seems likely that additional systematic survey will record even more of these early sites.

Ais Yiorkis is especially important since it is located in the uplands, whereas most known Neolithic sites are much closer to the coast (with the exception of those just noted). Although originally recorded as a small hunting site or hamlet (Fox 1987), excavation has shown it to be more than an ephemeral settlement. This is based primarily on the presence of a previously undocumented type of architectural feature for the Cypriot Neolithic: large circular plaster and stone platforms (fig. 8.3), as well as deep pits. Radiocarbon dates indicate an occupation during the mid–Cypro-PPNB and possibly into the early Khirokitia Culture. A large chipped-stone assemblage is similar to other Cypro-PPNB materials. Economically, *Ais Yiorkis* is intriguing. It contains some of the earliest directly dated domesticates in the Near East in the form of emmer and einkorn wheat. Of note is that very early domesticated plants also were recovered from *Mylouthkia*, and wild forms from *Shillourokambos*. While the paleobotanical data from *Ais Yiorkis* are of considerable significance,

FIGURE 8.3. Circular platform structure at *Ais Yiorkis.* (From Simmons 2007: fig. 9.4).

the amount of faunal remains (primarily sheep/goat, pig, and deer) is overwhelming and may suggest that animal husbandry was more important than farming at this upland locality. Furthermore, the association of fauna with exotic artifacts (e.g., imported obsidian, large ground-stone vessels, and ornaments) may be indicative of feasting activities.

Conventional wisdom was that the Neolithic settlers of Cyprus had a relatively simple economic system, arriving on the island with few resources. These early colonists introduced domesticated plants and domesticated sheep, goat, and pig, as well as wild deer for hunting (although see Horwitz et al. 2004 for an alternate interpretation, proposing that these animals were in fact imported wild, since morphological evidence for domesticated mainland counterparts are rare). Now, however, with the documentation of domestic plants that are roughly as early as those on the mainland, there is evidence for increasingly complex economic strategies during the Cypriot Neolithic. Adding to this is the presence of an animal that had been conspicuously absent from the Neolithic economic suite: cattle. It was widely believed that cattle were not imported to the island before the Bronze Age (Croft 1991:63; Knapp et al. 1994:418). At *Shillourokambos*, however, limited amounts of cattle are documented during the Cypro-PPNB, and *Ais Yiorkis* has collaborated this evidence. Since the site may extend into the Khirokitia Culture, cattle were possibly also used into the early part of that period. *Akantou* also has cattle (Frame 2002), although the chronological association is yet to be confirmed. Likely these animals were domesticated, although this has yet to be conclusively demonstrated.

The significance of cattle is not yet known. At *Akantou Shillourokambos* and *Ais Yiorkis*, these animals are represented thus far only in relatively small numbers. Certainly their importation to Cyprus may have been for economic reasons, but given the documented ritual association of cattle with many mainland sites (e.g., Cauvin 2000), we also cannot rule out some sort of symbolic significance as well. Perhaps the earliest colonizers of Cyprus may not have wished to entirely sever their mainland identities. Cattle could have been one ritual element, which also had economic benefits, that was imported to ensure symbolic ties with the homeland. It appears that their unique island identity was established by the Khirokitia Culture, and thus there was no need to retain cows as a material symbol of a ritual world. Such scenarios, of course, are speculative, and at this point, the role of cattle cannot be adequately evaluated in Cyprus.

Discussion

What are the implications of this new research? Broadly speaking, there are several. First, we now know that Cyprus was occupied prior to the Neolithic. Second, Neolithic peoples arrived on the island much earlier than suspected, thereby shortening the chronological gap between them and the Akrotiri phase by at least one thousand years. In fact, these new studies stimulate conjecture that the island may not have been abandoned after the Akrotiri phase. Third, this research is unfolding a story of an economically sophisticated Neolithic adaptation. We have learned that not all early settlements were restricted to the coastal areas of Cyprus, nor were they all villages in the traditional sense. Furthermore, the addition of cattle to the economic larder during the Cypro-PPNB, and their apparent subsequent disappearance before or during the Khirokitia Culture, is curious. Within the context of this volume, these new studies have significance in that they suggest ecological impacts, or lack thereof, that might not be readily apparent.

Given that the Neolithic was at least one thousand years older than previously believed, and that both animal husbandry and farming were the economic mainstays on a small island with few natural resources, we might reasonably expect to see an acceleration of human impacts during the Cypriot Neolithic. Curiously, however, evidence to date indicates that these Neolithic colonizers of Cyprus did not have a dramatic impact on the environment, either during the Cypro-PPNB or the Khirokitia Culture. Indeed, there really is not too much documentation of culturally induced environmental deterioration until the Chalcolithic (cf. Croft 1988; Peltenburg 2003b:261; Peltenburg et al. 1998a:241, 1998b:354–356).

This is somewhat of a surprise and contrasts with the mainland, where severe ecological impacts dramatically accelerated during the Neolithic. While climatic changes may have been partially responsible, many feel that humans were much more active agents in bringing this about (see, e.g., discussion in Simmons 2007:chap. 7). Some of our best data for such a human role in ecological degradation come from the "mega-sites" of Wadi Shu'eib and, especially, 'Ain Ghazal in Jordan. While farming and herding may initially have been compatible and complementary economic strategies that allowed for the expansion of these communities, continued growth and environmental mismanagement led to reduction of crop yields. This occurred at a time when populations were expanding and required more and more food. Thus, whereas the PPNB residents of these large communities had a remarkably varied subsistence base consisting of both domesticates and wild resources, there was a dramatic decrease in the number of species exploited from the PPNB into the Pottery Neolithic. Notable is that while the range of faunal resources was broad, the focus was on goats, a species so notoriously detrimental to vegetation that it has been referred to as "the Black Plague of the Near East" (Rollefson 1996:223). By the late Neolithic, there was a dramatic decrease in the number of species exploited. Goats continued in importance, but woodland and parkland species were absent, supporting the argument that such environments were no longer present, having been cleared for either fields or timber (Rollefson 1996:223–224; Simmons et al. 1988:37–38).

Additional evidence for environmental deterioration comes from architecture, where Rollefson has argued that the smaller size of postholes, or their complete absence, indicates that wood resources were becoming sparse. Furthermore, the nearly insatiable quest for lime plaster, so common in the PPNB, undoubtedly contributed to local degeneration, since lime has to be burned to form plaster. Indeed, late in the occupation of 'Ain Ghazal, the plaster is of a much inferior quality, supporting the argument that fuel was becoming scarce (Rollefson 1996:223; Rollefson and Köhler-Rollefson 1989:76–82).

Ultimately, these people essentially ate themselves out of their environments. A series of culturally induced environmental missteps, possibly coupled with increasingly deteriorated climatic conditions, contributed to the ultimate abandonment of these large communities, and likely was the beginning of the classic Near Eastern economic dichotomy between "the desert and the sown" (Köhler-Rollefson 1988; Köhler-Rollefson and Rollefson 1990; Rollefson 1992, 1996; Rollefson and Köhler-Rollefson 1989; Simmons 2000; Simmons et al. 1988).

Thus, there is considerable evidence that mainland Neolithic peoples had a dramatic environmental impact, some aspects of which are still being felt today. Why, then, did the Neolithic occupants of Cyprus apparently have such limited ecological degradation during the Cypriot Neolithic as opposed to the mainland? Although baseline data are still being established for the Cypro-PPNB, what we do know indicates that their sites were relatively small and that animal husbandry may have been more important than farming activities. If true, this could have avoided competing land-use strategies and minimized ecological impacts. I make this statement with some hesitation, however, since most evidence of the early Neolithic occupants of Cyprus points to a mixed economy in which farming was significant (Peltenburg 2003a:83–103). We simply do not know yet if agriculture was supplemental to animal husbandry or if both strategies were equally important. Perhaps, however, herds, although they often included goats, were properly managed to avoid the type of overgrazing so common in much of the mainland. Additionally, population levels may have been sufficiently low to minimize impacts, especially if agriculture was supplementary.

Such conclusions, however, must be made cautiously, since thus far in Cyprus, large-scale investigations attempting to determine human ecological impacts are relatively rare, especially for the prehistoric periods. Studies such as Atherden's (2000) in Crete, looking at human impacts in both lowland and upland grazing areas, are badly needed in Cyprus. *Ais Yiorkis* could be significant in similar studies, since Atherden's (2000:66) work suggests that upland sites may reflect the clearest evidence of the effects of grazing and browsing on local vegetation. What is clear is that *Ais Yiorkis*, as an upland Neolithic settlement, and *Shillourokambos*, *Mylouthkia*, and *Akantou*, all near the coast, contribute to a more balanced understanding of the overall diversity of settlement systems practiced by Neolithic peoples on the Mediterranean islands.

Another pattern that is emerging is that during the Cypro-PPNB, sites were quite distinct from one another. While they may represent small villages or hamlets of some sort, they are quite dissimilar one from the other. For example, *Mylouthkia* contains deep wells, *Shillourokambos* has features cut into the bedrock in addition to wells, *Akantou* has substantial open-air plastered surfaces as well as structures of some sort, *Tenta* also may have features cut into natural deposits, and *Ais Yiorkis* is located in the uplands, as opposed to the other sites. It also has unusual architectural features. Thus, these early Neolithic people apparently had not yet established a well-defined and consistent settlement type. Likely, their population levels were relatively low as well. Could these have been variables in their apparent lack of ecological impact?

But even if the Cypro-PPNB occupation of the island was relatively limited, why is there so little evidence for accelerated impacts during the subsequent Khirokitia Culture, when large and substantial villages are documented? Indeed, Khirokitia itself is one of the largest Neolithic sites in the Near East, and the decline of pigs and deer and increase of pine there could indicate local anthropogenic degradation (Davis 2003:263; Renault-Miskovsky 1989). This, however, appears localized, and on the island as a whole, there is limited evidence for such impacts. With the exception of Khirokitia and Kalavasos *Tenta*, most Khirokitia Culture sites are relatively small, and we do not see a great density of site clusters. Population growth on Cyprus, and the associated built environment in terms of settlements, fields, grazing areas, and land clearing, simply may still have been sufficiently low to avoid the ecological havoc witnessed on the mainland.

Certainly the earliest occupants of Cyprus, as reflected by Akrotiri *Aetokremnos*, had a more dramatic impact. Even if population levels were low, it appears that humans helped drive the endemic fauna to extinction. As populations grew in post-Neolithic times, the consequences of agriculture and animal husbandry also took their toll, particularly as Cyprus became increasingly important in copper production and its associated environmental impacts. By practicing diverse economic strategies and keeping populations low, however, Neolithic peoples on Cyprus may have been offered a respite from the ecological deterioration seen in both earlier and later periods. As such, we should not automatically assume that Neolithic economies and culturally induced environmental deterioration are linked in any simple cause-and-effect fashion.

There clearly was a lot going on throughout the Near East during the early Neolithic, and new evidence indicates continual and systematic contact with Cyprus, and perhaps other islands. There is no longer reason to believe in one vast Neolithic colonization attempt, and the concept of multiple "pioneer colonizers" (Perlès 2001:62) seems a much more likely scenario. It now is clear that the Cypriot Neolithic was a participant in a wider Neolithic interaction sphere (Peltenburg 2004). Despite this, however, the Neolithic residents of Cyprus apparently managed to live in harmony with their fragile island ecology.

Conclusion

How does the Cyprus example contribute to the theme of this volume, with its focus on what the editors call "socionatural archaeology"? In the introduction, they note that the root causes that underlie environmental issues involve long-term and complex interactions between humans and ecological processes. To fully examine these socionatural connections, scholars must account for human decisions, environmental change, and unintended consequences, and do so from multiple timescales. To my way of thinking, the latter variable, one of unintended consequences, is perhaps the most interesting and difficult to decipher. Indeed, as the editors note, Jared Diamond's (2005) coining of the phrase "ecocide" involves unintentional episodes of ecological havoc.

Within the timeframe of generational lifetimes, I doubt that those Neolithic people living at settlements such as 'Ain Ghazal directly realized that the ecological deterioration that they were living through was a direct result of their agro-pastoral activities as well as possibly shifting climatic conditions. They likely, however, had the realization that something was going horribly wrong over time; whether or not they linked this to their manipulation of the landscape may never be known, lacking written records. Thus, even though they had substantially altered the environment through time, much of this may have been unintentional, despite the accelerated need to use more and more natural resources to supply the needs of expanding populations.

In Cyprus, however, a different scenario emerged. Scholars now generally agree that there is no direct causal link between population growth and land depletion. Certainly those responsible for Akrotiri *Aetokremnos* probably had low population levels and a minimal built environment, and yet they likely were a major factor in the extinction of endemic mammalian fauna. Again, I doubt that during individual lifespans they realized that they were doing this. Ultimately, though, these resources were depleted, and alternate economic strategies had to be sought. Whether this involved returning to their mainland homes or staying on the island, however, is an issue beyond the scope of this chapter. What is important is that these people with a limited material "footprint" had a dramatic ecological impact.

But what about the Neolithic? Cypriot Neolithic populations likely continued to be relatively low and widely spread over the landscape, and this probably contributed to their lack of severe impacts. That these people were living on an island, with its constrained boundaries and limited resources, may also have been a factor enhancing ecological restraint. Was this perhaps an intentional form of conservation, rather than an unintended consequence of agro-pastoralism gone rampant? We likely never will know. The point of these contrasting case studies is that the interplay between humans and their environments is complex and should never be taken for granted based on presumed increased impact with more sophisticated economic strategies.

From a broader perspective, a prevailing theme throughout this volume is, "How can we link archaeological research to present land use and can our research be meaningful to scholars from other disciplines?" I think that the Cypriot case studies, as well as others presented in this volume, indicate this can be answered in the affirmative.

Although it is always a bit dangerous to link archaeological studies, especially those conducted in "deep time," to modern situations, it is clear that humans have been impacting the environment for quite some time. This certainly is not a profound observation, but we are able to demonstrate that simplistic one-to-one models, for example showing that hunting and gathering has limited ecological impact and that agriculture automatically ensures dramatic impacts, simply do not work. It certainly appears that the early Neolithic residents of Cyprus had relatively little impact, even though they must have had higher populations that those reflected by the Akrotiri *Aetokremnos* hippopotamus hunters.

We need to be cautious, however, any time that modern land-use planners turn to archaeologists for assistance. Archaeological examples must be considered from a case-by-case perspective. As just one example of the need for caution, there was considerable controversy and alternate perspectives when, in Central America, there was talk of returning to pre-Hispanic agricultural practices since these were presumed to have fewer ecological consequences. O'Hara et al. (1993), however, indicated that pre-Hispanic practices may have been more detrimental to the environment, although this conclusion was hotly contested (Fisher et al. 2003; Fisher, this vol.).

Finally, is this type of research useful to other scholars? Again, the answer to this should be a clear and unqualified yes. Archaeology offers time-depth and the ability to see long-term vs. short-term consequences. We have the benefit of long-term and shifting timescales. It also is clear that modern archaeology cannot exist without the interdisciplinary input of scholars from other disciplines. In order to understand fully the degree and nature of previous human impacts on the environment, we need the direct help of a variety of other fields. Likewise, disciplines addressing contemporary conservation issues can learn a great deal from archaeology. Combined, these perspectives offer powerful explanatory potential for understanding both past and future impacts that humans have inflicted upon the landscape.

9

Social Changes Triggered by the Younger Dryas and the Early Holocene Climatic Fluctuations in the Near East

O. Bar-Yosef

Chronological Correlation Is Not Causation

Near Eastern archaeologists and historians are generally reluctant to accept that climatic changes as expressed in environmental degradation or rapid improvement affected prehistoric and historic societies, for two reasons. First, these scholars claim, changes may emanate from intra- and inter-society political pressures, conflicts and wars, rapid population growth, technological innovations, and the like. Each of these, or a combination of several factors, may drive changes expressed in settlement patterns and social structures. Second, given the degree of chronological resolution for currently available radiometric techniques, those opposed to what is known in common jargon as "climatic determinism" point out that "time correlations between proxy paleo-climatic data and the dated events in recorded human history do not necessarily indicate causation." True. Demonstrating a general chronological contemporaneity between cultural shifts and changing paleoecological conditions as reflected in marine and terrestrial pollen cores or interpreted from other sources, such as cave speleothems, lake-level fluctuations, tree rings, alluvial sequences, and the like, is insufficient as an explanatory model for the observed archaeological phenomena. Two major components or informative steps in building models are missing from a host of current interpretations.

1. How did various human populations react to diverse conditions, either worsening or improving them (e.g., droughts versus increasing precipitation in Mediterranean lands)?

2. How can we be certain that the fluctuations as recorded in proxy paleo-climatic sequences impacted human societies?

We must respond soundly to these questions when we propose that, based on proxy climatic data, we consider societies, whether prehistoric or historic, to have been affected. For a substantive answer to the first question, we need the information concerning the social structure of a given society, its degree of resilience to face environmental challenges, and its history of past reactions to climatic fluctuations. Only then can we test whether there is a fit or none at all between the dated environmental and cultural changes. The second question involves bridging the dated paleo-climatic information and the dated archaeological sequences. The best positive correlation would be achieved by uncovering from the excavated sites the indicators of climatic fluctuations and their impact on human behavior. Each of these issues is discussed in the following pages and illustrated by my proposed interpretations of the role of climate change in the Near East, mainly focusing on the Younger Dryas (YD) and the 8,200 cal BP event (fig. 9.1).

The Cultural Filter

In studying human variable responses to changes in their environments, scholars often address natural disasters such as droughts and famines. An important source of information is derived from relief programs, which are forced to identify specific interactions between a society and its environment. Some reactions are common across the human spectrum, while others particularly express the individual character of the affected human group. In each case, anthropologists discovered that the social reactions resulted from previously held beliefs, social structure and organization, and the interaction with neighboring societies. The most generalized responses to environmental disasters or improvements are the consequences of the following societal capacities (e.g., Copans 1983; Glantz 1987; Glantz et al. 1998; Hewitt 1983; Hoffman and Oliver-Smith 2002):

1. The human control or intervention in the so-called "natural environment" that has changed, in particular since the colonization of all the continents, various aspects such as the size of wild animal

populations, the tending of particular fruit trees, the use of fire to increase the growth of wild stands of edible seeds, and the like.

2. The complexity and efficiency of the social organization of foragers, farmers, and herders and the articulation between the social unit and its members and their means of retaining the social network; the mode and structure of environmental exploitation, including the perception of the settlement, the extent of home ranges, and the presence of sacred localities.
3. The level of preparedness for natural disasters by those who inhabit ecologically marginal belts in the face of rapidly changing conditions—whether increased frequency of droughts or prolonged cold winters—and their effects on the region. Much depends on the survival of the "living memory" of the social unit (e.g., Minc and Smith 1989).
4. The inter-group or inter-tribal relationship within the larger geographic region and the ability of each population to sustain its biological survival for future generations. The existing variability of social organizations, alliances, and history of conflicts, as well as the different modes of food acquisition or production, often play an additional role in the course of societal adaptation to the new conditions.

The sum of all these traits or only a few is what constitutes the "cultural filter" through which environmental changes are mitigated within the affected society or negotiated with its neighbors, whether they belong to the same culture (and speak the same language or a dialect of the same language) or others, or are bearers of a different culture as expressed in their language, material culture, cosmology, and the like.

As archaeologists we struggle to identify the various "cultural filters" of each society, first by tracing its uniqueness (often expressed in special components of its material culture) and then by studying the socioeconomic system, and ideology or cosmology. It is the individual "cultural filter" which determines how the group may respond to a natural disaster or positive environmental amelioration such as the expansion and proliferation of vegetal and animal resources. In evaluating the impact of an abrupt change, a prolonged period of food stress or time of plenty, we take into account subsistence practices (including technology of food acquisition and preparation), as well as the social organization (including aspects of territorial perception, food-avoidance habits, and religion) of hunter-gatherers, farmers, and herders (e.g., Bar-Yosef 1996; Bar-Yosef and Belfer-Cohen 2002; Diamond 1997; Glantz 1987; Hawkes and O'Connell 1992; Jochim 1981; R. Kelly 1995; Kent 1992).

Dating Archaeological Contexts: Past and Future

Radiocarbon dates of archaeological samples are generally collected by the excavators during the excavation season. All radiocarbon dates serve the same purpose, namely, to place the material remains in a chrono-cultural sequence. Historically, most samples were charred-wood specks because the required sample size for the conventional dating technique was large. Wood samples are problematic because they date the age of a tree or a perennial bush and not the archaeological context. Dates of "dead wood" still create "noise" in the lists of radiocarbon dates, resulting in ambiguities or controversial chronological interpretations. Today, short-lived samples such as seeds or bones (both human and animal with reasonably preserved collagen) are often submitted for AMS (Accelerator Mass Spectrometer) dating. Another improvement was the calibration of radiocarbon measurements to calendrical years, a procedure now more commonly accepted by archaeologists, although not by all.

We face problems when we try to correlate cultural changes with climatic events because the published dates from archaeological sites are currently the sole source for corroborating natural and anthropogenic sequences. The task is difficult because often the available readings only refer to an archaeological layer (whether in a cave or a mound), without reference to the detailed stratigraphic position of each sample. This difficulty can be overcome if the reported dates are placed on a published stratigraphic section or digital photos of the relevant contexts. In addition, comments on the possible taphonomic history of each sample would be helpful.

For example, I will try to demonstrate below that the collapse of the Pre-Pottery Neolithic B (PPNB) civilization was caused by the 8,200 cal BP cold event (fig. 9.1). Most of the archaeological dates derive from Final PPNB layers (also called PPNC), but when calibrated, these dates

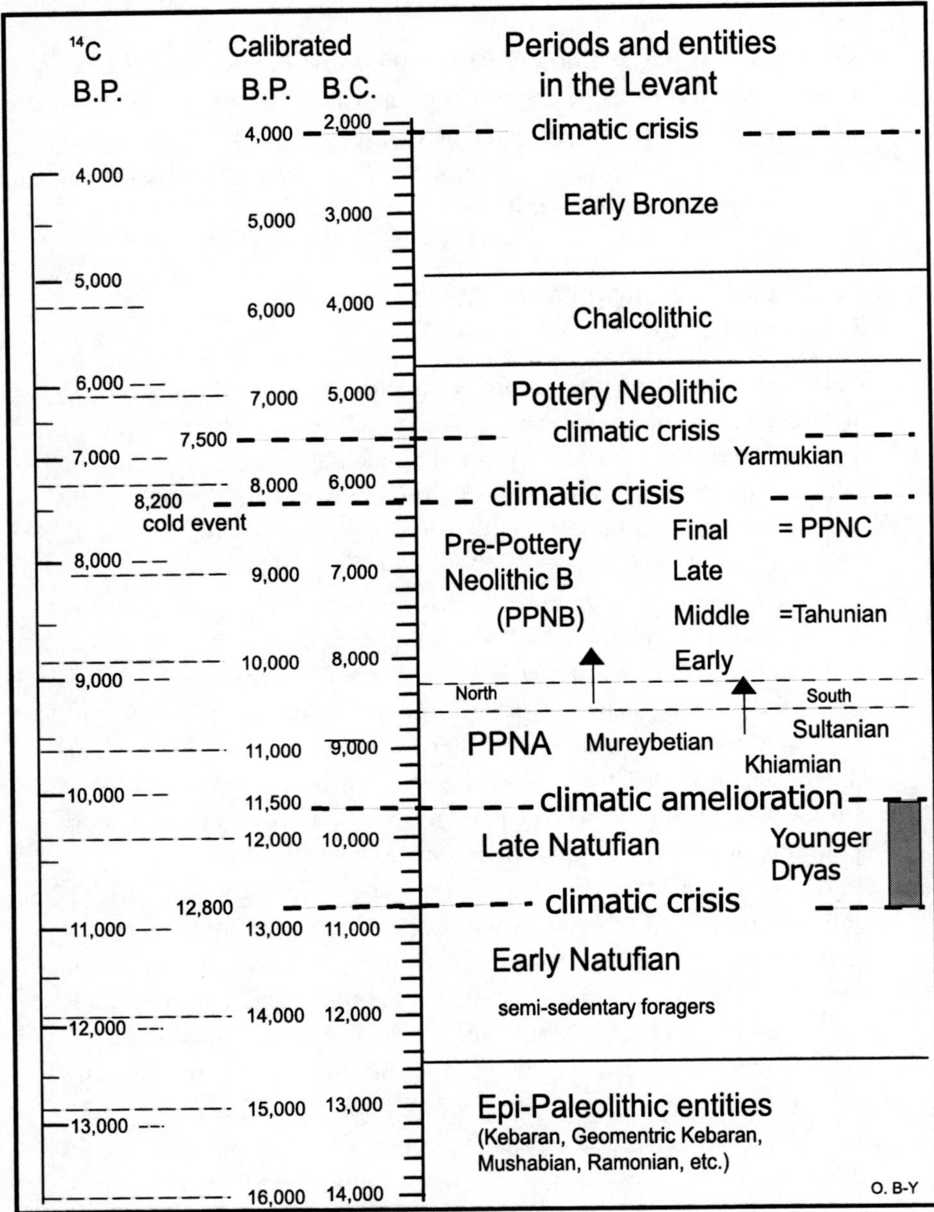

FIGURE 9.1. A chronological chart of periods and cultural entities in the Levant. Both ^{14}C and calibrated chronology are given. Ambiguities concerning the onset of the PPNB in the northern Levant relative to the southern Levant are marked with arrows. Suggested climatic changes are marked with the archaeological sequence.

fall in the range of 8,500–8,000 cal BP. However, in most cases, we have no idea if these dates mark the existence or the conclusion of an occupation. Based on my personal experience, the first interpretation is correct. Hence, we must do better by dating short-lived samples that will provide information concerning two short time spans: 1) the final years of the human occupation, and 2) the earliest years of the ensuing phase. In reality, this means dating the last abandoned houses and the first newly built houses, either in the same site or in a new village. Thus, we will be able to trace the date of the stratigraphic, and possibly cultural, unconformity. Otherwise, the time of the actual collapse, whether it lasted for one century or two, is not well recorded in the archaeological sequence, and those who prefer a sociocultural interpretation would deny the role of climate and its impact on the environment.

In addition, the investigation of biological evidence of harsh or improved conditions either before or during the 8,200 cal BP crisis should accompany the traditional archaeological approach. For example, looking for the signs of repeated droughts, evident through the response of cultivated grains to water availability, raised the alternative interpretations—increased precipitation or the development of irrigation systems during the PPNB (see Araus et al. 1997, 1999, 2001). Once the observations from different informational sources are combined in a coherent picture, the impact of a particular environmental change on human lifeways can be demonstrated.

How Good Are the Proxy Climatic Data from the Near East?

Before turning to the interpretation of the cultural sequence as reflecting the effects of environmental conditions, we need to examine the paleoclimatic record of Southwest Asia, also referred to as the Near (Middle) East. The information is derived from the following sources: cave speleothems, terrestrial pollen cores, and eastern Mediterranean marine cores. Intentionally, the archaeological examples I describe below are dated to the Late Pleistocene–Early Holocene. This will avoid the issue recently raised by Ruddiman (2003) concerning the anthropogenic impact on earth climate that was generated according to his analysis ca. 8,000–5,000 years ago by the agricultural societies across Eurasia and Mesoamerica.

The claim in his paper is based on incomplete archaeological evidence. For example, the well-documented palynological, geomorphological, and charcoal analysis records for the deforestation in the Mediterranean basin indicate that the massive destruction began in the Early Bronze Age (i.e., fourth millennium BC; e.g., Wilcox 1999). The antiquity of rice paddies in East Asia as sources for increased methane emissions is poorly known, although rice domestication may have begun some fourteen thousand years ago. Based on the archaeology of south China, the earliest paddies date within the range of seven thousand to five thousand years ago (Yasuda 2002a and papers therein).

The Levant is located on the edge of the eastern Mediterranean basin where latitudinal and longitudinal shifts of several atmospheric systems dictate changing climatic patterns. Most of the storm tracks that transport the winter rain to this region originate in the Atlantic Ocean and cross the Mediterranean in different paths (Goodfriend 1999). South of the 30–31° latitudes, the Levant is within the subtropical high pressure zone, and the influence of the monsoon system is considered minimal, reaching at the most the 28° latitude in the Sinai Peninsula. Hence, the stable oxygen and carbon isotopes recorded in the speleothems reflect past winter precipitation and its millennial fluctuations (Bar-Matthews et al. 2000; Bar-Matthews and Ayalon 2003; Frumkin et al. 2000; Vaks et al. 2003). By comparing the results of the isotopic composition ($\delta^{13}C$ and $\delta^{18}O$) between Soreq Cave on the western flanks of the central hilly ridge and Ma'aleh Efriam Cave on the eastern flanks, a paleo-climatic curve was obtained (Bar-Matthews and Ayalon 2003; Bar-Matthews et al. 1999; Vaks et al. 2003). In short, the Last Glacial Maximum (25,000–19,000 cal BP) saw a decline in precipitation, while the transition to a slightly warmer period was accompanied by increasing rainfall, although the growth rate of the speleothems, prior to the Younger Dryas, was the same on both flanks, indicating that the effects of the rain shadow were limited. This topographic impact, characteristic of the Levant Rift, operated only during fully interglacial conditions.

The Soreq Cave sequence revealed the impact of the YD (fig. 9.2), although the dates show a slightly longer range (ca. 13.1–11.0 cal BP) than the European averages (Bar-Matthews and Ayalon 2003), and the effects are somewhat attenuated when compared to northern latitudes.

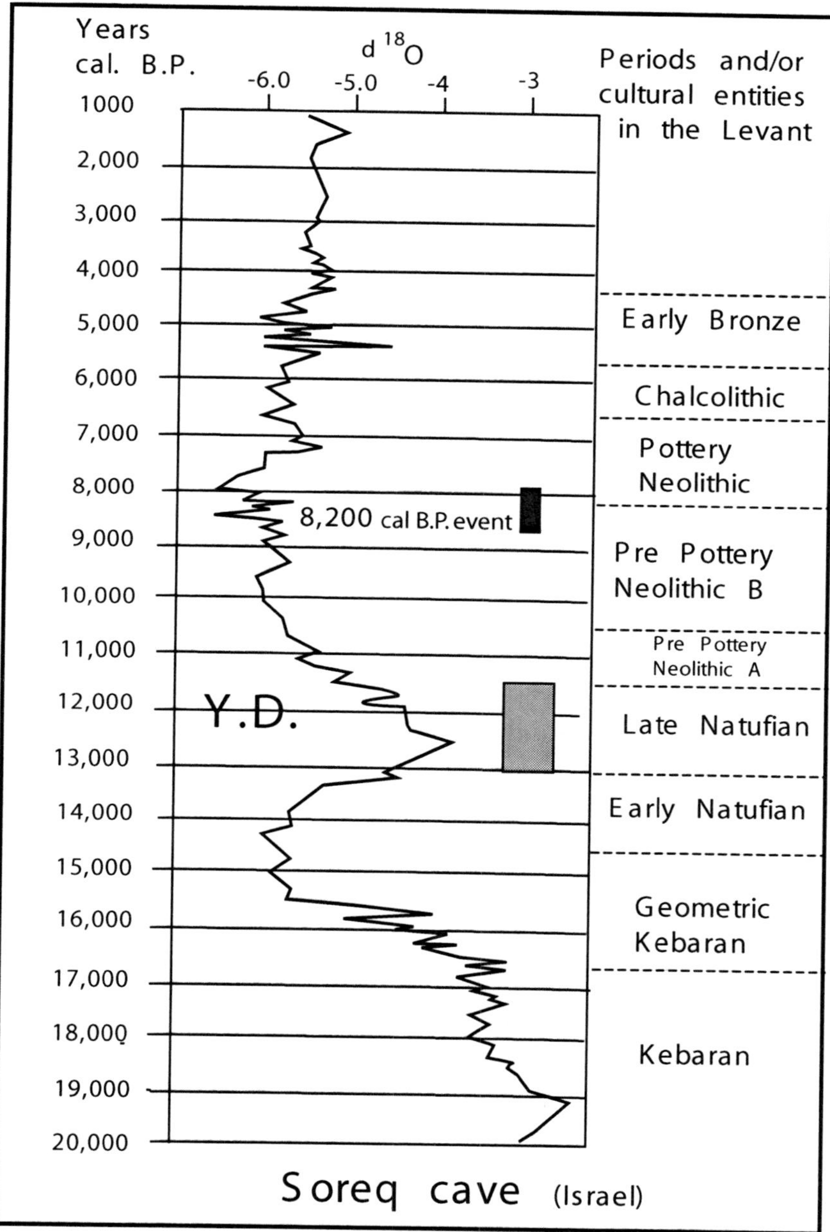

FIGURE 9.2. The climatic fluctuations according to the ∂^{18} O of the terrestrial speleothem in Soreq Cave and the suggested correlations with the ages of prehistoric entities or periods are given following M. Bar-Matthews and A. Ayalon (Israel Geological Survey; with permission).

The same sequence indicates also the impact of ca. 8,400–8,200 cal BP as a short and cold abrupt climatic change (Bar-Matthews et al. 1999; Mayewski et al. 2004).

The pollen records are more ambiguous proxies, perhaps because the available cores are from relatively lush areas such as the Ghab marshes and Hula Lake, located 350 km apart in the Levant Rift Valley, as well as the shores of Mount Carmel (Baruch and Bottema 1999; Kadosh et al. 2004; van Zeist and Bottema 1991; Yasuda 2002b). These localities are close to the Mediterranean Sea and were generally forested. The core of the Ghab (in the Orontes Valley), where the original study by Dutch researchers was later supported and clarified by Japanese researchers, presents a clear decline of arboreal pollen during the YD with a major recovery of the oak-pistachio forests. The drastic reduction in arboreal pollen is more poorly marked in the south Levantine cores (Hula Valley, coast of Mount Carmel), an observation that led to certain disagreements. A similar observation concerning the lesser impact of the YD was offered by Bottema (1995) for pollen cores from Anatolian lakes located in the steppic areas.

It should be noted that among the Near Eastern pollen cores the one from the Hula Valley has the largest number of radiocarbon dates. Even after the efforts to recalculate the effects of hard water on the reported ages (Cappers et al. 1998, 2002), the YD is reflected in a minor forest decline when compared to the Ghab area. J. Wright and Thorpe (2003), in analyzing the information from various pollen cores, accepted the identification of the YD in the Hula core and indicated that the conditions within the drainage basin of this valley were less arid than farther north. However, an entirely different interpretation was offered by Rossignol-Strick (1995, 1999). Rossignol-Strick suggested that the stratified pollen zones in the marine cores should be the type sequence for identifying the terrestrial vegetational changes because of their secure radiocarbon dates. The YD conditions were quasi-glacial in the eastern Mediterranean and were characterized by dominance of chenopods and *Artemisia* and the post-glacial, Early Holocene warming shown by the rapid expansion of *Quercus* and *Pistacia*. These forests enjoyed spring and summer rains, an interpretation supported by a previous study (Horowitz and Gat 1984). Based on her type-sequence, Rossignol-Strick (1995) suggested correcting the dates in almost every pollen core across the Anatolia and the

Levant, but her proposal for the main terrestrial cores was not accepted by others, in particular J. Wright and Thorpe (2003). Finally, it should be noted that the pollen samples retrieved from archaeological sites spanning the same period (ca. 17,000 through ca. 7,500 cal BP) support the trends from the same general trend of climatic fluctuations (Darmon 1996; Leroi-Gourhan and Darmon 1991).

Additional proxy data are provided by the marine cores across the eastern Mediterranean. In a survey of information from the Adriatic Sea through the southeast of the Aegean Sea to the Cyprus area, the cooling periods of the YD and the 8 ka BP event are clearly identified (e.g., Rohling et al. 2002). The temperature cline from the Atlantic Ocean through the Mediterranean Sea, as shown by the analysis of planktonic foraminifera (Hayes et al. 2005), demonstrates the general time-correlations of climatic fluctuations between the two water bodies. Comparisons between oxygen and stable carbon isotopes from the cave speleothems and the marine sequence of the Last Interglacial period lends further support to the recognition of the same sequence of climatic changes in the Levant (Bar-Matthews et al. 2002; fig. 9.2). Hence, in spite of the certain ambiguities and the probable attenuation of the local conditions in the eastern Mediterranean, it seems that one can employ with caution proxies from other western areas within the Northern Hemisphere.

The Impact of the YD

The YD has been recognized in marine and terrestrial cores across the Northern Hemisphere (e.g., Broecker 1999; De Rijk et al. 1999; Gosse et al. 1995; Mayewski et al. 2004; Rohling et al. 2002; Sima et al. 2004). The well-known cold and dry conditions have been the main causes that forced human groups in the Levant to have a series of *major social and economic decisions*, which resulted in the emergence of farming communities. Determining the length of this period depends on dating the Allerød/YD and the YD/Preboreal transitions. Based on the ice-core chronology, its estimated overall duration is ca. 1,300±70 years (Alley et al. 1993; Mayewski and Bender 1995; Taylor et al. 1997), from ca. 12,900 to ca. 11,600 or ca. 12,800 to ca. 11,500 cal BP, with a few discrepancies indicated by the Anatolian varve chronology (e.g., Lemcke and Sturm 1997).

Among the cultures of hunter-gatherers of the eastern Mediterranean, the Natufian culture, dated to the terminal Pleistocene, occupies a special place (Bar-Yosef 1998; Belfer-Cohen and Bar-Yosef 2000; Cauvin 2000; Valla 1995, 1999, 2003; fig. 9.3). Known from the southern Levant, due to paucity of fieldwork in Syria and lack of surveys aiming at locating contemporary foragers in southeastern Turkey, the early Natufian was a flourishing semi-sedentary society (14,500–13,000 cal BP). Not surprisingly, contemporary with the Bølling-Allerød, the local conditions in the Near East afforded the establishment of a complex foraging society, with sedentary or semi-sedentary hamlets, as shown by the presence of commensals such as mice and house sparrow (Auffray et al. 1998; Tchernov 1984). The Natufians built rounded pit houses in most sites within the Mediterranean vegetal belt, and the only public building was exposed in Eynan (Ain Mallaha), where the excavation size exceeds 600 m^2. All Natufian sites contain rich material culture of lithics, bones, and groundstone. Many of the dead were buried on-site, often wearing body decorations made of *Dentalium* sp. shells, bone beads, and pendants. The earliest Near Eastern prehistoric figurines were found in the Natufian sites, as well as a series of incised slabs displaying various patterns (e.g., Marshack 1997). Sickles and glossed blades indicate the harvesting of cereals, and grooved pebbles employed as "shaft straighteners" reflect the use of bows and arrows. The basic Natufian subsistence continued the already existing tradition of procurement of vegetal sources, well recorded in the waterlogged site of Ohalo II that dates to almost ten millennia earlier (e.g., Nadel et al. 2004; E. Weiss et al. 2004). The suite of gathered food included wild cereals, pulses, other seeds, and various fruits. Meat was obtained by hunting in the immediate environment; the main targets were the gazelle, fallow deer, and wild boar as well as a suite of small game such as hare, tortoise, and numerous birds (e.g., Bar-Oz et al. 2003; Munro 2004; Stiner and Munro 2002).

The YD had a major impact on the Natufian society. Under the fluctuating environmental conditions, with decreasing reliability and predictability of plant and animal resources, two polarized options faced these groups of foragers. The first was to increase mobility, assuming that it could be done by minimal physical conflicts with their territorial neighbors. The second was to settle down where resources are stable, such as near perennial streams, in order to defend their food supplies.

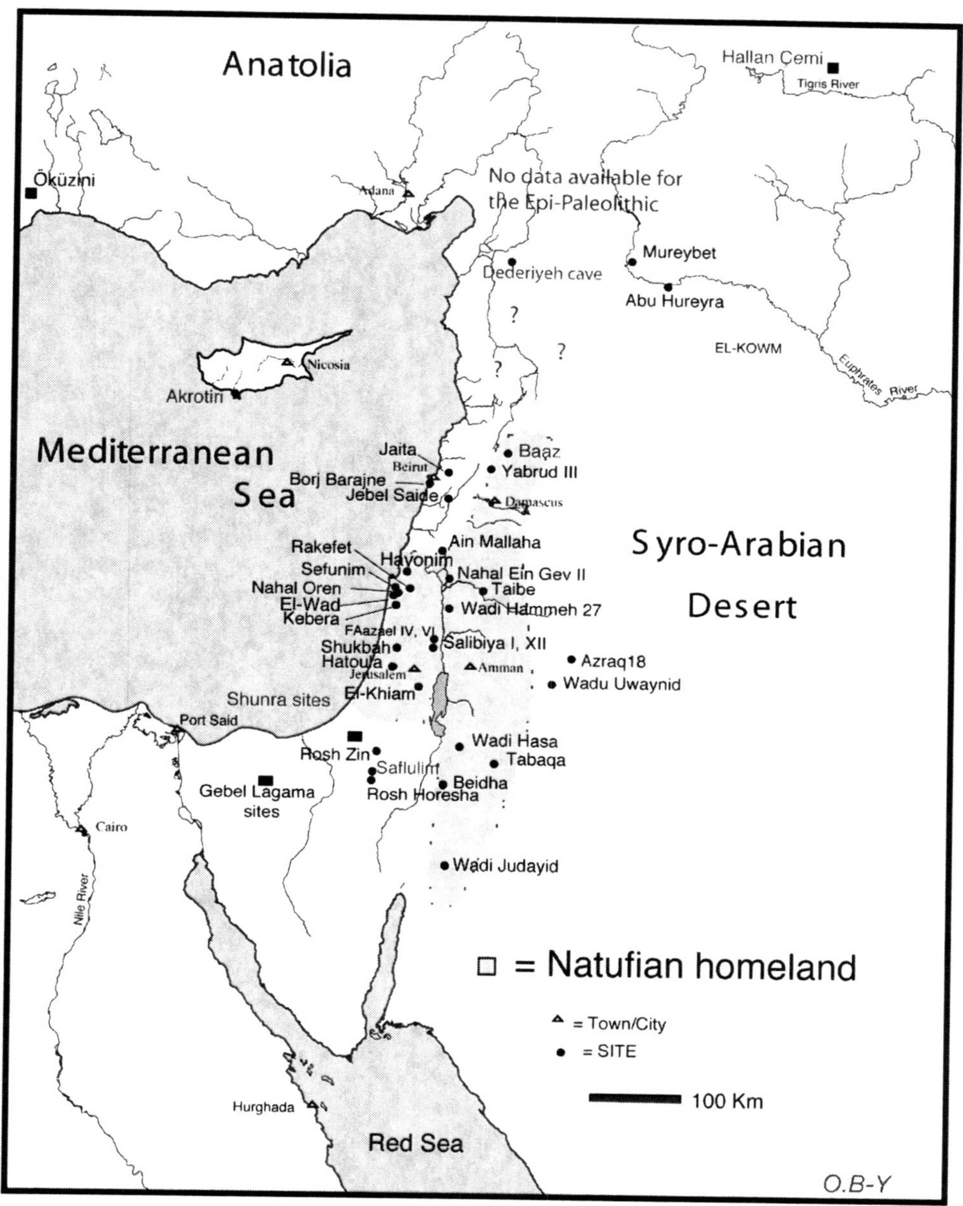

FIGURE 9.3. The distribution of Natufian sites in the Levant (O. Bar-Yosef).

The archaeology of the Near East provides examples for the two opposed solutions, namely, increased mobility and sedentism.

Late Natufian groups adopted a more mobile settlement pattern, rarely buried their dead with their adornments, and increased consumption of low-ranked resources such as bone grease, juvenile gazelles, and fast-moving small game such as hare (Munro 2004). In southeastern Turkey, on the bank of a tributary of the Tigris River, Rosenberg and Redding (2000) studied the late Paleolithic village of Hallan Çemi. Numerous radiocarbon readings date the site to the YD, and its contents indicate that it was a sedentary community exploiting variable plant and animal sources. Colledge et al. (2004) suggest that humans initiated in this local area the intentional cultivation in reaction to worsening climatic conditions, as proposed earlier (Bar-Yosef and Belfer-Cohen 2002; J. Wright and Thorpe 2003).

Whether the process of domestication of cultivated cereals occurred in a short time (twenty to two hundred years), as indicated by Hillman and Davies (1992), or a longer time (ca. one thousand years), as suggested by Kislev (1997), we can only say that the archaeological evidence of the earliest Pre-Pottery Neolithic A (PPNA; ca. 11,600–10,500 cal BP) demonstrates the presence of large villages up to 2.5 ha in size, supported by growing their staple food. This simply means that in the last centuries of the YD, cultivation was initiated by Natufian or contemporary forgers who took advantage of their knowledge of these plant life cycles. Systematic sawing and harvesting, along with the human selection, brought about the domination of the cereals' mutation that defines the domesticated species.

The Collapse of the PPNB Civilization

The development of early Neolithic villages through the full establishment of agriculture as the new economy, the processes of domestication of plants (cereals, pulses, flax, etc.) and herd animals (goat, sheep, cattle, and pigs), and the continuing activities of gathering and hunting by farmers occurred first in the western wing of the Fertile Crescent and then in the eastern wing (e.g., Aurenche and Kozlowski 1999; Bar-Yosef 2002; Cauvin 2000; fig. 9.4). The entire cultural evolution lasted from 11,500 through ca. 8,500/8,200 cal BP during what is known as the

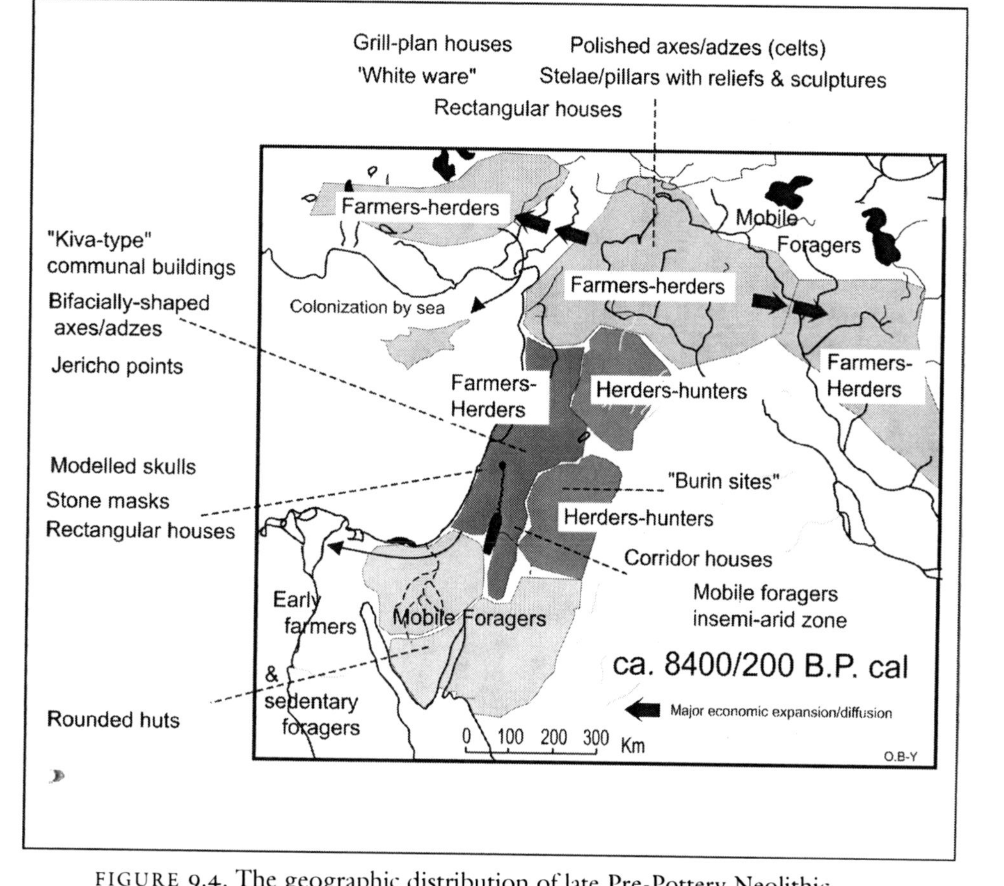

FIGURE 9.4. The geographic distribution of late Pre-Pottery Neolithic socio-economic entities or "tribes" in the Levant (O. Bar-Yosef).

PPNA and PPNB periods. No less impressive were the changes in social organization and ranking, the emergence of elites in several subregions, the building and maintenance of ceremonial and/or ritual centers in each village, and the formation of ceremonial centers in particular localities to which pilgrimage involving the burial of the dead took place. The mobilization of work, craft specialization in lithics and wood work, the knowledge of digging wells and possibly using irrigation, the development of complex exchange systems, the colonization of Cyprus, and other social traits culminated during the PPNB period (ca. 10,500–8,200 cal BP). Except for writing systems and full evidence for the existence of chiefdoms, the PPNB sites, in particular in southeastern Turkey, represent a set of cultural and social achievements not recognized by archaeologists a decade ago. Our new knowledge can be symbolized by the shrines/temples or gathering houses of Göbekli Tepe, where T-shaped limestone pillars, mostly 3 m high, held the buildings' roofs, many of which carry a series of carved animals on them (Peters and Schmidt 2004; K. Schmidt 2001).

This civilization came to an end in what seemed to be an abrupt collapse. The collapse of this civilization is documented by site abandonment and stratigraphical gaps in PPNB mounds and the establishment of new villages and farmsteads dated to what is known as the Pottery Neolithic period (ca. 8,200/8,000–6,500 cal BP; figs. 9.1, 9.2).

Various reasons may account for the abandonment of houses in a living village, from the death of the head of the family to the outcome of verbal and physical conflicts. However, when the entire village is deserted, the reasons could be more complex, from overexploitation of the immediate environment, to successful aggression by a neighboring village, to the impact of consecutive droughts. Only rare examples for conflicts that ended in burning the entire village are known from the PPNB period (e.g., Ganj Dareh; P. Smith 1976), although their paucity does not necessarily reflect the endurance of peaceful lifeways. On the contrary, data concerning physical conflicts are accumulating as more skeletal collections are published (Agelarakis 1993). Under any circumstances, the abandonment of one site and/or several may precipitate societal restructuring, especially among farming communities. It is, therefore, necessary first to document the timing of abandonment and to ascertain whether it is only a local phenomenon or a regional event. Second, we need to search for the reasons, which as mentioned above inspire lively debates among scholars.

Stratigraphic gaps between the latest PPNB deposits and the Pottery Neolithic were noticed in many sites such as Jericho, 'Ain Ghazal, Çayönü, etc. (Akkermans and Duistermaat 1996; Gopher and Gophna 1993; Kenyon 1957; A. Özdogan 1999; M. Özdogan 1997), as well as in sites across the Anatolian plateau.

The subsequent establishment of new hamlets and farmsteads in the various parts of the Levant is known among others from the southern Levant in the Yarmukian culture (E. B. Banning et al. 1994; E. G. Banning 1998; Garfinkel 1993, 1999).

Interpretations suggested for the abandonment of 'Ain Ghazal as caused by overexploitation of pastures by herding goats and tree felling for plaster production and building posts (Rollefson 1990; Rollefson and Köhler-Rollefson 1989) are problematic. To expect that overexploitation took place in both Anatolia and the Levant is to assume that the same destructive mechanism operated across every ecological belt within the entire eastern Mediterranean terrestrial landscapes. As this seems unlikely, another cause or, more likely, causes need to be tested as resulting in a wide range of geographical impacts.

Another perspective would be to see the collapse as motivated by societal overexploitation. Unfortunately, we have no evidence for the presence of a Big Man or other kinds of chiefs enslaving smaller communities, serving and supplying the larger villages. This is not to say that there is no evidence for social ranking or clear signs for the existence of personal property marked by stamps. Perhaps future excavations will reveal the presence of slaves, a known phenomenon from the sedentary villages of the northwest coast of North America (Ames 2001).

It seems to me that an abrupt climatic change was responsible for the rapid worsening of environmental conditions. I therefore propose that the climatic crisis around 8,400–8,200 cal BP as recorded in the ice, marine, and pollen cores, as well as in speleothems, was the culprit (Alley et al. 1997; Bar-Mathews et al. 1999; Mayewski et al. 2004; Rohling et al. 2002; Rossignol-Strick 1995; van Zeist and Bottema 1991).

In the event of a series of droughts, a complex society that subsisted on farming and herding in which the demands of more affluent individuals (or families) drove the flow of foreign goods, such as obsidian, marine shells, chlorite bowls, and the like, could not continue to accumulate surplus. The lack of central authorities and public storage of staple food meant the absence of support to affected populations. Shifts in the pattern of seasonal precipitation resulted in lower yields of summer harvests in the villages and imposed the search for pastures farther away. In brief, economic deterioration, as we learned from history, results in social upheaval. The change was inevitable. The disappearance of previously large villages and the establishment of smaller villages, hamlets, or farmsteads were probably the reactions of the people. Like foragers under similar circumstances, they increased their relative mobility. Enhanced reliance on more flexible subsistence strategies such as full adaptation of pastoral nomadism could have been one of the results. Needless to mention, central ceremonial centers were abandoned and most probably resulted in the early Pottery Neolithic period through the increased importance of the local shrine.

In Anatolia, the Levantine PPNB collapse, including most of southeastern Turkey, triggered another wave of colonizers moving westward, first into temperate Europe (Perlès 2003). Other colonizers brought the Levantine agricultural system and part of their ideological package to the delta of the Nile. Others moved into the regions of the Caucasus and beyond. Perhaps more important was the "push" given by those who had the knowledge developed during the PPNB in Upper Mesopotamia of simple irrigation control to areas such as southern Mesopotamia where the general water-rich environment was suitable for further modifications. With the hierarchical social structure in place, establishing "hydraulic civilization" all over Mesopotamia was the step that heralded the emergence of chiefdoms and city-states.

10

Abandoning the Garden

THE POPULATION/LAND DEGRADATION FALLACY AS APPLIED TO THE LAKE PÁTZCUARO BASIN IN MEXICO

Christopher T. Fisher

The Population/Land Degradation Fallacy

Increasingly, stakeholders, policy makers, and the lay public are recognizing the value of long-term perspectives on coupled human and natural systems (see the introduction to this volume). But much of this awareness comes from syntheses compiled by non-specialists, leading to assertions such as "few people, however, least of all our politicians, realize that a primary cause of the collapse of . . . [ancient] societies has been the destruction of the environmental resources on which they depended" (Diamond 2003:43).

One long-standing myth pervading popular conceptions about human-environment interconnections is the population/land degradation fallacy or the Malthusian-inspired "vicious-circle principle" for the evolution of humanity (Dilworth 2002:78–79). This "paradigm" of human development posits that population growth leads to technological innovation, which puts increasing pressure on finite resources. Ultimately, demographic pressure leads to unsustainable strategies that cause degradation and finally collapse.

The supposed connection between people and land degradation is still commonly invoked as a universal prime mover (see Chew 2001 for many examples), most notably for the Classic period Maya (see discussion in B. L. Turner 1993; D. Rice 1996; Webster 2002:chap. 9). While contemporary population growth is a serious matter, the supposed connection between demography and land degradation has long been demonstrated to be nonexistent (Blaikie and Brookfield 1987:chap. 2; Brookfield 2001; Denevan 2000; Fisher et al. 2003; T. J. Whitmore et al. 1990). Collapse-by-land-degradation arguments are attractive because they seem logical, they can be easily communicated through the sound-bite, and they take few leaps to be related to current environmental malaise.

To varying degrees, and at a multitude of scales in time and space, humans transform the "wild" into "garden" and in the process create a landscape that is largely anthropogenic. But what happens to the garden once it is abandoned? Here I argue that many accounts of ancient ecological suicide are actually confusing cause and effect and that massive land degradation is most commonly associated with the abandonment of built environments after societal collapse. The primary mechanism in this process is the activation of the land degradation time-clock associated with anthropogenic landscapes.

My discussion centers on three factors that sustain arguments implicating population pressure as an explanation for ancient land degradation: 1) continued adherence to the nature/society dichotomy, 2) modeling land degradation as an ecological rather than a socionatural process, and 3) perpetuation of the scientific "Great Divide." Then I present alternative ways that these factors can be conceptualized so that land degradation becomes a social rather than an ecological phenomenon. I discuss the implications of this new perspective using evidence from a recent landscape project exploring relationships between environmental and social transformations in the development of the pre-Columbian Tarascan (Purépecha) Empire centered in the Lake Pátzcuaro Basin, Mexico. The results from this project challenge common conceptions regarding the impact of agriculture, urbanism, and state collapse on ancient landscapes (see Fisher et al. 2003 and discussion in Redman 1999:146–148; T. M. Whitmore and Turner 2002:228–235). To conclude, I consider how this work can inform the concepts of sustainability, land degradation, and resilience.

The Nature/Society Dichotomy and the Recursive Solution

A major driver in the perpetuation of the land degradation/population connection has been the tendency to still follow the basic precepts of cultural ecology as it has been practiced in archaeology (Scarborough 2003a:4366). One of these basic precepts is a biophysical environment that is prioritized so that human societies are governed by the same basic laws that determine ecological relationships. "Man's extra-somatic means of adaptation" in this sense is culture (e.g., J. Steward 1955; L. White 1959). Another precept is that, as noted in a recent critique by Erickson, "in the human adaptation process, humans 'adapt to,' 'interact with,' 'impact' and 'influence'" (2000a:315) an environment that is seen as natural or largely outside of human control. Culture is the mechanism through which people try to maintain equilibrium with an environment that is conceptualized as static. Social change can be explained by a response to shifting parameters outside the purview of human control, such as climatic flux, natural disasters, or land degradation.

This has led to a fundamental disconnect between landscapes and people, and it perpetuates the traditional nature-culture opposition common to Western thought. The result is the separation of socioeconomic spheres from ecological ones, placing past (and present) environmental problems outside the span of human control, even though humans in many instances are seen as initiating many of the problems. In this view, the history of civilization can be seen as a "trajectory of numerous collisions with the natural environment" so that "the relations of Culture with Nature have been exploitative, engendered primarily to meet materialistic requirements of hierarchical systems of social organizations. The outcomes have been the loss of species diversity, polluted oceans and rivers, siltation, population losses due to flooding, health issues, and civilizational collapse" (Chew 2001:1). Here, land degradation (and many other environmental issues) are conceived of as environmental, rather than social, problems.

In a recent *American Antiquity* contribution, van der Leeuw and Redman trace the theoretical evolution of nature-society relationships from "reactive, via proactive, to interactive" (2002:501) and, quoting Foley (1987), see humans as "just another unique species," albeit one that can "learn how to learn" and change their behavior based on observation. This alternative recursive human-environment connection follows much thinking in the social sciences seeking to discard the nature-culture dichotomy to transform environmental problems such as land degradation into sociocultural phenomena (Blaikie and Brookfield 1987; Bryant 1992; Cronon 1996; Descola and Pálsson 1996; Escobar 1999; McGlade 1995; van der Leeuw et al. 1998, 2000). Thus, environment becomes a social phenomena constructed from generations of human observations and inherited via cultural transmission. This means that humans don't interact with their environment, but rather with their cultural perceptions of ecosystem processes (van der Leeuw et al. 2000). Or, as phrased eloquently by Pollan:

> As *Walden* itself teaches us, we humans are never simply in nature, like the beasts and trees and boulders, but always also in relation to nature: looking at it through the frames of our various preconceptions, our personal and collective histories, our self-consciousness, our words. . . . What other creature, after all, even has a relationship to nature? (Pollan 1997:264)

Humans in this recursive perspective have causal roles in shaping environments that are seen as dynamic rather than static. Drawing on the new ecology (Botkin 1990; Perry 2002; B.L.M. Turner et al. 2003; Vayda and McCay 1975; Zimmerer 1996, 2006), the concept of "ecosystems in balance" has been abandoned in favor of flux, non-equilibrium dynamics, and long-term change at many temporal and geographical scales (see Botkin 1990; Zimmerer 1994; Zimmerer and Young 1998). The result is a landscape that is viewed as a heterogeneous mosaic of patches undergoing distinct successional regimes (Perry 2002:341).

The mediator between *nature* (forces outside human control) and *culture* is landscape, conceived here as a unit of human occupation (Fisher and Thurston 1999). Even the smallest societies through time construct a physical and cognized socioenvironmental realm, which is part perception and part transformed nature, through which purposeful socioeconomic strategy is pursued. Since landscapes serve as the human/ecosystem fulcrum, an understanding of processes leading to their formation can yield unique and critical insights into societal development (van der Leeuw and Redman 2002). This also means that substantive anthropological issues can be addressed when landscapes are treated as artifacts (Fisher and Thurston 1999).

For landscapes, the seemingly contradictive normative notion of disequilibria means that humans constantly coped with flux while engineering intensive landscapes. One benefit of large-scale environmental modification would have been the elimination of risk by creating predictable, easily replicable, and relatively homogenous landscapes. Humans continually created and solved environmental crises, engineered environments, and repaired land degradation, entering into long-term socionatural relationships that determined the course of human ecodynamics at many scales in time and space.

Land Degradation Is a Socionatural Rather Than an Ecological Process

The second factor contributing to the perpetuation of the land degradation/population myth is the tendency to see ecological problems as something outside or separate from human societies. One example is land degradation, which is a common, but not necessarily immediate, outcome of landscape manipulation. Since land degradation is a "composite term" (Stocking and Murnaghan 2001:9)—it typically describes changes in a host of ecosystem parameters—there is no single identifier, making definitions difficult. Here I follow the UN/FAO in defining land degradation as the temporary or permanent decline in the productive capacity of the land. Land degradation, often synonymous with erosion, can include, but not be limited to, soil erosion, habitat loss, loss of biodiversity, or other physical environmental change initiated by humans, resulting in perceived productivity loss (D. Johnson and Lewis 1995; for examples and discussion, see Stocking and Murnaghan 2001). This makes land degradation, like the environment, a cognized, cultural phenomena (Barrow 1991:1; Kasperson et al. 1995; Stocking and Murnaghan 2001:11; van der Leeuw et al. 2000:362). Actors in the past may not experience environmental change—defined today as degradation—in the same way. Land degradation is a wholly human phenomenon and can theoretically be separated from natural change with intertwined intentional and unintentional components (D. Johnson and Lewis 1995:2).

Critical to any definition of land degradation is time and the ability of humans to ameliorate unproductive conditions, which can generally be done using simple technologies along with labor as capital. In modern studies, short-term land degradation is generally considered to occur within a person's lifetime and be "repairable," in contrast to long-term or permanent degradation persisting beyond a generation (50 years) (D. Johnson and Lewis 1995:6). For most archaeologists (those who do not have access to annual dating methods such as dendrochronology), discerning short-term degradation (<50 years) would be a dicey proposition given current dating methods and the likely evidence available making most human-induced landscape perturbation long-term land degradation (>50 years).

All complex societies are associated with some form of surplus, usually obtained from an engineered landscape, and these large-scale human constructions play a central role in ancient land degradation. Human-generated landscapes increase biodiversity, stability, and economic usefulness, and some would argue general health, solving many of the same maladies from which our current environments suffer (Brookfield 2000; Teutonico and Matero 2003). They also encode long-term strategies of land use and can act as repositories of traditional ecological knowledge, and culture (Erickson 2003:181–182). Whether by subtly manipulating natural fire regimes (Krech 1999; Pyne et al. 1996), keeping forests at bay while managing intensive wetland systems (Erickson 2000a), or comprehensively terra-forming sloped lands (Denevan 2000), humans generated cultural landscapes within a relatively narrow range of parameters to mediate much short- and intermediate-term risk, create economic and social capital, generate agricultural surplus, and build easily replicated ecosystems. Indeed, many argue that the transformation of environments is a process akin to and occurring before the genetic domestication of plants and animals (Terrel et al. 2003; Yen 1989).

Most ancient agricultural landscapes are the result of accretionary construction (Doolittle 1984) through which human capital is accumulated incrementally, generation by generation. Landesque capital is a concept developed by Brookfield (1984) and Blaikie and Brookfield (1987; also Kirch 1994) to characterize the process of environmentally banking labor for increased future returns. This landscape capital tracks labor banked through stone walls, terraces, drainage systems, irrigation systems, raised fields, or other landscape-intensive features. These constructions "pay off" by providing future output, creating environmental capital for generations if maintained, and making agro-ecosystems accretionary labor banks.

Built into many landesque capital landscapes is a degradation time clock that stops ticking when labor is pulled from the system. Abandonment has profound consequences for landesque capital because regular labor inputs are needed for stability. Land degradation often results from a failure to repair and maintain (Blaikie and Brookfield 1987; Denevan

2000; D. Johnson and Lewis 1995). Societal perturbations causing maintenance to be postponed or withdrawn can have disastrous environmental consequences. This causes a reliance on labor for environmental stability so that landesque capital systems may actually promote population growth. In this instance, "population pressure on resources is something that can operate on both sides, contributing to degradation, and aiding management and repair" (Blaikie and Brookfield 1987:34).

This moves degradation from the environmental realm to one of perception and cognition that is within, rather than outside, human control. For landesque capital, landscapes' land degradation most often results from the loss of labor through a sociopolitical rather than an ecological circumstance. As a consequence, explanations seeking the cause of ancient (or modern) land degradation, evidenced by changes in the landscape, must be sought within social rather than purely environmental domains.

Fast and Slow: Earth Science and Archaeological Compatibility

A third major contributing factor to the perpetuation of the population/land degradation myth is the perpetuation of what C. P. Snow called the "Great Divide" between the two scientific cultures (1959). Due to perceived differences in the pace of phenomena studied by natural and social scientists, there is a significant disconnect between the scales at which earth science and archaeological data are collected. Building on the work of Elias (1992), Newton has recently argued that there is an epistemological disconnect that sees environmental and physical evolution as slow in contrast to human societies, which are viewed as fast (2003:436–438). Processes involved in the evolution of the earth, such as tectonics, volcanism, weathering, erosion, soil development, etc., are generally perceived of as phenomena that operate at millennial or greater cycles of time. In contrast, social phenomena, such as the formation and collapse of states and empires, demographic growth, settlement formation, etc., are typically seen as operating in century or less timescales.

In reality, both geological and social phenomena operate on both slow and fast time. A catastrophic event such as an earthquake, volcanic eruption, or tsunami can be the dominant factor influencing landscape formation, while many social processes occur over long time spans such as the development of social complexity, migrations, and colonization. This means that there are complementary cycles of earth science and social processes at the timescale of generations, centuries, and millennia constantly acting on the landscape. Conjunctions between these cycles, which occur at a multitude of scales in time and space, are visible in the landscape record and must be explored better if we are to understand the co-evolution of society and environment.

The problem is that landscape reconstruction by necessity incorporates both archaeological and earth science components that are conceived, collected, and presented in disparate scales in time and space. Processes that are seen as "environmental" (land degradation, physical evolution of the earth) are most often described by "natural scientists" trained to view the phenomena they study in slow or deep time, while social scientists conceive, describe, and present their data in fast time (the timescale of human action). The result is confusion between the cause and effect of land degradation. Since the physical consequences of land degradation, such as soil erosion, are studied by natural scientists, the concept as a whole is most often thought of as an ecological rather then as a social phenomenon.

This leads to a disconnect between understandings of past landscapes and the human processes that are largely responsible for their creation. As an example, despite full-coverage survey for large areas of the Mediterranean (see Cherry et al. 1991; Keller and Rupp 1983; Renfrew and Wagstaff 1982; van Andel and Runnels 1987; B. Wells 1992), associated earth science data lack comparability, hindering interpretation, similar to the Mesoamerican record (i.e., Copan Valley, central Petén, and the Lake Pátzcuaro Basin).

A similar problem hinders interpretations of earth science data in general. Most environmental data is of two types: 1) lacustrine or marsh cores, and 2) terrestrial records. Both are associated with benefits and limitations. Cores record long sequences of continuous change, often lasting several millennia, providing generalized sequences of landscape evolution over large areas (Oldfield 1991). Interpretation is limited because core data reveals trends at broad spatial and temporal scales, masking short-duration events. Linking specific cause and effect is difficult, with wide-interval dating exacerbating this problem.

Terrestrial records, recovered from colluvial or alluvial fills, record individual episodes of landscape instability at small spatial scales (van Andel et al. 1990; van Andel and Runnels 1987, for the Mediterranean; Dunning et al. 2002, for Mesoamerica). These discontinuous records reflect single events spanning several centuries, but with limited spatial and temporal coverage. Landscape change, specifically soil erosion, is highly variable, and although terrestrial data can be linked to specific landscape features, and often ancient settlements, broader connections are difficult.

Because these sources of data show different parts of the same record, results often diverge, making correlation difficult. As an example, for the Mediterranean, over three dozen cores yield information concerning landscape change spanning six to eight thousand years (see K. W. Butzer 1996:144 for a review). Yet these generalized records diverge from terrestrial data showing contradictory results, illustrated by differing reconstructions of Lake Lerna in the Greek Argive Plain (Jahns 1993 versus Zangger 1991). Records from archaeological sites and cores from the same watershed also may differ (i.e., van Zeist and Bottema, 1991:fig. 41a versus 41b, as cited in K. W. Butzer 1996).

Thus, there are real issues of temporal and spatial scale that must be solved before anthropological questions centered on ancient land degradation can be addressed. Earth science data must be collected at the timescale of human action to better connect land degradation, which is an outcome of human decision making, with the actual societal processes that allowed it to happen. And both natural and social kinds of data must be understood at many spatial scales—from the specific to the general—to connect natural, social, and landscape evolution better. To answer questions centering on past degradation, you need a record correlated across a wide area, both in time and space, and across discipline and specialty niches.

The Columbus Polemic and the Latin American Example

Mesoamerica is one example of a region in which misconceptions regarding the relationship between human societies and land degradation have had an impact on modern environmental policy. Latin America in general is currently undergoing an environmental crisis caused by deforestation, soil erosion, and habitat loss rooted in past land-use processes (Guillermo et al. 1995). One limiting factor for conservation has been poorly understood historical processes responsible for landscapes popularly characterized as "endangered" (J. Simon 1997). Current research addressing past land-use impacts is galvanized around the "Columbus polemic" (summarized in K. W. Butzer 1992, 1993; Denevan 1992; Redman 1999; Sluyter 1999; T. M. Whitmore and Turner 2002:228–235), centering on debates pinning much of this environmental damage on either pre-Hispanic or Hispanic land practice.

Recent attempts at "polemic" resolution focus on ethnohistoric (K. Butzer and Butzer 1993; K. W. Butzer 1991; Endfield and O'Hara 1999; Sluyter 1999, 2002) and sediment-based (Metcalfe 1991; Metcalfe et al. 1989, 1994, 2000; O'Hara 1992; O'Hara et al. 1993) studies limited either by a lack of time depth or by data collected at geologic dimensions inadequate for anthropogenic questions (see critique in Denevan 1994; Fisher 2000; Fisher et al. 2003; H. P. Pollard et al. 1994). Consequently, this work cannot be linked to either site- or settlement-based archaeological investigation at comparable temporal and spatial scales. Furthermore, interpretations in many regions of the Americas are dominated by archaic notions of the population/degradation connection as discussed above.

An important location in this debate is the Lake Pátzcuaro Basin, which is located in west-central Mexico and is very similar to the more familiar Basin of Mexico in terms of geology, vegetation, elevation, and climate, although Pátzcuaro receives significantly more rainfall (Chacón Torres 1989). A long history of human occupation and a well-documented paleoenvironmental record for the Lake Pátzcuaro Basin have played pivotal roles in deciphering the impact of population, urbanism, and agriculture on the landscape (see summary in Fisher et al. 2003). At the time of European contact (~AD 1522; Warren 1985), the Lake Pátzcuaro Basin was the epicenter of the Tarascan (Purépecha) Empire, making it a Mesoamerican core zone (Palerm 1957), with a dense population and a heavily modified environment (H. P. Pollard 1993, 2003). The ecological impact of regional demographic expansion in the centuries prior to European Conquest has been a central question in the prehistory of the region. Two large-scale projects are critical to this debate.

The first culminated in the late 1980s when the Lake Pátzcuaro Basin was the core of an intensive interdisciplinary study of indigenous environmental knowledge, land use, and management. The goal of this research was to understand the "cultural, economic, ecological, and historical mechanisms or processes responsible for conservation of the natural habitats of the Lake Pátzcuaro Basin" (V. Toledo 1991:148). The major finding from this research was that the indigenous (Purépecha) culture in the region, direct descendants of their Tarascan forebearers, "possess a set of intrinsic features that have favored conservative uses of nature, thus allowing continuous maintenance of productive processes" (V. Toledo 1991:167).

The result of this work, *Plan Pátzcuaro 2000: Investigación multidisciplinaria para el desarrollo sostenido*, was an integrative conservation plan for the region based on the application of traditional ecological knowledge (TEK) (V. M. Toledo et al. 1992). From this and limited paleoecological investigation (Street-Perrott et al. 1989), and following other work in the Mexican Highlands (C. Gibson 1967; Melville 1990; Sale 1990; L. Simpson 1952), it was assumed that Hispanic land practice, rather than high precontact populations, was largely responsible for the modern degraded landscape. A major limiting factor for the Toledo project has been the lack of archaeological and paleoenvironmental data that could be compared with modern Purépecha land use to project TEK-derived conservation strategies into the future.

The second project involved the study of sediments from twenty-one lake cores combined with limited terrestrial investigation (O'Hara 1992). Published in 1993 as "Accelerated Erosion around a Highland Mexican Lake" in the Journal *Nature* (O'Hara et al. 2003), this study suggested that there were three major periods of human-induced erosion in the past: 1) associated with the adoption of agriculture sometime during the Preclassic period between 1900 and 1250 BC, 2) a more intense episode during the Late Classic period between AD 600 and 650, and 3) a final "destructive" event after AD 1200 caused by the large population in the region associated with the Tarascan (Purépecha) Empire (O'Hara et al. 1993; calibrated dates are from K. W. Butzer 1993:16). The study concluded by stating that

> there is a move by many environmental agencies both in Mexico and elsewhere for a return to traditional forms of agriculture, as they are

> considered to be better for the environment. As our findings indicate that traditional farming techniques cause significant erosion, it is unlikely that a return to prehispanic farming methods would solve the problem of environmental degradation. (O'Hara et al. 1993:50)

The results from the O'Hara et al. project had a broad appeal and were widely reported in the popular media, including Latin America, derailing the V. M. Toledo et al. *Pátzcuaro Plan 2000*, much of which was not implemented. From this, and related research (K. Butzer and Butzer 1993; Endfield and O'Hara 1999), many now contend that colonialists inherited landscapes ravaged by soil erosion, deforestation, and mismanagement. This work is also often cited as a clear-cut example of the assumed population/land degradation connection and appears widely in many general treatments of ancient environmental interaction (Redman 1999). The O'Hara et al. research was far from conclusive, with criticisms centering on the complete reliance on environmental data, inherent spatial limitations related to lake core research, the lack of a comparable archaeological record, and dating (see Fisher 2000; Fisher et al. 2003).

In an effort to elucidate connections among demographic growth, land degradation, and the development of social complexity better, a multidisciplinary program of landscape research in the southwest quarter of the Lake Pátzcuaro Basin was initiated in 1995, involving both settlement-pattern research and intensive geoarchaeological investigation conducted at comparable temporal and spatial scales. Much of this work was enabled by recent lowered lake levels that allowed paleoenvironmental investigation on the former lakebed below ancient Tarascan settlements, allowing the construction of a linked terrestrial- and lacustrine-based erosion record.

Central to this project was a conception of a recursive human-environment link, the casting of land degradation as a social problem, and the collection of natural and archaeological datasets at complementary scales. The findings from this research challenge aspects of both the V. M. Toledo et al. and O'Hara et al. projects and elucidate formerly ignored aspects of ancient built environments. These findings also serve as another example to nullify the population/land degradation myth with related contemporary policy implications.

The following discussion summarizes relevant findings from this research (table 10.1; figs. 10.1, 10.2); more specific information concerning methodology, data, and results can be found in Fisher 2000; Fisher et al. 1999, 2003; H. Pollard 2000; H. P. Pollard 2003; and H. Pollard and Cahue-Manrique 1999.

The Socionatural Connection in Pátzcuaro Prehistory

Initial settlement within the 250 km study area (see fig. 10.1) is first evident from surface remains during the Early Classic period (Loma Alta phase 2–3; 100 BC–AD 500). These early occupations were small (>5 ha), appearing either on islands or at the lakeshore. The first evidence for intensive wetland agriculture also appears, as evidenced by raised fields near the modern village of Nocutzepo (Fisher et al. 1999). Upland occupation is known from excavation at the sites of Urichu (H. Pollard and Cahue-Manrique 1998; H. P. Pollard 1993) and Erongarícuaro, which is located just outside the study area (H. P. Pollard 2003). During the Middle–Epiclassic periods (Jaracuaro–Lupe phases; AD 500–900), settlements are expanded, but the study area occupation remains small, with an estimated population for this period of 581–1,018 persons or 14–26 persons/km^2. During this period, a major drop in lake level is also indicated by the occupation of formerly inundated areas down to roughly 2,033 m above sea level (fig. 10.2d).

In two episodes (AD 120–590, 665–775), fans of eroded material, characterized by abrupt changes in color, texture, and structure (Unit 2, fig. 10.2d), were deposited below the two largest pre-Hispanic settlements of this period (Charahuén and Pareo; fig. 10.1). Away from areas of occupation the lakebed lacks eroded material. This early erosion event is the most severe of the pre-Hispanic period, occurring during a period of low population density (fig. 10.2d map; Loma Alta 3 phase 14–10 persons/km^2; Lupe 14–26 persons/km^2). Additionally, erosion during this period is a settlement rather than landscape-wide phenomenon, a trend that characterizes pre-Hispanic land disturbance. This detailed record indicates both landscape flux and lake-level change on the order of one-hundred-year intervals, meaning that early basin inhabitants coped with a highly dynamic environment.

TABLE 10.1. Summary of Trends by Archaeological Phase for the Lake Pátzcuaro Study Area (adapted from Fisher et al. 2003:table 1)

	Hispanic (1520–1650)	Postclassic (900–1520/1000)			Classic (900/350–1000)	
Period (AD)	Early	Late	Middle	Early	Epiclassic	Middle
Phases	Early	Tariacuri	Urichu	Urichu	Lupe	Loma Alta
Unit	5	4	3	3	2–3	1–2
Lake Level	2,040	<2,033	<2,033	<2,033–>2,035	>2,035	>2,035
Population	1,560–3,560	7,155–13,087	4,087–7,806	925–1,706	581–1,018	393–543
Settlement area (ha)	200	851.25	472.5	107.5	52.52	20
Persons/km^2	64	182–334	104–199	23–43	14–26	10–14
Erosion	4	2	2	2	4–5	5

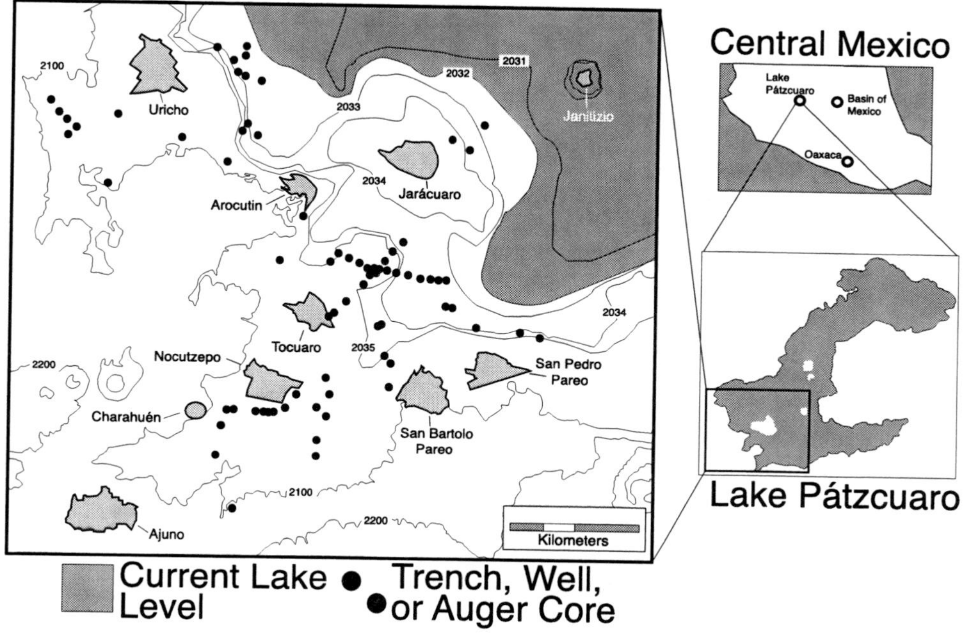

FIGURE 10.1. Location of the study area.

During the Early and Middle Postclassic (Urichu phase AD 900/1350), settlement grows steadily with a lake-edge focus and occupation positioned along the lakeshore up to the 2,033 m contour, indicating continued low lake levels (fig. 10.2c map). This is confirmed by soil formation in marsh sediments. The estimated population by AD 1350 is 4,087–7,806 persons or 104–199 persons/km². Erosion during this period is greatly reduced, demonstrating that basin inhabitants stabilized the landscape during a period of population growth.

The Tariacuri phase marks the most intensive pre-Hispanic occupation of the basin associated with the Tarascan Empire (Late Postclassic; AD 1350–1520). Tariacuri surface remains form an almost continuous scatter of material around the rim of the lakeshore similar to the Late Aztec period Basin of Mexico (Sanders et al. 1979). During the Late Postclassic (AD 1350–1520), shoreline and island occupations are constricted to locations above 2,040 m asl, indicating a major lake transgression (fig. 10.2b map). This event is confirmed in the geoarchaeological record by the burial of soils by marsh sediment, and it conforms to previous paleoenvironmental

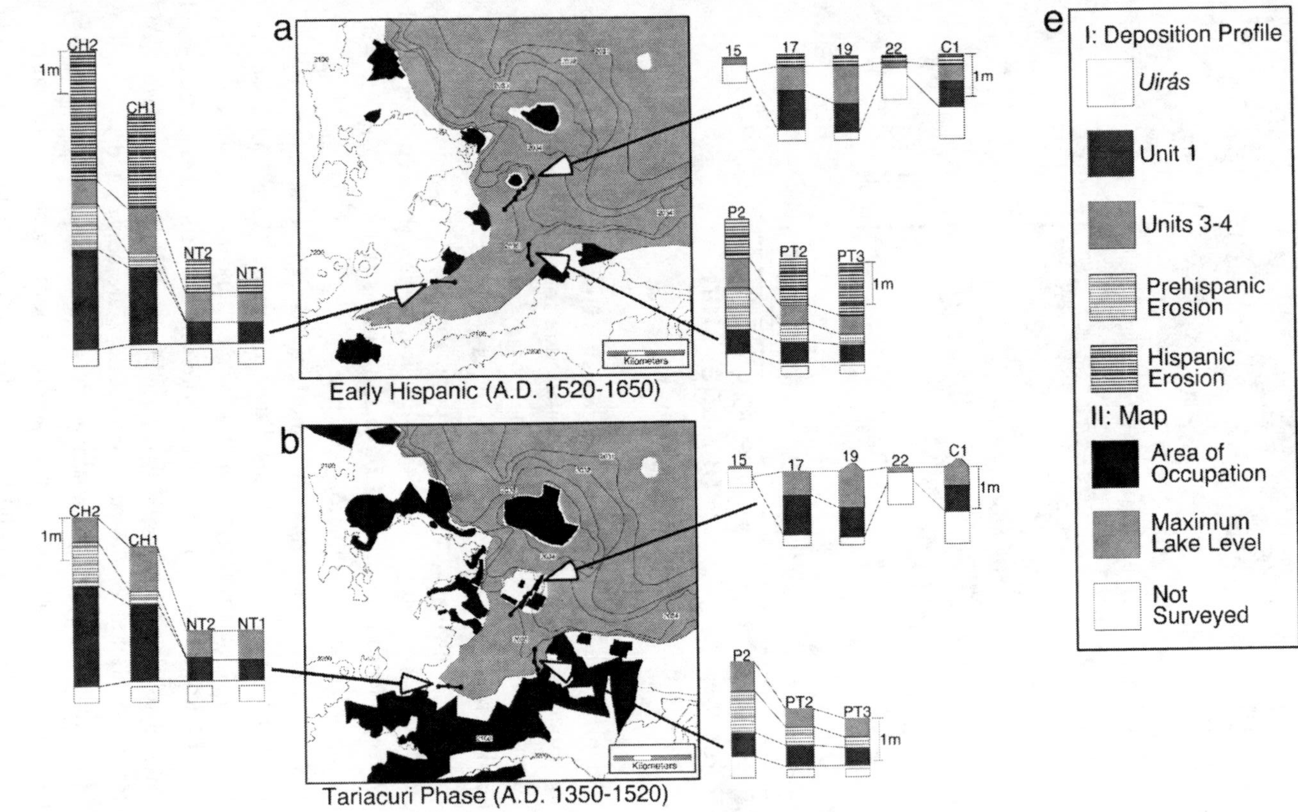
a
CH2
CH1
NT2
NT1
1m
15
17
19
22
C1
P2
PT2
PT3
Kilometers
Early Hispanic (A.D. 1520-1650)
b
Tariacuri Phase (A.D. 1350-1520)
e
I: Deposition Profile
Uirás
Unit 1
Units 3-4
Prehispanic Erosion
Hispanic Erosion
II: Map
Area of Occupation
Maximum Lake Level
Not Surveyed

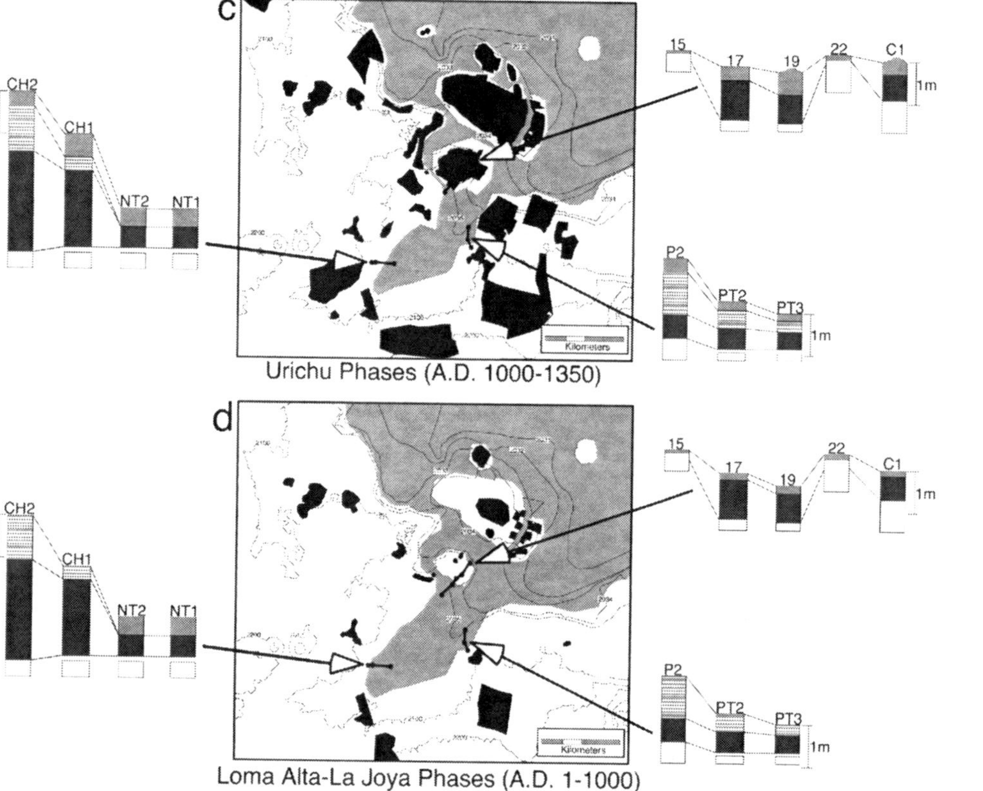

FIGURE 10.2. The co-evolution of landscape and settlement by major archaeological phases. a–d depict the interplay of lake level, settlement, and lithostratigraphic unit that characterize landscape development within the study region. The three catenas depicted in each inset are, clockwise from top right, Copujo, Pareo, Charahuén. eI (legend) shows shading indicating lithostratigraphic units. Central portion is a map of the study area. eII legend shows shading indicating settlement and lake level (adapted from Fisher et al. 2003).

research (Bradbury 2000; Metcalfe et al. 2000; O'Hara et al. 1993). Importantly, soil erosion remains low during the Tariacuri phase even though the Lake Pátzcuro Basin holds the largest pre-Hispanic occupation in the sequence (fig. 10.2b map; Tariacuri phase 182–334 persons/km^2) with a heavily terraced landscape.

The Colonial and Historic periods (AD 1520–present) mark a dramatic shift from the point-source deposition that characterized the pre-Hispanic to landscape-wide erosion that successively stripped soils from the landscape, exposing the loosely consolidated volcanic parent material underlying the escarpment of the basin. This caused some of the highest erosion rates in the sequence, even though the population of the basin was decimated by European-introduced disease (fig. 10.2a insets and map; 1,560–3,560 by AD 1650; Gorenstein and Pollard 1983; Warren 1984, 1985). Laminated clay sediments over soils and marsh sediments indicate the highest transgression in the sequence. This high stage is recorded in the ethnohistoric record beginning at the European Conquest and lasting until AD 1750–1800 (Gorenstein and Pollard 1983; O'Hara et al. 1993).

Discussion

The major implications of this work for modern policy are threefold. First, a long-term perspective can inform the V. M. Toledo et al. conservation plan by identifying the specific mechanisms that caused land degradation in the past. Our research corroborates aspects of earlier studies, demonstrating that there was significant past degradation (e.g., O'Hara et al. 1993). But unlike this previous research, we can actually identify specific land-degradation mechanisms. For the Classic period, this included the construction of large settlements rather than agriculture practice, while for the Early Conquest period the primary land degradation trigger was large-scale landscape abandonment.

In terms of conservation policy, this means that Purépecha TEK cannot be adopted out of whole cloth as a solution for current and future land degradation. Rather, informed by the record of long-term socionatural relations presented here, aspects of successful land use can be adopted for the modern Lake Pátzcuaro Basin economy. One major problem that will have to be solved before aspects of past land use can be solved is the current Lake Pátzcuaro Basin labor deficit. Traditional systems within the basin, past and present, are highly dependent on abundant and cheap labor, a form of human capital that is simply not present in the modern regional economy (Barrera-Bassols and Zinck 2003).

Second, large populations in the centuries leading to the European Conquest did not cause massive land degradation as argued by O'Hara et al. Instead, we are able to demonstrate that erosion episodes (AD 120–775, 1520–1960) occurred while the Lake Pátzcuaro Basin contained a low population density, but landscape stability (AD 776–1520) was maintained during population growth, urbanism, and massive environmental modification. This is attributable directly to the development of the humanized Pátzcuaro environment, which in the centuries leading to the conquest became increasingly dependent on labor for stability.

The degradation of the present-day landscape can be traced directly to the first landscape-wide erosion that occurred during the Early Hispanic period. This was caused by wholesale abandonment and was exacerbated by the introduction of the Euro-agro suite and high rainfall (Fisher 2000; Fisher et al. 2003). Here, it was indigenous land practice, rooted in abundant labor, that created an environment susceptible to degradation subsequent to demographic collapse.

Construction of large-scale terrace landscapes, which began in the Early Postclassic and was enabled by the growing population within the Lake Pátzcuaro Basin, was initiated to repair earlier land degradation. Like the Aztecs (B. Williams 1972) and the Classic period Maya (Dunning et al. 2002), Pátzcuaro land managers moderated past environmental damage to create sustainable, predictable, and intensive landscapes, with each successive episode of environmental modification conditioning the next.

Finally, perhaps the most significant mechanism contributing to the modern degraded Pátzcuaro environment centers on the effects of unintended consequences. For the Pátzcuaro Lake Basin, stability was maintained for centuries, while also creating a landscape susceptible to unforeseen risk. Tarascan land managers could not have foreseen the profound, and in many respects unintended, costs of the conquest of the Americas. Mid-nineteenth-century lumbering, followed by the political and economic instability of the Mexican Revolution and Cristero War (AD 1910–1940), only deepened the degradation already in process. Indeed, a parallel process occurred in sixteenth-century Spain. There, the expulsion of the Moors resulted in the abandonment of intensive landscape systems with associated land degradation (Latorre et al. 2001; van der Leeuw et al. 1998).

By the Late Postclassic, the Pátzcuaro landscape was an amalgam of consistent sociopolitical action that spanned centuries. Lake Pátzcuaro Basin inhabitants, like those in many other complex societies, lived in an ecosystem that was largely a human construct. This landscape was constantly shifting, significantly altering baseline environmental conditions on which human decisions were made. In this context, "geographical and ecological" constraints (Algaze 2001:199) were in large part determined by available labor and organization, often exacerbated by unintended consequences—which ultimately caused the unraveling of the Pátzcuaro system. In this sense, there are no villains and no heroes in the Lake Pátzcuaro Basin story. Or, in the words of Blaikie and Brookfield:

> Any attempt to find the cause of land degradation is somewhat akin to a 'whodunnit' except that no criminal will ultimately confess, and Hercule Poirot is unable to assemble the suspects on a Nile steamer or in the dining car of a snowbound Orient Express for the final confrontation. (Blaikie and Brookfield 1987:27)

Conclusion

When touting the contributions that a historical approach to modern conservation can make toward modern policy, an often-cited example is the ability to use long-term records to test for sustainability. In the final section of this contribution, I would like to explore briefly this proposition as informed by the Pátzcuaro work detailed above. Here, I argue that there are substantive failings in the sustainability concept that become apparent when long-term records of socionatural records are considered.

Though there is much dissension, most development policy generally follows the basic prescriptions laid out in United Nations–sponsored programs and meetings, such as the Brundtland Commission (WCED 1987) and its offshoots. In "Our Common Future," sustainable development is defined as "development that meets the needs of the present without compromising the ability of future generations to meet their own needs" (WCED 1987:8). The emphasis for sustainability is on maintaining a given lifeway, though the means to accomplish this end differ greatly. It is generally assumed that sustainability can be realized in one of two ways, either by 1) reducing human demands of the earth (strong sustainability), or 2) increasing resource production or using resources more efficiently (weak sustainability). Both are ultimately measured by evaluating land degradation (see Stocking and Murnaghan 2001).

Eventually, both lead to what C. Williams and Millington have coined "the environmental paradox," namely that there is a mismatch between what is demanded of the earth and what the earth is capable of supplying (2004:100). This disparity is due largely to the nature/culture dichotomy that has served to separate ourselves from environmental problems as described in the introduction to this chapter. Like the concept of environment, sustainability and land degradation are concepts largely defined by perception, making them both cultural and situational (Bell and Morse 1999; Keeney 1990; T. Kohler 1992a; Tainter 2000). This means that what is perceived today as sustainable land use may in a century be considered highly environmentally damaging.

For sustainability, space and time must be clearly defined and are critical for determining cause-and-effect relationships (K. W. Butzer 1996; van der Leuuw et al. 2000:363). Consideration of shorter temporal and spatial scales masks long-term trends, but allows human action and environmental consequence to be elucidated. Larger scales allow broad patterns to be discerned, but at the cost of causal discrimination.

D. Johnson and Lewis have recently proposed a useful dichotomy to categorize human land use across temporal scales (1995:chap. 7). *Creative destruction* refers to "the process by which the natural world is modified and sustainable land-use systems are developed" (1995:228). It is destruction in the sense that all human modification of the earth begins with the alteration of "natural" conditions. In contrast, *destructive creation* is a "failure to achieve long-term sustainability and by the initiation of progressively more serious patterns of land degradation" (D. Johnson and Lewis 1995:228–229).

Strikingly, when viewed from the *longue durée* (centuries), ancient human land use in the same region often oscillates between these two states, and this is related to the degradation time clock that is intrinsic to many engineered environments. In the Lake Pátzcuaro Basin example given above, Tarascan land managers maintained stable environments for centuries leading up to the period of European Conquest, while at the same time setting the stage for an environmental catastrophe. This cyclical pattern of past land degradation outlined for the Lake Pátzcuaro Basin is very similar to the Near East, Mediterranean, other parts of Europe, central Mexico, and the Maya region (see Redman 1999). In this sense, sustainable is in the eye of the beholder and is largely dependent on the scale of analysis, meaning that you can always find a scale at which land practice is sustainable management and another at which it can be considered land degradation.

Inherent to the sustainability concept is the need to prognosticate the output of the earth and the needs of future generations. One clear lesson that can be delivered from long-term records of socionatural change is the devastating impact of unplanned events, catastrophe, and the unintended consequences of human action. For the Lake Pátzcuaro Basin, there was no way to foresee the European Conquest, along with its devastating environmental consequences.

Thus, when viewed from the perspective of deep time, the concept of sustainability has some substantive failings. First, as a cognized phenomenon, any treatment of either is by definition culturally relative and an artifact of a specific social milieu. Second, as we learn more about nature and society, what today may seem sustainable for the long term may seem facile a century from now. Third, one of the largest messages that the historical approach can deliver is the impact of unintended consequences. If we cannot predict these perturbations, how can we incorporate them into modern management plans?

One possible solution comes in the concept of resilience, which can be defined simply as the ability of a socionatural configuration to successfully reorganize itself in the face of major perturbation (Redman, this vol.; Redman and Kinzig 2003; van der Leeuw et al. 2000, this vol.). Given the lessons above, if we are to be successful in the future as a species, we must be able to adapt quickly to unforeseen events, and this ability must be incorporated into considerations of sustainability.

As a completely human-induced phenomenon, land degradation—past and present—is a complex construct with many potential causes, consequences, and solutions, and only a historical perspective on human socionatural relations can decipher this tangled web of causality (Blaikie and Brookfield 1987:3–7; D. Johnson and Lewis 1995; Stocking and Murnaghan 2001). One common cause of ancient land degradation has been the abandonment of built environments as a consequence of societal collapse. In a recent essay in the journal *Science*, Jansen characterized human land manipulation as the "Gardenification of Nature," and like any garden, constant human intervention is needed for success (1998). Ancient landscapes are no exception, and as demonstrated here, when the garden is abandoned, the consequences can be disastrous.

11

Hohokam and Pima-Maricopa Irrigation Agriculturalists

MALADAPTIVE OR RESILIENT SOCIETIES?

John C. Ravesloot, J. Andrew Darling, and Michael R. Waters

For several thousand years, the inhabitants of the middle Gila River Valley were master farmers who constructed sophisticated agricultural systems that transformed the Sonoran Desert into a highly productive, sustainable socionatural ecosystem. The prehistoric Hohokam built the most extensive and large-scale irrigation system discovered by archaeologists in the pre-Columbian New World. Although smaller in scale than the canal systems of their Hohokam forebearers, the irrigation networks of the Pima-Maricopa were equally impressive.

Historical records reveal that the Pima-Maricopa Indians' ability to subsist using irrigation agriculture ended in the late 1800s with the upstream diversion of the Gila River, and the subsequent desertification of the middle Gila River Valley. The Gila River was the lifeblood of the middle Gila Valley, and its containment substantially altered and forever changed this ecosystem (Bigler 2005; Haury 1976; Ortiz 1973; Rea 1983). In the absence of historical records, our knowledge about the adaptation of the Hohokam comes from over one hundred years of archaeological investigations within the Salt and Gila river valleys. Some scholars see the Hohokam as having existed in ecological harmony with their desert environment, while others view them as a maladaptive society destined for collapse. In this chapter, we discuss and evaluate these two opposing viewpoints of Hohokam adaptation on the basis of over fifteen years of new research conducted in the middle Gila River Valley as part of the Pima-Maricopa Irrigation Project. We conclude that the Hohokam and their descendants, the Pima-Maricopa, are resilient societies and that several thousand years of occupation of the middle

FIGURE 11.1. First irrigations (Modified from Haury 1967; Peter Bianchi/ National Geographic Image Collection).

Gila River Valley—from the earliest stages of dependence on irrigation agriculture to the present—provides a rich and largely untapped laboratory for the long-term study of resiliency and sustainability of human societies.

Salinization and the Ecological Indian

Shepard Krech's (1999) radical critique of the nobilizing qualities of viewing Native Americans as ecologists and conservationists reduces the question of Sonoran Desert adaptation to two opposing viewpoints. The first, attributed to the late Emil Haury (1976:8), holds that the Hohokam were in "nearly perfect" balance with their environment, having established an equilibrium that was later lost with the arrival of the Euroamericans (fig. 11.1). The second position holds that the Hohokam literally "irrigated themselves to death" with mineral-laden waters that rendered the soils infertile. In this scenario, the demise of the Hohokam was as much a result of salinization as it was a result of their inability to comprehend the "systemic consequences" of irrigation on their ecosystem (1999:45–46).

In spite of the untested status of the salinization hypothesis, Krech's critique lacks the nuanced understanding of Gila River ecodynamics necessary to adequately assess Haury's position (cf. McGlade 1995; McIntosh et al. 2000; van der Leeuw and Redman 2002). Instead, Krech proposes that Haury's argument was motivated by 1960s political bias and intellectual viewpoints concerning the ecological Indian rather than his interpretation of 2,000 years of adaptation by the Hohokam and Pima-Maricopa to a riverine desert environment. For Krech, the Hohokam irrigation system lacked the sophistication necessary to cope with environmental hazards, culminating in social collapse.

A similar viewpoint is expressed by Hackenberg (1974) who characterizes Hohokam agriculture as labor intensive. Canal systems extended onto the upper terraces above the Gila River floodplain and avoided many of the maintenance problems presented by lower-lying canals and ditches due to annual flood damage. However, insufficient water supply limited their ability to flush out alkali and redeposit silt on previously irrigated fields. Like Krech, Hackenberg argues that the Hohokam adaptation was pre-programmed for failure.

In contrast, for Hackenberg, subsequent occupation of the floodplain by the Pima-Maricopa was labor extensive, but equally doomed. Agricultural production extended along the length of the riverbank, and canals and ditches were constantly re-excavated and replaced, but at a smaller scale by comparison with the Hohokam. Fields above the floodplain, rendered sterile by their prehistoric predecessors, remained fallow and unutilized. Unable to control the changes in the river and its banks, the Pima-Maricopa eventually failed, but for very different reasons.

Hackenberg argues that each successive adaptation to the local ecology suffered from the one that preceded it. For the Hohokam, extractive methods eventually outstripped the environment's capacity to support them. For the Pima-Maricopa, attempts at maintaining the soil and water balance in fields undamaged by the Hohokam eventually failed due to changes in the river. Since the time of Haury's work, theoretical statements about Hohokam and Pima-Maricopa adaptation have tended to emphasize the maladaptive qualities of each society.

Another frequently cited model deals with the effects of high-magnitude floods, as well as periods of drought, with similar catastrophic results for the Hohokam. Nials et al. (1989) suggest that the abandonment of Late Classic period Hohokam communities coincided with a period of drought and large floods (ca. AD 1350) that substantially impacted the canal systems on which these irrigation agriculturalists depended. Redman (1999) and Redman and Kinzig (2003) have built upon this idea to further consider such human ecosystem failures as hinge points between adaptive cycles corresponding to major periods in Hohokam development. They find that the forces for ecosystem change rely on the interaction of short- and long-term climatic variability. The proposed collapse of the Classic period Hohokam is viewed as the end of an adaptive cycle marked by the change from a period of hydrologic stability in the Salt and Gila rivers to a period of variable flow punctuated by drought and high-energy floods. Hohokam society ". . . already weakened by a century of disruptions, obviously did not overcome this one-two punch" (Redman 1999:155). The result was geographical contraction and sociopolitical fragmentation to the point that the Hohokam adaptation to the desert riverine environment could not be sustained.

With the exception of Haury, all models spell out impending ecological disaster. However, few of these models have been reasonably tested, and even fewer address the fact that the Pima and Maricopa populations that succeeded the Hohokam exhibited a new organizational configuration. Unlike their predecessors, Pima and Maricopa populations, in spite of unpredictable and low flows in the Gila, were able to manage the problems of floods, drought, salinization, and water balance.

Middle Gila: The Evidence

In 1993, the Gila River Indian Community initiated the planning to construct a modern water-delivery and -distribution system to serve 146,000 acres of allotted and tribal lands. The Pima-Maricopa Irrigation Project will ultimately consist of 82 miles of mainstem and 2,400 miles of secondary canals and associated irrigation features (fig. 11.2). This project incorporates tribal social memory in the design and construction of a gravity-fed water-delivery system. Like prehistoric and historic earthen canals, this modern irrigation system follows the alignment and the slope of where earlier canals had been constructed.

The Pima-Maricopa Irrigation Project will bring back into cultivation the 77,000 acres that represent the historically irrigated lands, plus an additional 69,000 acres. Projected agricultural output in terms of total acreage far exceeds previous totals at any time in the valley's history and prehistory by an order of magnitude. The sustainability of this new water-delivery system, like the Hohokam and Pima-Maricopa models, rests on the reliability and availability of water and labor required

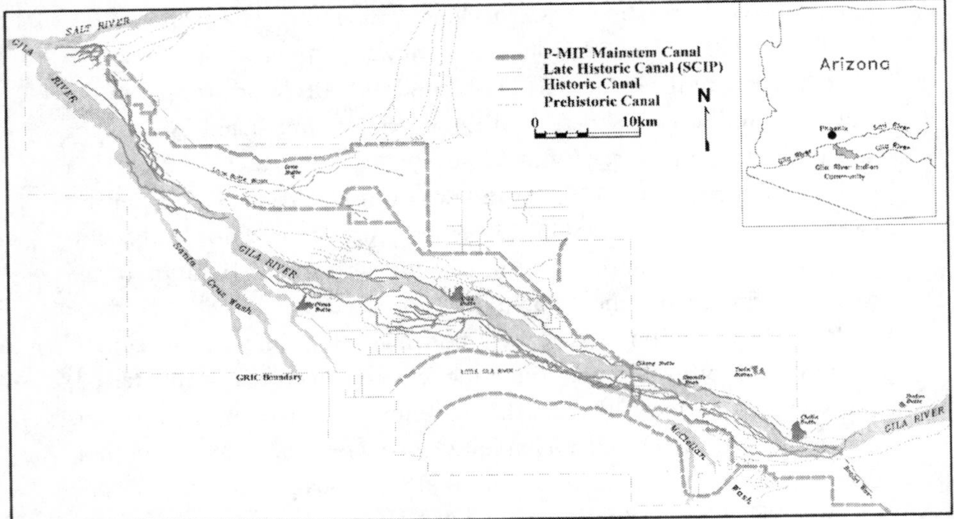

FIGURE 11.2. Prehistoric, historic, and modern irrigation systems on the middle Gila River.

to maintain such a system. Knowledge gained from the 2,000 years of prehistory and history in the middle Gila River Valley provide invaluable lessons for modern engineers, tribal administrators, and community farmers.

This modern irrigation project provides the community's Cultural Resource Management Program with the resources to document and investigate all prehistoric and historic sites that might be impacted or destroyed by the construction of new cement-lined canals, protective channels, dikes, and reservoirs. This is no minor detail, since the scale of the archaeological project being undertaken is truly massive. Ten years of archaeological surveys have resulted in the recording of nearly 1,000 sites, spanning Middle Archaic through Historic time periods (Ravesloot and Waters 2004; E. Wells et al. 2004). Over the next decade, a relatively large sample, 25 percent or more of these sites, is slated for testing and/or partial excavation.

One of the major research issues guiding these archaeological studies deals with describing the nature and extent of the prehistoric, protohistoric, and historic irrigation systems of the middle Gila River Valley (Woodson 2003, 2004). This research focus is necessary to examine the competing models for the organization and collapse of Hohokam, as presented above. These models, in turn, can be considered in relation to contemporary problems of irrigation and sustainable agricultural development in similar environments. Specific research questions being investigated by Gila River Indian Community's cultural program are provided below.

When and where were canals first constructed on the middle Gila?

How did canal systems on the middle Gila evolve through time?

How do prehistoric Hohokam canal systems on the middle Gila River Valley compare/contrast with those constructed in the lower Salt River Valley?

What were the organizational characteristics of Hohokam society and did they change between the Preclassic and Classic periods?

What effect did high- and low-frequency environmental processes, such as floods and droughts, have on the operation and maintenance of irrigation systems? What effect did these processes have on water balance and salinization?

Did the Pima practice irrigation agriculture during the Protohistoric period or only floodwater farming, as suggested by some scholars?

Was or is canal irrigation ecologically sustainable within the middle Gila River Valley?

Overview of Prehistoric and Historic Irrigation Systems

Irrigation has been a continuous feature of middle Gila River Valley adaptations since the first centuries AD to the present (Cummings 1926; M. Foster et al. 2002; Haury 1976; Midvale 1965; Turney 1929; Woodbury 1961; Woodson 2004). While a review of this history is beyond the scope of this chapter, a minimum of three general phases of irrigation may be identified: prehistoric Hohokam (AD 200–1450), historic Pima (AD 1600 [or earlier]–1920), and Euroamerican (1920–present). As mentioned earlier, the Pima-Maricopa Irrigation Project is drawing on the past to design and implement a water delivery system that will exceed in size and scope all previously constructed irrigation networks combined.

Geoarchaeological Research

A reconstruction of the late Quaternary landscape history of the middle Gila River's floodplain has been a major focus of our research. We have argued elsewhere (Waters and Ravesloot 2000, 2001) that a reconstruction of the alluvial history of the river was critical to elucidating the development and organization of the prehistoric Hohokam and historic Pima-Maricopa irrigation systems. The Gila River represented the only reliable source of water for Hohokam irrigation agriculturalists in an otherwise arid environment (Rea 1997).

Geoarchaeological investigations of the middle Gila River have revealed that after nearly 750 years of floodplain stability and a predictable streamflow regime, Hohokam farmers had to contend with a major environmental catastrophe (Waters and Ravesloot 2000, 2001, 2003). Sometime between AD 1020 and 1160, the alluvial history of the middle Gila River is characterized by a major sedimentological change (fig. 11.3). Down cutting and widening created a river channel similar to what we see today, which is at least 1 km wide. This regional catastrophic event would have had devastating consequences for Hohokam irrigation agriculturalists, made many canal headgates unusable, and forced the Hohokam to rely on fewer locations. Huckleberry (1995:177) has argued that the recovery of the Gila River from a high-energy down-cutting event may have taken thirty years or more before a wide streambed with braided conditions would be replaced by a single river channel.

While not the sole cause for the changes observed in the archaeological record between the Hohokam Preclassic and Classic periods, this low-frequency landscape process (sensu J. Dean 1988, 2000) may have accelerated social and political changes already underway (Waters and Ravesloot 2001, 2003). Contrary to the findings of Nials et al. (1989) (also embraced by Redman [1999] and Redman and Kinzig [2003]), there is no stratigraphic evidence for a major down-cutting event along the Gila River at AD 1350.

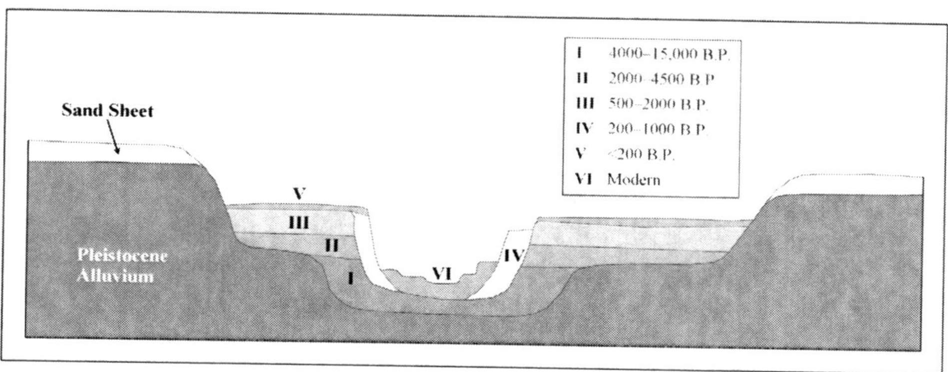

FIGURE 11.3. Gila River stratigraphic sequence (adapted from Waters and Ravesloot 2000, 2001).

One of the major weaknesses of stream-flow reconstructions (Graybill 1989; Graybill et al. 2006; Nials et al. 1989) is that we have no way of determining the configuration and discharge capacity of prehistoric river channels from dendrochronological data alone. This type of information can only be obtained from geological studies. Instead of inferring channel configuration and thus the effects of stream flow on canal systems, one should really determine from empirical data the size and configuration of the prehistoric channel. The stream-flow reconstruction should then be examined on the basis of this knowledge. If the channel was wide and deep, as demonstrated for the Preclassic to Classic transition, it can certainly carry more water than a single narrow channel. Thus, if you do not know the cross-sectional area of the channel, how can you determine if overbank flooding occurred and the effect on canal systems?

Recent geomorphic studies of the lower Salt River in the Phoenix Basin (Ciolek-Torrello et al. 2003; Onken et al. 2004) have uncovered evidence for a major down-cutting and channel-widening event during the Sedentary period, but like the Gila River (Waters and Ravesloot 2001), such evidence is lacking for the Classic period (Ravesloot and Rice 2004). Thus, there is stratigraphic evidence on both the Gila and Salt rivers for only a single down-cutting event that occurred between AD 1020 and 1160 during the Sedentary period. Models other than landscape change, therefore, must be considered to explain the reorganization of the Hohokam at the end of Classic period.

Stream-Flow Reconstructions

Dendrochronologic reconstructions of annual volume of stream flow in the Salt (Graybill 1989) and Gila rivers (Graybill et al. 2006), combined with geoarchaeological research, offer considerable insights into understanding how high- and low-frequency changes in the availability of water affected the development of prehistoric and historic irrigation systems (Ravesloot and Rice 2004). Stream-flow reconstructions for the Salt River (Graybill 1989) suggest that Hohokam farmers could expect in every ten-year cycle to have an annual flow that was 150 percent above the average flow and a low flow that was only 54 percent above the annual average. Hohokam agriculturalists were adapted to high-frequency events such as floods and periods of low flow or droughts (Ravesloot and Rice 2004; Waters and Ravesloot 2003). We believe that Hohokam populations were more than capable of summoning the labor required to repair canal systems relatively quickly following high-frequency floods—distinguished from down-cutting events. Furthermore, descriptions of historic Pima farmers demonstrate that over-bank flooding resulting from high flows of the river can be very beneficial to agricultural productivity (Castetter and Bell 1942; Rea 1978).

Rather than high-frequency flood events, we argue that the adaptation of Hohokam irrigation agriculturalists to the middle Gila River Valley was also affected by low-frequency variation in the availability of water or "prolonged periods of low flow." Graybill et al. (2006) define "prolonged periods of low flow" as any period of eight or more successive years during which the annual stream flow was consistently half a standard deviation beneath the average annual flow.

According to Castetter and Bell (1942), the Pima normally had a four-year surplus of foods in storage. On the basis of the Pima agricultural model, we doubt that a single year or even several years of drought were really a major problem for Hohokam farmers. Russell (1908:66) noted that the Pima were conditioned to diminished flow in the Gila River every fifth year during midwinter in historic times. However, eight years of prolonged drought would have seriously exhausted stored food surpluses for

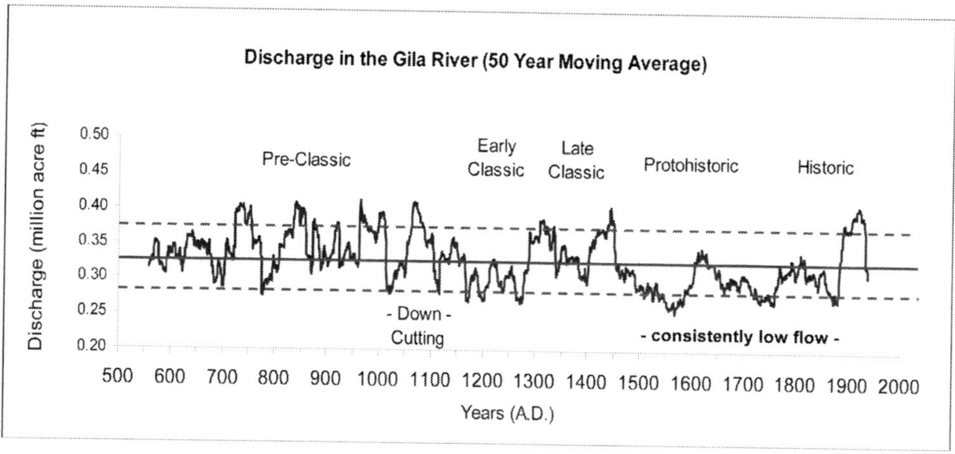

FIGURE 11.4. Streamflow reconstruction of the middle Gila River (AD 550–1950) (adapted from Ravesloot and Rice 2004 and Graybill et al. 2006).

both the Pima and the Hohokam. At such times, their diet would have consisted primarily of wild foods such as mesquite, saguaro fruit, cholla buds, and screwbean.

A graph of the fifty-year moving average of stream flow indicates that there are several century-long periods during which the mean remained consistently above or below the average (fig. 11.4).

AD 800 to 1000 was characterized by consistently above-average flow. Conditions were good for agriculture.

AD 1160 to 1280 was characterized by consistently below-average flows. Even with intensification, agriculture may have been less productive than previous centuries.

AD 1280 to 1450 was characterized by consistently above-average flows. Conditions were excellent for agriculture.

AD 1450 to 1870 was characterized by consistently below-average flows. During this four-hundred-year period, there was consistently less stream flow available for irrigation than anytime in the previous one thousand years. In addition, consistently less irrigation water was available for protohistoric and early historic populations than the Hohokam had during the previous two thousand years.

Critique of the Salinization Hypothesis

Periods of prolonged low flow (drought) may have contributed to the longer-term problem of salinization common to irrigation agriculturalists worldwide. Contrary to Krech or Hackenberg, who view the Hohokam collapse as a result of over-irrigation, or Nials et al. (1989) who describe flooding as destructive to the irrigation system, salinization is dependent on maintaining an effective water balance in which drainage is a critical factor. Insufficient water supplies for irrigation and low-flow regimes may have limited further the ability of farmers to leach destructive salts from their fields. Ackerly (1988) has demonstrated on the basis of a thorough study of the Lehi-Mesa canals that salinization was not a significant contributing factor in the collapse of the Hohokam—what he refers to as false causality. As illustrated in fig. 11.4, the period from AD 1280 to 1450 was characterized by above-average flows of water in the Gila River. Problems with salinization should arise within fifty years or less of the start of irrigation, so Hohokam society would have collapsed much earlier had they not been able to solve this problem.

Interestingly, low-flow regimes apparently did not present a problem for the Pima until there was no water in the river. ". . . they flooded the tract repeatedly and in this way washed the alkali out of it. They declare that they never abandoned a piece of ground because of it" (Russell 1908:87). Castetter and Bell (1942:123) also note that the Pima never abandon any farmland due to problems with the accumulation of salts. C. H. Southworth (1914) records significant agricultural recovery along the length of the middle Gila River. Subsequent to major flooding a decade earlier, by 1914 as much as 15,490 acres of agricultural land were placed back into cultivation, while 11,361 acres rested in fallow. This recovery occurred in spite of widespread soil contamination (increasing alkali/salinization) due to water imbalance and drought (Darling et al. 2004:fn. 16; Southworth 1914; fig. 11.5). "This . . . bespeaks their [Pima] ancient knowledge of how to manage the fields from this standpoint" (Castetter and Bell 1942:123).

Worldwide irrigation agriculturalists have used similar solutions to deal with the problem of salinization (Gelburd 1985; Henry Wright, personal communication 2003). Commonly used solutions include leaching fields with additional water, digging wells to lower the water table, and

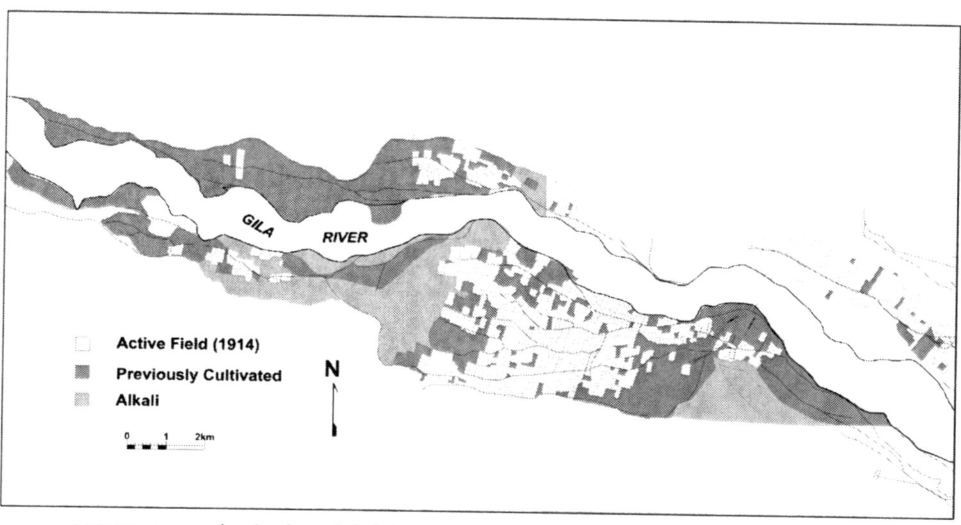

FIGURE 11.5. Agricultural fields along the middle Gila River in 1914 (adapted from Southworth 1914).

leaving fields fallow for regularly scheduled intervals (R. M. Adams 1978). Water logging and salt concentrations in fields due to over-irrigation may have been a factor in the collapse or reorganization of the Hohokam (e.g., Hackenberg 1974; Krech 1999), although future evaluation of this hypothesis within the middle Gila is required. However, we speculate based on Haury's and Ackerly's research and the Pima-Maricopa agricultural model that salinization was a minor issue for the Hohokam, as long as sufficient water was available to leech the fields.

New Model

The Hohokam entered a new adaptive cycle as a result of the declining availability of water at about AD 1450 or 1500 (see fig. 11.4). Irrigation agriculture could not sustain the population levels of the preceding Hohokam Classic period. Rather than a collapse, the Pima-Maricopa represent a reorganized society minus the Hohokam veneer of ballcourts and platform mounds. The so-called demise or collapse of the Hohokam may have been related in part to a lack of water to sustain a large agrarian population supported by irrigation. Hohokam populations adapted to one major low-frequency event, down cutting of the river, at the juncture between the Preclassic and Classic periods. Geoarchaeological evidence has demonstrated that history did not repeat itself again during the Classic period.

Ezell (1994:326) has argued that the Pima and Maricopa Indians in the middle of the nineteenth century were a hydraulic agricultural society ". . . thoroughly adjusted to its environment and circumstances and apparently well in control of its own destiny." The economic stability the Pima-Maricopa Indians had known for centuries was radically changed during the 1860s with the large-scale construction of canals and ditches, intensive dam building, and rapidly increasing upstream diversion of water off the Salt and Gila rivers. "The Pima-Maricopa culture was tied to the river, which was soon to become an erratic channel, sometimes swollen with floods, sometimes dry from natural drought, and increasingly dry from upstream diversion of water by increasing numbers of American and Mexican farmers" (Ezell 1994:365). In a relatively short period of time, a decade or so, the self-sufficient people who had adapted to the American economic system by producing major surpluses of wheat, corn, and barley experienced a steady decrease in the availability of water for irrigation agriculture and subsequent crop failures. Like their ancestors the Hohokam, the Pima-Maricopa were fully capable of adapting to changing major environmental and economic conditions (Darling et al. 2004).

Conclusions

From the standpoint of long-term adaptation by an indigenous society that co-evolved with the local ecosystem of the middle Gila River, the last great catastrophe to impact the valley was the upstream diversion of water in the mid-nineteenth century (Rea 1983). Prior to this, the river down cutting of the eleventh century brought on by a period of hydraulic instability initiated an extended period of reduced stream flow. The resultant social changes in the Hohokam described as the Classic period may have initiated a new organizational configuration, culminating in Pima-Maricopa society. We doubt this was a nearly perfect balance as suggested by Haury, but ten years of research demonstrate that contrary to Krech, Hackenberg, and Redman these societies were not maladaptive or insufficiently resilient.

Concurrent with the writing of this chapter, the Gila River Indian Community is entering a new era in its relationship with water. After more than a century of negotiation, a water settlement between the tribe and the U.S. government has been signed into law (Shaun McKinnon and Bill House, "Historic Arizona Water Deal," *Arizona Republic*, November 18, 2004). This historic settlement not only compensates the tribe for previous losses but also will restore the vitality of lands rendered infertile by non-Indian appropriation with large quantities of Central Arizona Project and other waters. Through the Pima-Maricopa Irrigation Project, the projected agricultural output in terms of total acreage will far exceed previous totals at any time in the valley's history.

Based on lessons learned from the past, sustainability of this project remains a major question. However, it is a problem of scale: the history of irrigation in the middle Gila has demonstrated a consistent trend toward the development of larger irrigation projects to increase productivity. Like the Hohokam and Pima-Maricopa models, successful implementation rests on the reliability and availability of water and the labor required to maintain a water-delivery system. It also depends on the role that water will play in the future for the Gila River Indian Community and for non-Indian communities that surround it.

In the 1920s, the failure of the San Carlos Irrigation Project (SCIP) to effectively bring an additional 50,000 acres above the land traditionally cultivated by the Pima-Maricopa Indians offers a case in point. In that instance, an insufficiency of water collected behind the Coolidge Dam, which also eliminated surface and subsurface flows downstream, marked the end of traditional farming and rendered the irrigation efforts of the SCIP largely unsustainable.

The burgeoning metropolis of modern-day Phoenix will, in time, fully encircle the Gila River Indian Community and already presents new environmental factors and significant landscape change. Such eventualities demand a change in viewpoint or a different strategy (Collins et al. 2000; van der Leeuw and Redman 2002). Water banking and multiple use includes not only agriculture (as agro-business) but also the sale of water, recreational uses, power generation, and environmental conservation (restoration), among other uses. New strategies for the use of water and its commoditization (Appadurai 1986) are evidence of the ecological resilience of Pima-Maricopa society and the new ecology of an urban landscape.

Conclusion

The Socionatural Connection

CLOSING COMMENTS

J. Brett Hill, Christopher T. Fisher, and Gary M. Feinman

THIS SYNTHETIC VOLUME serves to bring together prominent scholars discussing new research findings addressing issues in ancient human ecology and its relevance to contemporary environmental concerns. In so doing we have endeavored to shed new light on present misconceptions, simplifications, and uncertainties about the interconnected relationship we all share with our environment. We are not alone in our concern that past records of human-induced environmental change be invoked for considerations of modern policy. Indeed, our volume answers a recent call to arms by many prominent researchers (e.g., Denevan 1995; Dunning et al. 2002; Fisher and Feinman 2005; Kirch 2005; Lentz 2000; McIntosh et al. 2000; Redman et al. 2004; B.L.M. Turner et al. 2003; van der Leeuw and Redman 2002). Unique are the large geographic coverage and breadth of topics addressed by our case studies. Contributors to this volume bring insights gleaned from archaeology in multiple regions of the world including North America, Mesoamerica, Europe, the Near East, and Africa. They present evidence from time periods spanning the Holocene and from environments ranging from tropical forest to desert. Through these insightful examples, they offer their perspectives on the variety of socionatural connections that have evolved and changed through history. A dominant theme running through all of the chapters is that a more accurate and complete understanding of these connections is essential for evaluating current theories and models of environmental degradation and conservation.

Perhaps the single most important contribution from this volume is a consensual and documented recognition in all of the case studies presented here that calls into question and ultimately refutes popular notions of a simple cause-and-effect relationship between people and their environment. The studies here reject the notion of people as either hapless victims of unstoppable forces or as inevitable destroyers of natural harmony (see discussion in T. M. Whitmore and Turner 2002). Instead, we see repeatedly how culture intercedes in both the material and ideological connections between people and the landscapes they inhabit. Human culture invariably structures the way environmental change is perceived and acted upon in particular historical settings, and environmental conditions are increasingly managed to fit culturally structured human desires. In the process, socionatural dynamics co-evolve in ways that deny causal primacy to any single factor or type of factor and preclude concepts such as "natural disaster," in which either humans or nature are predestined to suffer the consequences of fate.

Instead, the archaeological record seems to suggest the multiplicity of both potential outcomes and human perceptions of their success. In addition, it contributes essential awareness of the connections among natural conditions and cultural practices that lead to such outcomes and perceptions. The contributors to this volume each offer a unique example of the ways in which a particular combination of ecological circumstance and cultural organization leads to systematic environmental change. Ultimately, these chapters strive to move beyond simple illustrations of past anthropogenic degradation to get at underlying concepts that have affected human ecodynamics over deep histories.

Three dominant conceptual themes emerge from archaeological studies of human impact on ancient environments represented here. First, the non-linear, recursive, and multiscalar qualities of ecodynamic processes clearly indicate that causal relationships exist in multiple dimensions and are inherently unsuitable to explanations relying on universal driving mechanisms. It appears unlikely that any simple explanation will provide a satisfying conclusion to fundamental questions of how and why processes play out the way they do. Rather, understanding will come only from the effort of examining the specifics of momentary circumstances and the historical trends that produced them.

Secondly, a limited number of process types may be defined and documented that explain a large part of the diversity springing from variable initial conditions. In this vein, several of the contributors introduce or elaborate on new theoretical principles useful to understanding fundamental socionatural processes. These principles may be characterized according to their focus on objective or subjective aspects of the dynamic. In other words, some focus on observable patterns of socionatural systems as they change through time, with an eye toward explaining what happened in the past as a systematic process. These chapters strive to place commonly observed phenomena such as adaptation, intensification, collapse, and abandonment into broadly applicable theoretical frameworks that provide insight into empirical matters of cause and effect. In addition, however, some chapters focus on the very important but underdeveloped aspects of human perception in ecodynamics. These include questions about the definitions of basic concepts like "natural" systems, degradation, environmental crisis, collapse, sustainability, and environmental determinism. The contributors here repeatedly expose the fallacy of common agreement on such concepts and underscore the need for more effective communication among environmental scientists about ontological matters.

Finally, the contributors to this volume offer new answers to old questions. Essential questions in archaeology often revolve around uncertainty over the fate of an ancient people and the role of the environment in their disappearance. These questions take the form of, Where did they go and who are their descendents? Did environmental degradation play a part and when did it become a problem? Was environmental degradation anthropogenic and/or natural, and how did particular people and populations respond to such challenges? The authors here present valuable insight into such questions for their specific study areas and discuss how such insights might be useful to understanding similar processes in other areas.

One challenge in bringing a volume like this to print is the necessity of organizing the chapters in a coherent and meaningful way. It can be clearly seen that the authors here frequently cross-cut the conceptual themes described above, rendering chapter organization problematic. In addition to the conceptual themes that structure the volume's present organization, individual chapters lend themselves to discussion in pragmatic terms that emphasize the distinct foci of their approach.

Some papers emphasize new constructs for socionatural interpretation. Redman and colleagues, van der Leeuw, and Scarborough focus on the theoretical and conceptual principles that underlie their research. In so doing, they draw attention to ways we might incorporate a more realistic and nuanced understanding of the socionatural connection and how archaeologists can communicate and work more effectively with other scientists.

Redman and colleagues discuss the contemporary state of interdisciplinary research and the potential for resilience theory in developing a theoretical structure that can help integrate archaeology with other disciplines. Using the example of Hohokam collapse, they illustrate the stages of an adaptive cycle as a regularized process of socionatural transformation with identifiable phases that are cause and consequence of other phases. The meta-language provided by resilience theory not only helps us organize and understand these phases but also facilitates communication with scholars identifying similar structural processes in other self-organizing systems.

Van der Leeuw clarifies the definition of environmental crisis as a relationship between society and its environment rather than as an event or a series of perturbations that occur purely in nature. He presents two case studies from Portugal and Greece to illustrate how changes in this relationship turned out differently because of different social circumstances. He follows with a discussion of crises and how they come about, drawing substantially on resilience theory. One important message is the need to change our attitudes and perceptions because all societies eventually go through such an adaptive cycle.

Scarborough presents two models of economic development and uses case studies from lowland Maya and Basin of Mexico contexts to illustrate the differences. The more-familiar technotasking emphasizes technological solutions to environmental constraints, focusing on resource extraction, consumption, and rapid change. The less-well-known labortasking emphasizes intensification, accretional development, and alteration of landscapes and resource harvesting. Scarborough argues that the latter is uncommon today outside of Southeast Asia, but may have been important in past humid tropical settings. He concludes that broadening our view of economy and the role of technology to include alternatives may offer important insights into questions of sustainability in both archaeological and modern contexts.

Issues of complexity, farming, and the built environment unite contributions focusing on the complex interactions among agriculturalists and the landscapes they construct through generations of problem solving and adaptation to local conditions. Ravesloot and colleagues, Dunning and colleagues, Fisher, and Thurston each provide fresh insights that contrast with commonly held views of the causal relationships between humans and their environment.

Ravesloot and colleagues offer an alternative to the view of Hohokam society as doomed by maladaptive qualities of its irrigation system. Based on geoarchaeological and ethnographic evidence, they argue that flooding and salinization were not significant problems for the Hohokam, but that sustained drought and channel incision were. They argue furthermore that people along the Gila River were able to successfully adapt to repeated changes in the hydrological regime of major rivers until nineteenth- and twentieth-century Euro-American irrigation and dam construction. Native American concerns over contemporary water-management programs must be viewed in the context of these past successes and failures, and must consider new strategies for the use of water in a changing environment.

Dunning and colleagues discuss the history of thought on Maya environment and land use, presenting a summary of the great variability of environments, land-use strategies, and consequences through Maya prehistory. They identify conditions in many areas that indicate the development of sophisticated and knowledgeable conservation practices structured by a land ethic that persists today. They furthermore identify sociopolitical conditions of conflict, land tenure, and intensification that contributed to the variety of both successful and unsuccessful practices over time. Knowledge of past land use and Maya adaptations to difficult conditions is essential to understanding present problems and local attitudes towards them.

Fisher deconstructs the population/land degradation fallacy through a discussion of the artificial separation of humans and nature in scientific inquiry. He then presents a case study from the Lake Pátzcuaro Basin to illustrate how land degradation did not follow from overpopulation, but rather from population decline. He discusses the ways in which the natural and the social must be integrated in analyses, and the importance of degradation as a social and perceptual problem. The concept of sustainability is found wanting as an objective goal, but must instead be seen in a social and temporal context. Fisher notes both the importance of a long-term view and of the role of unintended consequences in understanding what exactly is sustained.

Thurston engages the underdeveloped subject of anthropogenic soils and how modern attempts at soil enrichment can be informed by the past development of *plaggen* soils in northwest Europe. Through an examination of the early use of livestock byres, she illustrates the development of soil enrichment as an unintended consequence of recursive cultural practice rather than an intentional strategy. She documents the subsequently variable use and success of soil enrichment as a function of variable land-use histories, knowledge of local conditions, and socioeconomic structures. Caution is advised in the simplistic application of technology to contemporary problems without consideration of these same cultural and historical details.

Finally, some papers move beyond the agricultural system, bringing together views of greater systemic and temporal diversity. Unlike other chapters that focus on agricultural systems of relatively recent time periods, Kusimba, Simmons, Bar-Yosef, and Hill consider more fundamental transformations in the long-term relations between humans and their environment.

Kusimba looks at the role of iron-production technology and the effects of international trade on African environments. He illustrates how the practice of ivory hunting is producing unexpected consequences for vegetation and human habitability of East Africa. International markets, tourism, and conservation efforts in Africa come into conflict with indigenous peoples attempting to share the same resources. Kusimba's work illustrates the important long-term role of humans in the co-evolution and sustainability of environments that conservationists value so greatly today, underscoring the potential fallacies of protecting the environment from humans.

Simmons presents evidence for early human impacts in Cyprus, contrasting the Epipaleolithic with the Late Neolithic. In the former case, there is evidence for substantial impacts on the island's endemic fauna, while later occupations by larger populations in the Neolithic apparently caused much less degradation. This light impact during the Neolithic is also in contrast to other parts of the Levant where some of the most extreme cases of early anthropogenic degradation were occurring at the same time. These differences illustrate the inadequacy of simple linkages between technology, population, and environmental degradation.

They likewise draw our attention to the importance of temporal scale and unintended consequences afforded by an archaeological perspective.

Bar-Yosef takes an unusual and interesting position relative to many current archaeological discussions by focusing on the importance of climate change. He argues that archaeologists have been too quick to exclude climate change as a causal factor affecting ancient societies. Because of our interest in demonstrating the importance of social factors and avoiding accusations of climatic determinism, we have undervalued the role of climate in social change. Using evidence from the Younger Dryas and Early Holocene, he emphasizes the importance of the cultural filter on variable responses to climate change by Natufian and Neolithic societies, and their longer-term consequences for neighboring areas. This focus reminds us that the error of linear cause-and-effect interpretations is not mitigated by an error of omission when evaluating the importance of climate change on the socionatural relationship.

Hill uses a long-term view of the relationship between people and their environment in the Levant to illustrate the punctuated nature of change and to highlight important hinge points in socionatural history. He illustrates the transformative quality of these changes in the organization of the socionatural relationship, finding common focus on such change in multiple views of anthropological and ecological theory. This history highlights the need for greater clarity on the meaning of significance in our interpretations of environmental degradation. He argues that from the vantage point of humans, significance is a function of change in the structure of socionatural relationships rather than a quantitative change in one component of those relationships.

Given the rapidly changing world around us, it is all too easy to focus on the latest environmental headline at the expense of long-term trajectories of change. But it is necessary to fully understand the interplay between past human decisions, unintended outcomes, and forces outside human control to create strategies for future environmental conservation. One important conclusion that emerges from all of the chapters is that environmental degradation is not a problem resulting from either endogenous or exogenous causes, but is fundamentally a problem of the relationship between humans and their environment—the socionatural connection. Consequently, solutions cannot be found by addressing either aspect of the equation alone. Both are always in flux, and change in the relationships among them is inevitable.

A further observation that emerges from these chapters is that consequences are not merely unintended, but are often surprising, unexpected, and relatively sudden. This point highlights the importance of temporal scale in our understanding of human ecodynamics by illustrating the inadequacy of the recent past as a guide to the future. Archaeological analyses repeatedly illustrate the absence of linearity or gradualism in socioecological change. It appears at least as often that periods of apparent stability are interrupted by dramatic change, and the pattern of change is most visible in the long-term perspective. If a simple lesson for the future is to be found in the archaeological record, it is that the future is for the adaptively nimble. Attempts to plan for any particular future are probably misguided, and instead a plan for flexibility and a broad perspective is suggested.

How can general lessons such as these contribute to modern environmental policy? We are constantly inundated with statistics detailing our changing world and our role in this volatile process. In spite of a large literature detailing the broader connection between societal and environmental health—of which this volume is one part—we still lack complete narratives and concrete ways in which we can make a contribution.

Our case studies demonstrate that the unpredictable, unintended consequences of human action loom large in causing past environmental problems. At some risk of dating this volume for future scholars, we feel that the recent Gulf Coast hurricane catastrophe exemplifies many of the points we make in this conclusion. Such problems do occur in a specific time and place, but to draw useful lessons from them, we must distinguish between the event and the process that produced it. It serves no useful purpose to plan for the most recent event, but we can better understand future potentials if we examine general principles that underlie the process. The social and environmental impact of hurricanes Katrina and Rita was the dramatic endgame of a complex interplay of natural perturbations, such as climatic change, and human factors, such as poor responses to initial challenges, that played off each other for centuries. When we read headlines that question whether the recent catastrophe was natural or human induced, or witness the political blame game over bungled responses to the hurricanes, we believe that it is important to put things in a larger perspective. Over the *longue durée*, the Gulf disaster reminds us of cases of past societal change and collapse, several of which are outlined in this volume. In such situations, challenges of the environment were repeatedly met with partial and momentary solutions that changed other aspects of the socionatural relationship and even exacerbated the initial problem. The results were disasters far worse than the initial damage or threat caused by nature. To truly understand these present events, we believe that a long-term perspective must be taken to consider the interplay of human decisions, environmental change, and unintended consequences leading directly to the hurricane disasters.

Unarguably, the scope, severity, and broad reach of the Gulf Coast cataclysm make it one of the worst in U.S. history, but in the history of our species, such episodes are all too common. Similar catastrophes have often occurred with even more deadly results for the impoverished and vulnerable, and sometimes have consequences reaching far beyond the immediate damage and loss of life. It is premature to signal the downfall of Western civilization in this catastrophe, but it does highlight systematic weaknesses and presages similar problems in the future that may have epic consequences. It is a truism that all civilizations eventually collapse, and in many respects, each collapse is unique. Yet there are striking similarities in causal processes and in human responses to them.

Many believe that human societies, having become fixed in their responses to continual ecological and social change, lose the ability to react or adapt to crises outside the scope of shared memory. They become less resilient to destabilizing change through continual small-scale, short-term solutions to large-scale problems. Environmental catastrophes in this view are communication failures between elements of societies tasked with solving particular problems, but failing to understand general processes.

One lesson from this work is that in our effort to achieve sustainable solutions for modern problems we must leave room for the unintended and the unexpected. We must develop solutions that are flexible enough to react to the unforeseen, and by examining past records of human change, we can get some idea of the form that these large-scale cataclysms may take. At the same time, there are broader questions that should be addressed. How will we recognize future transformations, and how can we best understand the complex and long-term processes leading towards them?

The history of New Orleans, Hurricane Katrina, and the aftermath is a prime example of socionatural crisis as long-term process. This tragedy has deep roots, perhaps extending back to the founding of the city on delta land best suited to seaborne commerce and the early attempts by the U.S. Army Corps of Engineers and others to stop flooding. A 1927 flood led to the profound rebuilding of the original levee system, meeting a desire for stability. Meanwhile, in the following decades, New Orleans sank or subsided as the delta region was not replenished by the alluvial sediments formerly brought by annual floods. As New Orleans sank, it also became more vulnerable because of the loss of coastal marsh and barrier islands, as well as the increased urbanization of rural areas. In recent years, decreased federal funding for the levees curtailed short-term quick fixes and longer-term planning alike. At the same time, global warming enhanced the likelihood of major hurricanes. Through short-term thinking and politically influenced decisions, resources were not allocated for the strengthening of the levees despite these ominous signs, ignoring the lessons that might have been learned from science and history.

In a recent editorial in *Science*, Donald Kennedy, discussing the recent Hurricane Katrina disaster, states that "the various interrelationships among Nature, God, and the law are becoming more complex and confusing in the modern world" (2006:303). The problems on the Gulf Coast are particularly visible and distressing examples of problems in the socionatural relationship, but they are not isolated, and by the time our readers contemplate these paragraphs, others will undoubtedly have occurred. Most will not be as visible as Katrina, but many will share basic underlying processual qualities. Whether they are climate change, diminished soils, or loss of biodiversity, they will appear in the moment as unintended and surprising consequences of changes in the socionatural relationship spanning generations.

If we are to avoid repeating the problems of the past and more effectively and resiliently manage the future, then we must heed the many lessons provided by history. We must actively integrate this knowledge into our policies, take a larger perspective on problems, and anticipate the unintended. Only then do we have a chance to escape what the global record of humankind tells us has happened over and over again. People in the past have faced many of the same problems we face today, and this record can provide valuable insights into contemporary problems if our focus is directed at the appropriate scale.

References

Abbott, D. R. 2000. *Ceramics and Community Organization among the Hohokam*. Tucson: University of Arizona Press.

———. 2003. *Centuries of Decline during the Hohokam Classic Period at Pueblo Grande*. Tucson: University of Arizona Press.

Abrams, E. M., and D. J. Rue. 1988. The Causes and Consequences of Deforestation among the Prehistoric Maya. *Human Ecology* 16:377–395.

Abungu, G.H.O. 1990. *Communities on the River Tana, Kenya: An Archaeological Study of Relations between the Delta and the River Basin, 700–1890 AD*. PhD diss., Cambridge University.

Ackerly, N. W. 1988. False Causality in the Hohokam Collapse. *The Kiva* 53(4):305–319.

Adams, J. S., and T. O. McShane. 1996. *The Myth of Wild Africa: Conservation without Illusion*. Berkeley: University of California Press.

Adams, R.E.W., and W. D. Smith. 1981. Feudal Models for Classic Maya Civilization. In *Lowland Maya Settlement Patterns*, ed. W. Ashmore, 335–349. Albuquerque: University of New Mexico Press.

Adams, R. McC. 1978. Strategies of Maximization, Stability, and Resilience in Mesopotamian Society, Settlement, and Agriculture. *Proceedings of the American Philosophical Society* 122(5):329–335.

———. 1981. *Heartlands of Cities*. Chicago: University of Chicago Press.

———. 2006. Intensified Large-Scale Irrigation as an Aspect of Imperial Policy. In *Agricultural Strategies*, ed. J. Marcus and C. Stanish, 17–37. Los Angeles: Cotsen Institute of Archaeology at UCLA.

Adderley, W. P., and I. A. Simpson. 2005. Early-Norse Home-Field Productivity in the Faroe Islands. *Human Ecology* 33(50):711–736.

Adderley, W. P., I. A. Simpson, M. J. Lockheart, R. P. Evershed, and D. A. Davidson. 2000. Modeling Traditional Manuring Practice: Soil Organic Matter Sustainability of an Early Shetland Community? *Human Ecology* 28(3):415–431.

Adnanal-Bakhit, M. 1982. Jordan in Perspective: The Mamluk-Ottoman Period. In Vol. 1 of *Studies in the History and Archaeology of Jordan*, ed. A. Hadidi, 361–362. Amman, Hashemite Kingdom of Jordan: Department of Antiquities.

Agelarakis, A. 1993. Shanidar Cave Proto-Neolithic Human Population: Aspects of Demography and Paleopathology. *Journal of Human Evolution* 8(4):235–253.

Akama, J. S. 1996a. A Political Ecology Approach to Wildlife Conservation in Kenya. *Environmental Values* 5:335–347.

———. 1996b. Western Environmental Values and Nature-based Tourism in Kenya. *Tourism Management* 17(8):567–574.

Akkermans, P.M.M.G., and K. Duistermaat. 1996. Of Storage and Nomads: The Sealings from Late Neolithic Sabi Abyad, Syria. *Paléorient* 22(2):17–44.

Alden, P. C., R. D. Estes, D. Schlitter, and B. McBride. 1995. *National Audubon Society Field Guide to African Wildlife*. New York: Alfred A. Knopf.

Algaze, G. 2001. Initial Social Complexity in Southwestern Asia. *Current Anthropology* 42(2):199–233.

Allen, T.F.H., and T. W. Hoekstra. 1992. *Toward a Unified Ecology*. New York: Columbia University Press.

Allen, T.F.H., and T. B. Starr. 1982. *Hierarchy: Perspectives for Ecological Complexity*. Chicago: University of Chicago Press.

Alley, R. B., P. A. Mayewski, T. Sowers, M. Stuiver, K. C. Taylor, and P. U. Clark. 1997. Holocene Climatic Instability: A Prominent, Widespread Event 8200 yr ago. *Geology* 25(6):483–486.

Alley, R. B., D. A. Meese, C. A. Shuman, A. J. Gow, K. C. Taylor, P. M. Grootes, J.W.C. White, M. Ram, E. D. Waddington, P. A. Mayewski, and G. A. Zielinski. 1993. Abrupt Increase in Greenland Snow Accumulation at the End of the Younger Dryas Event. *Nature* 362:527–529.

Altieri, M. A., and P. Rosset. 1999. Ten Reasons Why Biotechnology Will Not Ensure Food Security, Protect the Environment and Reduce Poverty in the Developing World. *AgBioForum* 2(3&4):155–162.

Ames, K. M. 2001. Slaves, Chiefs and Labour on the Northern Northwest Coast. *World Archaeology* 33(1):1–17.

Ammerman, A., C. McCartney, and D. Sorabji. 2006. More on the Early Sites at Aspros and Nissi Beach. Paper presented at the 24th annual CAARI Archaeological Workshop, Nicosia, Cyprus, June 24.

Ammerman, A., and J. Noller. 2005. New Light on *Aetokremnos*. *World Archaeology* 37:533–543.

Andersen, S. T. 1992. Pollen Spectra from the Bronze Age Barrow at Egshvile, Thy, Denmark. *Journal of Danish Archaeology* 9:1990:153–156.

Anderson, A. 1991. *Prodigious Birds: Moas and Moa Hunting in Prehistoric New Zealand*. Cambridge: Cambridge University Press.

Anderson, D., and R. Grove. 1987. *Conservation in Africa: Peoples, Policies and Practice*. Cambridge: Cambridge University Press.

Anselmetti, F. S., D. A. Hodell, D. Aritegui, M. Brenner, and M. Rosenmeier. 2007. Quantification of Soil Erosion Rates Related to Ancient Maya Deforestation. *Geology* 35:915–918.

Appadurai, A. 1986. Introduction: Commodities and the Politics of Value. In *The Social Life of Things: Commodities in Cultural Perspective*, ed. A. Appadurai, 3–63. Cambridge: Cambridge University Press.

Araus, J. L., A. Febrero, R. Buxó, M. O. Rodríguez-Ariza, F. Molina, M. D. Camalich, D. Martín, and J. Voltas. 1997. Identification of Ancient Irrigation Practices Based on the Carbon Isotope Discrimination of Plant Seeds: A Case Study from the South-East Iberian Peninsula (as960153). *Journal of Archaeological Science* 24(8):729–740.

Araus, J. L., A. Febrero, M. Catala, M. Molist, J. Voltas, and I. Romagosa. 1991. Crop Water Availability in Early Agriculture: Evidence from Carbon Isotope Discrimination of Seeds from a Tenth Millennium BP Site on the Euphrates. *Global Change Biology* 5:201–212.

Araus, J. L., G. A. Slafer, I. Romagosa, and M. Molist. 2001. Estimated Wheat Yields during the Emergence of Agriculture Based on the Carbon Isotope Discrimination of Grains: Evidence from a 10th Millenium BP Site on the Euphrates. *Journal of Archaeological Science* 28(4):341–350.

Armillas, Pedro. 1971. Gardens on Swamps. *Science* 174:653–661.

Ashton, T. S. 1924. *Iron and Steel in the Industrial Revolution*. Economic History Series, no. 2. Manchester, UK: University of Manchester.

Asiema, J. 1994. Africa's Green Revolution. *Biotechnology and Development Monitor* 19:17–18.

Atherden, M. 2000. Human Impact on the Vegetation of Southern Greece and Problems of Palynological Interpretation: A Case Study from Crete. In *Landscape and Land Use in Postglacial Greece*, ed. P. Halstead and C. Frederick, 62–78. Sheffield Studies in Aegean Archaeology, 3. Sheffield, UK: Sheffield Academic Press.

Auffray, J. C., E. Tchernov, and E. Nevo. 1998. Origine du commensalisme de la souris domestique (mus musculus domesticus) vis-à-vis de l'homme. *Comptes rendus de l'Academie des Sciences, Paris* 307(Serie III):517–522.

Aurenche, O., and S. K. Kozlowski. 1999. *La naissance du Néolithique au Proche Orient ou le paradis perdu*. Paris: Editions Errance.

Bak, P. 1996. *How Nature Works: The Science of Self-organized Criticality*. New York: Copernicus Press.

Banning, E. B., D. Rahimi, and J. Siggers. 1994. The Late Neolithic of the Southern Levant: Hiatus, Settlement Shift or Observer Bias? The Perspective from Wadi Ziqlab. *Paléorient* 20(2):151–164.

Banning, E. G. 1998. The Neolithic Period: Triumphs of Architecture, Agriculture and Art. *Near Eastern Archaeology* 61(4):188–237.

Barker, G. 1995. Land Use and Environmental Degradation in Biferno Valley (Central Southern Italy) from Prehistoric Times to Present Day. In *L'homme et la dègradation de l'environment*. ed. S. van der Leeuw, 285–297. XVe recontres internationales d'archéologie d'historie d'Antibes. Sophia Antipolis, France: Éditions APDCA.

Bar-Matthews, M., and A. Ayalon. 2003. Climatic Conditions in the Eastern Mediterranean during the Last Glacial (60–10 ky) and Their Relations to the Upper Palaeolithic in the Levant as Inferred from Oxygen and Carbon Isotope Systematics of Cave Deposits. In *More than Meets the Eye: Studies on Upper Palaeolithic*

Diversity in the Near East, ed. A. N. Goring-Morris and A. Belfer-Cohen, 13–18. Oxford: Oxbow Books.

Bar-Matthews, M., A. Ayalon, M. Gilmour, A. Matthews, and C. Hawkesworth. 2002. Sea-Land Oxygen Isotopic Relationships from Planktonic Foraminifera and Speleothems in the Eastern Mediterranean Region and Their Implication for Paleorainfall during Interglacial Intervals. *Geochimica et Coxmochimica Acta* 66(24):1–19.

Bar-Matthews, M., A. Ayalon, and A. Kaufman. 2000. Timing the Hydrological Conditions of Sapropel Events in the Eastern Mediterranean, as Evident from Speleothems, Soreq Cave, Israel. *Chemical Geology* 169:145–156.

Bar-Matthews, M., A. Ayalon, A. Kaufman, and G. J. Wasserburg. 1999. The Eastern Mediterranean Region Paleoclimate as a Reflection of Regional Events: Soreq Cave, Israel. *Earth Planetary Science Letters* 166:85–95.

Bar-Oz, G., T. Dayan, D. Kaufman, and M. Weinstein-Evron. 2003. The Natufian Economy at el-Wad Terrace with Special Reference to Gazelle Exploitation Patterns. *Journal of Archaeological Science* 31:1–15.

Barrera-Bassols, N., and A. Zinck. 2003. "Land Moves and Behaves": Indigenous Discourse on Sustainable Land Management in Pichataro, Patzcuaro Basin, Mexico. *Geografiska Annaler* 85:229–245.

Barrow, C. 1991. *Land Degradation: Development and Breakdown of Terrestrial Environments.* Cambridge: Cambridge University Press.

Baruch, U. 1990. Palynological Evidence of Human Impact on the Vegetation as Recorded in Late Holocene Lake Sediments in Israel. In *Man's Role in the Shaping of the Eastern Mediterranean Landscape*, ed. S. Bottema, G. Entjes-Nieborg, and W. van Zeist, 283–293. Rotterdam: Balkema.

Baruch, U., and S. Bottema. 1999. A New Pollen Diagram from Lake Hula: Vegetational, Climatic, and Anthropologenic Implications. In *Ancient Lakes: Their Cultural and Biological Diversity*, ed. H. Kawanabe, G. W. Coulter, and A. C. Roosevelt, 75–86. Ghent, Belgium: Kenobe Productions.

Bar-Yosef, O. 1996. The Impact of Late Pleistocene–Early Holocene Climatic Changes on Humans in Southwest Asia. In *Humans at the End of the Ice Age: The Archaeology of the Pleistocene-Holocene Transition*, ed. L. G. Straus, B. V. Eriksen, J. M. Erlandson, and D. R. Yesner, 61–76. New York: Plenum.

———. 1998. The Natufian Culture in the Levant-Threshold to the Origins of Agriculture. *Evolutionary Anthropology* 6(5):159–177.

———. 2002. The Natufian Culture and the Early Neolithic: Social and Economic Trends in Southwestern Asia. In *Examining the Farming/Language Dispersal Hypothesis*, ed. P. Bellwood and C. Renfrew, 113–126. McDonald Institute Monographs, C. Scarre, general ed. Cambridge: McDonald Institute for Archaeological Research.

Bar-Yosef, O., and A. Belfer-Cohen. 1989. The Origins of Sedentism and Farming Communities. *Journal of World Prehistory* 3(4):447–498.

———. 2002. Facing Environmental Crisis: Societal and Cultural Changes at the Transition from the Younger Dryas to the Holocene in the Levant. In *The Dawn of Farming in the Near East*, ed. R.T.J. Cappers and S. Bottema, 55–66. Studies in Early Near Eastern Production, Subsistence, and Environment, vol. 6. Berlin: Ex oriente.

Bar-Yosef, O., and A. Khazanov, eds. 1992. *Pastoralism in the Levant, Archaeological Materials in Anthropological Perspectives.* Monographs in World Archaeology, 10. Madison, WI: Prehistory Press.

Bates, R. L., and J. A. Jackson. 1984. *Dictionary of Geological Terms.* 3rd ed. New York: Anchor Books Doubleday.

Bationo, A. 2004. *Managing Nutrient Cycles to Sustain Soil Fertility in Sub-Saharan Africa.* Nairobi: Academy Science Publishers, in association with the Tropical Soil Biology and Fertility Institute of CIAT.

Bayman, J. M. 2001. The Hohokam of Southwest North America. *Journal of World Prehistory* 15:257–311.

———. 2002. Hohokam Craft Economies and the Materialization of Power. *Journal of Archaeological Method and Theory* 9:69–95.

Bayman, J. M., and M. S. Shackley. 1999. Dynamics of Hohokam Obsidian Circulation in the North American Southwest. *Antiquity* 73:836–845.

Beach, T. 1998a. Soil Catenas, Tropical Deforestation, and Ancient and Contemporary Soil Erosion in the Petén, Guatemala. *Physical Geography* 19:378–405.

———. 1998b. Soil Constraints on Northwest Yucatán: Pedo-archaeology and Subsistence at Chunchucmil. *Geoarchaeology* 13:759–791.

Beach, T., and N. Dunning. 1995. Ancient Maya Terracing and Modern Conservation in the Petén Rain Forest of Guatemala. *Journal of Soil and Water Conservation* 50:138–145.

Beach, T., N. Dunning, S. Luzzadder-Beach, J. Lohse, and D. Cook. 2006. Ancient Maya Impacts on Soils and Soil Erosion. *Catena* 65:166–178.

Beach, T., N. Dunning, S. Luzzadder-Beach, and V. Scarborough. 2003. Depression Soils in the Lowland Tropics of Northwestern Belize: Anthropogenic and Natural Origins. In *Lowland Maya Area: Three Millennia at the Human-Wildland Interface*, ed. A. Gomez-Pompa, M. Allen, S. Fedick, and J. Jiménez-Osornio, 139–174. Binghamton, NY: Haworth Press.

Beach, T., S. Luzzadder-Beach, N. Dunning, J. Hageman, and J. Lohse. 2002. Upland Agriculture in the Maya Lowlands: Ancient Maya Soil Conservation in Northwestern Belize. *Geographical Review* 92:372–397.

Beach, T., S. Luzzadder-Beach, W. I. Woods, and N. P. Dunning. 2006. Soils and History in Mesoamerica and the Caribbean Islands. In *The Skin of the Earth: Environmental History of Soils*, ed. J. McNeill and V. Winiwarter, 51–90. London: White Horse Press.

Beard, P. 1988. *The End of the Game: The Last Word from Paradise.* London: Thames and Hudson.

Bech, J.-H., and M. Mikkelsen 1999. Landscape, Settlement and Subsistence in Bronze Age Thy, NW Denmark. In *Settlement and Landscape,* ed. C. Fabech and J. Ringtved, 69–77. Moesgård, Denmark: Jutland Archaeological Society.

Becquelin, P., and D. Michelet. 1994. Demografía en la Zona Puuc: El recurso del método. *Latin American Antiquity* 5:289–311.

Belfer-Cohen, A., and O. Bar-Yosef. 2000. Early Sedentism in the Near East: A Bumpy Ride to Village Life. In *Life in Neolithic Farming Communities: Social Organization, Identity, and Differentiation*, ed. I. Kuijt, 19–37. New York: Plenum Press.

Bell, S., and S. Morse. 1999. *Sustainability Indicators: Measuring the Immeasurable?* London: Earthscan Publications.

Bender, B. 1978. Gatherer-Hunter to Farmer: A Social Perspective. *World Archaeology* 10:204–220.

Berger, J.-F., F. Favory, T. Muxart, F.-P. Tourneux, and S. E. van der Leeuw. 2003. Comment identifier, analyser et évaluer les dynamiques d'interactions entre les sociétés et leurs environnements. In *Quelles natures voulons nous? Pour une approche socio-écologique du champ de l'environnement*, ed. C. Lévèque and S. E. van der Leeuw, 146–184. Paris: Elsevier.

Berglund, B. E., L. Larsson, N. Lewan, E.G.A. Olsson, and S. Skansjö. 1991. Ecological and Social Factors behind Landscape Changes. In *The Cultural Landscape during 6,000 Years in Southern Sweden—The Ystad Project*, ed. B. Berglund, 425–445. Ecological Bulletins 41. Copenhagen: Munksgaard International Publishers.

Berglund, J. 1998. The Excavations at the Farm beneath the Sand. In *Man, Culture and Environment in Ancient Greenland. Report on a Research Programme*, ed. J. Arneborg and H. C. Gullprv, 7–13. Copenhagen: The Danish National Museum and Danish Polar Center.

Berry, K. A., and P. A. McAnany. 2007. Reckoning with the Wetlands and Their Role in Ancient Maya Society. In *The Political Economy of Ancient Mesoamerica: Transformations during the Formative and Classic Periods*, ed. V. L. Scarborough and J. Clark, 40–52. Albuquerque: University of New Mexico Press.

Bienkowski, P. 1992. The Beginning of the Iron Age in Southern Jordan: A Framework. In *Early Edom and Moab: The Beginning of the Iron Age in Southern Jordan*, ed. P. Bienkowski, 1–12. 7th ed. Sheffield Archaeological Monographs. Oxford: The Alden Press.

Bigler, W. 2005. Historical Ecology of Arid Land Irrigation Agriculture: The Akimel O'odham (Pima) and the Gila River, Arizona. PhD diss., Department of Geography, Arizona State University, Tempe.

Binford, L. 2000. Review of *Faunal Extinctions in an Island Society: Pygmy Hippopotamus Hunters of the Akrotiri Peninsula, Cyprus* by A. Simmons. *American Antiquity* 65:771.

Binford, M. W., M. Brenner, T. J. Whitmore, A. Higuera-Gundy, E. Deevey, and B. Leyden. 1987. Ecosystems, Paleoecology, and Human Disturbance in Subtropical and Tropical America. *Quaternary Science Review* 6:113–128.

Bintliff, J. 2002. Time, Process and Catastrophism in the Study of Mediterranean Alluvial History: A Review. *World Archaeology* 33(3):417–435.

Blaikie, P., and H. Brookfield. 1987. *Land Degradation and Society*. New York: Methuen & Co.

Blumenschine, R. J. 1985. Early Hominid Scavenging Opportunities: Insights from the Ecology of Carcass Availability in the Serengeti and Ngorongoro Crater, Tanzania. PhD diss., University of California, Berkeley.

———. 1995. Percussion Marks, Tooth Marks, and Experimental Determinations of the Timing of Hominid and Carnivore Access to Long Bones at FLK Zinjanthropus, Olduvai Gorge, Tanzania. *Journal of Human Evolution* 29:21–51.

Blumenschine, R. J., and M. M. Selvaggio. 1988. Percussion Marks on Bone Surfaces as a New Diagnostic of Hominid Behavior. *Nature* 333:763–765.

Boardman, J., and M. Bell. 1992. Past and Present Soil Erosion: Linking Archaeology and Geomorphology. In *Past and Present Soil Erosion: Archaeological and Geographical Perspectives*, ed. M. Bell and J. Boardman, 1–8. Oxford: Oxbow Books.

Bosworth, C. E. 1967. *The Islamic Dynasties, A Chronological and Genealogical Handbook*. Islamic Surveys 5. Edinburgh: Edinburgh University Press.

Botkin, D. B. 1990. *Discordant Harmonies: A New Ecology for the Twenty First Century*. New York: Oxford University Press.

Bottema, S. 1995. The Younger Dryas in the Eastern Mediterranean. *Quaternary Science Reviews* 14(9):883–891.

Bottema, S., G. Entjes-Nieborg, and W. van Zeist, eds. 1990. *Man's Role in the Shaping of the Eastern Mediterranean Landscape*. Rotterdam: Balkema.

Bourdieu, P. 1977. *Outline of a Theory of Practice*. Cambridge: Cambridge University Press.

———. 1990. *The Logic of Practice*. Cambridge: Polity Press.

Bradbury, J. P. 2000. Limnologic History of Lago de Patzcuaro, Michoacan, Mexico for the Past 48,000 Years: Impacts of Climate and Man. *Palaeogeography Palaeoclimatology Palaeoecology* 163(1–2):69–95.

Brain, C. K. 1981. *The Hunters or the Hunted? An Introduction to African Cave Taphonomy*. Chicago: University of Chicago Press.

Brand, Stewart. 1999. *The Clock of the Long Now: Time and Responsibility*. New York: Basic Books.

Braudel, F. 1967. *Capitalism and Material Life: 1400–1600*. New York: Harper Colophon Books.

Braun, E. 1989. The Transition from the Chalcolithic to the Early Bronze Age in Northern Israel and Jordan: Is There a Missing Link? In *L'urbanization de la Palestine a l'Age du Bronze Ancien*, ed. P. D. Miroshedji, 7–28. British Archaeological Reports International Series 527. Oxford: Archaeopress.

Bray, F. 1986. *The Rice Economies: Technology and Development in Asian Societies*. Oxford: Basil Blackwell.

Brenner, M., M. F. Rosenmeier, D. A. Hodell, and J. H. Curtis. 2002. Paleolimnology of the Maya Lowlands. *Ancient Mesoamerica* 13:141–157.

Briggs, J. M., K. A. Spielmann, H. Schaafsma, K. W. Kintigh, M. Kruse, K. Morehouse, and K. Schollmeyer. 2006. Why Ecology Needs Archaeologists and Archaeology Needs Ecologists. *Frontiers in Ecology and the Environment* 4:180–188.

Broecker, W. S. 1999. What if the Conveyor Were to Shut Down? Reflections on a Possible Outcome of the Great Global Experiment. *GSA Today* 9(1):1–7.

Brokaw, N.V.L., and E. P. Mallory. 1993. *Vegetation of the Rio Bravo Conservation and Management Area, Belize.* Manomet, MA: Manomet Bird Observatory.

Broodbank, C. 2000. *An Island Archaeology of the Early Cyclades.* Cambridge: Cambridge University Press.

Brookfield, H. C. 1972. Intensification and Disintensification in Pacific Agriculture. *Pacific Viewpoint* 13:30–48.

———. 1984. Intensification Revisited. *Pacific Viewpoint* 25(1):15–44.

———. 2001. *Exploring Agrodiversity. Issues, Cases, and Methods in Biodiversity Conservation.* New York: Columbia University Press.

Bryant, R. 1992. Political Ecology: An Emerging Research Agenda in Third World Studies. *Political Geography* 11(1):12–36.

Buckles, D., A. Etèka, O. Osiname, M. Galiba, and N. Galiano, eds. 1998. *Cover Crops in West Africa: Contributing to Sustainable Agriculture.* Ottowa: IDRC/IITA/SG2000/Canada.

Buckles, D., B. Triomphe, and G. Sain. 1998. Cover Crops. In *Hillside Agriculture: Farmer Innovation with Mucuna*, ed. D. Buckles, B. Triomphe, and G. Sain, 60–72. Ottowa: IDRC/CIMMYT/Canada.

Bull, I. D., I. A. Simpson, P. F. van Bergen, and R. P. Evershed. 1999. Muck 'n' Molecules: Organic Geochemical Methods for Detecting Ancient Manuring. *Antiquity* 73(279):86–92.

Bunch, R. 2002. Green Manure in Belize and the Peten, the Mayan Homelands: Achieving Sustainability in the Use of Green Manures. *ILEIA Newsletter* 13(3):12.

Bunimovitz, S., and R. Barkai. 1996. Ancient Bones and Modern Myths: Ninth Millennium BC Hippopotamus Hunters at Akrotiri *Aetokremnos*, Cyprus? *Journal of Mediterranean Archaeology* 9:85–96.

Butzer, K. 1981. Rise and Fall of Axum, Ethiopia: A Geo-Archaeological Interpretation. *American Antiquity* 46:471–495.

Butzer, K., and E. Butzer. 1993. The Sixteenth-Century Environment of the Central Mexican Bajío: Archival Reconstruction from Colonial Land Grants and the Question of Spanish Ecological Impact. In *Culture, Form, and Place: Essays in Cultural Historical Geography*, ed. K. Mathewson, 89–124. Baton Rouge: Louisiana State University.

Butzer, K. W. 1982. *Archaeology as Human Ecology: Method and Theory for a Contextual Approach.* Cambridge: Cambridge University Press.

———. 1991. Spanish Colonization of the New World: Cultural Continuity and Change in Mexico. *Erkunde* 45:205–219.

———. 1992. The Americas before and after 1492: An Introduction to Current Geographical Research. *Annals of the Association of American Geographers* 82(3):345–369.

———. 1993. No Eden in the New World. *Nature* 362(6415):15–17.

———. 1996. Ecology in the Long View: Settlement, Agrosystem Strategies, and Ecological Performance. *Journal of Field Archaeology* 23(2):141–150.

Callmer, J. 1991. The Process of Village Formation. In *The Cultural Landscape during 6000 Years in Southern Sweden: The Ystad Project*, ed. B. Berglund, 337–349. Ecological Bulletins, vol. 41. Copenhagen: Munksgaard International Publishers.

Cameron, C. 2004. Anthropogenic Soils at Two Norse Farms in Greenland and Iceland. MA thesis, University of Alberta, Edmonton.

Capaldo, S. D. 1995. Inferring Hominid and Carnivore Behavior from Dual-Patterned Archaeofaunal Assemblages. PhD diss., Rutgers University.

Cappers, R.T.J., S. Bottema, and H. Woldring. 1998. Problems in Correlating Pollen Diagrams of the Near East: A Preliminary Report. In *The Origins of Agriculture and Crop Domestication*, ed. A. B. Damania, J. Valkoun, G. Willcox, and C. O. Qualset, 160–169. Aleppo, Syria: ICARDA.

Cappers, R.T.J., S. Bottema, H. Woldring, H. van der Plicht, and H. J. Streurman. 2002. Modeling the Emergence of Farming: Implications of the Vegetation Development in the Near East during the Pleistocene-Holocene Transition. In *The Dawn of Farming in the Near East*, ed. R.T.J. Cappers and S. Bottema, 3–14. Studies in Early Near Eastern Production, Subsistence, and Environment, vol. 6. Berlin: Ex oriente.

Carpenter, S., W. Brock, and P. Hanson. 1999. Ecological and Social Dynamics in Simple Models of Ecosystem Management. *Conservation Ecology* 3(2):4. http://www.consecol.org/vol3/|iss2/art4 (accessed February 10, 2009)

Carpenter, S. F., B. Walker, J. M. Anderies, and N. Abel. 2001. From Metaphor to Measurement: Resilience of What to What? *Ecosystems* 4:765–781.

Carpenter, S. R., and L. H. Gunderson. 2001. Coping with Collapse: Ecological and Social Dynamics in Ecosystem Management. *BioScience* 51(6):451–457.

Carter, S. P., and D. A. Davidson. 1998. An Evaluation of the Contribution of Soil Micromorphology to the Study of Ancient Arable Agriculture. *Geoarchaeology* 13(6):535–547.

Castetter, E. F., and W. H. Bell. 1942. Pima and Papago Indian Agriculture. In Vol. I of *Inter-American Studies*. Albuquerque: University of New Mexico Press.

Cauvin, J. 2000. *The Birth of the Gods and the Origins of Agriculture*, trans. T. Watkins (originally published in 1994). Cambridge: Cambridge University Press.

Cavallo, J. A., and R. J. Blumenschine. 1989. Tree-Stored Leopard Kills: Expanding the Hominid Scavenging Niche. *Journal of Human Evolution* 18:393–399.

Chacón Torres, A. 1989. A Limnological Study of Lake Pátzcuaro, Michoacán, Mexico. PhD diss., University of Stirling, United Kingdom.

Chami, F. A. 1988. The Coastal Iron Age Site in Kisarawe, Tanzania. MA thesis, Department of Anthropology, Brown University, Providence.

———. 1994. The Tanzanian Coast in the First Millenium A.D. *Studies in African Archaeology*, 7. Uppsala, Sweden: Societas Archaologica Upsaliensis.

———. 2002. Excavations at Kaole Ruins. In *Southern African and the Swahili World*, ed. F. Chami and G. Pwiti, 25–49. Dar es Salaam, Tanzania: Dar es Salaam University Press Ltd.

Charles, D. R. 1994. Comparative Climatic Requirements. In *Livestock Housing*, ed. C. M. Wathes and D. R. Charles, 3–24. Wallingford, UK: CABI Publishing.

Chase, A. F., and D. Z. Chase. 1998. Scale and Intensity in Classic Period Maya Agriculture: Terracing and Settlement at Caracol, Belize. *Culture and Agriculture* 20:60–77.

Cherry, J. 1981. Pattern and Process in the Earliest Colonisation of the Mediterranean Islands. *Proceedings of the Prehistoric Society* 47:41–68.

———. 1990. The First Colonization of the Mediterranean Islands: A Review of Recent Research. *Journal of Mediterranean Archaeology* 3:145–221.

———. 1992. Paleolithic Sardinians? Some Questions of Evidence and Method. In *Sardinia in the Mediterranean: A Footprint in the Sea*, ed. R. Tykot and T. Andrew, 29–39. Monographs in Mediterranean Archaeology 3. Oxford: Sheffield Academic Press.

Cherry, J., J. Davis, and E. Mantzourani. 1991. *Landscape Archaeology as Long-Term History: Northern Keos in the Cycladic Islands from the Earliest Settlement until Modern Times.* Los Angeles: University of California at Los Angeles, Institute of Archaeology.

Chew, S. C. 2001. *World Ecological Degradation: Accumulation, Urbanization, and Deforestation, 3000 B.C.–A.D. 2000*. Walnut Creek, CA: AltaMira Press.

Chianu, J. N., and H. Tsujii. 2004. Missing Links in Sustainable Food Production in West Africa: The Case of the Savannas of Northern NIGERIA. *Sustainable Development* 12:212–222.

Childe, V. G. 1928. *The Most Ancient East: The Oriental Prelude to European Prehistory.* New York: Alfred A. Knopf.

———. 1951. The Urban Revolution. *Town Planning Review* 21:3–17.

Chittick, N. H. 1974. *Kilwa: An Islamic Trading City on the East African Coast.* Nairobi: The British Institute in Eastern Africa.

———. 1984. *Manda: Excavations at an Island Port on the Kenya Coast.* Nairobi: The British Institute in Eastern Africa.

Ciolek-Torrello, R., J. A. Homburg, M. R. Waters, and J. Onken. 2003. Canals, Sediments, Streamflow, and Settlement on the Salt River, Arizona. Paper presented at the annual meeting of the Society for American Archaeology, Milwaukee, WI.

Cliff, M. B. 1982. Lowland Maya Nucleation: A Case Study from Northern Belize. PhD diss., Southern Methodist University.

———. 1986. Excavations in the Late Preclassic Nucleated Village. In *Archaeology at Cerros, Belize, Central America: Vol. I, An Interim Report*, ed. R. A. Robertson and D. A. Freidel, 45–64. Dallas: Southern Methodist University Press.

Coe, Michael D. 1964. The Chinampas of Mexico. *Scientific American* 211:90–98.

Cohen, M. N. 1977. *The Food Crisis in Prehistory: Overpopulation and the Origins of Agriculture.* New Haven: Yale University Press.

Coles, J. 2003. And on They Went . . . Processions in Scandinavian Bronze Age Rock Carvings. *Acta Archaeologica* 74:211–250.

Colledge, S., J. Conolly, and S. Shennan. 2004. Archaeobotanical Evidence for the Spread of Farming in the Eastern Mediterranean. *Current Anthropology* 45, Supplement:S35–S58.

Collins, J., A. Kinzig, N. Grimm, W. Fagan, D. Hope, J. Wu, and E. Borer. 2000. A New Urban Ecology. *American Scientist* 88:416–424.

Copans, J. 1983. The Sahelian Drought: Social Sciences and the Political Economy of Underdevelopment. In *Interpretations of Calamity from the Viewpoint of Human Ecology*, ed. K. Hewitt, 83–97. Boston: Allen and Unwin.

Copeland, L., and C. Vita-Finzi. 1978. Archaeological Dating of Geological Deposits in Jordan. *Levant* 10:10–25.

Cowgill, U. M. 1961. Soil Fertility and the Ancient Maya. *Transactions of the Connecticut Academy of Arts and Sciences* 42:1–56.

Croft, Paul. 1988. A Study of Some Faunal Remains from Neolithic and Chalcolithic Cyprus. Unpublished PhD thesis, University of Cambridge.

———. 1991. Man and Beast in Chalcolithic Cyprus. *Bulletin of the American Schools of Oriental Research* 282/283:63–79.

Cronon, W. 1983. *Changes in the Land: Indians, Colonists, and the Ecology of New England.* New York: Hill and Wang.

———. 1996. *Uncommon Ground: Rethinking the Human Place in Nature*. New York: W.W. Norton and Company.

Crown, P. L., and J. J. Judge, eds. 1991. *Chaco & Hohokam: Prehistoric Regional Systems in the American Southwest*. Santa Fe, NM: School of American Research Press.

Crumley, C. L., ed. 1994. *Historical Ecology: Cultural Knowledge and Changing Landscapes.* Santa Fe, New Mexico: School of American Research Press.

Culbert, T. P., and D. S. Rice, eds. 1990. *Precolumbian Population History in the Maya Lowlands.* Albuquerque: University of New Mexico Press.

Cummings, B. 1926. Ancient Canals of the Casa Grande. *Progressive Arizona* 3:9–10, 43.

Dahlin, B. H., T. Beach, S. Luzzadder-Beach, D. Hixson, S. Hutson, A. Magnoni, E. Mansell, and D. Mazeau. 2005. Reconstructing Agricultural Self-Sufficiency at Chunchucmil, Yucatan, Mexico. *Ancient Mesoamerica* 16:229–247.

Darling, J. A., J. C. Ravesloot, and M. R. Waters. 2004. Village Drift and Riverine Settlement: Modeling Akimel O'odham Land Use. *American Anthropologist* 106(2):282–295.

Darmon, F. 1996. Evolution de l'environment végétal et du climat de l'Épipaléolithique au début du Néolithique ancien, dans la Basse Vallée du Jourdain. *L'Anthropologie* 100:179–212.

Davis, S. 2003. The Zooarchaeology of Khirokitia (Neolithic Cyprus), Including a View from the Mainland. In *Le Néolithique de Chypre*, ed. J. Guilaine and A. Le-Brun, 253–268. Bulletin de correspondance Hellénique supplément 43. Athens: École française d'Athènes.

Dawes, M. 1999. Hundreds die in Uganda cattle raid. *BBC News*, September 13, 1999.

De Maret, P. 1985. The Smith Myth and the Origin of Leadership in Central Africa. In *African Iron-working: Ancient and Traditional*, ed. R. Haaland and P. Shinnie, 73–87. Oslo: Norwegian University Press.

Dean, J. S. 1988. A Model of Anasazi Behavioral Adaptation. In *The Anasazi in a Changing Environment*, ed. G. J. Gumerman, 25–44. Cambridge: Cambridge University Press.

———. 2000. Complexity Theory and Sociocultural Change in the American Southwest. In *The Way the Wind Blows: Climate, History, and Human Action*, ed. R. J. McIntosh, J. A. Tainter, and S. K. McIntosh, 89–118. New York: Columbia University Press.

Dean, S. 1994. The World of Pottery: A Conversation with Marian Naranjo. *Callaloo* 17(1):285–289.

DeBarros, P. 1986. Bassar: A Quantified Chronologically Controlled, Regional Approach to a Traditional Iron Production Center in West Africa. *Africa* 56:148–174.

———. 1988. Societal Repercussions of the Rise of Traditional Iron Production: A West African Example. *African Archaeological Review* 6:91–113.

Deevey, E. S., D. S. Rice, P. M. Rice, V. Hague, M. Brenner, and M. S. Flannery. 1979. Maya Urbanism: Impact on a Tropical Karst Environment. *Science* 206:298–306.

Demarest, A. A. 2004. After the Maelstrom: Collapse of the Classic Maya Kingdoms and the Terminal Classic in Western Peten. In *The Terminal Classic in the Maya Lowlands: Collapse, Transition, and Transformation*, ed. A. Demarest, P. M. Rice, and D. S. Rice, 102–124. Boulder: University Press of Colorado.

Demarest, A. A., P. M. Rice, and D. S. Rice. 2004. The Terminal Classic in the Maya Lowlands: Assessing Collapses, Terminations, and Transformations. In *The Terminal Classic in the Maya Lowlands: Collapse, Transition, and Transformation*, ed. A. Demarest, P. M. Rice, and D. S. Rice, 545–571. Boulder: University Press of Colorado.

Demoncal, P. B., and E. R. Cook. 2005. Perspectives on Diamond's Collapse: How Societies Choose to Fail or Succeed. *Current Anthropology* 46(Supplement Dec. 2005):S91–S99.

Denevan, W. M. 1992. The Pristine Myth: The Landscape of the Americas in 1492. *Annals of the Association of American Geographers* 82(3):369–386.

———. 1994. Comments on Archaeology and Public Policy. *American Anthropological Association Newsletter* June:2.

———. 1995. Prehistoric Agricultural Methods as Models for Sustainability. In *Advances in Plant Pathology. Vol. 11*, ed. J. H. Andrews and I. C. Tommerup, 21–43. New York: Academic Press.

———. 2000. *Cultivated Landscapes of Native Amazonia and the Andes.* Oxford; New York: Oxford University Press.

De Rijk, S., A. Hayes, and E. J. Rohling. 1999. Eastern Mediterranean Sapropel S1 Interruption: An Expression of the Onset of Climatic Deterioration around 7 ka BP. *Marine Geology* 153:337–343.

Descola, P., and G. Pálsson. 1996. *Nature and Society: Anthropological Perspectives.* London: Routledge.

Dever, W. G. 1987. The Middle Bronze Age: The Zenith of the Urban Canaanite Era. *Biblical Archaeologist* 50:149–177.

Diamond, J. M. 1997. *Guns, Germs, and Steel: The Fates of Human Societies.* New York: W. W. Norton.

———. 2003. The Last Americans: Environmental Collapse and the End of Civilization. *Harper's Magazine* June:43–51.

———. 2005. *Collapse: How Societies Choose to Fail or Succeed.* New York: Viking.

Dickson, D. B. 1987. Circumscription by Anthropogenic Environmental Destruction: An Expansion of Carneiro's (1970) Theory of the Origin of the State. *American Antiquity* 52(4):709–716.

Dilworth, C. 2002. Population, Technology, and Development: The Vicious-Circle Principle and the Theory of Human Development. In *On the Edge of Scarcity: Environment, Resources, Population, Sustainability, and Conflict*, ed. M. N. Dobkowski and I. Wallimann, 77–92. Syracuse, NY: Syracuse University Press.

Donahue, J. 1985. Hydrologic and Topographic Change during and after the Early Bronze Occupation at Bab edh-Drah and Numeira. In *Studies in the History and Archaeology of Jordan II*, ed. A. Hadidi, (2)131–140. Amman, Hashemite Kingdom of Jordan: Department of Antiquities.

Doolittle, W. E. 1984. Agricultural Change as Incremental Process. *Annals of the Association of American Geographers* 74:124–137.

———. 1990. *Canal Irrigation in Prehistoric Mexico.* Austin: University of Texas Press.

———. 2000. *Cultivated Landscapes of Native North America.* New York: Oxford University Press.

Doyel, D. E., S. K. Fish, and P. R. Fish, eds. 2000. *The Hohokam Village Revisited.* Fort Collins, CO: Southwestern and Rocky Mountain Division of the American Association for the Advancement of Science.

Drew, D. 1999. *The Lost Chronicles of the Maya Kings.* Berkeley: University of California Press.

Dudal, R., F. O. Nchtergaele, and M. F. Purnall. 2002. The Human Factor of Soil Formation. Paper presented at the 17th World Congress of Soil Science, Bangkok, Thailand, August 14–21.

Dugmore, A. J., M. J. Church, P. C. Buckland, K. J. Edwards, I. T. Lawson, T. H. McGovern, E. Panagiotakopulu, I. A. Simpson, P. Skidmore, and G. Sveinbjarnardóttir. 2005. The Norse Landnám on the North Atlantic Islands: An Environmental Impact Assessment. *Polar Record* 41:21–37.

Dunning, N. P. 1992a. The Implication of Folk Soil Taxonomies for Agricultural Change in Middle America. *Conference of Latin Americanist Geographers* 17/18:42–44.

———. 1992b. Lords of the Hills: Ancient Maya Settlement in the Puuc Region, Yucatan, Mexico. Monographs in World Archaeology, no. 15. Madison, WI: Prehistory Press.

———. 1995. Coming Together at the Temple Mountain: Environment, Subsistence, and the Emergence of Classic Maya Segmentary States. In *The Emergence of Classic Maya Civilization: Preclassic to Classic*, ed. N. Grube, 61–70. Acta Mesoamericana 8. Möckmühl, Germany: Verlag von Flemming.

Dunning, N. P. 2003. Birth and Death of Waters: Environmental Change, Adaptation, and Symbolism in the Southern Maya Lowlands. In *Espacios Mayas: Representaciones, usos, creencias*, ed. A. Breton, A. Monod-Becquelin, and M. H. Ruz, 49–75. Mexico City: Universidad Autónoma de México.

———. 2004. Down on the Farm: Classic Maya "Homesteads" as "Farmsteads." In *Ancient Maya Commoners*, ed. J. C. Lohse and F. Valdez Jr., 97–116. Austin: University of Texas Press.

Dunning, N. P., and T. Beach. 1994. Soil Erosion, Slope Management, and Ancient Terracing in the Maya Lowlands. *Latin American Antiquity* 5:51–69.

———. 2000. Stability and Instability in Prehispanic Maya Landscapes. In *Imperfect Balance: Landscape Transformations in the Precolumbian Americas*, ed. D. L. Lentz, 179–202. New York: Columbia University Press.

———. 2003. Fruit of the *Luum*: Lowland Maya Soil Knowledge and Agricultural Practices. *Mono y Conejo* 2:1–25.

———. 2004. Noxious or Nuturing Nature? Maya Civilization in Environmental Context. In *Continuities and Change in Maya Archaeology (A Millennial Perspective)*, eds. C. Golden and G. Borgstede, 125–141. New York; London: Routledge.

———. Forthcoming. *An Ancient Maya Landscape: Environmental Archaeology and Ancient Settlement of the Petexbatun Region, Guatemala.* Nashville: Vanderbilt University Press.

Dunning, N. P., T. Beach, P. Farrell, and S. Luzzadder-Beach. 1998. Prehispanic Agrosystems and Adaptive Regions in the Maya Lowlands. *Culture and Agriculture* 20:87–101.

Dunning, N. P., T. Beach, and S. Luzzadder-Beach. 2006. Environmental Variability among Bajos in the Southern Maya Lowlands and Its Implications for Ancient Maya Civilization and Archaeology. In *Precolombian Water Management*, ed. L. J. Lucero and B. W. Fash, 111–133. Tucson: University of Arizona Press.

Dunning, N. P., T. Beach, and D. Rue. 1997. The Paleoecology and Ancient Settlement of the Petexbatun Region, Guatemala. *Ancient Mesoamerica* 8:185–197.

Dunning, N. P., J. G. Jones, T. Beach, and S. Luzzadder-Beach. 2003. Physiography, Habitats, and Landscapes in the Three Rivers Region. In *Heterarchy, Political Economy, and the Ancient Maya: The Three Rivers Region of the East-Central Yucatán Peninsula*, ed. V. L. Scarborough, F. Valdez Jr., and N. P. Dunning, 14–24. Tucson: University of Arizona Press.

Dunning, N. P., S. Luzzadder-Beach, T. Beach, J. Jones, V. Scarborough, and T. P. Culbert. 2002. Arising from the Bajos: The Evolution of a Neotropical Landscape and the Rise of Maya Civilization. *Annals of the Association of American Geographers* 92:267–283.

Dunning, N. P., D. Rue, T. Beach, A. Covich, and A. Traverse. 1998. Human-Environment Interactions in a Tropical Watershed: The Paleoecology of Laguna Tamarindito, Peten, Guatemala. *Journal of Field Archaeology* 25:139–151.

Earle, T. 2002. *Bronze Age Economics: The Beginnings of Political Economies.* Boulder, CO: Westview Press.

———. 2004. Culture Matters in the Neolithic Transition and Emergence of Hierarchy in Thy, Denmark: Distinguished Lecture. *American Anthropologist* 106(1):111–125.

Earle, T. K., and J. Haas, eds. 1991. *Chiefdoms: Power, Economy, and Ideology*. Cambridge: Cambridge University Press.

Ekström, G. 1950. *Skånes åkerjordsområden (Scania's Agricultural Soil Regions)*. Sockerhandlingar. Svenska sockerfabriksaktiebolagets skrifter, vol. 6, no. 3. Malmö, Sweden: Riksantikvarieämbetet.

Eldredge, N., and S. J. Gould. 1972. Punctuated Equilibria: An Alternative to Phyletic Gradualism. In *Models in Paleobiology*, ed. T.J.M. Schopf, 82–115. San Francisco: Freeman Cooper.

Elias, N. 1992. *Time: An Essay*. Oxford: Blackwell.

Emanuel, K. 2005a. Emanuel Replies. *Nature* 438(22):E13.

———. 2005b. Increasing Destructiveness of Tropical Cyclones over the Past 30 Years. *Nature* 436(4):686–688.

Emery, K. F., L. E. Wright, and H. Schwarcz. 2000. Isotopic Analysis of Ancient Deer Bone: Biotic Stability in Collapse Period Maya Land-Use. *Journal of Archaeological Science* 27:537–550.

Endfield, G., and S. O'Hara. 1999. Degradation, Drought, and Dissent: An Environmental History of Colonial Michoacán, West Central Mexico. *AAAG* 89(3):402–419.

Erickson, C. 2000a. An Artificial Landscape-Scale Fishery in the Bolivian Amazon. *Nature* 408:190–193.

———. 2000b. The Lake Titicaca Basin: A Precolumbian Built Landscape. In *Imperfect Balance: Landscape Transformations in the Precolumbian Americas*, ed. D. L. Lentz, 311–357. New York: Columbia Unversity Press.

———. 2003. Agricultural Landscapes as World Heritage: Raised Field Agriculture in Bolivia and Peru. In *Managing Change: Sustainable Approaches to Conservation of the Built Environment: 4th Annual US/ICOMOS International Symposium*, organized by US/ICOMOS, the Graduate Program in Historic Preservation of the University of Pennsylvania, and the Getty Conservation Institute, Philadelphia, Pennsylvania, April, 2001, ed. J. M. Teutonico and F. G. Matero, 181–204. Los Angeles: Getty Conservation Institute.

Eriksen, S., E. Ouko, and N. Marekia. 1996. Land Tenure and Wildlife Management. In *In Land We Trust: Environment, Private Property, and Constitutional Change*, ed. C. Juma and J. B. Ojwang, 199–230. Nairobi: Initiative Publishers.

Escobar, A. 1999. After Nature: Steps to an Antiessentialist Political Ecology. *Current Anthropology* 40:1–30.

Evans-Pritchard, E. E. 1940. *The Nuer*. Oxford: Oxford University Press.

Ezell, P. H. 1994. Plants without Water: The Pima-Maricopa Experience. *Journal of the Southwest* 36(4):315–392.

Fairhead, J., and M. Leach. 1996. Enriching the Landscape: Social History and the Management of Transition Ecology in the Forest, Savanna Mosaic of the Republic of Guinea. *Africa: Journal of the International African Institute* 66(1):14–36.

Fall, P. L., S. E. Falconer, L. Lines, and M. C. Metzger. 2004. Environmental Impacts of the Rise of Civilization in the Southern Levant. In *The Archaeology of Global Change: The Impacts of Humans on Their Environment,* ed. C. L. Redman, S. R. James, P. R. Fish, and J. D. Rogers, 141–157. Washington, D.C: Smithsonian Books.

Fall, P. L., L. Lines, and S. Falconer. 1996. Seeds of Civilization: Bronze Age Rural Economy and Ecology in the Southern Levant. *Annals of the Association of American Geographers* 88(1):1–23.

FAO. 1978. *FAO-Unesco Soil Map of the World.* Rome: Food and Agriculture Organization of the United Nations.

———. 1981. *FAO-Unesco Soil Map of the World* 1:5 000 000 vol. 5–Europe. Rome: Food and Agriculture Organization of the United Nations.

———. 1997. Women and Food Security. *FAO Focus on the Issues* http://www.fao.org/FOCUS/E/Women/WoHm-e.htm (accessed February 10, 2009).

———. 1998. *Rural Women and Food Security: Current Situation and Perspectives.* Rome: Food and Agriculture Organization of the United Nations.

Fash, W. L., E. W. Andrews, and T. K. Manahan. 2004. Political Decentralization, Dynastic Collapse, and the Early Postclassic in the Urban Center of Copan, Honduras. In *The Terminal Classic in the Maya Lowlands: Collapse, Transition, and Transformation*, ed. A. Demarest, P. M. Rice, and D. S. Rice, 260–287. Boulder: University Press of Colorado.

Fedick, S. L., B. A. Morrison, B. J. Andersen, S. Boucher, J. C. Acosta, and J. P. Mathews. 2000. Wetland Manipulation in the Yalahau Region of the Northern Maya Lowlands. *Journal of Field Archaeology* 27:131–152.

Fish, P. R., and S. K. Fish. 1992. Prehistoric Landscapes of the Sonoran Desert Hohokam. *Population and Environment: A Journal of Interdisciplinary Studies* 13:269–283.

Fish, S. K., and P. R. Fish. 2000. The Institutional Contexts of Hohokam Complexity and Inequality. In *Alternative Leadership Strategies in the Prehispanic Southwest*, ed. B. J. Mills, 154–167. Tucson: University of Arizona Press.

Fisher, C. T. 2000. Landscapes of the Lake Pátzcuaro Basin. PhD diss., University of Wisconsin, Madison.

Fisher, C. T., and G. M. Feinman. 2005. Introduction to "Landscapes over Time: Resilience, Degradation, and Contemporary Lessons." *American Anthropologist* 107(1):62–69.

Fisher, C. T., H. P. Pollard, and C. Frederick. 1999. Intensive Agriculture and Socio-Political Development in the Lake Pátzcuaro Basin, Michoacán, Mexico. *Antiquity* 73(281):642–649.

Fisher, C. T., H. P. Pollard, I. Israde-Alcántara, V. H. Garduño-Monroy, and S. K. Banerjee. 2003. A Reexamination of Human-Induced Environmental Change within the Lake Pátzcuaro Basin, Michoacán, Mexico. *PNAS* 100:4957–4962.

Fisher, C. T., and T. Thurston. 1999. Dynamic Landscapes and Socio-Political Process: The Topography of Anthropogenic Environments in Global Perspective. *Antiquity* 73:630–631.

Flannery, K. V. 1968. Archaeological Systems Theory and Early Mesoamerica. In *Anthropological Archaeology in the Americas*, ed. B. J. Meggers, 67–87. Washington, D.C.: Anthropological Society of Washington.

———. 1972. The Cultural Evolution of Civilizations. In *Annual Review of Ecology and Systematics* 3:339–426.

Fleisher, M. L. 1998. Cattle Raiding and Its Correlates: The Cultural-Ecological Consequences of Market-Oriented Cattle Raiding among the Kuria of Tanzania. *Human Ecology* 26(4):547–572.

Fletcher, R. 2000. Seeing Angkor: New Views on an Old City. *Journal of the Oriental Society of Australia* 32–33:1–27.

Flores, J. S., and I. Espejel Carvajal. 1994. *Tipos de vegetación de la Peninsula de Yucatán*. Etnoflora Yucatanese, no. 3. Mérida, Mexico: Universidad Autónoma de Yucatán.

Fokkens, H. 1997. The Genesis of Urnfields: Economic Crisis or Ideological Change? *Antiquity* 71:360–373.

Foley, R. A. 1987. *Just Another Unique Species*. Cambridge: University of Cambridge Press.

Folke, C., S. Carpenter, T. Elmqvist, L. Gunderson, C. S. Holling, and B. Walker. 2002. Resilience and Sustainable Development: Building Adaptive Capacity in a World of Transformations. *Ambio* 31:437–440.

Fontana, W. 2002. The Topology of the Possible. Paper presented at the workshop "Paradigms of Change," Bonn, Germany, May 23–25.

Foster, D., F. Swanson, J. Aber, I. Burke, N. Brokaw, D. Tilman, and A. Knapp. 2003. The Importance of Land-Use Legacies to Ecology and Conservation. *Bioscience* 53:77–88.

Foster, D. R. 2000. Conservation Lessons and Challenges from Ecological History. *Forest History Today* Fall:2–11.

Foster, M. S., M. K. Woodson, and G. Huckleberry. 2002. *Prehistoric Water Utilization and Technology in Arizona*. Phoenix: State Historic Preservation Office, Arizona State Parks.

Fowler, C. S. 2000. "We Live by Them": Native Knowledge of Biodiversity in the Great Basin of Western North America. In *Biodiversity and Native America*, ed. P. E. Minnis and W. J. Elisens, 99–132. Norman: University of Oklahoma Press.

Fox, W. 1987. The Neolithic Occupation of Western Cyprus. In *Western Cyprus: Connections*, ed. David Rupp, 19–44. Studies in Mediterranean Archaeology, vol. 77. Gothenburg, Sweden: Paul Åströms Förlag.

Frame, S. 2002. Island Neolithics: Animal Exploitation in the Aceramic Neolithic of Cyprus. In *World Islands in Prehistory*, ed. W. Waldren and J. Ensenyat, 233–238. British Archaeological Reports International Series 1095. Oxford: Archaeopress.

Fredskild, B. 1978. Paleobotanical Investigations of Some Peat Deposits of Norse Age at Qagssiarssuk, South Greenland. *Meddelelser om Grønland* 204(5):1–41.

Freeman-Grenville, G.S.P. 1962. *The East African Coast: Select Documents from the First to the Earlier Nineteenth Century*. Oxford: Clarendon Press.

Freidel, D., L. Schele, and J. Parker. 1993. *Maya Cosmos: Three Thousand Years on the Shaman's Path.* New York: Morrow.

Frumkin, A. 1997. The Holocene History of Dead Sea Levels. In *The Dead Sea: The Lake and Its Setting,* ed. T. M. Niemi, Z. Ben-Avraham, and J. R. Gat, 237–248. Oxford: Oxford University Press.

Frumkin, A., D. C. Ford, and H. P. Schwarcz. 2000. Paleoclimate and Vegetation of the Last Glacial Cycles in Jerusalem from a Speleothem Record. *Global Biogeochemical Cycles* 14(3):863–870.

Garfinkel, Y. 1993. The Yarmukian Culture in Israel. *Paléorient* 19(1):115–134.

———. 1999. Radiometric Dates from Eighth Millennium B.P. Israel. *BASOR* 315:1–13.

Gauntlett, D. 2002. *Media, Gender and Identity: An Introduction.* London; New York: Routledge.

Gelbspan, R. 1998. *The Heat Is On: The Climate Crisis, the Cover-up, the Prescription.* Updated ed. Reading, MA: Perseus Books.

———. 2004. *Boiling Point: How Politicians, Big Oil and Coal, Journalists, and Activists Are Fueling the Climate Crisis–And What We Can Do to Avert Disaster.* 1st ed. New York: Basic Books.

Gelburd, D. E. 1985. Managing Salinity: Lessons from the Past. *Journal of Soil and Water Conservation* 40(4):329–331.

Gibson, C. 1967. *The Aztecs under Spanish Rule.* Stanford, CA: Stanford University Press.

Gibson, M. 1974. Violation of Fallow and Engineered Disaster in Mesopotamian Civilization. In *Irrigation's Impact on Society,* ed. T. E. Downing and M. Gibson, 7–19. Anthropological Papers of the University of Arizona 25. Tucson: University of Arizona Press.

Giddens, A. 1984. *The Constitution of Society: Outline of the Theory of Structuration.* Cambridge: Polity Press.

———. 1993. *New Rules of Sociological Method: A Positive Critique of Interpretive Sociologies.* Stanford, CA: Stanford University Press.

Gill, R. B. 1995. *The Great Maya Droughts.* PhD diss., University of Texas.

Gillson, L. 2005. A "Large Infrequent Disturbance" in an East African Savanna. *African Journal of Ecology* 44(4):458–467.

Glantz, M. H., ed. 1987. *Drought and Hunger in Africa.* Cambridge: Cambridge University Press.

Glantz, M. H., D. G. Streets, T. R. Stewart, N. Bhatti, C. M. Moore, and C. H. Rosa. 1998. *Exploring the Concept of Climate Surprises: A Review of the Literature on the Concept of Surprise and How It Is Related to Climate Change.* U.S. Department of Energy, Office of Energy Research.

Goldberg, P., and O. Bar-Yosef. 1990. The Effect of Man on Geomorphological Processes Based upon the Evidence from the Levant and Adjacent Areas. In *Man's Role in the Shaping of the Eastern Mediterranean Landscape,* ed. S. Bottema, G. Entjes-Nieborg, and W. van Zeist, 71–86. Rotterdam: Balkema.

Gomez-Pompa, A., M. Allen, S. Fedick, and J. Jiménez-Osornio, eds. 2003. *Lowland Maya Area: Three Millennia at the Human-Wildland Interface.* Binghamton, NY: Haworth Press.

Goodfriend, G. A. 1999. Terrestrial Stable Isotope Records of Late Quaternary Paleoclimates in the Eastern Mediterranean Region. *Quaternary Science Reviews* 18(4–5):501–514.

Gopher, A., and R. Gophna. 1993. Cultures of the Eighth and Seventh Millennium BP in Southern Levant: A Review for the 1990's. *Journal of World Prehistory* 7(3):297–351.

Gophna, R. 1995. Early Bronze Age Canaan: Some Spatial and Demographic Observations. In *The Archaeology of Society in the Holy Land*, ed. T. E. Levy, 269–282. New York: Facts on File.

Gorenstein, S., and H. P. Pollard. 1983. *The Tarascan Civilization: A Late Prehispanic Cultural System.* Nashville, TN: Vanderbilt University Press.

Gosse, J. C., E. B. Evenson, J. Klein, B. Lawn, and R. Middleton. 1995. Precise Cosmogenic 10Be Measurements in Western North American: Support for a Global Younger Dryas Cooling Event. *Geology* 23(10):877–880.

Graf, D. F. 1997. *Rome and the Arabian Frontier: From the Nabateans to the Saracens.* Aldershot, Hampshire, UK: Ashgate Publishing.

Gray, S., M. Sundal, B. Wiebusch, M. A. Little, P. W. Leslie, and I.L. Pike. 2003. Cattle Raiding, Cultural Survival, and Adaptability of East African Pastoralists. *Current Anthropology* 44(Supplement):S3–S30.

Graybill, D. A. 1989. The Reconstruction of Prehistoric Salt River Streamflow. In *The 1982–1984 Excavations at Las Colinas: Environment and Subsistence*, ed. D. A. Graybill, D. A. Gregory, F. L. Nials, S. K. Fish, R. E. Gasser, C. H. Miksicek, and C. R. Szuter, 25–38. Archaeological Series 162, vol. 5. Tucson: Arizona State Museum, University of Arizona.

Graybill, D. A., D. A. Gregory, G. S. Funkhouser, and F. Nials. 2006. Long-Term Streamflow Reconstruction, River Channel Morphology, and Aboriginal Irrigation Systems along the Salt and Gila Rivers. In *Environmental Change and Human Adaptation in the Ancient American Southwest*, ed. D. Doyel and J. Dean, 69–123. Salt Lake City: University of Utah Press.

Greller, A. M. 2000. Vegetation on the Floristic Regions of North and Central America. In *Imperfect Balance: Landscape Transformations in the Precolumbian Americas*, ed. D. L. Lentz, 39–88. New York: Columbia University Press.

Guderjan, T. H., J. Baker, and R. J. Lichtenstein. 2003. Environmental and Cultural Diversity at Blue Creek. In *Heterarchy, Political Economy, and the Ancient Maya: The Three Rivers Region of the East-Central Yucatán Peninsula*, ed. V. L. Scarborough, F. Valdez Jr., and N. Dunning, 77–91. Tucson: University of Arizona Press.

Guilaine, J. 2003. Parekklisha-*Shillourokambos*: Périodisation et aménagements domestiques. In *Le Néolithique de Chypre*, ed. J. Guilaine and A. LeBrun, 4–14. Bulletin de correspondance Hellénique supplément 43. Athens: École française d'Athènes.

Guilaine, J., and A. LeBrun, eds. 2003. *Le Néolithique de Chypre*. Bulletin de correspondance Hellénique supplément 43. Athens: École française d'Athènes.

Guillermo Aguilar, A., E. Excurra, T. Garciá, M. Mazari Hiriart, and I. Pisanty. 1995. The Basin of Mexico. In *Regions at Risk: Comparisons of Threatened Environments*, ed. R. E. Kasperson, J. X. Kasperson, B. L. Turner III, K. Dow, and W. B. Meyer, 304–307. New York: United Nations University Press.

Gunderson, L. H., and C. S. Holling, eds. 2002. *Panarchy: Understanding Transformations in Human and Natural Systems*. Washington, D.C.; London: Island Press.

Gunn, J. D., W. J. Folan, and H. Robichaux. 1995. A Landscape Analysis of the Candelaria Watershed in Mexico: Insights into Paleoclimates Affecting Upland Horticulture in the Southern Yucatan Peninsular Semi-Karst. *Geoarchaeology* 10:3–42.

Gunn, J. D., J. E. Foss, W. J. Folan, M. del Rosario Domínguez, and B. B. Faust. 2002. Bajo Sediments and the Hydraulic System of Calakmul, Campeche, Mexico. *Ancient Mesoamerica* 13:297–315.

Haag, A. 2007. Is This What the World's Coming To? *Nature Reports Climate Change* doi:10.1038/climate.2007.56 *Nature* online.

Hackenberg, R. A. 1974. Ecosystemic Channeling: Cultural Ecology from the Viewpoint of Aerial Photography. In *Aerial Photography in Anthropological Research*, ed. E. Z. Voght, 28–39. Cambridge: Harvard University Press.

Hageman, J. B., and J. C. Lohse. 2003. Heterarchy, Corporate Groups, and Late Classic Resource Management in Northwestern Belize. In *Heterarchy, Political Economy, and the Ancient Maya: The Three Rivers Region of the East-Central Yucatán Peninsula*, ed. V. L. Scarborough, F. Valdez Jr., and N. P. Dunning, 109–121. Tucson: University of Arizona Press.

Halperin, R. H. 1994. *Cultural Economies: Past and Present*. Austin: University of Texas Press.

Hammond, N. 1978. The Myth of the Milpa: Agricultural Expansion in the Maya Lowlands. In *Pre-Hispanic Maya Agriculture*, ed. P. D. Harrison and B. L. Turner II, 23–34. Albuquerque: University of New Mexico Press.

Hammond, N., and G. Tourtellot III. 2004. Out with a Whimper: La Milpa in the Terminal Classic. In *The Terminal Classic in the Maya Lowlands: Collapse, Transition, and Transformation*, ed. A. Demarest, P. M. Rice, and D. S. Rice, 288–301. Boulder: University Press of Colorado.

Hammond, N., G. Tourtellot III, S. Donaghey, and A. Clarke. 1998. No Slow Dusk: Maya Urban Development and Decline at La Milpa, Belize. *Antiquity* 72:831–837.

Hammond, P. C. 1973. The Nabataeans—Their History, Culture and Archaeology. Studies in Mediterranean Archaeology 37. Gothenburg, Sweden: Paul Astroms Forlag.

Hanbury-Tenison, J. W. 1986. *The Late Chalcolithic to Early Bronze I Transition in Palestine and Transjordan*. British Archaeological Reports International Series 311. Oxford: Archaeopress.

Hannon, G. E., S. Wastegård, E. Bradshaw, and R.H.W. Bradshaw. 2001. Human Impact and Landscape Degradation on the Faroe Islands. *Biology and Environment: Proceedings of the Royal Irish Academy* 101B(1–2):129–139.

Hansen, R. D., S. Bosarth, R. Byrne, J. Jacob, D. Wahl, and T. Schreiner. 2002. Climatic and Environmental Variability in the Rise of Maya Civilization: A Preliminary Perspective from Northern Petén. *Ancient Mesoamerica* 13:273–295.

Harlan, J. R. 1985. The Early Bronze Age Environment of the Southern Ghor and the Moab Plateau. In *Studies in the History and Archaeology of Jordan II*, ed. A. Hadidi, (2)125–129. Amman, Hashemite Kingdom of Jordan: Department of Antiquities.

———. 1988. Natural Resources. In *The Wadi el Hasa Archaeological Survey 1979–1983, West-Central Jordan*, ed. B. MacDonald, 40–48. Waterloo, Ontario, Canada: Wilfred Laurier University Press.

Harrison, P. D. 1990. The Revolution in Ancient Maya Subsistence. In *Vision and Revision in Maya Studies*, ed. F. S. Clancy and P. D. Harrison, 99–113. Albuquerque: University of New Mexico Press.

———. 1993. Aspects of Water Management in the Southern Maya Lowlands. In *Economic Aspects of Water Management in the Prehispanic New World*, ed. V. L. Scarborough and B. L. Isaac, 71–119. Research in Economic Anthropology, Supplement 7. Greenwich, CT: JAI Press.

Harrison, P. D., and B. L. Turner II, eds. 1983. *Pulltrouser Swamp: Ancient Maya Habitat, Agriculture and Settlement in Northern Belize*. Austin: University of Texas Press.

Hartshorn, G. S. 1988. Tropical and Subtropical Vegetation of Meso-America. In *North American Terrestrial Vegetation*, ed. M. G. Barbour and W. D. Billings, 365–390. New York: Cambridge University Press.

Hartwell, R. 1963. *Iron and Early Industrialism in Eleventh-Century China*. PhD diss., University of Chicago.

Haug, G. H., K. A. Hughen, D. M. Sigman, L. C. Peterson, and U. Röhl. 2001. Southward Migration of the Intertropical Convergence Zone through the Holocene. *Science* 293:1304–1308.

Haury, E. W. 1967. First Masters of the American Desert: The Hohokam. *National Geographic* 131(5):670–695.

———. 1976. *The Hohokam: Desert Farmers and Craftsman-Excavations at Snaketown, 1964–1965*. Tucson: University of Arizona Press.

Hawkes, K., and J. O'Connell. 1992. On Optimal Foraging Models and Subsistence Transitions. *Current Anthropology* 23(1):63–66.

Hayes, A., M. Kucera, N. Kallel, L. Sbaffi, and E. J. Rohling. 2005. Glacial Mediterranean Sea Surface Temperatures Based on Planktonic Foraminiferal Assemblages. *Quaternary Science Reviews* 24:999.

Head, L. 2000. *Cultural Landscapes and Environmental Change*. London: Arnold.

Heckenberger, M. J., A. Kuikuro, U. Tabata Kuikuro, J. C. Russell, M. Schmidt, C. Fausto, and B. Franchetto. 2003. Amazonia 1492: Pristine Forest or Cultural Parkland? *Science* 301:1710–1714.

Hegmon, M., M. Peeples, S. Ingram, A. Kinzig, S. Kulow, C. Meegan, and M. Nelson. 2007. *Social Transformation and Its Human Costs in the Prehispanic US Southwest.* Manuscript in possession of authors.

Held, S. 1989. Colonization Cycles on Cyprus, 1: The Biogeographic and Paleontological Foundations of Early Prehistoric Settlement. *Report of the Department of Antiquities, Cyprus, 1989*: 7–28.

Hewitt, K., ed. 1983. *Interpretations of Calamity from the Viewpoint of Human Ecology.* Boston: Allen and Unwin.

Hill, J. B. 2004a. Land Use and an Archaeological Perspective on Socio-Natural Studies in the Wadi al-Hasa, West-Central Jordan. *American Antiquity* 69(3):389–412.

———. 2004b. Time, Scale and Interpretation: 10,000 Years of Land Use on the Transjordan Plateau, Amid Multiple Contexts of Change. In *Mediterranean Archaeological Landscapes: Current Issues*, ed. E. F. Athanassopoulos and L. Wandsnider, 125–142. Philadelphia: University of Pennsylvania Museum Publications.

———. 2006. *Human Ecology in the Wadi al-Hasa: Land Use and Abandonment through the Holocene.* Tucson: University of Arizona Press.

Hillman, G. C., and M. S. Davies. 1992. Domestication Rate in Wild Wheats and Barley under Primitive Cultivation: Preliminary Results and the Archaeological Implications of Field Measurements of Selection Coefficient. In *Préhistoire de l'agriculture*, ed. P. C. Anderson-Gerfaud, 119–158. Monographie du CRA, no. 6. Paris: CNRS.

Hitchcock, R. K. 1994. International Human Rights, the Environment, and Indigenous Peoples. *Colorado Journal of International Environmental Law and Policy* 5(1):1–22.

———. 1995. Centralization, Resource Depletion, and Coercive Conservation among the Tyua of the Northeastern Kalahari. *Human Ecology* 23(2):169–198.

Hodell, D. A., M. Brenner, J. H. Curtis, and T. Guilderson. 2001. Solar Forcing of Drought Frequency in the Maya Lowlands. *Science* 292:1367–1370.

Hodell, D. A., J. H. Curtis, and M. Brenner. 1995. Possible Role of Climate in the Collapse of Classic Maya Civilization. *Nature* 375:391–394.

Hoffman, S. M., and A. Oliver-Smith, eds. 2002. *Catastrophe and Culture: The Anthropology of Disaster.* Santa Fe, NM: School of American Research Press.

Holling, C. S. 1973. Resilience and Stability of Ecological Systems. *Annual Review of Ecology and Systematics* 4:1–23.

———. 1986. The Resilience of Terrestrial Ecosystems: Local Surprise and Global Change. In *Sustainable Development of the Biosphere*, ed. W. C. Clark and R. E. Munn, 292–317. Cambridge: Cambridge University Press.

———. 2001. Understanding the Complexity of Economic, Ecological, and Social Systems. *Ecosystems* 4(5):394–405.

Holling, C. S., and L. H. Gunderson. 2002. Resilience and Adaptive Cycles. In *Panarchy: Understanding Transformations in Human and Natural Systems*, ed. L. H. Gunderson and C. S. Holling, 25–62. Washington, D.C.: Island Press.

Holling, C. S., L. H. Gunderson, and D. Ludwig. 2002. In Quest of a Theory of Adaptive Change. In *Panarchy: Understanding Transformations in Human and*

Natural Systems, ed. L. H. Gunderson and C. S. Holling, 3–24. Washington, D.C.: Island Press.

Horne, L. 1982. Fuel for the Metal-Worker: The Role of Charcoal and Charcoal Production in Ancient Metallurgy. *Expedition* 25(1):6–13.

Horowitz, A., and J. R. Gat. 1984. Floral and Isotopic Indications for Possible Summer Rains in Israel during Wetter Climates. *Pollen et Spores* 26(1):61–68.

Horton, M. 1996. *Shanga: A Muslim Trading Community on the East African Coast.* Nairobi: The British Institute in Eastern Africa.

Horwitz, L., E. Tchernov, and H. Hongo. 2004. The Domestic Status of the Early Neolithic Fauna of Cyprus: A View from the Mainland. In *Neolithic Revolution: New Perspectives on Southwest Asia in Light of Recent Discoveries on Cyprus*, ed. E. Peltenburg and A. Wasse, 35–48. Levant Supplementary Series 1. Oxford: Oxbow Books.

Houston, S. D. 1993. *Hieroglyphs and History at Dos Pilas: Dynastic Politics of the Classic Maya*. Austin: University of Texas Press.

Howard, J. B., and G. Huckleberry. 1991. *The Operation and Evolution of an Irrigation System: The East Papago Canal Study.* Soil Systems Publication in Archaeology, no. 18. Report submitted to Arizona Department of Transportation, Environmental Planning Services, Phoenix.

Huberman, B., ed. 1988. *The Ecology of Computation*. Amsterdam: North Holland Pub. Co.

Huckleberry, G. 1995. Archaeological Implications of Late-Holocene Channel Changes on the Middle Gila River, Arizona. *Geoarchaeology* 10(3):159–182.

Hughbanks, P. J. 1998. Settlement and Land Use at Guijarral, Northwestern Belize. *Culture and Agriculture* 20:107–120.

Hughes, A. R. 1958. Some Ancient and Recent Observations on Hyaenas. *Koedoe* 1:105–114.

Hüttermann, A. 1999. *The Ecological Message of the Torah: Knowledge, Concepts, and Laws Which Made Survival in a Land of "Milk and Honey" Possible*. South Florida Studies in the History of Judaism 199. Atlanta, GA: Scholars Press.

Hutteroth, W. 1975. The Pattern of Settlement in Palestine in the Sixteenth Century: Geographic Research on Turkish Defter-i Mufassal. In *Studies on Palestine during the Ottoman Period*, ed. M. Ma'oz, 3–10. Jerusalem: Magnes Press, Hebrew University and Yad Izhak Ben-Zvi.

Inalcik, H. 1997. Part I: The Ottoman State: Economy and Society, 1300–1600. In Vol. 1 of *An Economic and Social History of the Ottoman Empire*, ed. H. Inalcik and D. Quataert, 1–409. Cambridge: Cambridge University Press.

Ingram, S. E. 2008. Streamflow and Population Change in the Lower Salt River Valley of Central Arizona, ca. A.D. 775 to 1450. *American Antiquity* 73(1):136–165.

Inomata, T. 2004. The Spatial Mobility of Non-elite Populations in Classic Maya Society and Its Political Implications. In *Ancient Maya Commoners*, ed. J. C. Lohse and F. Valdez Jr., 175–196. Austin: University of Texas Press.

International Federation of Red Cross and Red Crescent Societies. 2001. *World Disasters Report.* Geneva: Red Cross.

Ives, A. R. 1998. Population Ecology: The Waxing and Waning of Populations. In *Ecology*, ed. S. I. Dodson, 12–15. Oxford: Oxford University Press.

Jabbur, J. S. 1995. *The Bedouins and the Desert: Aspects of Nomadic Life in the Arab East.* Trans. L. I. Conrad. SUNY Series in Near Eastern Studies. Albany: State University of New York Press.

Jacob, J. S. 1995. Archaeological Pedology in the Maya Lowlands. In *Pedological Perspectives in Archaeological Research.* Soil Science Society of America Special Publication 44:51–79. Madison, WI: Soil Science Society of America.

Jacobsen, T., and R. McC. Adams. 1958. Salt and Silt in Ancient Mesopotamian Agriculture. *Science* 128:1251–1258.

Jahns, S. 1993. On the Holocene Vegetation of the Argive Plain (Peloponnese Southern Greece). *Vegetation History and Archaeobotany* 2:187–203.

Jakobsen, B. H. 1991. Soil Erosion in the Norse Settlement Area of Østerbygden in Southern Greenland. *Acta Borealia* 8:56–68.

James, S. R. 1994. Hunting, Fishing, and Resource Depletion: Prehistoric Cultural Impacts on Animals in the Southwest. Paper presented at the 1994 Southwest Symposium, Tempe, Arizona, January 7–8.

———. 2003. Hunting and Fishing Patterns Leading to Resource Depletion. In *Centuries of Decline during the Hohokam Classic Period at Pueblo Grande*, ed. D. R. Abbott, 70–81. Tucson: University of Arizona Press.

Jansen, D. 1998. Gardenification of Wildland Nature and the Human Footprint. *Science* 279(5355):1312–1313.

Janssen, M.A.K., A. Timothy, and M. Scheffer. 2003. Sunk-Cost Effects and Vulnerability to Collapse in Ancient Societies. *Current Anthropology* 44(5):722–728.

Jiggins, J. 1986a. *Gender-related Impacts and the Work of the International Agricultural Research Centres.* Washington, D.C.: World Bank.

———. 1986b. *Special Problems of Female Heads of Households in Agriculture and Rural Development in Asia and the Pacific.* Rome: Food and Agriculture Organization of the United Nations.

Jochim, M. A. 1981. *Strategies for Survival: Cultural Behavior in an Ecological Context.* New York: Academic Press.

Johnson, A., and T. Earle. 1987. *The Evolution of Human Societies: From Foraging Groups to Agrarian States.* Stanford, CA: Stanford University Press.

Johnson, D. L., and L. A. Lewis. 1995. *Land Degradation: Creation and Destruction.* Oxford: Blackwell.

Johnson, K. J. 2003. The Intensification of Pre-industrial Cereal Agriculture in the Tropics: Boserup, Cultivation Lengthening, and the Classic Maya. *Journal of Anthropological Archaeology* 22:126–161.

Johnston, K. J., A. J. Breckenbridge, and B. C. Hansen. 2001. Paleoecological Evidence of an Early Postclassic Occupation in the Southwestern Maya Lowlands: Laguna Las Pozas, Guatemala. *Latin American Antiquity* 12:149–166.

Jones, G. 1987. *A History of the Vikings.* Oxford: Oxford University Press.

Jones, J. G., and N. P. Dunning. n.d. Aguadas of the Pre-Hispanic Central Maya Lowlands as Paleoenvironmental Sources. *Ancient Mesoamerica.* In review.

Joyce, A. A., and R. G. Mueller. 1992. The Social Impact of Anthropogenic Landscape Modification in the Rio Verde Drainage Basin, Oaxaca, Mexico. *Geoarchaeology: An International Journal* 7(6):503–526.

Kadosh, D., D. Sivan, H. Kutiel, and M. Weinstein-Evron. 2004. A Late Quaternary Paleoenvironmental Sequence from Dor, Carmel Coastal Plain, Israel. *Palynology* 28:143–157.

Kaegi, W. 1992. *Byzantium and the Early Islamic Conquests.* Cambridge: Cambridge University Press.

Kasperson, J. X., R. E. Kasperson, and B. L. Turner. 1995. *Regions at Risk: Comparisons of Threatened Environments.* Tokyo; New York: United Nations University Press.

Kauffman, S. 1993. *The Origins of Order.* Oxford: Oxford University Press.

Keeney, D. 1990. Sustainable Agriculture: Definition and Concepts. *Journal of Production Agriculture* 3(3):281–285.

Keller, D., and D. Rupp. 1983. *Archaeological Survey in the Mediterranean Area.* British Archaeological Reports International Series 155. Oxford: Archaeopress.

Kelly, R. 1995. *The Foraging Spectrum: Diversity in Hunter-Gatherer Lifeways.* Washington, D.C.: Smithsonian Institution Press.

Kelly, R. C. 1985. *The Nuer Conquest: The Structure and Development of an Expansionist System.* Ann Arbor: University of Michigan Press.

Kennedy, D. 2006. Acts of God? *Science* 311:303.

Kent, S. 1992. The Current Forager Controversy: Real Versus Ideal Views of Hunter-Gatherers. *Man* 27(1):45–70.

Kenya Wildlife Services. 1994–1995. *Report from Review Group on Human-Wildlife Conflict.* Nairobi: Government Press.

Kenyon, K. 1957. *Digging Up Jericho.* London: Benn.

King, E. M., and L. C. Shaw. 2003. Heterarchical Approach to Site Variability: The Maax Na Archaeological Project. In *Heterarchy, Political Economy, and the Ancient Maya: The Three Rivers Region of the East-Central Yucatán Peninsula,* ed. V. L. Scarborough, F. Valdez Jr., and N. Dunning, 64–76. Tucson: University of Arizona Press.

Kingdon, Jonathan. 1982. *East African Mammals. Vol. IIIC: Bovids.* Chicago: University of Chicago Press.

———. 1997. *The Kingdon Field Guide to African Mammals.* London: Academic Press.

Kirch, P. V. 1994. *The Wet and the Dry: Irrigation and Agricultural Intensification in Polynesia.* Chicago: University of Chicago Press.

———. 2005. Archaeology and Global Change: The Holocene Record. *Annual Review of Environmental Resources* 30:409–440.

Kirch, P. V., J. R. Flenley, D. Steadman, F. Lamont, and S. Dawson. 1992. Ancient Environmental Degradation. *National Geographic Research and Exploration* 8(2):166–179.

Kislev, M. E. 1997. Early Agriculture and Paleoecology of Netiv Hagdud. In *An Early Neolithic Village in the Jordan Valley. Part I: The Archaeology of Netiv*

Hagdud, ed. O. Bar-Yosef and A. Gopher, 209–236. Cambridge, MA: Peabody Museum of Archaeology and Ethnology, Harvard University.

Klein, R. G. 1983. Palaeoenvironmental Implications of Quaternary Large Mammals in the Fynbos Region. In *Fynbos Palaeoecology: A Preliminary Synthesis*, ed. H. J. Deacon, Q. B. Hendey, and J.J.N. Lambrechts, 116–133. South African National Science Programmes Report 75. Pretoria, South Africa: CSIR.

Knapp, A. B., S. Held, and S. Manning. 1994. The Prehistory of Cyprus: Problems and Prospects. *Journal of World Prehistory* 377:377–453.

Kohler, T. 1992a. Prehistoric Human Impact on the Environment in Upland North American Southwest. *Population and Environment: A Journal of Interdisciplinary Studies* 13(4):255–268.

———. 1992b. The Prehistory of Sustainability. *Population and Environment* 13(4): 237–243.

Köhler-Rollefson, I. 1988. The Aftermath of the Levantine Neolithic Revolution in Light of Ecologic and Ethnographic Evidence. *Paleorient* 14:87–93.

———. 1993. Camels and Camel Pastoralism in Arabia. *Biblical Archaeologist* 56(4): 180–188.

Köhler-Rollefson, I., and G. Rollefson. 1990. The Impact of Neolithic Subsistence Strategies on the Environment: The Case of 'Ain Ghazal, Jordan. In *Man's Role in the Shaping of the Eastern Mediterranean Landscape*, ed. S. Bottema, G. Entjes-Nieborg, and W. van Zeist, 3–14. Rotterdam: Balkema.

Krech, S., III. 1999. *The Ecological Indian: Myth and History*. New York: W.W. Norton.

Kristiansen, K. 1988. Stenalder, Bronzealder (Stone Age, Bronze Age). In *Den Danske Landbugs Historie I* (Danish Agricultural History I), ed. A. Anderson, 13-3–107. Copenhagen: Landbohistorsk Selskab.

Kuijpers, A., N. Abrahamsen, G. Hoffmann, V. Hühnerbach, P. Konradi, H. Kunzendorf, N. Mikkelsen, J. Thiede, and W. Weinrebe. 1999. Climate Change and the Viking-Age Fjord Environment of the Eastern Settlement, South Greenland. *Geology of Greenland Survey Bulletin* 183:61–67.

Kuijpers, A., J. M. Lloyd, J. B. Jensen, R. Endler, M. Moros, L. A. Park, B. Schulz, K. G. Jensen, and T. Laier. 2001. Late Quaternary Circulation Changes and Sedimentation in Disko Bugt and Adjacent Fjords, Central West Greenland. *Geology of Greenland Survey Bulletin* 189:41–47.

Kunen, J. L., T. P. Culbert, V. Fialko, B. R. McKee, and L. Grazioso. 2000. Bajo Communities: A Case Study from the Central Peten. *Culture and Agriculture* 22(3):15–31.

Kunen, J. L., and P. Hughbanks. 2003. Bajo Communities as Resource Specialists. In *Heterarchy, Political Economy, and the Ancient Maya: The Three Rivers Region of the East-Central Yucatán Peninsula*, ed. V. L. Scarborough, F. Valdez Jr., and N. P. Dunning, 92–108. Tucson: University of Arizona Press.

Kusimba, C. M. 1993. *The Archaeology and Ethnography of Iron Metallurgy of the Kenya Coast*. PhD diss., Bryn Mawr College.

———. 1996. *The Social Context of Iron Forging on the Kenya Coast. Africa* 63(3): 386–419.

———. 1997a. Swahili and Coastal City-States. In *Encyclopedia of Africa: Archaeology, History, Languages, Cultures and Environments*, ed. J. Vogel, 507–512. Walnut Creek, CA: Altamira Press.

———. 1997b. A Time Traveler in Kenya. *Natural History* 106(5):38–47.

———. 1999a. The Rise of Elites among the Precolonial Swahili of the East African Coast. In *Material Symbols in Prehistory*, ed. J. Robb, 318–341. Carbondale: Southern Illinois University Press.

———. 1999b. *The Rise and Fall of Swahili State.* Walnut Creek, CA: Altamira Press.

———. 2004. The Archaeology of Slavery. *African Archaeological Review* 21: 59–88.

Kusimba, C. M., and D. Killick. 2003. Iron Age Ironworking on the Swahili Coast of Kenya. In *Current Research Themes in Later Prehistory of Kenya, Tanzania, and Uganda*, ed. C. M. Kusimba and S. B. Kusimba, 100–111. Philadelphia: University Museum of Pennsylvania.

Kusimba, C. M., D. Killick, and R. G. Creswell. 1994. Indigenous and Imported Metals on Swahili Sites of Kenya. *MASCA Papers in Science and Archaeology* 11(Supplement):63–77.

Kusimba, C. M., and S. B. Kusimba. 2001. Hinterlands of Swahili Cities: Archaeological Investigations of Economy and Trade in Tsavo, Kenya. In *Africa 2000: Forty Years of African Studies in Prague*, ed. L. Kropacek and P. Skalnik, 203–230. Prague: Romna Misek.

Kusimba, C. M., S. B. Kusimba, and D. K. Wright. 2005. The Development and Collapse of Precolonial Ethnic Mosaics in Tsavo, Kenya. *Journal of African Archaeology* 3(2):243–265.

Kwiatkowski, S. M. 2003. Evidence for Subsistence Problems. In *Centuries of Decline during the Hohokam Classic Period at Pueblo Grande*, ed. D. R. Abbott, 48–69. Tucson: University of Arizona Press.

Lal, R. 1987. Managing the Soils of Sub-Saharan Africa. *Science* 236:1069–1076.

Lamprey, R., and R. Waller. 1990. The Loita-Mara Region in Historical Times: Patterns of Subsistence, Settlement and Ecological Change. In *Early Pastoralists of Southwestern Kenya*, ed. P. Robertshaw, 21–43. Nairobi: British Institute in Eastern Africa.

Landsea, C. W. 2005. Hurricanes and Global Warming. *Nature* 438(22):E11–E13.

Lappé, F. M., J. Collins, and P. Rosset, with L. Esparza. 1998. *World Hunger: Twelve Myths.* New York: Grove Press.

Lassen, S., K. G. Jensen, A. Kuijpers, H. Kunzendorf, J. Heinemeier, and P. Konradi. 2000. Late Holocene Climate Signals in South Greenland Waters: Preliminary Results from Igaliku Fjord. *Rapid Oceanographic Changes in the Arctic: Causes and Effects*, 30–36. Copenhagen: Nordic Arctic Research Program, Danish Meteorological Institute.

Latorre, J. García, J. Garciá-Latorre, and A. Sanchez-Picón. 2001. Dealing with Aridity: Socio-Economic Structures and Environmental Changes in an Arid Mediterranean Region. *Land Use Policy* 18:53–64.

LeBrun, A., S. Cluzan, S. Davis, J. Hansen, and J. Renault-Miskovsky. 1987. Le Néolithique précéramique de Chypre. *L'Anthropologie* 91:283–316.

Le Hourou, H. N. 1981. Impact of Man and His Animals on Mediterranean Vegetation. In *Mediterranean Type Ecosystems*, ed. L. DiCastri and R. W. Hooney, 479–521. Berlin: Springer-Verlag.

Lemcke, G., and M. Sturm. 1997. $\partial^{18}O$ and Trace Element Measurements as Proxy for the Reconstructions of Climate Changes at Lake Van (Turkey): Preliminary Results. In *Third Millennium BC Climate Change and Old World Collapse*, ed. H. N. Dalfes, G. Kukla, and H. Weiss, 653–678. NATO ASI Series, vol. I, 49. Berlin: Springer-Verlag.

Lentz, D. L. 2000. *Imperfect Balance: Landscape Transformations in the Precolumbian Americas*. The Historical Ecology Series. New York: Columbia University Press.

Leon-Portilla, M. 1988. *Time and Reality in the Thought of the Maya*. Norman: University of Oklahoma.

Leroi-Gourhan, A., and F. Darmon. 1991. Analyses polliniques de stations natoufiennes au Proche-Orient. In *The Natufian Culture in the Levant*, ed. O. Bar-Yosef and F. R. Valla, 21–26. Ann Arbor, MI: International Monographs in Prehistory.

Leveau, P., F. Trement, K. Walsh, and G. Barker, eds. 1999. *Environmental Reconstruction in Mediterranean Landscape Archaeology*. The Archaeology of Mediterranean Landscapes 2. Oxford: Oxbow Books.

Lévèque, C., and S. E. van der Leeuw. 2003. *Quelle nature voulons-nous? Pour une approche socio-écologique du champ de l'environnement*. Paris: Elsevier.

Levin, S. A. 1999. *Fragile Dominion: Complexity and the Commons*. Reading, MA: Perseus Books.

Levy, T. E. 1983. The Emergence of Specialized Pastoralism in the Southern Levant. *World Archaeology* 15(1):15–36.

Lewandowski, A., M. Zumwinkle, and A. Fish 1999. *Assessing the Soil System: A Review of Soil Quality Literature*. St. Paul, MN: Minnesota Department of Agriculture Energy and Sustainable Agriculture Program.

Lewis, D., and N. Carter, eds. 1993. *Voices from Africa: Local Perspectives on Conservation*. Washington, D.C.: World Wildlife Fund.

Lindner, M., and E. A. Knauf. 1997. Between the Plateau and the Rocks: Edomite Economic and and Social Structure. In Vol. 6 of *Studies in the History and Archaeology of Jordan VI: Landscape Resources and Human Occupation in Jordan throughout the Ages*, ed. G. Bisheh, M. Zaghloul, and I. Kehrberg, 261–264. Amman, Hashemite Kingdom of Jordan: Department of Antiquities.

Lipe, W., and C. Redman. 1996. Conference on "Renewing Our National Archaeological Program." *SAA Bulletin* 14(4):14–17.

Lipton, M., and R. Longhurst. 1989. *New Seeds and Poor People*. London: Unwin Hyman.

Little, P. D. 1996. Pastoralism, Biodiversity, and the Shaping of Savanna Landscapes in East Africa. *Africa* 66:37–50.

Liu, J., T. Dietz, S. Carpenter, M. Alberti, C. Folke, E. Moran, A. Pell, P. Deadman, T. Kratz, J. Lubchenco, E. Ostrom, Z. Ouyang, W. Provencher, C. Redman, S. Schneider, and W. Taylor. 2007. Complexity of Coupled Human and Natural Systems. *Science* 317:1513–1516.

Lohse, J. C. 2004. Inter-site Settlement Signatures and Implications for Late Classic Maya Commoner Organization at Dos Hombres, Belize. In *Ancient Maya Commoners*, ed. J. C. Lohse and F. Valdez Jr., 117–146. Austin: University of Texas Press.

Lohse, J. C., and P. N. Findlay. 2000. A Classic Maya House-Lot Drainage System in Northwestern Belize. *Latin American Antiquity* 11:175–185.

Luhmann, N. 1992. *Ecological Communication*. London: Polity Press.

Luzzadder-Beach, S. 2000. Water Resources of the Chunchucmil Maya. *Geographical Review* 90:493–510.

Luzzadder-Beach, S., and T. Beach. 2009. Arising from the Wetlands: Mechanisms and Chronology of Landscape Aggradation in the Northern Coastal Plain of Belize. *Annals of the Association of American Geographers* 99(1):1–26.

Lynnerup, N., and S. Nørby. 2004. The Greenland Norse: Bones, Graves, Computers, and DNA. *Polar Record* 40(213):107–111.

Macilwain, C. 2004. Head to Head. *Nature* 431(7006):238–243.

Maguire, J., D. Pemberton, and M. H. Collett. 1980. The Makapansgat Limeworks Grey Breccia: Hominids, Hyaenas, Hystricids or Hillwash? *Palaeontologia Africana* 23:75–98.

Mann, C. 2002a. 1491. *The Atlantic Monthly* 289(3):41–53.

———. 2002b. The Real Dirt on Rainforest Fertility. *Science* 297:920–923.

———. 2005. *1491: New Revelations of the Americas before Columbus*. New York: Knopf.

Marean, C. W. 1991. Measuring the Post-Depositional Destruction of Bone in Archaeological Assemblages. *Journal of Archaeological Science* 18:677–694.

Marean, C. W., and L. M. Spencer. 1991. Impact of Carnivore Ravaging on Zooarchaeological Measures of Element Abundance. *American Antiquity* 56:645–658.

Marks, S. A. 1976. *Large Mammals and a Brave People*. Seattle: University of Washington Press.

Marseen, O. 1959. Lindholm Hoje. *Kuml* 1959:53–68.

Marshack, A. 1997. Paleolithic Image Making and Symboling in Europe and the Middle East: A Comparative Review. In Vol. 23 of *Beyond Art: Pleistocene Image and Symbol*, ed. M. Conkey, O. Soffer, D. Stratmann, and N. G. Jablonski, 53–91. Memoirs of California Academy of Sciences. Berkeley: University of California Press.

Martin, P., and R. Klein, eds. 1984. *Quaternary Extinctions: A Prehistoric Revolution*. Tucson: University of Arizona Press.

Matheny, R. T. 1987. El Mirador: An Early Maya Metropolis Uncovered. *National Geographic* 172:316–339.

Mayerson, P. 1994. The Desert of Southern Palestine According to Byzantine Sources. In *Monks, Martyrs, Soldiers and Saracens: Papers on the Near East in Late Antiquity (1962–1993)*, ed. P. Mayerson, 40–52. Jerusalem: The Israel Exploration Society in Association with New York University.

Mayewski, P. A., and M. Bender. 1995. The GISP2 Ice Core Record-Paleoclimate Highlights. *Reviews of Geophysics, Supplement* July:1287–1296.

Mayewski, P. A., E. E. Rohling, J. C. Stager, W. Karlén, K. A. Maasch, L. D. Meeker, E. A. Meyerson, F. Gasse, S. van Kreveld, K. Holmgren, J. Lee-Thorp, G. Rosqvist, F. Rack, M. Staubwasser, R. R. Schneider, and E. J. Steig. 2004. Holocene Climate Variability. *Quaternary Research* 62:243–255.

McCartney, C. 2004. Cypriot Neolithic Chipped Stone Industries and the Progress of Regionalization. In *Neolithic Revolution: New Perspectives on Southwest Asia in Light of Recent Discoveries on Cyprus*, ed. E. Peltenburg and A. Wasse, 103–122. Levant Supplementary Series 1. Oxford: Oxbow Books.

———. 2005. Preliminary Report on the Re-survey of Three Early Neolithic Sites in Cyprus. *Report of the Department of Antiquities, Cyprus 2005*:1–21.

McGlade, J. 1995. Archaeology and the Ecodynamics of Human-Modified Landscapes. *Antiquity* 69:113–132.

———. 1999. Archaeology and the Evolution of Cultural Landscapes: Towards an Interdisciplinary Research Agenda. In *The Archaeology and Anthropology of Landscape*, ed. P. J. Ucko and R. Layton, 53–61. London: Routledge.

McGovern, T. 1990. The Archaeology of the Norse North Atlantic. *Annual Review of Anthropology* 19:331–351.

———. 1992. Bones, Buildings, and Boundaries: Paleoeconomic Approaches to Norse Greenland. In *Norse and Later Settlement and Subsistence in the North Atlantic*, ed. C. D. Morris and J. Rackham, 157–186. Glasgow: Glasgow University Press.

McGovern, T. H., G. Bigelow, T. Amorosi, and D. Russell. 1988. Northern Islands, Human Error, and Environmental Degradation: A View of Social and Ecological Change in the Medieval North Atlantic. *Human Ecology* 16(3):225–269.

McGowan, B. 1997. Part III: The Age of the Ayans, 1699–1812. In Vol. 2 of *An Economic and Social History of the Ottoman Empire*, ed. H. Inalcik and D. Quataert, 639–758. Cambridge: Cambridge University Press.

McGuire, A. 2003. Green Manuring Mustard: Improving an Old Technology. *Food, Farm, & Natural Resource Systems: Sustaining the Pacific Northwest* 1(3):6–9.

McIntosh, R. J., J. A. Tainter, and S. K. McIntosh, eds. 2000. *The Way the Wind Blows*. The Historical Ecology Series. New York: Columbia University Press.

Meggars, B. J. 1954. Environmental Limitation on the Development of Culture. *American Anthropologist* 56:801–824.

Mehlman, M. J. 1989. *Late Quaternary Archaeological Sequences in Northern Tanzania*. PhD diss., University of Illinois, Urbana-Champaign.

Melville, E.G.K. 1990. Environmental and Social Change in the Valle del Mezquital, Mexico, 1521–1600. *Comparative Studies in Society and History* 32:24–53.

Merker, M. 1910. *Die Masai: Ethnographische Monographieeines Ostafrikanischenes Semitenvolkes.* 2nd ed. Berlin: Dietrich Reimer.

Merritt, H. E. 1975. *A History of the Taita of Kenya to 1900*. PhD diss., Department of History, Indiana University, Bloomington.

Metcalfe, S. E. 1991. The Human Impact on the Environment. *Geography* 76(1): 59–60.

Metcalfe, S. E., S. L. O'Hara, M. Caballero, and S. J. Davies. 2000. Records of Late Pleistocene-Holocene Climatic Change in Mexico–A Review. *Quaternary Science Reviews* 19(7):699–721.

Metcalfe, S. E., F. A. Street-Perrott, R. B. Brown, P. E. Hales, R. A. Perrott, and F. M. Steininger. 1989. Late Holocene Human Impacts on Lake Basins in Central Mexico. *Geoarchaeology* 4:119–141.

Metcalfe, S. E., F. Street-Perrot, S. O'Hara, P. Hales, and F. Perrot. 1994. The Paleolimnological Record of Environmental Change: Examples from the Arid Frontier of Mexico. In *Environmental Change in Drylands: Biogeographical and Geomorphological Perspectives*, ed. A. Millington and K. Pye, 131–147. London: John Wiley and Sons.

Middleton, J., and M. Horton. 2000. *The Swahili*. Boston: Blackwell Publishers.

Midvale, F. 1965. Prehistoric Irrigation of the Casa Grande Ruins Area. *Kiva* 30:82–86.

Mikkelsen, N., A. Kuijpers, S. Lassen, and J. Vedel. 2001. Marine and Terrestrial Investigations in the Norse Eastern Settlement, South Greenland. *Geology of Greenland Survey Bulletin* 189:65–69.

Millon, R. 1973. The Teotihuacan Map. In Vol. 1 of *Urbanism at Teotihuacan, Mexico*, ed. R. Millon, 1–154. Austin: University of Texas.

Minc, L. D., and K. P. Smith. 1989. The Spirit of Survival: Cultural Response to Resource Variability in North Alaska. In *Bad Year Economics: Cultural Responses to Risk and Uncertainty*, ed. P. Halstead and J. O'Shea, 8–39. Cambridge: Cambridge University Press.

Montgomery, D. R. 2007. *Dirt: The Erosion of Civilizatons*. Berkeley: University of California Press.

Moore, S. F., and P. Puritt. 1977. *The Chagga and Meru of Tanzania*. London: International African Institute.

Moran, E. 1990. *The Ecosystem Approach in Anthropology: From Concept to Practice*. Ann Arbor: University of Michigan Press.

Moritz, M., P. Sholte, and S. Kari. 2002. The Demise of the Nomadic Contract: Arrangements and Rangelands under Pressure in the Far North of Cameroon. *Nomadic Peoples* 6(1):127–146.

Morley, S. G. 1946. *The Ancient Maya*. Stanford, CA: Stanford University Press.

Motzkin, G., D. Foster, and A. Allen. 1999. Vegetation Patterns in Heterogeneous Landscapes: The Importance of History and Environment. *Journal of Vegetation Science* 10(6):903–920.

Munro, N. D. 2004. Zooarchaeological Measures of Hunting Pressure and Occupation Intensity in the Natufian. *Current Anthropology* 45, Supplement:S5–S33.

Musiba, C., and A. Mabulla. 2003. Politics, Cattle, and Conservation: Ngorongoro Crater at the Crossroads. In *East African Archaeology: Foragers, Potters, Smiths, and Traders*, ed. C. Kusimba and S. Kusimba, 1343–1348. Philadelphia: University of Pennsylvania Museum of Anthropology and Archaeology.

Musonda, F. 1989. Cultural and Social Patterning in Economic Activities and Their Implications to Archaeological Interpretation: A Case from the Kafue Basin, Zambia. *African Studies* 48(1):55–69.

Mutundu, K. 1998. *Ethnohistoric Archaeology of the Mukogodo in North-Central Kenya: Contemporary Hunter-Gatherer Subsistence and the Transition to Pastoralism in Secondary Settings*. PhD diss., Washington University, St. Louis.

Myrdal, J. 1984. Elisenhof och jarnalderns boskapsskottsel i Nordvesteuropa (Cattle Sheds and Iron Age Husbandry in Northwest Europe). *Fornvännen* 1984(2):73–92.

———. 1988. Agrarteknik och samhälle under två tusen år (Agriculture and Community during Two Thousand Years). In *Folkvandringstiden i Norden. En kristid mellem ældre og yngre jernalder* (The Folkswandering in the North. A Crisis-Time between the Older and Younger Iron Ages), ed. U. Näsman and J. Lund, 187–200. Aarhus, Denmark: Moesgård.

Nadel, D., E. Weiss, O. Simchoni, A. Tsatskin, A. Danin, and M. Kislev. 2004. Stone Age Hut in Israel Yields World's Oldest Evidence of Bedding. *PNAS* 101(17):6821–6826.

Naveh, Z., and J. Dan. 1973. The Human Degradation of Mediterranean Landscapes in Israel. In *Mediterranean Type Ecosystems: Origin and Structure*, ed. F. D. Castri and H. A. Mooney, 373–389. Springer: Verlag.

Neev, D., and K. O. Emery. 1995. *The Destruction of Sodom, Gomorrah and Jericho: Geological, Climatological and Archaeological Background*. Oxford: Oxford University Press.

Nef, J. U. 1932. *The Rise of the British Coal Industry*. London: Routledge.

Nelson, M. C., M. Hegmon, S. Kulow, and K. Gust Schollmeyer. 2006. Archaeological and Ecological Perspectives on Reorganization: A Case Study from the Mimbres Region of the US Southwest. *American Antiquity* 71(3):403–432.

Nelson, S. H. 1994. *Colonialism in the Congo Basin, 1880–1940*. Ohio State University Monographs in International Studies, Africa Series Number 64. Columbus: Ohio State University.

Newton, T. 2003. Crossing the Great Divide: Time, Nature and the Social. *Sociology* 37(3):433–457.

Nials, F. L., D. A. Gregory, and D. A. Graybill. 1989. Salt River Stream Flow and Hohokam Irrigation Systems. In *The 1982–1998 Excavations at Las Colinas: Environment and Subsistence*, ed. D. A. Graybill, D. A. Gregory, F. L. Nials, S. Fish, R. Gasser, C. Miksicek, and C. Szuter, 59–78. Arizona State Museum Archaeological Series, no. 162. Tucson: Cultural Resource Management Division, Arizona State Museum, University of Arizona.

Nichols, D. L. 1987. Risk, Uncertainty, and Prehispanic Agricultural Intensification in the Northern Basin of Mexico. *American Anthropologist* 89:596–616.

Nichols, D. L., C. D. Fredrick, L. Morett Alatorre, and F. Sanchez Martinez. 2006. Water Management and Political Economy in Formative Period Central Mexico. In *Precolumbian Water Management: Ideology, Ritual, and Power*, ed. L. J. Lucero and B. W. Fash, 40–51. Tucson: University of Arizona Press.

Niederberger, C. B. 1979. Early Sedentary Economy in the Basin of Mexico. *Science* 203:131–142.

Nørlund, P. 1924. Buried Norsemen at Herjolfsnes: An Archaeological and Historical Study. *Meddelelser om Grønland* 67(1):270.

O'Hara, S. 1992. *Late Holocene Environmental Change in the Basin of Pátzcuaro, Michoacán, Mexico*. PhD diss., Oxford Unversity.

O'Hara, S., F. A. Street-Perrott, and T. P. Burt. 1993. Accelerated Soil Erosion around a Mexican Highland Lake Caused by Prehispanic Agriculture. *Nature* 362:48–51.

Olausson, M. 1999. Herding and Stalling in Bronze Age Sweden. In *Settlement and Landscape*, ed. C. Fabech and J. Ringtved, 319–328. Aarhus: Jutland Archaeological Society.

Olsson, E.G.A. 1991. The Agrarian Landscape of the Köpinge Area in the Late Bronze Age. In *The Cultural Landscape during 600 Years in Southern Sweden. The Ystad Project*, ed. B. Berglund, 128–132. Ecological Bulletins, vol. 41. Copenhagen: Munksgaard International.

O'Mansky, M., and N. Dunning. 2004. Settlement and Late Classic Political Disintegration in the Petexbatun Region, Guatemala. *The Terminal Classic in the Maya Lowlands: Collapse, Transition, and Transformation*, ed. A. Demarest, P. Rice, and D. S. Rice, 83–101. Boulder: University Press of Colorado.

O'Neill, R. V., D. L. DeAngelis, J. B. Waide, and T.F.H. Allen. 1986. *A Hierarchical Concept of Ecosystems*. Princeton: Princeton University Press.

Onken, J., M. R. Waters, and J. A. Homburg. 2003. Geoarchaeological Assessment for the Tres Rios Project, Maricopa County, Arizona. Statistical Research, Inc. Technical Report 03–68. Tucson: Statistical Research, Inc.

Ortiz, A. 1973. The Gila River Piman Water Problem: An Ethnohistorical Account. In *Changing Ways of Southwestern Indians*, ed. A. H. Schroeder, 245–257. El Corral de Santa Fe Westerners Brand Book 1973. Glorieta, NM: Rio Grande Press.

Ortner, S. B. 1984. Theory of Anthropology since the Sixties. *Comparative Studies in Society and History* 126(1):126–166.

———. 1989. *High Religion: A Cultural and Political History of Sherpa Buddhism*. Princeton: Princeton University Press.

Oyen, L. 1995. Aggressive Colonizers Work for the Farmers: Experiences from South-East Asia. *ILEIA Newsletter* 11(3):10–13.

Özdogan, A. 1999. Çayönü. In *Neolithic in Turkey: Cradle of Civilization. New Discoveries*, ed. M. Özdogan and N. Basgelen, 35–64. Istanbul: Arkeoloji ve Sanat Yayinlari.

Özdogan, M. 1997. Anatolia from the Last Glacial Maximum to the Holocene Climatic Optimum: Cultural Formations and the Impact of the Environmental Setting. *Paléorient* 23(2):25–38.

Padoch, C., E. Harwell, and A. Susanto. 1998. Swidden, Sawah, and In-Between: Agricultural Transformation in Borneo. *Human Ecology* 26(1):3–20.

Palerm, A. 1955. The Agricultural Basis of Urban Civilization in Mesoamerica. In *Irrigation Civilizations: A Comparative Study*, ed. J. H. Steward, 28–42. Washington, D.C.: Pan American Union.

Palerm, A., and E. R. Wolf. 1957. Ecological Potential and Cultural Development in Mesoamerica. *Pan American Union Social Science Monograph* 3:1–37.

Pålsson, H., and P. Edwards. 1986. *Knytlinga Saga*, trans. S.B.E. Palson. Odense, Denmark: Odense University Press.

Pandey, D. N., A. K. Gupta, and D. M. Anderson. 2003. Rainwater Harvesting as an Adaptation to Climate Change. *Current Science* 85:46–59.

Pape, J. C. 1970. Plaggen Soils in the Netherlands. *Geoderma* 4:229–256.

Parker, I., and M. Amin. 1983. *Ivory Crisis*. London: Chatto & Windus.

Pattee, H. H., ed. 1973. *Hierarchy Theory. The Challenge of Complex Systems*. New York: Georges Braziller.

Patton, M. 1996. *Islands in Time: Island Sociogeography and Mediterranean Prehistory*. London; New York: Routledge.

Pearson, M. N. 1998. *Port Cities and Intruders: The Swahili Coast, India, and Portugal in the Early Modern Era*. Baltimore, MD: John Hopkins University Press.

Peltenburg, E., ed. 2003a. *The Colonisation and Settlement of Cyprus. Investigations at Kissonerga-Mylouthkia, 1976–1996*. Studies in Mediterranean Archaeology, 70:4. Sävedalen, Sweden: Paul Aströms Förlag.

———. 2003b. Post-Colonisation Settlement Patterns: The Late Neolithic-Chalcolithic Transition. In *The Colonisation and Settlement of Cyprus. Investigations at Kissonerga-Mylouthkia, 1976–1996*, ed. E. Peltenburg, 257–276. Studies in Mediterranean Archaeology, 70:4. Sävedalen, Sweden: Paul Aströms Förlag.

Peltenburg, E., et al. 1998a. Lemba Archaeological Project II.1A. Excavations at Kissonerga-Mosphilia 1977–1995. *Studies in Mediterranean Archaeology* 70:2.

———. 1998b. *Lemba Archaeological Project II.1B. Excavations at Kissonerga-Mosphilia 1979–1992*. 2 vols. Edinburgh: Dept. of Archaeology, University of Edinburgh. http://www.arcl.ed.ac.uk/arch/publications/cyprus/kissonerga/dir.htm (accessed February 10, 2009).

Peltenburg, E., S. Colledge, P. Croft, A. Jackson, C. McCartney, and M. Murray. 2000. Agro-Pastoralist Colonization of Cyprus in the 10th Millennium BP: Initial Assessments. *Antiquity* 74:844–853.

Peltenburg, E., P. Croft, A. Jackson, C. McCartney, and M. Murray. 2001. Neolithic Dispersals from the Levantine Corridor: A Mediterranean Perspective. *Levant* 33:35–64.

Peltenburg, E., and A. Wasse. 2004. *Neolithic Revolution: New Perspectives on Southwest Asia in Light of Recent Discoveries on Cyprus*. Levant Supplementary Series 1. Oxford: Oxbow Books.

Perlès, C. 2001. *The Early Neolithic in Greece*. Cambridge World Archaeology. Cambridge: Cambridge University Press.

———. 2003. Le rôle du Proche-Orient dans la Néolithisation de la Grèce. In *Échanges et diffusion dans la préhistoire Mediterranéenne*, ed. B. Vandermeersch, 91–104. Paris: Comité des travaux historiques et scientifiques.

Perry, G.L.W. 2002. Landscapes, Space and Equilibrium: Shifting Viewpoints. *Progress in Physical Geography* 26(3):339–359.

Peters, J., and K. Schmidt. 2004. Animals in the Symbolic World of Pre-Pottery Neolithic Göbekli Tepe, Southeastern Turkey: A Preliminary Assessment. *Anthropozoologica* 39(1):179–218.

Pick, W. P. 1990. Meissner Pasha and the Construction of Railways in Palestine and Neighboring Countries. In *Ottoman Palestine 1800–1914, Studies in Economic and Social History*, ed. G. G. Gilbar, 179–218. Leiden: E. J. Brill.

Pielke, R. A., Jr. 2005. Are There Trends in Hurricane Destruction. *Nature* 438(22):E11.

Pielke, R. A., Jr., C. Landsea, M. Mayfield, J. Laver, and R. Pasch. 2005. Hurricanes and Global Warming. *American Meteorological Society* November(2):1571–1575.

Pielke, R. A., Jr., and R. A. Pielke, Sr. 1997. Hurricanes: Their Nature and Impacts on Society. New York: John Wiley and Sons.

Pohl, M. D., K. O. Pope, J. G. Jones, J. S. Jacob, D. R. Piperno, S. deFrance, D. L. Lentz, J. A. Gifford, M. E. Danforth, and J. K. Josserand. 1996. Early Agriculture in the Maya Lowlands. *Latin American Antiquity* 7:355–372.

Pollan, M. 1997. *A Place of My Own: The Education of an Amateur Builder*. New York: Delta.

Pollard, H. 2000. Tarascans and Their Ancestors: Prehistory of Michoacán. In *Greater Mesoamerica: The Archaeology of West and Northwest Mexico*, ed. S. Gorenstein and M. S. Foster, 59–71. Salt Lake City: University of Utah Press.

Pollard, H., and L. Cahue-Manrique. 1999. Mortuary Patterns of Regional Elites in the Lake Patzcuaro Basin of Western Mexico. *Latin American Antiquity* 10(3):259–281.

Pollard, H. P. 1993. *Tariacuri's Legacy, The Prehispanic Tarascan State*. Norton: University of Oklahoma Press.

———. 2003. Central Places and Cities in the Core of the Tarascan State. In *Urbanism in Mesoamerica. Volume 1*, ed. W. T. Sanders, A. G. Mastache, and R. H. Cobean, 345–390. Philadelphia: Pennsylvania State University.

Pollard, H. P., C. T. Fisher, and G. M. Feinman. 1994. Archaeology and Public Policy. *Newsletter of the American Anthropological Association* June:2–4.

Postgate, J. N. 1992. *Early Mesopotamia: Society and Economy at the Dawn of History*. London: Routledge.

Powell, M. A. 1985. Salt, Seed, and Yields in Sumerian Agriculture: A Critique of the Theory of Progressive Salinization. *Zeitschrift fur Assyriologie* 75:7–38.

Pred, A. 1984. Place as Historically Contingent Process: Structuration and the Time Geography of Becoming Places. *Annals of the Association of American Geographers* 74(2):279–297.

———. 1986. *Place, Practice and Structure*. New York: Barnes & Noble.

Prigogine, I. 1980. *From Being to Becoming: Time and Complexity in the Physical Sciences*. San Francisco: W. H. Freeman.

Prins, G. 1980. *The Hidden Hippopotamus*. Cambridge: Cambridge University Press.

Puleston, D., and O. S. Puleston. 1971. An Ecological Approach to the Origins of Maya Civilization. *Archaeology* 24:330–337.

Pyne, S., P. Andrews, and R. Laven. 1996. *Introduction to Wildfire*. New York: John Wiley & Sons.

Rappaport, R. A. 1978. Maladaptation in Social Systems. In *The Evolution of Social Systems*, ed. J. Friedman and M. J. Rowlands, 49–87. Pittsburgh, PA: University of Pittsburgh Press.

Rasch, M., and J. Fog Jensen. 1997. Ancient Eskimo Dwelling Sites and Holocene Relative Sea Level Changes in Southern Disko Bugt, Central West Greenland. *Polar Research* 16(2):101–115.

Ravesloot, J. C., and G. E. Rice. 2004. The Growth and Consolidation of Settlement Complexes and Irrigation Communities on the Middle Gila. Paper prepared for Hohokam Trajectories in World Perspective: An Advanced Seminar, Amerind Foundation, Dragoon, Arizona, January 27–31.

Ravesloot, J. C., and M. R. Waters. 2004. Geoarchaeology and Archaeological Site Patterning on the Middle Gila River, Arizona. *Journal of Field Archaeology* 29(1 and 2):203–214.

Rea, A. M. 1978. Ecology of Pima Fields. *Environment Southwest* 484:8–13.

———. 1983. *Once a River: Bird Life and Habitat Changes on the Middle Gila*. Tucson: University of Arizona Press.

———. 1997. *At the Desert's Green Edge*. Tucson: University of Arizona Press.

Redman, C., and A. Kinzig. 2003. Resilience of Past Landscapes: Resilience Theory, Society and the *Longue Durée*. *Conservation Ecology* 7(1):14.

Redman, C. 1992. The Impact of Food Production: Short-Term Strategies and Long-Term Consequences. In *Human Impact on the Environment: Ancient Roots, Current Challenges*, ed. J. E. Jacobsen and J. Firor, 35–49. Boulder, CO: Westview Press.

———. 1999. *Human Impact on Ancient Environments*. Tucson: University of Arizona Press.

———. 2000. The Human Factor in Paleoclimate. *PAGES Newsletter* 8(3):4–5.

———. 2005. Resilience Theory in Archaeology. *American Anthropologist* 107(1): 70–77.

Redman, C., P. R. Fish, J. D. Rogers, S. R. James, eds. 2004. *Introduction to the Archaeology of Global Change: The Impact of Humans on Their Environment*. Washington, D.C.: Smithsonian Institution Press.

Rejmankova, E., K. O. Pope, M. D. Pohl, and J. M. Rey-Benayas. 1995. Freshwater Wetland Plant Competition in Northern Belize: Implications for Paleoecological Studies of Maya Wetland Agriculture. *Biotropica* 27:28–36.

Renault-Miskovsky, J. 1989. Étude paléobotanique, paléoclimatique et palethnographique du site Néolithique de Khirokitia dans le sud-ouest de l'île de Chypre. In *Fouilles récentes à Khirokitia (Chypre) 1983–1986*, ed. A. LeBrun, 251–263. Éditions Recherche sur les Civilisations Mémoire 81. Paris: ADPF.

Renfrew, C. 1978. Trajectory Discontinuity and Morphogenesis: The Implications of Catastrophe Theory for Archaeology. *American Antiquity* 43:203–222.

Renfrew, C., and M. Wagstaff, eds. 1982. *An Island Polity: The Archaeology of Exploitation on Melos*. Cambridge: Cambridge University Press.

Resilience Alliance. http://www.resalliance.org (accessed February 10, 2009).

Reynolds, J., M. Smith, E. Lambin, B. L. Turner II, M. Mortimore, S. Batterbury, T. Downing, H. Dowlatabadi, R. Fernández, J. Herrick, E. Huber-Sannwald, H. Jiang, R. Leemans, T. Lynam, F. Maestre, M. Ayarza, and B. Walker. 2007. Global Desertification: Building a Science for Dryland Development. *Science* 316:847–851.

Rice, D. S. 1993. Eighth-Century Physical Geography, Environment, and Natural Resources in the Maya Lowlands. In *Lowland Maya Civilization in the Eighth Century A.D.*, ed. J. A. Sabloff and J. A. Henderson, 11–63. Washington, D.C.: Dumbarton Oaks.

———. 1996. Paleolimnological Analysis in the Central Peten, Guatemala. In *The Managed Mosaic: Ancient Maya Agriculture and Resource Use*, ed. S. L. Fedick, 193–206. Salt Lake City: University of Utah Press.

Rice, D. S., and P. M. Rice. 1990. Population Size and Population Change in the Central Peten Lakes Region, Guatemala. In *Precolumbian Population History in the Maya Lowlands*, ed. T. P. Culbert and D. S. Rice, 123–148. Albuquerque: University of New Mexico Press.

Rice, G. 1998. War and Water: An Ecological Perspective on Hohokam Irrigation. *Kiva* 63(3):263–301.

Rice, P. M., and D. S. Rice. 2004. Late Classic to Postclassic Transformations in the Peten Lakes Region, Guatemala. In *The Terminal Classic in the Maya Lowlands: Collapse, Transition, and Transformation*, ed. A. Demarest, P. M. Rice, and D. S. Rice, 125–139. Boulder: University Press of Colorado.

Richard, S. 1987. The Early Bronze Age: The Rise and Collapse of Urbanism. *Biblical Archaeologist* 50(1):22–43.

Ridderspore, M. 1988. Settlement Site-Village Site: Analysis of the Toft-Structure in Some Medieval Villages and Its Relation to Late Iron Age Settlements. A Preliminary Report and Some Tentative Ideas Based on Scanian Examples. *Geografisk Annaler* 70B(1):75–85.

Roberts, N. 1998. *The Holocene: An Environmental History*. 2nd ed. Oxford: Blackwell.

Rohling, E. J., J. Casford, R. Abu-Zied, S. Cooke, D. Mercone, J. Thomson, I. Croudace, F. J. Jorissen, H. Brinkhuis, J. Kallmeyer, and G. Wefer. 2002. Rapid Holocene Climate Changes in the Eastern Mediterranean. In *Drought Food and Culture: Ecological Change and Food Security in Africa's Later Prehistor ,*, ed. F. A. Hassan, 35–46. New York: Kluwer Academic/Plenum.

Rollefson, G. O. 1990. The Uses of Plaster at Neolithic 'Ain Ghazal, Jordan. *Archeomaterials* 4(1):33–54.

———. 1992. Early Neolithic Exploitation Patterns in the Levant: Cultural Impact on the Environment. *Population and Environment* 13:243–254.

Rollefson, G. O. 1996. The Neolithic Devolution: Ecological Impact and Cultural Compensation at 'Ain Ghazal, Jordan. In *Retrieving the Past*, ed. J. Seger, 219–229. Cobb Institute of Archaeology, Mississippi State University. Winona Lake, IN: Eisenbrauns.

Rollefson, G. O., and I. Köhler-Rollefson. 1989. The Collapse of Early Neolithic Settlements in the Southern Levant. In *People and Culture in Change: Proceedings of the Second Symposium on Upper Palaeolithic, Mesolithic and Neolithic Populations of Europe and the Mediterranean Basin*, ed. I. Hershkovitz, 73–89. British Archaeological Reports International Series 508. Oxford: Archaeopress.

———. 1992. Early Neolithic Exploitation Patterns in the Levant: Cultural Impact on the Environment. *Population and Environment: A Journal of Interdisciplinary Studies* 13(4):243–254.

Rollefson, G. O., A. H. Simmons, and Z. Kafafi. 1992. Neolithic Cultures at 'Ain Ghazal, Jordan. *Journal of Field Archaeology* 19:443–470.

Rosenberg, M., and R. W. Redding. 2000. Hallan Çemi and Early Village Organization in Eastern Anatolia. In *Life in Neolithic Farming Communities: Social Organization, Identity, and Differentiation*, ed. I. Kuijt, 39–61. New York: Plenum Press.

Ross, W. 2003. Dozens Die in Kenyan Cattle Raids. *BBC News*, April 11, 2003.

Rosset, P., J. Collins, and F. M. Lappé. 2000. Lessons from the Green Revolution. *Tikkun* March/April 2000.

Rossignol-Strick, M. 1995. Sea-Land Correlation of Pollen Records in the Eastern Mediterranean for the Glacial-Interglacial Transition: Biostratigraphy Versus Radiometric Time-Scale. *Quaternary Science Reviews* 14:893–915.

———. 1999. The Holocene Climatic Optimum and Pollen Records of Sapropel 1 in the Eastern Mediterranean, 9000–6000 BP. *Quaternary Science Reviews* 18(4–5): 515–530.

Ruddiman, W. E. 2003. The Anthropogenic Greenhouse Era Began Thousands of Years Ago. *Climatic Change* 61:261–293.

Runnels, C. 2000. Anthropogenic Soil Erosion in Prehistoric Greece. In *The Archaeology of Natural Disaster and Human Response*, ed. G. Bawden, 11–20. Sante Fe: University of New Mexico Press.

Russell, F. 1908. The Pima Indians. In *Twenty-Sixth Annual Report of the Bureau of American Ethnology, Smithsonian Institution, 1904–1905*, 3–389. Washington, D.C.: United States Printing Office.

Ruttan, L. M., and M. B. Mulder. 1999. Are East African Pastoralists Truly Conservationists? *Current Anthropology* 40(5):621–652.

Sahlins, M. 1981. *Historical Metaphors and Mythical Realities: Structure in the Early History of the Sandwich Islands Kingdom.* Ann Arbor: University of Michigan Press.

———. 2000. The Return of the Event, Again. In *Culture in Practice: Selected Essays of Marshal Sahlins*, 293–351. New York: Zone Books.

Sampson, G. C. 1998. Tortoise Remains from a Later Stone Age Rock Shelter in the Upper Karoo, South Africa. *Journal of Archaeological Science* 25:985–1000.

———. 1999. Late Holocene Amphibian Remains from Karoo Rock Shelters, South Africa. Paper presented at the INQUA XV International Congress, Durban, South Africa.

Sanders, W. T., J. R. Parsons, and R. S. Santley. 1979. *The Basin of Mexico: Ecological Processes in the Evolution of a Civilization.* New York: Academic Press.

Sanders, W. T., and B. J. Price. 1968. *Mesoamerica: The Evolution of a Civilization.* New York: Random House.

Sanders, W. T., and D. Webster. 1978. Unilinealism, Multilinealism, and the Evolution of Complex Societies. In *Social Archaeology: Beyond Subsistence and Dating*, ed. C. L. Redman, M. J. Berman, E. V. Curtin, W. T. Langhorne Jr., N. M. Versaggi, and J. C. Wanser, 249–302. New York: Academic Press.

Sandgren, P., and B. Fredskild. 1991. Magnetic Measurements Recording Late Holocene Man-Induced Erosion in South Greenland. *Boreas* 20:315–331.

Sarewitz, D., and R. A. Pielke Jr. 2005. Rising Tide: The Tsunami's Real Cause. *The New Republic* Jan. 17:10.

Scarborough, V. L. 1993. Water Management in the Southern Maya Lowlands: An Accretive Model for the Engineered Landscape. In *Economic Aspects of Water Management in the Prehispanic New World*, ed. V. L. Scarborough and B. L. Isaac, 17–69. Research in Economic Anthropology, Supplement 7. Greenwich, CT: JAI Press.

———. 1994. Maya Water Management. *National Geographic Research and Exploration* 10:184–199.

———. 1998. Ecology and Ritual: Water Management and the Maya. *Latin American Antiquity* 9:135–159.

———. 2000. Resilience, Resource Use, and Socioeconomic Organization: A Mesoamerican Pathway. In *Natural Disaster and the Archaeology of Human Response*, ed. G. Bawden and R. Reycraft, 195–212. Albuquerque: Maxwell Museum of Anthropology and the University of New Mexico Press.

———. 2003a. *The Flow of Power: Ancient Water Systems and Landscapes.* Santa Fe, NM: School of American Research Press.

———. 2003b. How to Interpret an Ancient Landscape. *Proceedings of the National Academy of Sciences* 100:4366–4368.

———. 2003c. Real-Time Maya. *Cambridge Journal of Archaeology* 13(2):286–288.

———. 2005a. Introduction. In *A Catalyst for Ideas: Anthropological Archaeology and the Legacy of Douglas W. Schwartz*, ed. V.L. Scarborough, 3–18. Santa Fe, NM: School of American Research Press.

———. 2005b. Landscapes of Power. In *A Catalyst for Ideas: Anthropological Archaeology and the Legacy of Douglas W. Schwartz*, ed. V. L. Scarborough, 209–228. Santa Fe, NM: School of American Research Press.

———. 2006a. An Overview of Mesoamerican Water Systems. In *Precolumbian Water Management: Ideology, Ritual and Power*, ed. B. L. Fash and L. J. Lucero, 223–235. Tucson: University of Arizona Press.

———. 2006b. The Rise and Fall of the Ancient Maya: A Case Study in Political Ecology. In *Integrated History and Future of People on Earth (IHOPE)*, ed. R. Costanza,

L. Gramlich, and W. Steffen, 51–59. Dahlem Workshop Report 96R. Cambridge: MIT Press.

———. 2007. Colonizing a Landscape: Water and Wetlands in Ancient Mesoamerica. In *The Political Economy of Ancient Mesoamerica: Transformations during the Formative and Classic Periods*, ed. V. L. Scarborough and J. Clark, 163–174. Albuquerque: University of New Mexico Press.

Scarborough, V. L., M. E. Becher, J. L. Baker, G. Harris, and F. Valdez Jr. 1995. Water and Land at the Ancient Maya Community of La Milpa. *Latin American Antiquity* 6:98–119.

Scarborough, V. L., R. P. Connolly, and S. P. Ross. 1994. The Pre-Hispanic Maya Reservoir System at Kinal, Peten, Guatamala. *Ancient Mesoamerica* 5:97–106.

Scarborough, V. L., and G. G. Gallopin. 1991. Water Storage Adaptation in the Maya Lowlands. *Science* 251:658–662.

Scarborough, V. L., J. W. Schoenfelder, and J. Stephen Lansing. 1999. Early Statecraft on Bali: The Water Temple Complex and the Decentralization of the Political Economy. *Research in Economic Anthropology* 20:299–330.

Scarborough, V. L., and F. Valdez Jr. 2003. The Engineered Environment and Political Economy of the Three Rivers Region. In *Heterarchy, Political Economy, and the Ancient Maya: The Three Rivers Region of the East-Central Yucatán Peninsula*, ed. V. L. Scarborough, F. Valdez Jr., and N. Dunning, 1–13. Tucson: University of Arizona Press.

Scarborough, V. L., F. Valdez Jr., and Nicholas Dunning, ed. 2003a. *Heterarchy, Political Economy, and the Ancient Maya: The Three Rivers Region of the East-Central Yucatán Peninsula*. Tucson: University of Arizona Press.

———. 2003b. Introduction. In *Heterarchy, Political Economy, and the Ancient Maya: The Three Rivers Region of the East-Central Yucatán Peninsula*, ed. V. L. Scarborough, F. Valdez Jr., and N. Dunning, xiii–xx. Tucson: University of Arizona Press.

Scheffer, M., S. Carpenter, J. A. Foley, C. Folke, and B. Walker. 2001. Catastrophic Shifts in Ecosystems. *Nature* 413(6856):591–596.

Schele, L., and M. E. Miller. 1986. *The Blood of Kings: Dynasty and Ritual in Maya Art*. Fort Worth, TX: Kimbell Art Museum.

Schmidt, K. 2001. Göbekli Tepe, Southeastern Turkey: A Preliminary Report on the 1995–1999 Excavations. *Paléorient* 26(1):45–54.

Schmidt, P. 1978. *Historical Archaeology*. Westfield, CT: Greenwood Press.

———. 1995. Using Archaeology to Remake History in Africa. In *Making Alternative Histories*, ed. P. Schmidt and T. C. Patterson, 119–147. Santa Fe, NM: School of American Research Press.

———. 1997. *Symbolic and Material Views of Iron Technology in East Africa*. Bloomington: Indiana University Press.

Schmidt, P. R., and B. B. Mapunda. 1997. Ideology and the Archaeological Record in Africa: Interpreting Symbolism in the Iron Smelting Technology. *Journal of Anthropological Archaeology* 16:127–157.

Schubert, H. R. 1957. *History of the British Iron and Steel Industry from ca. 450 BC to AD 1775*. London: Routledge and Kegan Paul.

Schuldenrein, J., and G. A. Clark. 1994. Landscape and Prehistoric Chronology of West-Central Jordan. *Geoarchaeology* 9(1):31–55.

Schweger, C. E. 1998. Geoarchaeology of the GUS Site: A Preliminary Framework. In *Man, Culture and Environment in Ancient Greenland: Report on a Research Programme,* ed. J. Arneborg and H. C. Gullprv, 14–17. Copenhagen: The Danish National Museum and Danish Polar Center.

Scoones, I. 1999. New Ecology and the Social Sciences: What Prospects for Future Engagement? *Annual Review of Anthropology* 28:479–507.

Scott, J. C. 1990. *Domination and the Arts of Resistance: Hidden Transcripts.* New Haven: Yale University Press.

———. 1998. *Seeing Like a State: How Certain Schemes to Improve the Human Condition Have Failed.* New Haven: Yale University Press.

Secaira, E. 1992. Conservation among the Q'eqchi'-Maya: A Comparison of Highland and Lowland Agriculture. MA thesis, Conservation Biology and Sustainable Development Program, University of Wisconsin, Madison.

Sept, J. 1986. Plant Foods and Early Hominids at Site FxJj 50, Koobi Fora. *Journal of Human Evolution* 15:751–770.

Service, E. R. 1962. *Primitive Social Organization: An Evolutionary Perspective.* New York: Random House.

———. 1971. *Profiles of Ethnology.* New York: Harper and Row.

Sevketoglu, M. 2002. Akanthou-Arkosyko (Tatlisu-Çiftlikdüzü): The Anatolian Connections in the 9th Millennium BC. In *World Islands in Prehistory*, ed. W. Waldren and J. Ensenyat, 98–106. British Archaeological Reports International Series 1095. Oxford: Archaeopress.

Shaban, M. A. 1976. *Islamic History: A New Interpretation 2, A.D. 750-1055 (A.H.132–448).* Cambridge: Cambridge University Press.

Sheldrick, D. 2000. Vegetation Changes in Tsavo National Park, Kenya, 1885–1996: Elephant Densities and Management. *Elephant* 26–32.

Shellenberger, M., and T. Nordhaus. 2005. The Death of Environmentalism: Global Warming Politics in a Post-environmental World. The Daily Grist Online 01/13, http://www.grist.org/news/maindish/2005/01/13/doe-reprint/ (accessed February 10, 2009).

Sima, A., A. Paul, and M. G. Schultz. 2004. The Younger Dryas: An Intrinsic Feature of the Late Pleistocene Climate Change at Millennial Timescales. *Earth and Planetary Science Letters* 222:741–750.

Simmons, A. 1991. One Flew Over the Hippos' Nest: Extinct Pleistocene Fauna, Early Man, and Conservative Archaeology in Cyprus. In *Perspectives on the Past*, ed. G. Clark, 282–304. Philadelphia: University of Pennsylvania Press.

———. 1998a. Exposed Fragments, Buried Hippos: Assessing Surface Archaeology. In *Surface Archaeology*, ed. A. Sullivan, 159–167. Albuquerque: University of New Mexico Press.

Simmons, A. 1998b. Of Tiny Hippos, Large Cows, and Early Colonists in Cyprus. *Journal of Mediterranean Archaeology* 11:232–241.

———. 1999. *Faunal Extinctions in an Island Society: Pygmy Hippopotamus Hunters of Cyprus.* New York: Kluwer Academic/Plenum Publishers.

———. 2000. Villages on the Edge: Regional Settlement Change and the End of the Levantine Pre-Pottery Neolithic. In *Life in Neolithic Farming Communities: Social Organization, Identity, and Differentiation*, ed. I. Kuijt, 211–230. New York: Kluwer Academic/Plenum Publishers.

———. 2001. The First Humans and Last Pygmy Hippopotami of Cyprus. In *The Earliest Prehistory of Cyprus. From Colonization to Exploitation*, ed. S. Swiny, 1–18. Cyprus American Archaeological Research Institute Monograph Series, vol. 2. American Schools of Oriental Research Archeological Reports, no. 5. Boston: American Schools of Oriental Research.

———. 2002. The Role of Islands in Pushing the Pleistocene Extinction Envelope: The Strange Case of the Cypriot Pygmy Hippos. In *World Islands in Prehistory*, ed. W. Waldren and J. Ensenyat, 406–414. British Archaeological Reports International Series 1095. Oxford: Archaeopress.

———. 2003. 2003 Excavations at Kritou Marottou *Ais Yiorkis*, an Early Neolithic Site in Western Cyprus: Preliminary Report. *Neolithics* 2/03:8–12.

———. 2004. Bitter Hippos of Cyprus: The Island's First Occupants and Last Endemic Animals: Setting the Stage for Colonization. In *Neolithic Revolution: New Perspectives on Southwest Asia in Light of Recent Discoveries on Cyprus*, ed. E. Peltenburg and A. Wasse, 1–14. Levant Supplementary Series 1. Oxford: Oxbow Books.

———. 2007. *The Neolithic Revolution in the Near East: Transforming the Human Landscape.* Tucson: University of Arizona Press.

———. 2008. American Researchers and the Earliest Cypriots. *Near Eastern Archaeology* 71:21–29.

Simmons, A., I. Köhler-Rollefson, G. Rollefson, R. Mandel, and Z. Kafafi. 1988. 'Ain Ghazal: A Major Neolithic Settlement in Central Jordan. *Science* 240:35–39.

Simmons, A., and R. Mandel. 2007. Not Such a New Light: A Response to Ammerman and Noller. *World Archaeology* 39:475–482.

Simon, H. A. 1969. 2nd ed. 1981. *The Sciences of the Artificial.* Cambridge, MA: MIT Press.

Simon, J. 1997. *Endangered Mexico: An Environment on the Edge.* San Francisco: Sierra Club Books.

Simpson, I. A. 1997. Relict Properties of Anthropogenic Deep Top Soils as Indicators of Infield Management in Marwick, West Mainland, Orkney. *Journal of Archaeological Science* 24:365–380.

Simpson, I. A., W. P. Adderley, G. Guðmundsson, M. Hallsdóttir, M. Sigurgeirsson, and M. Snæsdóttir. 2002. Soil Limitations to Agrarian Land Production in Premodern Iceland. *Human Ecology* 30(4):423–443.

Simpson, I. A., J. H. Barrett, and K. B. Milek. 2005. Interpreting the Viking Age to Medieval Period Transition in Norse Orkney through Cultural Soil and Sediment Analyses. *Geoarchaeology* 20(4):355–377.

Simpson, I. A., R. J. Bryant, and U. Tveraabak. 1998. Relict Soils and Early Arable Land Management in Lofoten, Norway. *Journal of Archaeological Science* 25: 1185–1198.

Simpson, I. A., S. J. Dockrill, I. D. Bull, and R. P. Evershed. 1998. Early Anthropogenic Soil Formation at Tofts Ness, Sanday, Orkney. *Journal of Archaeological Science* 25:729–746.

Simpson, I. A., A. J. Dugmore, A. Thomson, and O. Vésteinsson. 2001. Crossing the Thresholds: Human Ecology and Historical Patterns of Landscape Degradation. *Catena* 42:175–192.

Simpson, I. A., P. F. Van Bergen, V. Perret, M. M. Elhmmali, D. J. Roberts, and R. P. Evershed. 1999. Lipid Biomarkers of Manuring Practice in Relict Anthropogenic Soils. *Holocene* 9(2):223–229.

Simpson, L. B. 1952. *Exploitation of Land in Central Mexico in the Sixteenth Century.* Berkeley: University of California Press.

Sisk, T. D., and B. R. Noon. 1995. Land Use History of North America: An Emerging Project of the National Biological Service. *SAA Bulletin* 13(3):21.

Sluyter, Andrew. 1999. The Making of the Myth in Postcolonial Development: Material-Conceptual Landscape Transformation in Sixteenth Century Veracruz. *AAAG* 89(3):377–401.

———. 2002. Colonialism and Landscape: Postcolonial Theory and Applications. Lanham, MD: Rowman & Littlefield.

Smith, E. A., and M. Wishnie. 2000. Conservation and Subsistence in Small-Scale Societies. *Annual Reviews of Anthropology* 29:493–524.

Smith, P.E.L. 1976. Reflections on Four Seasons of Excavations at Tapeh Ganj Dareh. In *Proceedings of the IVth Annual Symposium on Archaeological Research in Iran*, ed. F. Bagherzadeh, 11–22. Tehran: Iranian Centre for Archaeological Research.

Smith, R. H. 1990. The Southern Levant in the Hellenistic Period. *Levant* 22:123–130.

Snow, C. P. 1959. *The Two Cultures and the Scientific Revolution.* New York: Cambridge University Press.

Soil Survey Staff. 2006. *Keys to Soil Taxonomy*, 10*th* ed. USDA—Natural Resources Conservation Service, Washington, D.C.

Sømme, A. 1968. *A Geography of Norden.* London: Heinemann.

Southworth, C. H. 1914. Gila River Survey, Pinal/Maricopa County, Arizona. Plane Table Topographic Survey Showing Irrigated and Irrigable Lands under Ditches Taking Water from the Gila River. Surveyed by C. H. Southworth. Thirteen Sheets from T5S R8E to T1N & T1S R1E, G&SRM. Sacaton, AZ: Cultural Resource Management Program, Gila River Indian Community.

Spencer, P. 1973. *Nomads in Alliance: Symbiosis and Growth among the Rendille and Samburu of Kenya.* London: Oxford University Press.

Spores, R. 1969. Settlement, Farming Technology, and Environment in the Nochixtlan Valley. *Science* 166(3905):557–569.

Steadman, D. 1995. Prehistoric Extinctions of Pacific Island Birds: Biodiversity Meets Zooarchaeology. *Science* 267:1123–1131.

Steinhart, E. I. 2000. Elephant Hunting in Nineteenth-Century Kenya: Kamba Society and Ecology in Transition. *International Journal of African Historical Studies* 33:32–56.

Steward, J. 1955. *Theory of Culture Change: The Methodology of Multilinear Evolution.* Urbana: University of Illinois Press.

Steward, J. H., R. Mc. Adams, M. D. Collier, A. Palerm, K. A. Wittfogel, and R. Beals. 1955. *Irrigation Civilizations: A Comparative Study.* Social Science Monograph, no. 1. Washington, D.C.: Pan American Union.

Stiner, M. C., and N. D. Munro. 2002. Approaches to Prehistoric Diet Breadth, Demography, and Prey Ranking Systems in Time and Space. *Journal of Archaeological Method and Theory* 9(2):181–214.

Stocking, M., and N. Murnaghan. 2001. *Handbook for the Field Assessment of Land Degradation.* London: Earthscan Publications.

Stone, G. D. 1993. Agricultural Abandonment: A Comparative Study in Historical Ecology. In *Abandonment of Settlements and Regions*, ed. C. M. Cameron and S. A. Tomka, 4–84. Cambridge: Cambridge University Press.

Stone, J. J. 1998. The Green Revolution Today: Agriculture Still Faces Big Challenges. *Global Issues in Agricultural Research* 1:12–20.

Street-Perrott, F. A., R. A. Perrott, and D. D. Harkness. 1989. Anthropogenic Soil Erosion around Lake Patzcuaro, Michoacan, Mexico, during the Preclassic and Late Postclassic Hispanic Periods. *American Antiquity* 54:759–766.

Swiny, S., ed. 2001. *The Earliest Prehistory of Cyprus: From Colonization to Exploitation.* American Schools of Oriental Research Archaeological Reports, no. 5. Boston: American Schools of Oriental Research.

Tainter, J. A. 1990. *The Collapse of Complex Societies.* Cambridge: Cambridge University Press.

———. 2000. Global Change, History, and Sustainability. In *The Way the Wind Blows: Climate, History, and Human Action*, ed. R. McIntosh, J. Tainter, and S. K. McIntosh, 331–357. New York: University of Columbia Press.

Tarayia, G. N. 2004. The Legal Perspectives of the Maasai Culture, Customs, and Traditions. *Arizona Journal of International & Comparative Law* 21(1)183–222.

Taylor, K. C., P. A. Mayewski, R. B. Alley, E. J. Brook, A. J. Gow, P. M. Grootes, D. A. Meese, E. S. Saltzman, J. P. Severinghaus, M. S. Twickler, J.W.C. White, S. Whitlow, and G. A. Zielinski. 1997. The Holocene-Younger Dryas Transition Recorded at Summit, Greenland. *Science* 278:825–827.

Tchernov, E. 1984. Commensal Animals and Human Sedentism in the Middle East. In *Animals and Archaeology 3. Early Herders and Their Flocks*, ed. J. Clutton-Brock and C. Grigson, 91–115. British Archaeological Reports International Series 202. Oxford: Archaeopress.

Terrell, J. E., J. P. Hart, S. Barut, N. Cellinese, A. Curet, T. Denham, C. Kusimba, K. Latinis, R. Oka, J. Palka, M. Pohl, K. Pope, P. Ryan, H. Haines, and J. Staller. 2003. Domesticated Landscapes: The Subsistence Ecology of Plant and Animal Domestication. *Journal of Archaeological Method and Theory* 10(4):323–368.

Teutonico, J. M., and F. G. Matero. 2003. *Managing Change: Sustainable Approaches to the Conservation of the Built Environment.* 4th Annual US/ICOMOS International Symposium organized by US/ICOMOS, the Graduate Program in Historic Preservation of the University of Pennsylvania, and the Getty Conservation Institute, Philadelphia, Pennsylvania, April 2001. Los Angeles: Getty Conservation Institute.

Thompson, J.E.S. 1954. *The Rise and Fall of Maya Civilization.* Norman: University of Oklahoma Press.

Thompson, M., R. Ellis, and A. Widawski. 1990. *Cultural Theory.* Boulder, CO: Westview Press.

Thomson, J. 2001. Modern Technology for African Agriculture. In *2020 Focus 7 Appropriate Technology for Sustainable Food,* ed. P. Pinstrup-Andersen, 10–11. Washington, D.C.: International Food Policy Research Institute (IFPRI).

Thorbahn, F. P. 1979. *The Precolonial Trade of East Africa: Reconstruction of a Human-Elephant Ecosystem.* PhD diss., University of Massachusetts, Amherst.

Thrane, H. 1984. *Lusehøj ved Voldtofte: En sydvestfynsk storhøj fra yngre broncealde* (Lusehøj at Voldtofte: A Large Southwest-Fyn Mound from the Younger Bronze Age). Odense, Denmark: Odense bys museer.

Thurston, T. L. 1999. The Knowable, the Doable, and the Undiscussed: Tradition, Submission, and the "Becoming" of Rural Landscapes in Denmark's Iron Age. *Antiquity* 72 (281):661–671.

———. 2001. *Landscapes of Power, Landscapes of Conflict: State Formation in the South Scandinavian Iron Age.* Fundamental Issues in Archaeology. New York: Kluwer/ Plenum Publishing.

———. 2006. *The Barren and the Fertile: Central and Local Intensification Strategies across Variable Landscapes.* In *Agriculture and Society,* ed. J. Marcus and C. Stanish, 42–56. Los Angeles: Cotsen Institute of Archaeology Press.

———. 2007. Infields, Outfields, and Broken Lands: Agricultural Intensification and the Ordering of Space in Iron Age Denmark. In *Seeking a Richer Harvest: The Archaeology of Subsistence Intensification, Innovation and Change,* ed. T. Thurston and C. Fisher, 69–78. Human Ecology and Adaptation Book Series. New York: Springer Scientific Publishing.

Todd, I. 2003. Kalavasos-Tenta: A Reappraisal. In *Le Néolithique de Chypre,* ed. J. Guilaine and A. LeBrun, 35–44. Bulletin de Correspondance Hellénique Supplément 43. Athens: École française d'Athènes.

Toledo, V. 1991. Pátzcuaro's Lesson: Nature, Production, and Culture in an Indigenous Region of Mexico. In *Biodiversity: Culture, Conservation, and Ecodevelopment,* ed. M. Oldfield and J. Alcorn, 146–171. Boulder, CO: Westview Press.

Toledo, V. M., P. Alvarez-Icaza, and P. Avila. 1992. *Plan Pátzcuaro 2000: Investigación multidisciplinaria para el desarrollo sostenido.* Mexico, D.F.: Fundación Friedrich Ebert, Representación en México.

Tourtellot, G., F. Estrada Belli, J. J. Rose, and N. Hammond. 2003. Late Classic Maya Heterarchy, Hierarchy, and Landscape at La Milpa, Belize. In *Heterarchy, Political*

Economy, and the Ancient Maya: The Three Rivers Region of the East-Central Yucatán Peninsula, ed. V. L. Scarborough, F. Valdez Jr., and N. P. Dunning, 37–51. Tucson: University of Arizona Press.

Trigger, B. G. 1989. *A History of Archaeological Thought*. Cambridge: Cambridge University Press.

Turner, B. L., II. 1978a. Ancient Agricultural Land Use in the Central Lowlands. In *Pre-Hispanic Maya Agriculture*, ed. P. D. Harrison and B. L. Turner II, 163–183. Albuquerque: University of New Mexico Press.

———. 1978b. The Development and Demise of the Swidden Hypothesis. In *Pre-Hispanic Maya Agriculture*, ed. P. D. Harrison and B. L. Turner II, 13–22. Albuquerque: University of New Mexico Press.

———. 1983. *Once Beneath the Forest: Prehistoric Terracing in the Rio Bec Region of the Maya Lowlands*. Boulder, CO: Westview Press.

———. 1990. Population Reconstruction for the Central Maya Lowlands. In *Precolumbian Population History in the Maya Lowlands*, ed. T. P. Culbert and D. S. Rice, 301–323. Albuquerque: University of New Mexico Press.

———. 1993. Rethinking the "New Orthodoxy": Interpreting Ancient Maya Agriculture and Environment. In *Culture, Form, and Place: Essays in Cultural and Historical Geography*, ed. K. W. Mathewson, 57–88. Geoscience and Man 32. Baton Rouge: Louisiana State University.

Turner, B.L.M., P. A. Matson, J. J. McCarthy, et al. 2003. Illustrating the Coupled Human-Environment System for Vulnerability Analysis: Three Case Studies. *PNAS* 100:8080–8085.

Turner, M. G., S. L. Collins, A. L. Lugo, J. J. Magnuson, S. Rupp, and F. J. Swanson. 2003. Disturbance Dynamics and Ecological Response: The Contribution to Long-Term Ecological Research. *Bioscience* 53(1):46–56.

Turner, S. 1994. *The Social Theory of Practices*. Chicago: University of Chicago Press.

Vaks, A., M. Bar-Matthews, A. Ayalon, B. Schilman, M. Gilmour, C. J. Hawkesworth, A. Frumkin, A. Kaufman, and A. Matthew. 2003. Paleoclimate Reconstruction Based on the Timing of Speleothem Growth and Oxygen and Carbon Isotope Composition in a Cave Located in the Rain Shadow in Israel. *Quaternary Research* 59:182–193.

Valdés, J. A. 1997. Tamarindito: Archaeology and Regional Politics in the Petexbatun Region. *Ancient Mesoamerica* 8:321–335.

Valla, F. R. 1995. The First Settled Societies—Natufian (12,500–10,200 BP). In *The Archaeology of Society in the Holy Land*, ed. T. Levy, 169–189. London: Leicester University Press.

———. 1999. The Natufian: A Coherent Thought? In *Dorothy Garrod and the Progress of the Palaeolithic*, ed. W. Davies and R. Charles, 224–241. Oxford: Oxbow Books.

———. 2003. La tradition natoufienne et les progrès de la néolithisation au Levant. In *Échanges et diffusion dans la préhistoire Méditerranéenne*, ed. B. Vandermeersch, 15–27. Paris: Comité des travaux historiques et scientifiques.

van Andel, T. H., and C. N. Runnels. 1987. *Beyond the Acropolis: A Rural Greek Past.* Stanford: Stanford University Press.

van Andel, T. H., E. Zangger, and A. Demitrack. 1990. Land Use and Soil Erosion in Prehistoric and Historical Greece. *Journal of Field Archaeology* 17:379–396.

van der Leeuw, S. E. 1998. *The ARCHAEOMEDES Project: Understanding the Natural and Anthropogenic Causes of Land Degradation and Desertification in the Mediterranean Basin.* Luxembourg: Office of Publications of the European Union.

van der Leeuw, S. E., and the ARCHAEOMEDES Research Team. 2000. Land Degradation as a Socionatural Process. In *The Way the Wind Blows: Climate, History, and Human Action*, ed. R. McIntosh, J. Tainter, and S. K. McIntosh, 357–383. New York: Columbia University Press.

van der Leeuw, S. E., F. Favory and J.-L. Fiches, eds. 2003. *Archéologie et systèmes socio-environnementaux: Études multi–scalaires sur la vallée du Rhône dans le programme ARCHAEOMEDES.* Monographies du CRA. Valbonne: CNRS.

van der Leeuw, S. E., and C. L. Redman. 2002. Placing Archaeology at the Center of Socio-natural Studies. *American Antiquity* 67:597–605.

van der Merwe, N. J. 1980. The Advent of Iron in Africa. In *The Coming of the Age of Iron*, ed. T. A. Wertime and J. D. Muhly, 146–506. New Haven, CT: Yale University Press.

van der Merwe, N. J., and D. H. Avery. 1988. Science and Magic in African Technology: Traditional Ironsmelting in Malawi. In *The Beginning of the Use of Metals and Alloys*, ed. R. Maddin, 245–260. Cambridge: MIT Press.

van Zeist, W., and S. Bottema. 1991. *Late Quaternary Vegetation of the Near East.* Beihefte zum Tübinger Atlas des Vorderen Orients, Reihe A (Naturwissenschaft), Nr. 18. Weisbaden, Germany: Dr. Ludwig Reichert Verlag.

Vayda, A. P., comp. 1969. *Environment and Cultural Behavior: Ecological Studies in Cultural Anthropology.*, Garden City, NY: Natural History Press, Published for American Museum of Natural History.

Vayda, A. P., and B. J. Mckay. 1975. New Directions in Ecology and Ecological Anthropology. *Annual Review of Anthropology* 4:293–306.

Wakefield, T. 1870. Routes of Natives from the Coast to the Interior of East Africa. *Journal of the Royal Geographical Society* 40:303–338.

Walsh, B. 2007. "A Green Tipping Point." *Time* Magazine, October 12. http://www.time.com/time/world/article/0,8599,1670871,00.html (accessed March 17, 2009).

Warren, J. B. 1984. *La administración de los negocios de un encomendero en Michoacán.* Michoacán, Mexico: SEP Michoacán/UMSNH.

———. 1985. *The Conquest of Michoacan: The Spanish Domination of the Tarascan Kingdom in Western Mexico, 1521–1530.* Norman: University of Oklahoma Press.

Waters, M. R., and J. C. Ravesloot. 2000. Late Quaternary Geology of the Middle Gila River, Gila River Indian Reservation, Arizona. *Quaternary Research* 54:49–57.

———. 2001. Landscape Change in the Cultural Evolution of the Hohokam along the Middle Gila River and Other River Valleys in South-Central Arizona. *American Antiquity* 66(2):285–299.

Waters, M. R., and J. C. Ravesloot. 2003. Disaster or Catastrophe: Human Adaptation to High- and Low-Frequency Landscape Processes: A Reply to Ensor, Ensor, and De Vries. *American Antiquity* 68:400–405.

Watkins, T. 1981. The Economic Status of the Aceramic Neolithic Culture of Cyprus. *Journal of Mediterranean Anthropology and Archaeology* 1:139–149.

Watson, R. A., and P. J. Watson. 1969. *Man and Nature: An Anthropological Essay in Human Ecology*. New York: Harcourt, Brace & World.

Watts, D. 2007. A Twenty-first Century Science. *Nature* 4451:489.

WCED (World Commission on Environment and Development). 1987. *Our Common Future*. Oxford: Oxford University Press.

Webster, D. 2002. *The Fall of the Ancient Maya: Solving the Mystery of the Maya Collapse*. London; New York: Thames and Hudson.

Webster, D., and A. Freter. 1990. The Demography of Late Classic Copan. In *Precolumbian Population History in the Maya Lowlands*, ed. T. P. Culbert and D. S. Rice, 37–62. Albuquerque: University of New Mexico Press.

Webster, D., A. Freter, and R. Storey. 2004. Dating Copan Culture-History: Implications for the Terminal Classic and the Collapse. In *The Terminal Classic in the Maya Lowlands: Collapse, Transition, and Transformation*, ed. A. Demarest, P. M. Rice, and D. S. Rice, 231–259. Boulder: University Press of Colorado.

Weiss, E., W. Wetterstrom, D. Nadel, and O. Bar-Yosef. 2004. The Broad Spectrum Revisited: Evidence from the Plant Remains. *PNAS* 109(26):9551–9555.

Weiss, H., and R. S. Bradley. 2001. What Drives Societal Collapse? *Science* 291(5504): 609–610.

Weiss-Krejci, E., and T. Sabbas. 2002. The Potential Role of Small Depressions as Water Storage Features in the Central Maya Lowlands. *Latin American Antiquity* 13:343–357.

Wells, B., ed. 1992. *Agriculture in Ancient Greece*. 4 Series, 42. Stockholm: Swedish Institute of Athens.

Wells, E. C., G. R. Rice, and J. C. Ravesloot. 2004. Peopling Landscapes between Villages in the Middle Gila River Valley of Central Arizona. *American Antiquity* 69(4):627–652.

Western, D., and R. M. Wright. 1994. *Natural Connections: Perspectives in Community-based Conservation*. Washington, D.C.: Island Press.

Westley, F., S. R. Carpenter, W. A. Brock, C. S. Holling, and L. H. Gunderson. 2002. Why Systems of People and Nature Are Not Just Social and Ecological Systems. In *Panarchy: Understanding Transformations in Systems of Humans and Nature*, ed. L. H. Gunderson and C. S. Holling, 103–120. Washington, D.C.: Island Press.

White, D. R. Forthcoming. Networks and Hierarchies. In *Complexity Perspectives on Innovation and Social Change*, ed. D. Lane, D. Pumain, S. E. van der Leeuw, and G. West. Methodos series. Berlin: Springer.

White, H. 2001. *Markets from Networks: Socioeconomic Models of Production*. Princeton, NJ: Princeton University Press.

White, L. A. 1959. *The Evolution of Culture*. New York: McGraw-Hill.

Whitmore, T. J., B. L. Turner III, D. L. Johnson, R. W. Kates, and T. R. Gottschang. 1990. Long-Term Population Change. In *The Earth as Transformed by Human Action: Global and Regional Changes in the Biosphere over the Past 300 Years*, ed. B. L. Turner, 25–39. Cambridge; New York: Cambridge University Press with Clark University.

Whitmore, T. M., and B. L. Turner. 2002. *Cultivated Landscapes of Middle America on the Eve of Conquest*. Oxford Geographical and Environmental Studies. Oxford; New York: Oxford University Press.

Wigand, P., and A. Simmons. 1999. The Dating of Akrotiri *Aetokremnos*. In *Faunal Extinctions in an Island Society: Pygmy Hippopotamus Hunters of the Akrotiri Peninsula, Cyprus*, ed. A. Simmons, 193–215. New York: Plenum Academic/Kluwer Publishers.

Wilcox, G. 1999. Charcoal Analysis and Holocene Vegetation History in Southern Syria. *Quaternary Science Reviews* 18(4–5):711–716.

Wilk, R. R., and H. L. Wilhite. 1982. Community of Cuello: Patterns of Household and Settlement Change. In *Cuello: An Early Maya Community in Belize*, ed. N. Hammond, 118–133. Cambridge: Cambridge University Press.

Wilkie, D. S. 1989. Impact of Roadside Agriculture on Subsistence Hunting in the Ituri Forest of Northeastern Zaire. *American Journal of Physical Anthropology* 78:485–494.

Williams, B. J. 1972. Tepetate in the Valley of Mexico. *Annals of the Association of American Geographers* 62:618–626.

Williams, C. C., and A. C. Millington. 2004. The Diverse and Contested Meanings of Sustainable Development. *Geographical Journal* 170(2):99–104.

Williams, J. G., and N. Arlott. 1980. *A Field Guide to the Birds of East Africa*. London: William Collins Sons.

Wingard, J. D. 1996. Interactions between Demographic Processes and Soil Resources in the Copan Valley, Honduras. In *The Managed Mosaic: Ancient Maya Agriculture and Resource Use*, ed. S. L. Fedick, 207–235. Salt Lake City: University of Utah Press.

Woodbury, R. B. 1961. A Reappraisal of Hohokam Irrigation. *American Anthropologist* 63:550–560.

Woodson, M. K. 2003. *A Research Design for the Study of Prehistoric and Historic Irrigation Systems in the Middle Gila Valley, Arizona*. P-MIP Technical Report no. 2003–10. Sacaton, AZ: Cultural Resource Management Program, Gila River Indian Community.

———. 2004. Constraints and Capacities of Hohokam Canal Systems in the Salt and Gila River Valleys, South-Central Arizona. Paper presented at the Inaugural Symposium of the Archaeological Sciences of the Americas, Tucson, AZ.

Wright, H. 2005. The Polycentricity of the Archaic Civilizations. In *A Catalyst for Ideas: Anthropological Archaeology and the Legacy of Douglas Schwartz*, ed. V. L. Scarborough, 149–168. Santa Fe, NM: School of American Research Press.

Wright, J.H.E., and J. L. Thorpe. 2003. Climatic Change and the Origin of Agriculture in the Near East. In *Global Change in the Holocene*, ed. A. Mackay, R. W. Battarbee, J. Birks, and F. Oldfield, 100–110. London: Arnold.

Wu, J., and O. L. Loucks. 1995. From Balance of Nature to Hierarchical Patch Dynamics: A Paradigm Shift in Ecology. *Quarterly Review of Biology* 70(4):439–466.

Yasuda, Y. 2002a. Origins of Pottery and Agriculture in East Asia. In *The Origins of Pottery and Agriculture*, ed. Y. Yasuda, 119–142. Yangtze River Civilization Programme, International Research Center for Japanese Studies. New Dehli: Roli Books/Lustre Press.

———. 2002b. The Second East Side Story: Origin of Agriculture in West Asia. In *The Origins of Pottery and Agriculture*, ed. Y. Yasuda, 15–38. Yangtze River Civilization Programme, International Research Center for Japanese Studies. New Dehli: Roli Books/Lustre Press.

Yen, D. E. 1989. The Domestication of the Environment. In *Farming and Foraging: The Evolution of Plant Exploitation*, ed. D. R. Harris and G. C. Hillman, 55–78. Boston: Unwin Hyman.

Yoffee, N. 1991. Orienting Collapse. In *The Collapse of Ancient States and Civilizations*, ed. N. Yoffee and G. L. Cowgill, 1–19. Tucson: University of Arizona Press.

Yoffee, N., and G. L. Cowgill, ed. 1988. *The Collapse of Ancient States and Civilizations*. Tucson: University of Arizona Press.

Zangger, E. 1991. Prehistoric Coastal Environments in Greece: The Vanished Landscape of Dimini Bay and Lake Lerna. *Journal of Field Archaeology* 18:1–15.

Zimmerer, K. S. 1991. Labor Shortages and Crop Diversity in the Southern Pervian Sierra. *Geographical Review* 81(4):415–432.

———. 1993. Soil Erosion and Labor Shortages in the Andes with Special Reference to Bolivia, 1953–91: Implications for "Conservation-With-Development." *World Development* 21(10):1659–1675.

———. 1994. Human Geography and the "New Ecology": The Prospect and Promise of Integration. *Annals of the Association of American Geographers* 84(1):108–125.

———. 1996. Ecology as Cornerstone and Chimera in Human Geography. In *Concepts in Human Geography*, ed. C. M. Earle and M. S. Kenzer, 161–188. Lanham MD: Rowman & Littlefield.

———. 2006. *Globalization & New Geographies of Conservation*. Chicago: University of Chicago Press.

Zimmerer, K. S., and K. R. Young. 1998. *Nature's Geography: New Lessons for Conservation in Developing Countries*. Madison: University of Wisconsin Press.

Zimmermann, W. H. 1999. Why Was Cattle-Stalling Introduced in Prehistory? The Significance of the Byre and Stable and of Outwintering. In *Settlement and Landscape*, ed. C. Fabech and J. Ringtved, 301–318. Aarhus: Jutland Archaeological Society.

About the Editors

Gary M. Feinman is curator of Mesoamerican anthropology at the Field Museum of Natural History in Chicago. Previously, he taught for sixteen years at the University of Wisconsin–Madison. He received his doctorate from the City University of New York–Graduate Center and his undergraduate degree from the University of Michigan. Feinman has written and edited more than fifteen books and has prepared over 150 scientific publications on topics ranging from an overview of world archaeology (*Images of the Past*) to settlement-pattern research to domestic life and economies, and from ceramic production to shell-ornament manufacture to frameworks to conceptualize and examine inter-regional exchange and interaction. For more than twenty-five years, he has been conducting archaeological field research on the rise of (and long-term changes in) pre-Hispanic Zapotec civilization in the valley of Oaxaca, Mexico. In Oaxaca, he has led regional surveys, intensive site surveys, and excavations at Ejutla de Crespo and El Palmillo. He also co-directs a collaborative thirteen-year regional archaeological project on the rise of civilization in eastern Shandong, China. Through his focus on settlement patterns, he has developed an active concern regarding the long-term recursive relationship between humans and the natural world in which they live. Over the years, a series of grants from the National Science Foundation, the National Geographic Foundation, and other agencies have supported his research efforts. Feinman was the recipient of a Presidential Recognition Award from the Society for American Archaeology for his editorial work with *Latin American Antiquity.* He also has received a special teaching internship at the Universidad Nacional Autónoma de México and a Li-Ching professorship at Shandong University.

Christopher T. Fisher is an associate professor of anthropology at Colorado State University. He received his doctorate from the University of Wisconsin–Madison and his undergraduate degree from Michigan State University. His work appears in edited volumes, including a co-edited book on intensification, *Seeking a Richer Harvest: An Introduction to the Archaeology of Subsistence Intensification, Innovation, and Change* (Springer, 2007), and journals such as the *Proceedings of the National Academy of Sciences* and the *American Anthropologist.* Through his research, Fisher seeks to unravel the complex relationship between human societies and their landscapes. His fieldwork utilizes a variety of archaeological and earth science techniques to map the distribution of ancient settlements, document past and present soil erosion, investigate ancient agricultural features, and excavate archaeological sites. He has conducted fieldwork in several areas of the United States, Mexico, Portugal, and Albania. Recent research in Mexico traces patterns of ancient, human-caused, environmental change in the Lake Pátzcuaro Basin, Michoacán, Mexico, and in the Malpaso Valley, Zacatecas, Mexico. In 2007, he initiated long-term survey work in the Lake Pátzcuaro Basin focused on questions related to the formation of the ancient Tarascan (Purepécha) Empire. His work is supported by grants from the National Science Foundation, Heinz Foundation, and other agencies. In 2007 Fisher received the prestigious Gordon R. Willey Award from the American Anthropological Association.

J. Brett Hill has conducted archaeological fieldwork in several areas of the Near East, Europe, and the North American Southwest. He received his doctorate from Arizona State University and currently holds positions at the Center for Desert Archaeology in Tucson, Arizona, and Hendrix College in Conway, Arkansas. His previous work on ancient human ecology has appeared in several publications including articles in *American Antiquity*, *Journal of Field Archaeology*, *Journal of Anthropological Archaeology*, *Human Ecology*, and a book, *Human Ecology in the Wadi al-Hasa* (University of Arizona Press, 2006). He has conducted numerous studies using geographic information systems (GIS) to evaluate how environment structured the economic and social opportunities available to ancient farmers and herders, and how people degraded their environment. Current projects include research supported by the National Science Foundation in the Mediterranean Basin and in the North American Southwest. In the Mediterranean Basin, he is working with a multidisciplinary team to conduct comparative analyses between areas of similar natural environment, but different culture history, in Jordan and Spain. In the Southwest, he is using macro-regional data to evaluate settlement patterns and demography from the Early Agricultural period to the collapse of the Classic period Hohokam. In both cases, complex ecological histories are approached from a standpoint emphasizing broad temporal and spatial scales. This macro-scale view of human ecology affords new perspectives on concepts such as degradation, adaptation, resilience, and sustainability that are critical to understanding contemporary environmental dilemmas.

About the Contributors

Ofer Bar-Yosef is the MacCurdy Professor of Prehistoric Archaeology in the Department of Anthropology at Harvard University. He obtained his academic degrees at the Hebrew University in Jerusalem, studying archaeology and physical geography, and taught there from 1968 to 1987. In his early years, he jointly conducted a series of Paleolithic and Epi-Paleolithic excavations at 'Ubeidiya, Hayonim Cave, and Ein Gev, addressing, among others, the issue of building a cultural chronology for the Levantine Epi-Paleolithic. In the 1980s, he became interested in formatting the dynamic socioeconomic map of Levantine Neolithic and conducted joint excavations at Netiv Hagdud, Nahal Hemar Cave, and several sites in Sinai. The issue of early appearance of modern humans in the Levant and the presence of late Neanderthals got him involved in joint excavations at Qafzeh, Kebara, and Hayonim Caves where the archaeological contexts were studied and dated. Joint excavations at Dzudzuana and Kotias Klde Caves in the Republic of Georgia led to clarifying the late disappearance of Neanderthals and the arrival of Modern humans, bearers of Upper Paleolithic industries, in the Caucasus region. Currently, he is involved in the study of the late prehistory of China aimed at uncovering archaeological evidence for rice exploitation and cultivation. He has co-edited several volumes and extensively published site reports and general overviews. He is the co-editor of the *Eurasian Prehistory*, a journal for primary archaeological data. His most recent co-edited volume with L. Meignen is *Kebara Cave, Mt. Carmel: The Middle and Upper Paleolithic Archaeology* (Vol. I, The American School of Prehistoric Research, Peabody Museum, Harvard University, 2006).

Timothy Beach was director of Georgetown University's Center for the Environment from 1999 to 2007 and is a professor of geography in the School of Foreign Service's Program in Science, Technology & International Affairs (STIA). He has conducted field research on soils, geomorphology, and environmental archaeology in the Corn Belt of the United States, Mexico, Belize, Guatemala, Syria, Turkey, and Germany. Based on these field studies, he has published numerous articles and chapters, has an accepted book on environmental archaeology in the Petén of Guatemala, and has given scientific presentations in fourteen countries around the world. He was elected fellow of the American Association for the Advancement of Science and received fellowships from Georgetown University, the Pre-Columbian Studies

Program at Dumbarton Oaks, and the Guggenheim Foundation. He is currently writing a book on the environments and environmental change of the Maya world. He also teaches courses on environmental science and physical geography (climatology, hydrology, soils, geomorphology, and geoarchaeology) and how these relate to international management and policy.

J. Andrew Darling was born in Williamsburg, Virginia, where he first became involved in archaeology at the age of eight as a member of the Virginia Archaeological Society. He is a graduate of Swarthmore College and received his PhD in Anthropology in 1998 from the University of Michigan–Ann Arbor. Dr. Darling is a co-founder of the Mexico-North Research Network, a nonprofit organization for the support of cross-border research and education, and a former fellow of the National Museum of Natural History, Smithsonian Institution, and the Pre-Columbian Studies Program at Dumbarton Oaks in Washington, D.C. His fieldwork experiences include locations in the United States, Mexico, Peru, and Hungary. Dr. Darling is currently the coordinator for the Cultural Resource Management Program of the Gila River Indian Community in central Arizona. In addition to historic and prehistoric trails systems, his interests include the archaeology of violence, obsidian and ceramic archaeometry, and landscape archaeology. He has published in the *American Anthropologist* on the archaeology of witch execution in the American Southwest and on settlement patterns of the historic Akimel O'odham (Pima) and the Hohokam.

Nicholas Dunning grew up on the island of Oahu in Hawaii, where he developed a fascination with tropical environments and cultural adaptation. By virtue of once having picked up the wrong book in the library (and reading it anyway), he developed a passionate interest in Maya civilization. Dunning has spent the past twenty-five years studying the intriguing environment of the Maya Lowlands and the nature of human environmental adaptations, both past and present, in this region. Along the way, he earned BA and MA degrees from the University of Chicago and a PhD from the University of Minnesota, all in geography. Dunning has authored two books and some sixty articles and book chapters on the Maya world. Occasionally, he does research in eastern North America, the eastern Mediterranean, and the Caribbean. Currently, Dunning is a professor of geography at the University of Cincinnati, where his students affectionately (he hopes) refer to him as "Dr. Dirt," because of his fascination with soil. He resides in Cincinnati with his wife, Betsy Lazaron, a practicing family physician, and three daughters—all of whom like to play in the dirt, but none of whom want to become dirt doctors.

John G. Jones is an archaeologist and palynologist who has been researching agricultural origins and early settlement throughout the New World tropics. He is currently serving as assistant professor in the Department of Anthropology at Washington State University where he is conducting research in Belize, Guatemala, Ecuador, Peru, and throughout the Caribbean. His research in Tabasco has documented some of the earliest evidence for *Zea mays* cultivation in the lowlands of Mexico. One of his more interesting current projects involves investigating prehistoric population dynamics and agricultural practices throughout the Lesser Antilles. Dr. Jones is also working on several historical archaeology projects, including the examination of late-seventeenth-century beeswax recovered on the coast of Oregon, and the reconstruction of historical landscapes at Monticello, the home of Thomas Jefferson.

Ann P. Kinzig is an associate professor in the School of Life Sciences at Arizona State University (ASU). She received her BA in physics from the University of Illinois–Urbana-Champaign, her MA in physics from University of California at Berkeley, and her PhD in energy and resources from Berkeley. Before arriving at ASU, she was a post-doctoral researcher and lecturer at Princeton University, and she served in Washington, D.C., at the Office of Science and Technology Policy in the executive office of the president. Her research interests focus broadly on ecosystem services, conservation-development interactions, and the resilience of natural-resource systems. She is currently involved in three major research projects, including 1) advancing conservation in a social context (examining the trade-offs between conservation and development goals in developing nations), 2) the resilience of prehistoric landscapes in the American Southwest, and 3) assessments of ecosystem services, their valuation, and mechanisms for ensuring their continued delivery. She is an Aldo Leopold Leadership Fellow and was selected as the first AAAS Roger Revelle Fellow in Global Stewardship in 1998. She is also a member of Ecological Society of America, the American Association for the Advancement of Science, and the Rocky Mountain Biological Laboratory. Her recent publications include articles in *Ecology and Society*, *Landscape and Urban Planning*, *Ambio*, and *Conservation Ecology*. She is also co-editor of the 2002 book *Functional Consequences of Biodiversity: Empirical Progress and Theoretical Extensions* published by Princeton University Press.

Chapurukha M. Kusimba received his BEd from Kenyatta University, Kenya, and his MA and PhD in anthropology from Bryn Mawr College. He a dual resident of Kenya and the United States and studies the historical relationships of East African people with each other and wildlife. Since 1986 he has conducted research on the Kenya coast with the aim of understanding the development of complex polities of the East African coast from 700 AD to 1500 AD. He completed the first phase of a project that involved the archaeological and ethnoarchaeological study of iron production in 1992. Since joining the Field Museum of Natural History in 1994, he has continued archaeological fieldwork on the Kenya Coast with the aim of understanding 1) the role of local craft production, especially iron production, in the development of political and economic relationships between the East African coast and its Indian Ocean trading partners, 2) the early Indian Ocean trade as a stimulus for technical innovation, economic profit, and as a conduit for the bi-directional transfer of technologies between East Africa, the Middle East, and South Asia, and 3) the role of coastal and interior peoples in the organization, production, use, and trade of local crafts, and the role of productive organization in the development of social stratification.

Sheryl Luzzadder-Beach received her BA from Chico State University and her MA and PhD in physical geography from the University of Minnesota. She taught at Humboldt State University and the University of Georgia before taking her current position at George Mason University in Fairfax, Virginia, where she is presently associate provost for general education. Her research interests have been focused on the impact of groundwater quality on the contemporary and ancient Maya. Over the past decade, she has traveled to Belize, Turkey, and Syria for geoarcheology field research. Beach is featured in the 1999 book *Women in Earth Science Careers* by J. Kahn (Mankato, MN: Capstone High/Low Books, 1999). Her recent publications include articles in *Annals of the Association of American Geographers*, *Geomorphology*, *Catena*, *Geographical Review* and *Professional Geographer*, as well as numerous book chapters.

Margaret C. Nelson conducts research on long-term cycles of change in human organization and land use. Her current interest is on changing economic and social strategies associated with population aggregation and dispersion among pueblo dwellers of the eleventh through fourteenth centuries in the Mogollon region. This research has been funded by the National Geographic Society, the National Institutes of Health, the U.S. Department of Education, and private foundations. In addition, she is lead principal investigator of an interdisciplinary research group from ecology and anthropology examining cycles of stability and transformation across the last one thousand years in the North American Southwest and northern Mexico. Also, she has examined aspects of the current status of women in archaeology. She has served on the executive board of the Society for American Archaeology and as treasurer for the Archaeology Division of the American Anthropological Association. She is a member and past chair of the Society for American Archaeology's Committee on the Status of Women in Archaeology. Her teaching emphasizes critical thinking and effective communication. In 2001 she was named Centennial Professor by the Associated Students of Arizona State University. In 2005 she was selected Parents Association Professor of the Year. She is the president of the Distinguished Teaching Academy at Arizona State University.

John C. Ravesloot is a principal with William Self Associates, Inc., and serves as a visiting scholar at the Arizona State Museum, University of Arizona. For the past thirty years, Dr. Ravesloot has participated in and directed archaeological fieldwork in the southwestern United States. He received his PhD in anthropology from Southern Illinois University–Carbondale in 1984. From 1993–2005 he served as founding director of the Gila River Indian Community's Cultural Resource Management Program. In that capacity, he directed cultural resource studies for the Pima-Maricopa Irrigation Project and served as the community's owners' representative for the construction of the Huhugam Heritage Center. Dr. Ravesloot's research interests include settlement patterns, geoarchaeology, landscape archaeology, social organization, and public archaeology. He has authored or co-authored articles in numerous journals, monographs, and books on these research topics.

Charles L. Redman has been committed to interdisciplinary research since he worked closely in the field with botanists, zoologists, geologists, art historians, and ethnographers as an archaeology graduate student. Redman received his BA from Harvard University and his MA and PhD in anthropology from the University of Chicago. He taught at New York University and at SUNY–Binghamton before coming to Arizona State University (ASU) in 1983. Since then, he served nine years as chair of the Department of Anthropology, seven years as director of the Center for Environmental Studies and, in 2004, was chosen to be the Julie Ann Wrigley Director of the newly formed Global Institute of Sustainability. In July 2007, Redman became the inaugural director of ASU's School of Sustainability. Redman's interests include human impacts on the environment, sustainable landscapes, rapidly urbanizing regions, urban ecology, environmental education, and public outreach. He is the author or co-author of fourteen books including *Explanation in Archaeology*, *The Rise of Civilization*, *People of the Tonto Rim*, *Human Impact on Ancient Environments* and, most recently, co-edited *The Archaeology of Global Change and Applied Remote Sensing for Urban Planning, Governance and Sustainability*. Redman is currently working on building upon the extensive research portfolio of the Global Institute of Sustainability to develop the new School of Sustainability, which will educate a new generation of leaders through collaborative learning, transdisciplinary approaches, and problem-oriented training to address the environmental, economic, and social challenges of the twenty-first century.

Vernon L. Scarborough is a professor of anthropology at the University of Cincinnati. His topical interests remain settlement, land use, and water management in the context of the archaic state. To achieve this end, he has emphasized cross-disciplinary exchange and international fieldwork. He has taught and conducted fieldwork at the University of Khartoum, Sudan, the University of Peshawar, Pakistan, and the University of Texas at El Paso. In addition to ongoing land-use and water-management studies in Belize and Guatemala, he has worked in the Argolid, Greece, and Bali, Indonesia. He has been funded by the National Science Foundation, the National Geographic Society, and the Wenner-Gren Foundation, in addition to several grants from the Taft Foundation Fund and the University of Cincinnati. He received a Weatherhead Fellowship and two summer resident scholarships from the School of American Research in Santa Fe, New Mexico. In 2004, he was awarded the All-University Faculty Rieveschl Award for Creative and Scholarly Works from the University of Cincinnati. Most recently, he received a Taft Center Fellowship for the academic year 2006–2007. He has published seven books and over seventy book chapters and journal articles. He is currently editing the volume *Water and Humanity: A Historical Overview* for UNESCO, a major initiative of their International Hydrological Program (Delft). He is also involved with IHOPE (Integrated History for the Future of the People of Earth; an effort of the IGBP [International Geosphere and Biosphere Programme, Stockholm]) for both the global and the regional Asia and Americas initiatives. Since 1992, he has been co-director of the Programme for Belize Archaeological Project, a large, annually active research project in northwestern Belize.

Alan H. Simmons received his PhD in anthropology from Southern Methodist University. He has worked at a variety of institutions, including the Navajo Nation Cultural Resource Management Program, the Universities of Kansas and Arizona, and the Desert Research Institute in Reno, Nevada. He presently is a professor in the Department of Anthropology and Ethnic Studies at the University of Nevada, Las Vegas. Simmons has worked extensively with Neolithic and other materials throughout the Near East, including Jordan, Lebanon, Egypt, and Israel. He also has investigated the early occupation of Cyprus and has worked on a variety of sites in the U.S. Southwest and elsewhere in North America. Simmons has received funding for this research from a variety of agencies, including the National Science Foundation, the National Endowment for the Humanities, and the National Geographic Society, as well as private foundations. He is particularly interested in the origins and consequences of Neolithic economies, the initial colonization of the Mediterranean islands, adaptations to harsh environments, archaeological ethics, interdisciplinary research, chipped-stone analyses, heritage management, and the ecological impacts resulting from sedentary food-producing societies. He has numerous publications in a range of professional journals, including *Science*, *Nature*, *American Antiquity*, *Antiquity*, and the *Journal of Field Archaeology*. He also has authored several monographs/books, including *Faunal Extinction in an Island Society-Pygmy Hippopotamus Hunters of Cyprus* (Kluwer/Plenum, 1999) and *The Neolithic Revolution in the Near East–Transforming the Human Landscape* (University of Arizona Press, 2007).

Tina L. Thurston received her BA and MA in anthropology from Hunter College of the City University of New York and her PhD in anthropology from the University of Wisconsin–Madison. She is an associate professor of anthropology at The University at Buffalo, State University of New York. An archaeologist who works regularly in northern Europe, her research and publications concern sociopolitical development during the Iron Age and early medieval periods—studied through a combination of historically situated local data and comparative, cross-cultural theories of political development—and the relationships between rulers and subjects—studied through topics such as the agroecology of states and their regions, domination and resistance, force versus power, and the role of ethnicity and cultural identity in mediating sociopolitical participation and exclusion.

Sander E. van der Leeuw, an archaeologist and historian by training, taught at the universities of Leyden, Amsterdam, Cambridge (UK), the Sorbonne, and the Institut Universitaire de France. He held visiting positions at the University of Michigan, the University of Reading (UK), Australian National University, the University of Massachussetts at Amherst, and lectured in many parts of the world. His research interests include archaeological theory, ancient ceramic technologies, regional archaeology, (ancient and modern) man-land relationships, GIS and modelling, and complex systems theory. He did archaeological fieldwork in Syria, Holland, and France and conducted ethno-archaeological studies in the Near East, the Philippines, and Mexico. Since 1992, he has coordinated a series of interdisciplinary research projects (financed by the European Union) on socionatural interactions and environmental problems. Up to sixty-five researchers from eleven European institutions were involved, ranging from theoretical physicists and mathematicians to historians and rural sociologists. The fieldwork spanned all the countries along the northern Mediterranean rim. Since February 2004, he has been professor of anthropology and director of the School of Human Evolution and Social Change of Arizona State University. He is an external professor of the Santa Fe Institute and a corresponding member of the Royal Dutch Academy of Sciences. Currently, he is treasurer of the International Human Dimensions in Global Environmental Change Programme. His publications include sixteen books and over a hundred papers and articles on archaeology, ancient technologies, socioenvironmental and sustainability issues, as well as invention and innovation.

Michael R. Waters is a professor of anthropology and geography at Texas A&M University. He is the holder of the Endowed Chair in First American Studies, director of the Center for the Study of the First Americans, and executive director of the North Star Archaeological Research Program. Dr. Waters specializes in the study of the First Americans, geoarchaeology, and late prehistoric agricultural societies in the American Southwest. He has published extensively in journals and books on these topics. He is well known for his book, *Principles of Geoarchaeology: A North American Perspective* (University of Arizona Press, 1997). Dr. Waters was awarded the Kirk Bryan Award of the Geological Society of America in 2003 and the Rip Rapp Archaeological Geology Award of the Geological Society of America in 2004.

Index

CPSIA information can be obtained at www.ICGtesting.com
Printed in the USA
LVOW13s0901240114

370719LV00004B/10/P